Listening in Paris

STUDIES ON THE HISTORY OF SOCIETY AND CULTURE

Victoria E. Bonnell and Lynn Hunt, Editors

Listening in Paris

A Cultural History

James H. Johnson

UNIVERSITY OF CALIFORNIA PRESS

Berkeley / Los Angeles / London

University of California Press
Berkeley and Los Angeles, California

University of California Press, Ltd.
London, England

Johnson, James H., 1960–
    Listening in Paris : a cultural history / James H. Johnson.
        p. cm.—(Studies on the history of society and culture ; 21)
    Based on author's dissertation (doctoral)—University of Chicago,
    1988.
    Includes bibliographical references and index.
    ISBN 0-520-08564-7 (cloth : alk. paper)
    ISBN 0-520-20648-7 (pbk. : alk. paper)
    1. Music—France—History and criticism.   2. Music and society.
    3. Music appreciation.   I. Title.   II. Series.
    ML270.J64   1995
    780'.944—dc20   94-6492
                                                                  CIP
                                                                   MN

Portions of this work have previously appeared in the following articles:
"Musical Experience and the Formation of a French Musical Public,"
Journal of Modern History 64 (1992): 191–226 (© 1992 by the
University of Chicago); "Revolutionary Audiences and the Impossible
Imperatives of Fraternity," in *Re-Creating Authority in Revolutionary
France*, ed. Bryant T. Ragan, Jr., and Elizabeth A. Williams (New
Brunswick: Rutgers University Press, 1992); "Beethoven and the Birth
of Romantic Musical Experience in France," *19th-Century Music* 15
(1991): 23–35.

Printed in the United States of America
9 8 7 6 5 4 3 2 1

For Robert A. Nye

Contents

Illustrations

Musical Examples

Acknowledgments

Without the generous help of friends and colleagues this book could never have appeared. May these thanks stand as a small expression of my appreciation. For their wise guidance of my doctoral dissertation, I thank Keith Michael Baker, Jan Goldstein, and Ellen T. Harris; I was fortunate to have such extraordinary models of professionalism in scholarship. For support in dissertation and post-dissertation research, I am grateful to the Hays-Fulbright Foundation, the American Council of Learned Societies, and the John M. Olin Program for the History of Political Culture at the University of Chicago. I am grateful as well for research support provided by the Kahn Award for junior faculty at Boston University, with special appreciation to Esther Kahn.

Among those whose insights have changed my thinking for the better over the course of this project are James Smith Allen, Steven Englund, Brian Jorgensen, and William Weber. I am grateful to William W. Kunze and James T. Dutton, whose computer expertise saved me from doing any further damage in certain desperate moments. Thanks also to Dore Brown of the University of California Press, who oversaw the production of this book with efficiency, grace, and good humor.

Finally, my heartfelt thanks to two friends whose learning and dedication are a constant inspiration: to Jim Whitman, who first proposed the idea for this project in the dingy congeniality of Jimmy's Woodlawn Tap on Fifty-fifth Street in Chicago and who can be relied upon for sound advice on just about everything; and to Bob Nye, whose immense gifts as a teacher and scholar, sustained always by his unfailing humanity, still inspire in me the same admiration I felt listening to his lectures as a college sophomore. This book is for Bob, in gratitude for his having enriched my life in so many ways. Every student should be so lucky.

Introduction

The theater is neither a school nor a portrait of manners,
but it can be considered their mirror in the sense that it is
the place where they are concentrated and reflected. There
you see the play of passions, prejudices and public opinion
most clearly. The choice of works to be performed most
often, the manner in which one listens, the type of pleasure
or discomfort that the mass of spectators feels most readily,
the lines most vigorously applauded, the silliness mocked,
the moods one shows at the theater, the behavior one
assumes, the people with whom one goes: all of these are so
many observations to be collected—observations according
to which, without the slightest knowledge of events or
incidents, one could form a complete picture of national
habits.

Étienne de Jouy, *L'Hermite de la Guiane*
(1816)

This book grew from a simple question. Why did French
audiences become silent? Eighteenth-century travelers' accounts of the
Paris Opéra and memoirs of concertgoers describe a busy, preoccupied
public, at times loud and at others merely sociable, but seldom deeply
attentive. Why, over the hundred years between 1750 and 1850, did
audiences stop talking and start listening? The answer is anything but
simple. This transformation in behavior was a sign of fundamental

1

change in listening, one whose elements included everything from the physical features of the hall to the musical qualities of the works. These elements slowly pacified musical experience from the Old Regime to romanticism, a remarkable feature of which was growing silence.

The cultural history of listening encompasses change in aesthetic response and public behavior. In writing this history of perception, I have worked within a general conceptual framework inspired by the idealist philosophical tradition, which places the perceiver at the center of meaning. This means, simply, that we cannot hear a Haydn symphony the same way Haydn's contemporaries did. Musical meaning does not exist objectively in the work—or even in its composer's intentions. It resides in the particular moment of reception, one shaped by dominant aesthetic and social expectations that are themselves historically structured. To paraphrase the philosopher Hans-Georg Gadamer, meaning occurs when sound meets prejudice.[1] That charged word "prejudice" is important, for it reminds us that there is no musical meaning without interpretation.[2]

I have resisted following the extreme application of this logic, however, to conclude that there are as many *Don Giovanni*s as there have been listeners. Nor do I think that denying a fixed musical meaning necessarily warrants this conclusion. For just as important as the culturally embedded associations a listener brings to a performance is the structure of the actual musical work. Wolfgang Iser, the literary theorist, is insightful on this point. His view is that a text allows for different meanings while also restricting the possibilities.[3] I believe the same can be said of music, though the matter is more complicated here, given the more elusive nature of musical signification. The insistent oboe playing the dotted eighth-sixteenth note pattern in Haydn's Symphony No. 83 is the image of a hen to some, the expression of merriment to others, and an essential thread in a web of indescribable content to others. But it would be hard to argue credibly that it is a funeral dirge, or paints the storming of the Bastille, or promotes slavery.[4]

The way audiences have listened over time can be generalized according to these sorts of categories: sounds, images, ideas, emotions, vague feelings, and so forth. It is also possible to sketch the process by which a cohort of spectators passes from one type of listening to another. This is a matter of discovering how the musical structures and styles of a given generation helped to create listeners' expectations for musical expression, speculating about what the listeners heard (and couldn't have heard) within the boundaries of those expectations, and determining what sort of individual engagement that content compelled. Set in the stream of time, listening becomes a dialectic between aesthetic expectations and musical innovations. It is a continuous negotiation conducted at the boundaries of musical sense. Change occurs when music accessible enough to meet listeners' criteria for meaning is at the same time innovative enough to prod them into revising and expanding those assumptions.

Intellectuals writing on the relationship between text and reader have called the mental set that orients the reading of a given generation a horizon of expectations. That phrase should also be applied to listening.[5] A music lover of 1750 magically transported in time could no more appreciate Beethoven's Ninth at first hearing than a contemporary of Titian might comprehend *Nude Descending a Staircase* at first sight: these works would be so far beyond the horizon of expectations as to seem another language, pleasant to hear or see, perhaps, but nonetheless foreign, indecipherable, and therefore meaningless. From the public's point of view (if we might telescope several generations of responses into a single conceptual moment), the perceptual change from Rameau to Beethoven, or from Titian to Duchamp, represents the steady expansion in boundaries of possible meaning. The popular comprehension of new aesthetic styles stands for more than just artistic innovation. It signifies the emergence and refinement of new modes of perception. This helps to explain why listening—no less than reading or seeing—is historically constituted and changes over time.

A rough correlation can be made between the horizon of expectations among listeners and their degree and depth of engagement while listening: to oversimplify, listening for storms, birds, and battles, as Rameau's audiences did, demanded much less attention than did listening for indescribable feelings and urges, as Beethoven's audiences did. By comparing the expectations for meaning with the compositional features of the works French audiences heard, I have constructed a conceptual framework to explain the shift from superficial to engaged listening and, by extension, from talkative to silent audiences.

But musical experience is never just musical. Beyond the particular negotiation between the listener and the music, it also implies a performance space, with its own particular personality, and a unique historical moment, with its styles of expression and political preoccupations. All public expression of musical response—even silence—is inevitably social. Public expression, although freely chosen, is drawn from a finite number of behaviors and styles of discourse shaped by the culture.

Le Sacre du printemps did not cause a riot on its premiere at the Théâtre du Champs Elysées in 1913; fighting in the theater, rather, was one of several possible responses expressing extreme divergence in taste. Why fighting in the aisles was an available behavior in 1913—and, indeed, why the spectators that night opted for this rather than other expressions of mutual contempt—is a question better posed to politics and society than to the music of Stravinsky.

I have used two broad categories to understand the political and social influences upon public responses to music, the structural and the personal. On the largest scale, structures of society—monarchical, aristocratic, meritocratic, democratic—produce patterns of behavior that underlie everyday interactions. To these structures can be attributed certain patterns of behavior during musical performances, patterns that occasionally spill over into the aesthetic and influence how the music is heard. Hence the aesthetically distracting habit of commenting upon other spectators during performances in a society structured by a courtly etiquette rooted in reputation, or the imperative of bourgeois politeness not to bother other spectators. Working very generally from the methodological framework employed by Norbert Elias in *The Civilizing Process*, wherein social configurations are seen to create behavioral constraints that individuals internalize as self-restraints, I have attempted to understand behavioral shifts as part of larger social transformations.[6]

At the same time, spectators' behavior during performances includes conscious responses to immediate stimuli—everything from the latrines overflowing in eighteenth-century halls, to the threat of decapitation for insufficient patriotism during the Revolution, to explosions coming from the new gas lamps. For this reason I open each major section of the book with chapters recreating the physical and psychological atmosphere of the hall from the spectator's point of view. The German musicologist Carl Dahlhaus has written that insofar as reception history attempts to illuminate how competing views of a work represent an age, a nation, a class, or a social group, the rhetorical mode of that history must be broadly narrative.[7] This view has guided much of my writing, which takes selected themes in social and intellectual history as reference points.

This book is not an institutional history of French opera or concert life. Nor is it a thorough account of French music. Rather, I have tried to isolate significant moments in the historical construction of listening. I have therefore discussed *opéra-comique* only in the section treating the French Revolution, the period when the form had its greatest impact upon musical experience. For the same reason I have chosen to treat the Théâtre Italien chiefly in the 1820s but do not follow its audiences into the 1830s. The Opéra is present throughout the book, although as a defining force in musical experience it recedes in importance during the Restoration years. For social and aesthetic reasons that will become clear, concert life figures with increasing prominence in the nineteenth-century sections. I hope that this approach will not seem distractingly selective.

Each major section contains passages of musical analysis in which I attempt to locate those salient musical features that reinforced, challenged, or changed existing aesthetic assumptions. I offer these sections as a musically literate listener rather than as a musicologist, which I am not. For the most part they point to the obvious, or what I think was obvious for spectators with a particular horizon of expectations, in an attempt to distinguish between the familiar and the foreign.

Inevitably, questions will arise concerning the legitimacy of generalizing about the experience of audiences based upon the musical descriptions of critics and journalists. Even taking into account the surprising number of ordinary spectators who recorded their musical perceptions in letters to newspapers or whose remarks were heard and used by others, the fact remains that the aesthetic evolution described here is drawn largely from those with a particular reason to listen critically and think systematically about what they heard.

Yet if the chapters on horizons of expectations are understood as attempts to isolate what made certain interpretive stances possible, as well as which musical innovations broadened those expectations and in what direction, then the use of critics and journalists is as valid an indicator of the mechanism of change in perceptions as any. Moreover, by correlating these aesthetic assumptions with their manifestations in behavior as I have attempted to do, one may perhaps make useful generalizations about the musical perceptions of those spectators whose behavior we see but whose thoughts are silent. That sort of logic is dangerous, I know, especially when one is also sensitive to the social—and often imitative—nature of behavior. Still, if applied prudently, the method is not entirely without merit.

There may appear to be a tension at the center of this book between two visions of history, one characterized by slow, piecemeal change and the other composed of clean breaks and successive structures. In the narrative sections I describe particular moments that contain a variety of perceptions and behaviors, while in the sections of social and musical

analysis I give the impression that the culture compelled identical response in thought and action. I am aware of the two souls in my method
(Macaulay and Foucault?) and have embraced each for a specific reason,
which I hope is not Mephistophelean. In fact I believe that historical
change occurs slowly and steadily and not by Foucault's discursive leaps.
But if narration alone can paint the details of experience in vivid colors,
it is insufficient as a rhetorical mode to illuminate the structures of
experience, which is the aim of the analytic sections. The historian's
choice, wrote the anthropologist Claude Lévi-Strauss, is always between
history "which teaches us more and explains less, and history which
explains more and teaches less."[8] In this book I've resisted choosing,
preferring instead to do a little of each.

PART ONE

The Rendezvous of the Rich

At the opera Roland *that I saw recently*
The duc de Grammont and the count Périgny
Stood transfixed in the pit by the great Subligny.
Madame Présidente had a first-level view;
In the box next to hers sat the abbé Chaulieu,
Who recited aloud all the songs that he knew
For the length of the show never missing a cue.
I saw in the balcony Monsieur du Breuil,
Then I climbed to the second-row loges straightaway,
And found blonds and brunettes and a happy abbé.
At last, tired of strolling, I returned to the floor
And found two-hundred officers speaking of war.
Brillac soon left and, with him, Sully,
They elbowed and pushed and disdained courtesy,
Which made at the door quite a loud shivaree.

From the *Chansonnier Clérambault*
(17th Century)

1

Opera as Social Duty

In 1750 it was unfashionable to arrive at the opera on time. Some *grandes dames* and noblemen preferred to stroll in the gardens outside the opera hall until darkness forced them indoors. Others lingered over their weak ale or chocolate in the opera's dark café just off the vestibule and down a few steps. Of those who entered the cavernous hall in the Palais Royal before the overture began—which was more or less at 5:15, depending upon whether all the singers had arrived—many circulated in the candlelit corridors outside their boxes to arrange for visits during the performance.

While most were in their places by the end of the first act, the continuous movement and low din of conversation never really stopped. Lackeys and young bachelors milled about in the crowded and often boisterous parterre, the floor-level pit to which only men were admitted. Princes of the blood and dukes visited among themselves in the highly visible first-row boxes. Worldly abbés chatted happily with ladies in jewels on the second level, occasionally earning indecent shouts from the parterre when their conversation turned too cordial. And lovers sought the dim heights of the third balcony—the paradise—away from the probing lorgnettes. Forty soldiers with loaded muskets roamed the pit and patrolled each floor, ensuring, in the words of an edict from Versailles, "the order due a Royal House."[1] The tone—superior, omniscient, unimpeachably correct—made it sound like putting troops in

Part-opening illustration: Detail of Gabriel de Saint-Aubin, *"Armide," représenté au Palais Royal*, 1761. Boston Museum of Fine Arts. Photograph courtesy of the Hermitage, Saint Petersburg.

the opera house was the most ordinary thing in the world. In the eighteenth century it was, and for good reason.

Few complained about the noise and bustle. In the Old Regime attending the opera was more social event than aesthetic encounter. In fact, eighteenth-century audiences considered music little more than an agreeable ornament to a magnificent spectacle, in which they themselves played the principal part. Like carrying a sword, which only noblemen could do, attending the opera was a proud display of identity in the Old Regime. It announced privilege in a society built upon rank and hierarchy. From its sumptuous decor to the impressive array of spectators assembled there, the Opéra seemed, of the three royal theaters, most exclusively the pastime of the Parisian aristocracy. The "small hint of commoner" at the Comédie-Française, as one observer delicately phrased it, was imperceptible at the Opéra.[2]

At mid-century the Opéra—known officially as the Académie Royale de Musique—was a royal spectacle, tailored to fit the tastes of the king's most distinguished subjects: his closest relatives held their boxes in the most visible rows, royal administrators and palace functionaries seldom missed performances, and Louis XV himself came with some regularity. "Accompanied by his great family," the *Mercure* sang after one such visit, "Louis deigns in these happy days to share our joys. . . . There is nothing as sweet as admiring the Monarch, the Father, the Citizen himself in you."[3] After his appearances at the Opéra the king and his entourage would sometimes walk through the gardens of the Palais Royal, past the *appartements* of the duc d'Orléans and his retainers, surrounded by spectators from the opera.

It was no wonder that detractors of the Opéra's pomp complained of the "court etiquette" that reigned among audiences there.[4] Everywhere you looked, from the fleur-de-lys on the proscenium to the personalities on display, you saw reminders of Versailles. Louis XIV had established the Académie Royale de Musique in 1669 at the height of the academy-building drive that effectively turned the arts and sciences into so many planets orbiting the sun and took a personal hand in music-making there, confirming personnel, selecting libretti, and occasionally sitting in on rehearsals: the works that appeared during Louis XIV's lifetime were permeated with his presence.[5] That model of centralization prevailed until late in the eighteenth century, as approval of virtually all administrative decisions at the Opéra—everything from annual budgets to the more trivial concerns of singers' contracts and which complimentary tickets would go to whom—snaked its way down the bureaucratic maze from Versailles. The singer Mlle Le Maure had proof of royal operatic oversight in an autograph from the king himself. It was affixed to her prison sentence for having insulted unappreciative spectators before storming off the stage in the middle of Montéclair's *Jephté*.[6]

The hall that drew the upper crust of the Old Regime was situated on the rue St.-Honoré, between the rue de Richelieu and the rue des Bons-Enfants (see Figure 1). The theater had belonged to the Académie Royale de Musique since 1673, when the court composer Jean-Baptiste Lully, famous for his tyrannical temper, convinced Louis XIV that the opera could make better use of the hall than its intended occupants, Molière's troupe of actors. The company used the theater until a fire destroyed the hall nearly a century later, giving first three and later four performances a week.[7]

By the mid-eighteenth century, eighty years of candlelit performances had dulled the theater's original luster, but contemporaries still spoke of its impressive look. The interior was done in greens and golds: the stage curtain was green with gold fringe, the corridor walls white with green trim, and the boxes swathed in green satin embroidered with golden flowers. The decor showed great attention to detail, with each class of seats done up in its own particular style. The six boxes on the sides of the stage—by far the most public in the house—were decorated along the front with interlacing designs in gold. Painted allegories of music interwoven with garlands appeared on the front of the first-level boxes. The ceilings of these first boxes were richly painted with figures from mythology, a clear mark of distinction over the plain turquoise-blue ceilings of the seconds.[8]

Sumptuous allegorical paintings covered the ceiling of the opera hall. Along the perimeter ran a *trompe l'oeil* marble balustrade supporting urns and vases brimming with flowers. Above it was a circuit of twelve panels depicting the Muses. And against a sky-blue background in the center of the ceiling was a resplendent Apollo borne through the clouds on a horsedrawn chariot that trailed flowers.[9]

Although the theater was notorious for its dark recesses, the oil lamps and candles gave off enough light for spectators to identify acquaintances from across the hall, so long as they kept to the front of their boxes. Wax candles burned continuously both outside and inside the boxes. A combination of tallow candles and oil lamps in panels along the front of the stage and suspended on scaffolding in the wings gave off more intense light for the performers, but they also filled the front of the theater with thick, ill-smelling smoke—a sort of "intervening

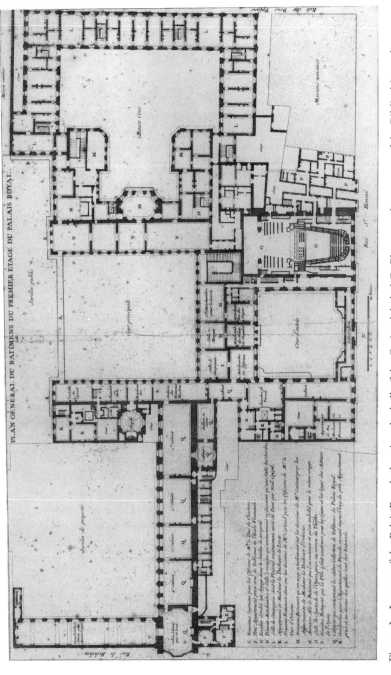

Figure 1. Layout of the Palais Royal, showing the hall of the Opéra, labeled O. Photograph courtesy of the Bibliothèque de l'Opéra.

haze," as one man described it, "between the actors and the spectators."[10] (It must have been an awful embarrassment when the opera
management received a letter from Marie Antoinette complaining
about the smoke, but what could be done? It was, after all, the most
advanced technique in lighting.)[11] Two crystal chandeliers studded with
candles hung from the ceiling; through an elaborate system of ropes and
pulleys it could be raised when the performance began. The maneuver
was designed to give spectators an unobstructed view of the stage rather
than dim the hall, since the candles continued to burn throughout the
performance.[12] Depending upon the smoke in front of the stage, spectators sometimes saw one another more clearly than the performers.

Like most early eighteenth-century Parisian theaters, the hall in the
Palais Royal was in the form of a rectangle with rounded corners. Three
levels of boxes lined the walls of the auditorium, so that spectators on
either side faced one another and had to turn their chairs to one side to
view the stage. Unlike most other European theaters, the partitions between the boxes pointed not toward the stage but toward the center of
the hall, a construction that gave a clear line of sight to virtually every
other box but made seeing the stage all the more difficult (see Figure 2). ("One has to stand to see the stage in all our theaters," an architect complained in the 1760s. "It's as if they placed the partitions there
intentionally to obstruct one's view of the stage.")[13] The forward-most
box on the right as you faced the stage was the king's, and the box
directly across the hall was the queen's. There were twenty-eight other
first-level boxes, including the six on the stage, with fewer on the second
and third levels. The last two levels also contained open seating in
balconies.

The boxes varied in size to contain four to twelve people and could
be rented for as long as spectators wished; most contracts in the mid-
eighteenth century ran for two to three years. It was common for acquaintances to share the cost of the box and alternate using it. On certain nights in the 1750s, for instance, Mme la duchesse de Biron
appeared in box no. 7 on the king's side in the first tier, while the duc
de Luxembourg sat there on other nights.[14] Each box acquired its own
character and circle of associations. If a subscriber stayed in the same
box long enough, the name might find its way into official documents,
as though the box were his personal property. In 1712 the duc de
Ventadour and Monseigneur Guzenet concluded an agreement to
decorate the interior of the onstage box they shared, installing their own
furniture, their own lock on the door, and a blind over the front that

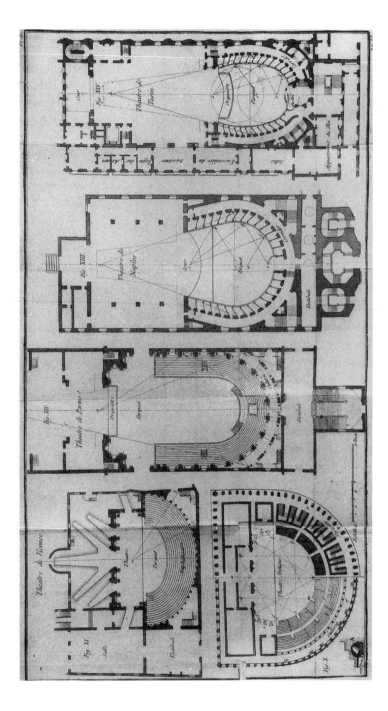

Fig. XIV. — Théâtre de Turin
Fig. XIII. — Théâtre de Naples
Fig. XII. — Théâtre de Parme
Fig. XI. — Théâtre de Vicence
Fig. X. — Théâtre Antique

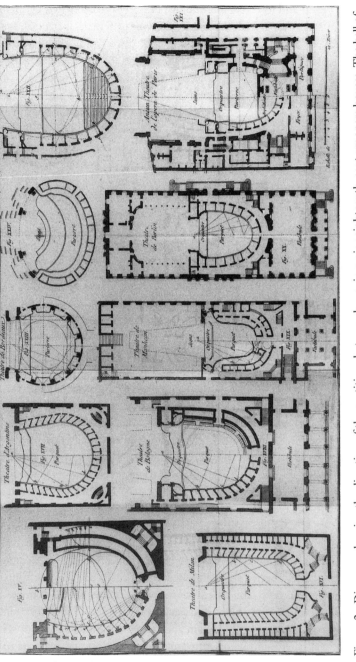

Figure 2. Diagrams showing the direction of the partitions between boxes in major eighteenth-century opera houses. The hall of the Paris Opéra is on the far right, lower level. From Patte, *Essai sur l'architecture théâtrale* (1782). Photograph courtesy of the Joseph Regenstein Library, University of Chicago.

could be raised and lowered.[15] Some boxes were so closely tied to their renters, in fact, that their *ouvreuses*—the young female ushers of the eighteenth century—carried lists of who could enter and kept all others away by locking the doors.[16]

The pleasures in possessing a box at the Opéra could be private or public, and French spectators explored all possibilities. It could serve as a secret little cocoon where confidantes talked "the whole time without having to worry about anyone hearing" (as Cécile Volanges describes in *Les Liaisons dangereuses*) or a sociable salon overflowing with warmth and high spirits.[17] From the boxes women reviewed the fashions in dress and coiffure, men learned the most recent military developments, and the young alternately sought and showed off lovers.

The six boxes on the stage were the most prestigious in the theater. They were the most expensive but provided a terrible view of the spectacle, as the lamps on the stage shone directly into the spectators' eyes, and much of the action took place farther upstage. Princes of the blood, foreign diplomats or the king's inner circle of advisers typically sat here: in the 1750–51 season, Louis XV's future minister of state (the duc de Choiseul), his minister of war (the comte d'Argenson), and the duc d'Aumont regularly appeared in these boxes.[18] Of course, being blinded by the oil lamps had its advantages for these spectators: their dress, their behavior, and their reactions to the performance were every bit as visible to the rest of the audience as were the singers and dancers.

Not that a clear view of the opera was of paramount importance anyway: to be seen was a higher priority. Subscription lists from the middle of the eighteenth century reveal a general correspondence between visibility to others and relative position in the social hierarchy. To attend the opera in the middle of the century was to see social power displayed. Hence the prestige of the first-level boxes, the "distinguished seats, those that the vain are eager to occupy," where "one can be seen and observed." [19] On Friday nights the first boxes framed the luminaries of the Old Regime: the prince de Clermont and the prince de Soubise, the duc de Luxembourg and the duc d'Orléans, the princesse de Sens and the marquise de Polignac all maintained boxes there at the same time. Virtually all noble tastes and styles had representatives in the first boxes. Only one box separated the rakish maréchal de Richelieu—who married three wives under three kings, was in and out of the Bastille three times before he was thirty, and whose unremitting seductions led Laharpe to label him "a master of the science of depravity"—from the frugal and upright Chrétien-Guillaume Lamoignon de Malesherbes, the lawyer who was to lose his life arguing Louis XVI's case before the revolution-ary tribunal later in the century.[20] The marquise de Boufflers, mistress of Louis XV and friend of Voltaire and Montesquieu, sat directly across the theater from the duchesse de Maine, whose salon drew Fontenelle, Marmontel, Diderot, Crébillon, and Raynal.[21]

Of the 135 annual subscribers in the first-level boxes between 1749 and 1757, 4 were commoners, and 3 were wealthy bourgeois of Paris. The rest were aristocrats. Of the latter, 51 percent were *grands* and comprised princes of the blood, dukes and peers, major army officers and royal counselors. The next largest group was the *grands officiers du Roi*, which included court financiers, magistrates, and other administra-tors. A number of parlementaires held boxes annually, as did a handful of farmers-general.[22]

The certain prestige conferred by the first boxes at mid-century was altogether missing in the second- and third-level boxes, which were higher, darker, and less expensive. This was the domain of wealthy priests, grisettes with benefactors, and lesser nobles. These boxes were rarely held annually at this time; many rented a box or a portion of one for a single performance. Honest bachelors were cautioned against sit-ting in the third boxes among "the chamber girls and demimondaines," and Mme de Genlis claimed that the practice of sharing boxes here kept many virtuous girls away from the opera altogether in the eighteenth century for fear of being seated next to a courtesan.[23]

Those spectators who delighted in the sensual brilliance of the Opéra had no doubt experienced it from the boxes and not the parterre, where the misery of standing for hours on end was compounded by routine overcrowding. By all accounts the parterre was always too full (the ticket office capped entries there at an even thousand) and, with its healthy share of drunken servants and spoiled dandies, was perpetually on the verge of pandemonium.[24] It was in the parterre that Rousseau received "kicks in the rear" after his withering attack on French music in "Lettre sur la musique française." ("The French do not and cannot have their own music," he had written; "and if they ever do it will be all the worse for them.")[25]

Men stood, strolled, sang, and sometimes danced here during the opera. Dogs were occasionally let loose in the parterre. The more fas-tidious tried to keep up by following along with the libretto, though the effort must have required heroic concentration. Mercier describes see-ing spectators "fall on top of one another" at the least shock, and the *Mercure* claimed that men were sometimes carried from the middle of the floor "half dead, so thoroughly soaked with sweat that even their clothes were wet."[26] In principle a shoulder-high barrier separated the parterre from the orchestra, but it couldn't always contain the crowd: one night in 1744 the crush to see a rare performance of a comic opera at the Académie Royale was so great that a knot of spectators went crashing into the orchestra pit and spilled onto the stage.[27] "Shoved, pushed, enraged," a police commissioner writes, "I try to make the best of things in the parterre."[28]

The parterre contained the fringes of the Parisian elites, whom the more polished elements of society viewed with disdain: frivolous younger sons of seigneurs with much money and little prudence, pages for the great houses, intellectuals, literary hacks, soldiers on leave.[29] Grimm, d'Alembert, and Diderot gathered under the queen's box to bait supporters of French music and encourage the Italians during the rowdy *querelle des bouffons* in 1752–54; their rivals the traditionalists—Fréron, Cazotte, Pidansat de Mairobert, and others—stood opposite them on the king's side.[30] Early in the century composers and poets watched their productions from the parterre, but the Paris police, suspecting that much of the hooting and whistling there came from jealous authors, ordered them to sit in the amphitheater, a raised area with benches at the rear of the auditorium, "where their conduct can be better observed."[31]

The *paradis*, an open balcony that faced the stage on the third level, was not particularly comfortable either, although here at least the spectators could sit on one of the three long benches nailed to the floor. Appreciated chiefly for its darkness, the paradise attracted those who for whatever reason preferred to stay out of view. Safer than the parterre, the paradise still had its own unpleasant aspects: the opera's toilets—in truth nothing more than wooden tubs in tiny closets—encircled the paradise and sometimes smelled so bad that the entire balcony emptied en masse.[32]

This elaborate spatialization of power was in part the natural effect of ticket prices, but an additional mechanism controlled the placement of the public according to social position. Although Louis XIV had explicitly forbidden spectators from attending the Opéra without paying, Louis XV and Louis XVI regularly granted distinguished subjects the privilege of free entry.[33] During Louis XV's reign, each honored name was assigned a place in the theater in these carefully prepared lists that traveled yearly from Versailles to opera administrators. Thus in 1720 the controllers-general of the Treasury and those of the *menus plaisirs du*

Roi could enter free and sit on the stage. Officers of the king's muske-teers, former actresses of the Opéra, and certain notaries could sit in the amphitheater. *Maréchaux des logis*, brigadiers, and sub-brigadiers were directed to stand in the parterre—a dubious honor, to be sure.[34]

Despite strong objections from the opera's directors over the lost revenue, the lists grew larger throughout the eighteenth century; by 1750 over two hundred of the king's guests could enter without paying. Confined mostly to the parterre and amphitheater, these spectators in-cluded Voltaire and Turgot, royal surgeons and scientists from the Aca-démie, actors from the Comédie-Française, and a generous array of mili-tary officers, *huissiers*, royal valets, and architects.[35] By giving the infrastructure of absolutism privileged entries to the Opéra, Louis XV and Louis XVI filled out the public map of social power, on which princes and countesses were merely the more prominent points.

The *coup d'archet* of the orchestra, a loud and mostly futile attack in-tended to silence the audience for the overture, signaled the start of the spectacle.[36] In the orchestra pit, a conductor of sorts beat the mea-sure by striking one of the wooden music stands in rhythm with a big stick from start to finish, through loud and soft passages alike. (Since Lully's untimely death by gangrene of the foot, pounding the podium with a sharpened log had been unadvisable.) Rousseau complained of the "terrible racket," and Grimm joked about the "woodchopper" among the violins, but all agreed that the incessant clatter was a neces-sary evil: even with it the orchestra, huddled as they were around com-mon "pulpits" and reading by candlelight, had a hard time staying together.

The spectacles here were not properly "operas," if the term is taken to mean musical dramas with coherent plots that consist primarily of singing. The most popular genre at the middle of the eighteenth cen-tury—the *opéra-ballet*—in fact contained more dancing than singing. Originated in 1679 by André Campra (1660–1744) with *L'Europe galante*, the *opéra-ballet* began with an overture and contained recita-tives and *airs*, but its greatest attractions were the numerous diver-tissements—minuets, gavottes, rigadoons, chaconnes. Each act of the *opéra-ballet* had its own independent action (as opposed to continuous dramatic movement over the length of the work) and at least one major sequence of dances.[37] During the Regency (1715–23), when tradition-alists like Saint-Simon saw the monarchy's gravitas threatened by the duc d'Orléans's dissolute morals and an overall neglect of ceremony, the characters who peopled *opéras-ballets* grew more earthly and ordinary than the deities who had graced the stage before, although the mythical heroizing returned as soon as Louis XV assumed the throne. The public apparently preferred the former style, as *opéras-ballets* from the Regency enjoyed more eighteenth-century revivals than the post-1723 works.[38] Closely related to the *opéra-ballet* in structure was the *pastorale*, a genre that evoked rural goodness and rosy-cheeked love. The enduring popularity of *opéras-ballet* and *pastorales* meant that for most of the eighteenth century the Académie Royale de Musique was as well known for its dancing as for its singing.

Dance in its various forms was certainly the most lucrative genre offered by the Opéra in the middle years of the century. In the years 1749–56 there were thirty-one ballets in the active repertory of the Académie Royale as opposed to eight *tragédies-lyriques*, a genre more explicitly devoted to singing. In this seven-year period the Opéra gave nearly 800 performances of ballet and only 204 performances of *tragédie-lyrique*.[39] Even in the *tragédie-lyrique*, dancing accounted for almost half the action.[40]

The *tragédie-lyrique*, the genre of greatest musical significance in the eighteenth century, was forged in the late seventeenth by Jean-Baptiste Lully (1633–87). Lully was far and away the most-performed composer of *tragédies-lyriques* in the early eighteenth century, and his works stayed in the repertoire to be revived over a longer time than those of any contemporary: *Thésée* (1675) enjoyed 13 revivals over 107 years, *Amadis* (1684) 8 over 97 years, and *Armide* (1686) 8 over 88 years. Such revivals came roughly once a decade; *Alceste* was fairly typical, coming back into production after its 1674 premiere in 1678, 1682, 1716, 1728, 1739, and 1757.[41] The endurance of Lully's works points to an important fact about eighteenth-century musical taste: even as more modern composers appeared and disappeared—Collasse, Desmarets, Salomon, and others—audiences continued to take their musical bearings from the solid, stately Lully. He was familiar and satisfying in ways the more ephemeral *opéras-ballets* and *pastorales* couldn't approach, a testament certainly to his musical gifts but the result as well of a royal edict from 1714 stipulating that a *tragédie* by Lully should always be in the repertoire should a new work fail.[42]

Lully's librettist Philippe Quinault chose subjects from ancient mythology and chivalric tales, building his plots on the amorous intrigue of kings, queens, gods, and goddesses. Tragic in name, many of Lully's *tragédies-lyriques* betray their title by ending with a deus ex machina rescue or miraculous resurrection from the dead, turns that permitted the spectacle to end with a whole stageful of characters dancing a happy chaconne.[43] Human passion is present in these libretti—most often high and remote, like distant thunder on Olympus—but Quinault frequently undercuts the grand with small concerns and pretty phrases.

The overall mood of the *tragédies-lyriques* is more *galant* than sad. Moments of potential dramatic intensity are tempered with lightness. In *Alceste*, for example, Admetus and Alcestis are not yet married, presumably so a courtly suitor named Alcide instead of Euripides' stuffy Hercules can retrieve Alcestis from Hades; Charon beckons passengers to his boat with an altogether fetching tune surely intended to draw laughter ("Pay up, pass through; pay up, pass through"); and in one of the ballets at the end a flirtatious attendant tells her two suitors that she cannot choose between them since "marriage destroys all tenderness."[44] Two notable works, *Atys* and *Phaéton*, end with genuine tragedy, which dispels any notion that the *tragédies-lyriques* always end happily. But the suffering of most of Lully's characters is the sweet torment of love rendered perilous by circumstances; and more often than not love triumphs in the end. The worst fate is not to love at all. Lully's works are filled with nymphs and shepherds who mourn the life without pleasure. "Ah what madness, what delusion, not to delight in life," sings a chorus in *Armide*. Though never frivolous, Lully's works convey a ruddy youthfulness whose credo is Carpe diem. "Enjoy the bliss that is lost so soon; in the winter of our years love no longer reigns." Lully is much closer to Watteau than to Racine. It's no wonder Boileau condemned the "lubricious morality" of Lully's operas.[45]

But if the works didn't always inspire tragic emotions, they were capable of stirring political passions. The prologue to *Thésée*, for example, takes place in the gardens of Versailles as Love, Grace, Pleasure, and Games regret the King's absence while Mars sings of his victories in war. In *Isis* Neptune refers to battles with Holland and Spain. Other prologues bear transparent references to politics and personalities at Versailles.[46] Lully's use of the prologue for political references was so widely assumed in the early part of the century that spectators found analogies in other works where the rapport was less certain. The *Mercure* was sure it had discovered the true meaning of the prologue to Destouches's *Issé*: the garden of the Hesperides was Abundance, the Dragon guarding it was War, and Hercules was "the exact image of the King, who only fights to end war and give his people . . . the abundance they desire."[47]

With the 1733 premiere of *Hippolyte et Aricie* by Jean-Philippe

Rameau (1683–1764) the Lullian tradition was threatened, or so the dogged defenders of Lully gave to believe. In fact, the basic Lullian-dramatic mold remained. This first work comes the closest to classical tragedy; the familiar lessons in love and galant divertissements dilute the tragic force of Rameau's later *tragédies-lyriques*. It was Rameau's musical style that seemed so jarring to Lullistes—a crop of nasty poems condemning "modern music" inevitably greeted his premieres—but gradually Rameau's audiences grew accustomed to the new sound. Rameau was versatile, and he knew his public: in his seventeen works longer than one act, six were *opéras-ballets*, five were *tragédies-lyriques*, three were *pastorales*, two were *comédies*, and one was the incidental music for a play.[48] By 1750 his works were staples of the repertoire. After a lukewarm reception in the early years, *Dardanus* (1739) ran to over one hundred performances with a revival as late as 1768. *Castor et Pollux* (1737), probably the most popular of Rameau's *tragédies-lyriques*, appeared into the 1780s and enjoyed ten different revivals in fifty years.[49]

By mid-century the political references had begun to fade, as though Louis XV couldn't exert the pressure the way his great-grandfather had. The prologue to Lully's *Thésée* was dropped in its 1754 revival, that of *Alceste* was suppressed in 1757, and in 1758 *Proserpine* went up without its prologue. Rameau's early *tragédies-lyriques—Hippolyte et Aricie, Castor et Pollux, Dardanus*—had prologues, but they were less pointed in their references to the monarchy. With *Zoroastre* (1749) Rameau stopped writing prologues—the first French operatic composer to do so—and beginning in the 1760s the prologues to his earlier works were omitted as well in performance.[50] These were the first signs of dissolution in the royal presence at the Opéra so carefully cultivated by Louis XIV, an early warning that aristocratic bearings in taste and sociability were shifting from Versailles to Paris.[51]

The great green and gold curtain rose to reveal a stage filled with the fantastical. (Once the curtain was up it stayed up, so spectators not only watched singers and dancers but saw the illusion-shattering scene changes between acts.) Decorations were lavish and costumes exuberant. The characters included clowns, sultans, demons, peasants (always happy), gods, a monkey or two, wood-nymphs, mermaids, and Indians. When François Chastelus, Sebastien Slodtz, and Pierre Dumesnil inventoried the Opéra's scenery in 1748, the task consumed two weeks and produced 161 items, including a Palace of Victory, a Palace of Ceres, a desert, twelve rustic countrysides, a Palace of Armide, a Palace of Neptune, one transparent garden, two rainbows, a grotto, six green fields with flowers, a Temple of Isis, a Temple of Destiny, a Temple of Memory, the port of Marseilles, a Throne of Theseus, a Palace of Persius, three altars, two ships, and a forest.[52]

At times the special effects made the Opéra seem more like a house of novelties than a temple of high art. Chariots bearing singers descended from the ceiling above the stage, surrounded by sparkling clouds strategically placed to hide the ropes. Altars billowed smoke through trap doors. Great creaking, multihinged floors were rolled out for nautical scenes, and water flowed through fountains, rivers, and grottoes. By the second act of Lully's *Isis* the eponymous goddess has already descended in a peacock-drawn chariot six times; a small orchestra floats down on a cloud in *Atys*. In Rameau's ballet *Naïs* mountains grow from the earth and giants climb them to fight with the gods; the climax comes when a thunderbolt from Jupiter reduces everything to rubble.[53] All of which was just one more thing for the *philosophes* to complain about at the Opéra: Diderot wrote that the realm of magic might well please the children but the real world lived by reason.[54]

The classical dramatic imperative for unity of time, place, and action made little difference to audiences (or, apparently, to librettists), for whom to watch the spectacle was "to traverse the seas without danger, to sweep through the four corners of the earth without fatigue, . . . [to be] transported from a superb palace into a charming and delicious glade."[55] To see machines sweep dancers through France, Spain, Italy, and Turkey, as in the enormously popular *L'Europe galante*, or singers pass from palace gardens to Hades in an instant was what audiences expected from the Opéra: "the parterre, enchanted by the novelty," François Antoine de Chevrier observed, "forgets in this instant of pleasure the boredom they have been suffering for the previous three hours."[56]

The attitude of spectators as they watched it all was more amusement than absorption. The stage director's loud whistle to change scenes, a signal that later audiences would find so annoying, was accepted at midcentury as part of the show. "The Opéra is an enchanted journey," wrote Charles Dufresny in a guide to Parisian entertainments; "it is a land of metamorphoses, and there one sees some of the most bizarre. . . . Are you lost in a frightful desert? A whistle will send you back to the land of the gods; another whistle, and you're in the land of fairies."[57] The risk in such maneuvers brought an undeniable touch of excitement. On one occasion a flying chariot dumped its load, and the tenor fell on his head in the middle of the stage. La Fontaine witnessed similar scenes:

> Even the prettiest chariot breaks free,
> Or a god gets caught in the ropes and yells;
> A fragment of forest falls in the sea,
> Or half of heaven ends up in hell.[58]

After the machines it was the dancers that attracted the attention of the spectators. A certain mystique surrounded Louis Dupré, who performed until he was sixty and appeared onstage with a mask, flowing black hair that reached halfway down his back, and a heavy mantle that swept the floor as he danced.[59] Another celebrity, Gaétan Vestris, was so popular—or so he believed—that when a woman accidentally stepped on his foot in the gardens of the Palais Royal he howled that all of Paris would mourn for two weeks.[60]

But the greater interest lay with the female dancers, the *filles d'opéra*, whose reputation for loose living inspired innumerable accounts of the Opéra. Just after the ballet corps raised the length of dresses for the *filles*, who, moreover, were for the first time leaping into the air on the stage of the Opéra, Casanova and his friend Patu visited the parterre to report triumphantly that the famous lead Marie-Anne Camargo was wearing no underwear. The claim was certainly in the spirit of the spectacle, but it was hardly verifiable, as the dancers' dresses now hit them just above the ankle.[61]

Still, people talked. Pidansot de Mairobert claimed that men milled about on the stage after performances for "négotiations de volupté" with the dancers; others received dancers in their boxes during performances (see Figure 3).[62] These *danseuses entretenues*, often orphans or runaways, were said to arrive at the Opéra in richly appointed carriages; they sometimes struck up conversations with the renters of the onstage boxes, and they were blamed for the ruin of "young foreigners and old financiers."[63] Eighteenth-century ladies of society reserved the epithet *fille d'opéra* for particularly forceful insults.[64] Their reputation was not entirely unearned: Mme Lévesque felt she couldn't entirely enjoy the opera since the dancers invariably struck poses "that would make the greatest libertine blush," and the marquis de Surville, aide-de-camp to the duc de Vendôme, describes the visit of several dancers to Vendôme's country estate, where they "danced stark naked all the entrées of the most celebrated operas" before Vendôme and the duc d'Orléans.[65]

Figure 3. Moreau le Jeune, *La Petite loge*. Engraving, n.d. Spectators receive a *fille d'opéra* in their box during a performance. Photograph courtesy of the Bibliothèque Nationale.

Some uprightly condemned the Opéra as "an asylum of vice" and the dancers as "serpents hidden in a flower-basket," but the pious warnings apparently cost the institution little: the ballet drew crowds like no other spectacle at the Opéra.[66]

Eighteenth-century audiences watched the opera if they felt like it—and had plenty of other options if they didn't. Mme de Sévigné's account of crying during the third act of Lully's *Alceste* and Lecerf de la

Viéville's descriptions of audiences immobile and scarcely able to breathe during certain scenes of *Armide* discourage any simple generalizations about spectators' supposed indifference to operatic drama.[67] But it is also true that both descriptions come from the time of Lully, and there is ample evidence that French taste in the middle years of the eighteenth century increasingly favored display over dramatic intensity. One telling indication of this came in the "improvements" the Opéra management made in works dating from the late seventeenth and early eighteenth centuries. Lully's *Armide* provides an eloquent case study: for the 1713 revival a minuet was inserted into the fourth act, in 1746 the dramatic action of the act was reduced to make room for more dancing, and in 1761 dramatic dialogue in the opera as a whole was condensed to make room for still more new divertissements.[68] Neither *Atys* nor *Phaéton*, Lully's two works that end tragically, appeared on the Paris stage after 1742.[69]

In the mid-eighteenth century an evening at the Opéra was more likely to be diverting than particularly somber. Gripping moments in the drama or especially renowned airs brought silence and genuine attention, but on the whole the Opéra in 1750 was a public setting for private salons, for which the music, dancers, and machines provided an excellent backdrop. Rémond de Saint-Mard, writing on contemporary opera in 1741, claimed that one watched the performance "perhaps the first time one goes, but thereafter the effect was no longer noticed." Between the unexpected distractions of fistfights or wisecracks shouted above the music and the more routine preoccupations of keeping social appointments, it was possible to forget about the performance altogether. "One listens to a song, one watches a fete, and sometimes one does neither one nor the other."[70] Voltaire called the Opéra a "public rendezvous" where everyone meets "no matter how terrible the singer or how boring the performance."[71] The common view, repeated in accounts from the period many times over, was that music touched the senses but not the soul.

Not surprisingly the parterre was the source of endless amusement for the boxes and infinite anguish for the performers. Arrests were frequent there for public drunkenness, which as often led to loud singing as to violence. In 1700 the captain of the King's Dragoons showed up in the parterre and "demonstrated his drunkenness by cries that troubled the opera."[72] The next year, "a young *gentilhomme* from Normandy whose head had been slightly warmed by the wine of Champagne" earned three weeks in prison for attacking a military officer with a walking stick in the parterre.[73] The Opéra guards were apparently less prompt to arrest more prominent members of the nobility. When Monsieur le marquis de Rochechouart wandered drunk onto the parterre and began shouting insults, the sergeant on duty "saw it necessary to represent to him his inconsideration," to which the marquis responded by "abusing" the sergeant. No arrest was made.[74] Singing was common in the parterre: Rameau tested his theories about the innate sense of harmony there by listening to spectators humming along with the music, and at the 1751 revival of Rameau's *Les Indes galantes* the parterre joined in singing the most famous chorus, "Brillant soleil." Addison likened the actors at such moments to parish clerks drowned out by their own congregation.[75]

Nor were spectators in the parterre hesitant to express their artistic judgments, despite the edicts from the king attempting to quell loud and unruly displays. The original 1699 ban forbidding spectators from "interrupting the actors in any manner whatever" was published and posted in various versions eleven additional times in the first half of the eighteenth century. The version printed in 1728 was the most refined in describing the forbidden activity: "All who attend spectacles, and particularly those who place themselves in the parterre, are prohibited from committing any disorder entering or leaving, from shouting and making noise before the spectacle begins and during the entr'actes, from whistling, hooting, wearing hats upon the head, and interrupting the actors during the performance in any way and under any pretext whatever, under penalty of disobedience."[76]

The ordinances had little effect. When a substitute singer replaced the lead in Marin Marais's *L'Ariane et Bacchus* without notice, whistles from the parterre quickly forced him to stop singing. After an awkward silence the singer composed himself and asked the parterre how they expected him to have a thousand-écu voice when he was paid only six hundred livres, a response that so delighted the troublemakers that they cheered him to the end of the opera.[77] The parterre's antics shattered any sort of dramatic engagement the performers might hope to encourage. When Caron demanded a coin from a shade crossing over to Hades in a performance of Lully's *Alceste*, a spectator called out "Throw him a banknote!"[78] (He must have had John Law in mind.) And in perhaps the grandest insult of all, one gifted spectator in the parterre thwarted a police crackdown on whistling by announcing his disapproval with a long, loud fart.[79] It may well have been true that the armed guards stationed prominently throughout the theater created "an unpleasant ambiance of despotism," as one spectator phrased it, but in the eighteenth century few thought that the spectacle could stay calm without them.[80]

The greatest pastime at the opera was conversation, and no place was better equipped than inside an opera box. Depending upon one's guests the topics ranged from war to religion to who was in favor at court. But most of the time the subject was other spectators. The memoirs of Anne-Marie de Moras contain vivid descriptions of the victims of her box's delectation: they included an abbé with yellow skin and an erect peruke, a reddish woman "very made up, very ugly, and very indecent," and the pale boy who sat next to her.[81] An account purportedly by a baron from Bordeaux describes a similar conversation. Although the baroness was too agitated by the number of lorgnettes focused on her either to listen to the music or to talk, the others in the party gossiped about other spectators from the instant the music started: the octogenarian as brave now in love as he once was in battle, the officer wearing an outfit that should never be worn in public, the stylish priest wearing a sword on one hip and a purse on the other.[82]

Rétif de la Bretonne gives a spectacular account of conversation during the opera in his *Tableaux de la bonne compagnie*. The setting is the box of an unnamed *parlementaire*'s wife, and her guests include a countess, a marquis, and Rétif. Before the music starts the présidente begins a spicy story about a soldier who seduces the very farm girl his commanding officer had earlier tried (unsuccessfully) to bed. As the story is drawing to an end—with the soldier in a cloister, the girl in a convent, and the officer doubly inconsolate—the music starts. The conversation continues for a time, but the music grows loud enough to silence them momentarily. ("The sacrifice of pleasure that a pretty piece of music can cause," Rétif observes, "costs us nothing if we are trying to please a woman who wishes to listen to it.")

A sharp peal of laughter from the countess soon dispels any notion that the women want to listen. A vicar from the adjoining box enters to announce that the music is preventing him from hearing their conversation. The group takes up the politics of Holland and Austria, the personalities of Catherine the Great and Frederick of Prussia, the chances for war, and the possible identity of the foreign ministers in the forestage boxes. In time the group notices spectators moving toward the doors and realizes the opera is over. "At length we also left, to judge at our own leisure the poem, the music, the actors, and the spectators."[83] For all the hyperbole Rétif's account likely contains, it touches what others described at the Opéra. "A conversation as loud as it was continuous covers the voices of the actors," commented a visitor to the Opéra late in the century.[84]

But for all the chaos at the Académie Royale there reigned a kind of order, one deeply shaped by modes of aristocratic sociability. Despite the rough edges and vulgar elements, contemporaries viewed the Opéra in the eighteenth century as a place to learn social graces, "to polish manners and make society more friendly."[85] The best way to do that was to watch others scrupulously. Opera glasses were *de rigueur*, necessary not so much for seeing the stage as for observing other spectators. One author estimated that half of the spectators present at any opera were "men and women of the lorgnette," and another wrote that there was nothing "so bourgeois and common" as a nobleman without his lorgnette at the Opéra.[86]

Noble girls who made their first appearance in society at the Opéra quickly learned to endure the gaze of the opera glasses with grace. The smallest details of their behavior were subject to ruthless inspection by dandies or rivals or fathers seeking wives for their sons. Their behavior, as Chevrier describes in exquisite detail, was expected to be both coquettish and controlled: if she "blushed in conversation," "lowered her eyes," or showed "a reserved manner in ignorance of all usage," the *grand monde* judged her "ridiculous and damned."[87] An account of the Opéra in 1738 gives a vivid description of the right response. "In the middle of the building were a number of men who stood and examined with the aid of lorgnettes the countenance and apparel of all women present. As the glasses alighted on a lady she would turn her eyes gently, smile in a friendly manner, play coyly with her muff or her fan. The game continued until the lorgnettes moved on to her neighbor, who would promptly take up the same role."[88] *Petits-maîtres*—young aristocrats of fussy tastes and precious manners—were virtuosi of the lorgnette. The comtesse de Courbon captured their unique mix of social power and silliness when she described them as the "idol of society and the scourge of good sense." The countess felt she had borne up fairly well under their scrutiny: one *petit-maître* gave her a look that seemed to say, "Oh yes, Mademoiselle, you will be obeyed; I adore you; I see nothing as beautiful as you; can you possibly know the ardor that devours me?"[89] She does not say what happened then.

Spectators also used their lorgnettes to keep an eye on the first boxes. That was the place to spot important personalities of the court or society. When the king, princes of the blood, or military heroes appeared in their boxes the audience would interrupt the music to applaud them. "The self love of almost everyone disappears before these privileged beings whom nature has created to lead," enthused the *Almanach musical* after an ovation for the comte d'Estaing at the Opéra. "As soon as they appear, all stare at them eagerly: one devours the pleasure of seeing them."[90] The entry of such beings regularly interrupted performances in the eighteenth century: the maréchal de Saxe received "resounding applause" when the audience spotted him at the Opéra after his 1745 victory at Fontenoy, and the prince de Condé's arrival near the end of the first act of a performance in 1763 produced an ovation so loud it covered the chorus.[91] At the very least such appearances disrupted the flow of performances, but occasionally actors dropped their roles altogether. After having begun the prologue to *Armide* the night the maréchal de Saxe celebrated his triumph, the characters Glory and Wisdom climbed to the balcony where he sat to crown him with laurel.[92] And when the comte d'Estaing appeared in the box of the duc de Chartres after he had led French troops in recapturing Grenada, one of the dancers took the crown intended for the mythical king in the ballet to the first-level boxes and crowned him instead.[93]

If the *honnêtes gens* of Paris took advantage of the Opéra to see and be seen, less reputable types also exploited the visibility for their own purposes. There were persistent reports of prostitutes renting the prominent first-balcony seats for professional reasons. Other shady characters appeared there, too. Because the opera is "essentially a school for gallantry and luxury," Pidansat de Mairobert warned, it inevitably has its vile elements: "men dishonored by lost women . . . [who] continually bring licence, debauchery and corruption."[94] The young especially were instructed to beware of older women of easy virtue who went to the opera seeking riches. Unsuspecting financiers, young officers in the army, and foreign visitors met these "sham princesses" at the Opéra, who seduced them, took their money, and moved on to others. "The victims they sacrifice are young Americans, little Englishmen, and the sons of good merchants who are treating themselves royally in Paris."[95]

Yet if spectators were free to arrive late, talk, watch others, and circulate, there was plenty at the Opéra that proper etiquette did not permit. Spectators, for example, mocked particularly arrogant or brusque behavior, as when the maréchal de Noailles wrongfully tried to evict a spectator from his seat.[96] When priests sat too near a companion, cries of "Monsieur abbé, let's see your hands!" would ring out.[97] And while all were aware of the prostitutes present, the audience tolerated only a limited display of familiarity between them and their clients. When an officer from the regiment of Lowendal escorted a woman of the demimonde into his first-level box in 1745, the audience turned their lorgnettes on the pair and began to murmur. "He gave her many scandalous caresses," a guard on duty soberly reported. The officer persisted, the murmurs turned to catcalls, and only after two visits by the sergeant of the interior guard was the couple persuaded to leave.[98]

Some maintained that it was bad form to stay for the entire opera. The young dandy Almair in La Morlière's *Angola*, described as "a scrupulous observer of etiquette [*bienséance*]," claims that there is "nothing *so indecent* as staying to the end" of an opera.[99] The practice was apparently common enough for the *Mercure* to mention it disapprovingly: it was a "disgrace," the paper wrote, for women to leave during the last acts of *Atys* and *Roland*.[100] Others held a prejudice against listening too intently to the music. A traveler to Paris who was quick to grasp the dynamics of behavior at the Opéra wrote with some derision that the only spectators who listened to the music were "several clerics, several shopkeepers, several schoolboys, sucklings of the muses and soldiers just returning from or about to leave for a tour of duty."[101] And a young nobleman explained to his guest that listening to the music with focused attention was "bourgeois." "There is nothing so damnable," he went on, "as listening to a work like a street merchant or some provincial just off the boat."[102]

For these spectators, attentiveness was a social *faux pas*, as the *Mercure* observed: spectators who attempted to listen to a work before judging it, the paper claimed, were regarded by the rest as "creatures from another world."[103] Circulating, conversing, arriving late, and leaving early were an accepted part of eighteenth-century musical experience, grudgingly tolerated by some and positively encouraged by others. "We listen at most to two or three pieces consecrated by fashion," as a character in *Angola* declares, "and at the end we excessively praise or thoroughly damn the whole work."[104]

As one of the few public places where Parisian nobility could gather, the Opéra was a place to take stock, a neutral field to size up rivals or secure allies. It shouldn't be surprising that spectators wielded their etiquette like a rapier. As at court, the accepted patterns of behavior at the Opéra left room for nuances that could carry esteem, reproach, or disdain. The duchesse d'Orléans, for example, sent the young prince de Condé an eminently artful rebuke at the Opéra when he appeared there too soon after leading his troops to defeat. The duchess loudly announced to a neighbor that reports of the humiliation must surely have been "fairy tales": "I just can't bring myself to believe it, and the proof that the news is untrue is that I see M. le prince de Condé sitting right here." The remark quickly made its way to the box of Condé, where his aunt Mme de Harsan scolded him so severely that he promptly burst into tears.[105]

But when individuals slipped outside the magic circle of esteem by losing favor in the sight of the powerful, the façade of *politesse* fell. The marquis d'Argenson recalls in his *Mémoires* the vicious change in the treatment of Mme de Pompadour at the Opéra when the rumor circulated that she was about to be dismissed as the king's mistress: people jeered her "with gross and mocking applause such as would never greet a woman of quality in the place she [formerly] occupied."[106]

The behavior that prevailed at the Opéra in the Old Regime was tied to the social structure of the upper nobility. The original impetus of precise etiquette had grown from Cardinal Richelieu's attempts in the seventeenth century to ensure respectful behavior toward the monarch from an unruly and irreverent aristocracy. In monitoring their every movement and scrutinizing each glance or grimace for hints of disloyalty, Richelieu subtly extended the control of the crown. Duty became distinction, and nobles soon relished the etiquette that gilded their subservience.[107] The uses of refined behavior grew. Proper etiquette minimized the risk of alienating the powerful with egregious mistakes by assigning comprehensive rituals to everyday behavior. It helped to assure predictable relations when so much depended upon the evaluation of others. "Without confirmation of one's prestige through behavior, this prestige is nothing," Norbert Elias has written of court society. "The immense value attached to the demonstration of prestige and the observation of etiquette does not betray an attachment to externals, but to what was virtually important to individual identity."[108] Courtly etiquette, moreover, permitted subtle variations that when skillfully delivered conveyed one's estimation of others, or perhaps dissembled one's judgment.[109]

Eventually, controlled behavior became an instrument of rule among the aristocracy themselves, a way of distributing and maintaining power within a social structure prone to rapid shifts in status. As even the most minute aspects of behavior carried social meaning—the manner in which one greeted the wife of a fellow noble, for example, or the respective depths of the bow when two courtiers brushed by each other in the corridors of Versailles—it was imperative to learn all aspects of politeness.[110] Refinements were forever possible. "It is certain that however frequently one associates with the most capable men and gallant ladies of the court . . . it is very difficult to reach perfection," as the chevalier de Méré wrote. "I will even maintain that however skilled one is in the subject of *bienséance* one is always in danger of making a false step."[111]

Thus the great need to observe, at court, in salons, and at the Opéra. This was how one learned conventions, discerned who was in favor and why, discovered whom to please, whom to avoid, and whom to insult. It was also essential in knowing which music to praise and which to damn. "One never judges things by what they are," wrote the great guardian of social etiquette Saint-Simon, "but by the people they concern."[112] Throughout performances spectators scanned the faces of the arbiters of taste—noblemen and *grandes dames* in the first boxes, princes of the blood and diplomats in the boxes on the stage, young *seigneurs* in the parterre—for signs of pleasure or disgust. The most widely read book of etiquette for the aristocracy in the eighteenth century, Antoine de Courtin's *Nouveau traité de la civilité*, was explicit on this point:

When it be your fortune at any play, or ball, or spectacle, to be placed next to a person of quality it is ungraceful to fly out into any rapture or extravagant acclamation at every passage that pleases you: you must give him leave to judge first, by attending his approbation. For though many times you may have reason enough, and it may show your capacity, yet it will be a greater evidence of your want of breeding and respect. It is the best way therefore to forbear till that person of quality applauds or condemns it, and then you may fall in as you see occasion.[113]

Lecerf de la Viéville, whose massive opus comparing French and Italian music was reprinted four times in the first half of the eighteenth century, gave essentially the same advice in matters of musical judgment, albeit couched more delicately: "To acquire good taste, we accustom ourselves to judging everything by listening to our natural sentiment and by confirming it with big and little rules. . . . At the opera we study with care the movements of spectators and let ourselves identify the judgements of the public and our own by the judgement of time."[114]

One consequence of this pattern of behavior at the Opéra was that taste came to be defined by groups rather than by individuals. Collective judgment held a legitimacy not granted to private opinion. "It is the job of the author to win our approval in advance, for we are the ones who decide their fate," declares a nobleman in a novel of the period, claiming that composers had "no merit if they are not fortunate enough to please us."[115] The mercurial nature of prestige, however, produced rival claims of authority, for the opinion of one group was only as definitive as others acknowledged it to be. One spectator asserted that composers must strive to please the women, who "hold the fate of the authors in the palm of their hands."[116] Others claimed that "young, overconfident *seigneurs* who ramble on about taste like invalids after glory" set opinions in taste.[117] Chevrier revealed the dynamic of judgment when he claimed that every foyer had "its haughty critic," a title in possession of either "the well-born man who pretends to have intelligence, or of the parvenu who is . . . familiar with the *grands*."[118]

Like the balls, banquets, coronations, and ceremonies of absolutism, musical experience in the Old Regime served the ideological function of temporarily illuminating the invisible power structure of the system.[119] If the Académie Royale de Musique in 1750 was less explicitly the king's spectacle than it had been in the late seventeenth century, it was still a pageant of nobility on display. As a result it was most typically the socially powerful—not always the most musically discerning spectators— who set taste. To manage the needed insouciance of casual visits and pleasant talk while also knowing which airs to praise required the prodigious skills of observation the nobility had learned to perfect.

It also relied upon knowing that those groups who set taste could be easily spotted in their accustomed places, a task made easier by the placement of the highest born in the most visible boxes and their tendency to keep the same box for years. As one observer wrote in 1735: "The parterre, formerly such a sovereign legislator, now seeks its suffrages in the gazes of the first boxes."[120]

Jean-Jacques Rousseau complained that in polite society the opinions of favored groups rode roughshod over individual taste. So it was at the Opéra, too, where fashion held sway over private judgment.[121] Dramatically, the plots and music were not suited to engage the deepest emotions of listeners. And just as at court, it was ill-advised and unnecessary at the Opéra to leap before you looked. But if musical experience in the Old Regime was scarcely private, it was anything but unified. The visible social hierarchy in the theater, as well as the arrangement of private boxes shut off from one another, reinforced the feeling that the public was an aggregate of coteries and cliques. For all its fairies and gardens, musical experience in the Old Regime was strangely mundane, neither intimate enough to transport the soul nor majestic enough to unite its fragmented public.

2

Expression as Imitation

In *La Nouvelle Héloïse* Saint-Preux gives a rather dismissive assessment of the effects of music. "Music is nothing but a vain sound that can flatter the ear and acts only indirectly on the soul; the impression of the chords is purely mechanical and physical. What do the chords have to do with sentiment, and why should I hope to be more strongly touched by a pretty harmony than by a pleasant combination of colors?"[1] In his simple declaration Saint-Preux speaks for a whole generation of audiences, describing a package of assumptions pertaining both to musical expression and to individual experience. Music washed over the senses and seldom touched the souls of spectators in the mid-eighteenth century. In fact, their understanding of musical expression virtually excluded the possibility of profound musical experience.

For those who shared the aesthetic expectations of Saint-Preux regarding the expressive impotence of harmony—and there were many such listeners in the middle of the eighteenth century—sentiment was a quality of the plot and not an effect of the tones. The behavior of audiences at mid-century was in part a manifestation of these views. Music dazzled, flattered, and enchanted, but rarely did it draw its hearers away from their other preoccupations to impose an absorbed, attentive silence. "A concert is to the ears what a feast is to taste, what perfumes are to smell, and what fireworks are for the eyes," wrote one spectator of the sensual experience of music.[2] And, he might have added, concerts, feasts, perfumes, and fireworks create a splendid setting for conversation.

Listeners in Paris in the middle years of the century spoke of musical

expression in terms of images or recognizable sounds, with music painting its particular meaning. To them, music presented a clear picture in a
one-to-one correspondence of tone to image or it had no expression at
all. "All music must have a signification and a meaning, the same as
poetry," reads the *Manuel de l'homme du monde* from 1761; "thus the
sounds must conform to the things they express."[3] For d'Alembert music was "hopeless noise" when the composer failed to paint clearly in his
music.[4] Marmontel wrote virtually the same thing—"Music that paints
nothing is insipid"—while Bâton declared music to be an art by virtue
of its capacity to imitate. "The object of every art is to paint nature: to
the mind for poetry, to the eyes for painting, and to the ears for music."[5]
The abbé Morellet devoted a book to musical expression in 1759 to
conclude that music is expressive insofar as it is imitative.[6]

Spectators often focused on words in the libretto when they described musical expression. As one listener said of Lully's *Armide*: "At
the word '*perçait*' I see, it seems to me, Renaud as he stabs the suppliant
Armide through the heart." "Beautiful words are the first foundation of
beautiful music."[7] It followed that if you couldn't describe what the
music meant, it had no meaning. Although the phrase would take on
different implications later in the century, spectators accepted as axio-
matic the principle that music was the slave of poetry. And what they
heard only seemed to confirm it. Eighteenth-century audiences also
cited natural sounds—birds chirping, brooks babbling, storms—when
they described musical expression apart from word painting. One listener claimed that music could "paint all that is capable of making
noise," listing thunder, wind, the surging of the sea, the clang of weapons, the songs of birds, a waterfall, and a river.[8] He added that he had
never listened to the overture to Rameau's *Pygmalion* without seeing in
his mind's eye a sculptor chiseling a block of marble.[9] Rulhière, a musician in the orchestra of the Opéra, heard honeybees and hornets in the
"Ballet de la Rose" of Rameau's *Les Indes galantes* and faulted the composer for the annoying associations they raised.[10]

Expecting to hear familiar sounds in the music, audiences invariably
heard them, sometimes in extraordinary quantities. The abbé de Morambert, a self-described harmonophile, relates hearing bells, cannon
blasts, wind, the roar of animals, even cries of "Vive le Roi!" in instrumental overtures.[11] Others identified more abstract images. Cazotte
praised the music in the first act of Mondonville's popular ballet *Titon
et l'Aurore* for depicting a beautiful sunrise, flowers opening, the dew

lifting, and the awakening of nature at dawn.[12] But in all cases the musical link with the extramusical idea—whether word, sound or image— had to be clear if the music was to hold one's attention.

Charles Batteux, an intellectual who discussed the relation between natural sounds and their musical imitation in *Les Beaux-arts réduits à un même principe* (1746), lent the weight of philosophy to these listeners' descriptions. For Batteux, listening was discovery and nature was the model. "The musician is no more free than the painter," he writes. "If he paints a storm, a brook, or a gentle breeze, the tones are all in nature. He can take them only from her. . . . If we cannot understand the sense of the expressions music contains, it has no wealth for us."[13]

Such literalism occasionally approached the ludicrous. One critic faulted Mondonville for not distinguishing clearly enough between the depiction of titans, demons, and the cyclops. Another discerning listener admired a musical passage that "painted the painful and hopeless effort of a dying eighty-year-old trying to spit up a piece of phlegm in his chest."[14] It also made audiences highly subject to suggestion, primed as they were to hear images. In the libretto to his *tragédie-lyrique Zoroastre* Rameau summarized what he intended the overture to depict: "The first part paints a most moving picture of Abramamus's barbaric might and the lamentations of the nations he oppresses. A gentle stillness ensues, and hope is reborn. The second part is a lively, cheerful description of the magnanimity of Zoroastre and the happiness of the nations he has delivered from bondage." And this was exactly what one listener who wrote to *Les Cinq années littéraires* in 1749 heard![15] Popular accounts of Rameau's music from mid-century are filled with unexpected images: d'Aquin de Châteaulyon wrote that the "bursting of shells, speeding rockets, a sparkling sky, tumult, shouts of joy, are all depicted in the manliest hues"; Clément complained that the overture to *Zaïs* "paints so well the unraveling of chaos" that the effect was unpleasant; and Chabanon wrote that the overture to *Naïs* "paints . . . the Titans' attack."[16]

Listeners in the first three-quarters of the century sometimes claimed that music could go beyond images to evoke human sentiments, but their starting point was almost always a clear painting that generated emotions by association: the imitation of birds might bring peaceful emotions associated with the countryside, for instance, or the sound of a raging sea might inspire terror by bringing to mind shipwrecks and drownings. In his *Critical Reflections on Poetry, Painting and Music*

(1719), Jean-Baptiste Dubos wrote that works imitating storms "engage us to the action by making almost the same impression upon us as would arise from the very sound they imitate."[17]

That route to emotional effect might seem roundabout, especially since Dubos acknowledged that the tones, accents, sighs, and inflections of the human voice could be imitated in music. But spectators of the period did not conceive of music evoking sentiment in the vague, generalized way later listeners described, so the mere reproduction of human tones couldn't guarantee an emotional effect. Any emotional response from the music alone, for those who experienced it, was a two-step process that required recognizing the imitation before one felt its associations: Ruhlière had to recognize the hornets in Rameau before his skin could crawl. As one listener wrote, "Sounds by themselves are incapable of representing anything other than sounds; they succeed in arousing ideas only as a result of established conventions that . . . associate a particular sound with a particular idea."[18]

These aesthetic assumptions had specific musical implications. First, they placed the burden of emotional and thematic expression upon the text. By and large, listeners regarded the musical tableaux they described as supplements to the libretto; whatever enhancement they provided to the emotional impact of the drama was purely secondary. This made the recitatives and airs the locus of the drama. "Accompaniment is vicious each time it distracts the ear and captures the principal attention," wrote Jacques Lacombe.[19] For the political thinker Mably, the accompaniment "is made only to support the voice" and serves its function best "only when the spectator, paying no attention to it so to speak, is yet more sensitive to the charms of the voice."[20]

Second, listeners regarded harmony as incapable of any but the crudest sorts of expression, for in most cases it was the melodic line that painted words, imitated the sounds of birds, or indicated the rise and fall of a churning sea. For audiences until the 1770s, harmony was a meaningless combination of sounds, "a prism that presents the most beautiful colors but does not constitute a painting," as Batteux put it.[21] "What happens when composers rely upon harmony?" asked a letter addressed to the *Mercure*. "The most beautiful scenes are disfigured, tenderness is stifled, all interest is lost, the ear only is satisfied—or rather deadened—while the mind and heart are left with nothing."[22] Spectators described harmony as empty arithmetic, a kind of syllogism appropriate for scholars to dissect and examine but wholly without expressive nuance. Fontenelle's trenchant phrase was the common currency when spectators heard interludes or overtures without obvious images: "Sonate, que me veux-tu?"—What do you want from me, Sonata?

Denis Diderot and Jean-Jacques Rousseau each pushed the imitative model to the breaking point in their works on musical expression.[23] They both wrote extensively about music—Diderot in essays, Rousseau in the *Encyclopédie* and his own musical dictionary. Their perceptions were based upon the same music the rest of the Parisian public heard, but their characteristic genius of spinning philosophy from the everyday—a stolen ribbon, an actor's gesture, the human voice—led them to expose the logic, and the limitations, of the imitative view.

Both shared their contemporaries' insistence upon musical painting, even as the images they perceived approached the insubstantial. Rousseau's famous line that music can depict even silence comes from a passage filled with images: for a composer endowed with the gift of "placing the eye in the ear," he writes, slumber, solitude, a prison, a tempest, a cool grove of trees, and fire are all worthy of "great musical tableaux."[24] Diderot similarly cited sunrise, nightfall, cruelty, and innocence as examples of musical painting, emphasizing, with Rousseau, the imitative mode by describing them in terms of the composer's palette.[25] Neither had much patience for music without clear images; for Rousseau it failed to carry the slightest emotion to the heart, and Diderot called it a sensory pleasure at best.

Yet Rousseau and Diderot both described emotional effects as they listened to music. Their attempts to account for them are perhaps more illuminating for what they fail to explain than for what they say. For just how does music *imitate* solitude or innocence? Isn't the metaphor of painting, already mixed when applied to storms or bird calls, altogether inappropriate for conveying what cannot be heard?

Rousseau resolved the dilemma after a fashion by referring to his anthropology of language, a theory that sketched the roots of human speech in intuitive, passionate utterances. For Rousseau, in the beginning were the passions, so that even before words appeared humans sang a natural language—a sigh of love or pity, a cry of pain, an ejaculation of anger. Recoverable in music, these most natural of sounds are imprinted on the heart like a genetic code of tones. Music thus acts through sympathetic arousal, revivifying our truest and highest passions. (The golden thread that runs throughout Jean-Jacques's oeuvre, how to approximate Eden in our own cursed state, glimmers here.) The great task for composers is to imitate the natural sounds of human passion, which will instantly move listeners without their necessarily knowing why.[26] For Rousseau, only melody can imitate these primal passions. He therefore condemns both polyphony (the sentiments of two simultaneous melodies cancel each other out and the effect is "null," he writes) and rich harmonies ("gothic," "barbaric," without any imitative capacity).[27]

Rousseau does not stop here, though, convinced as he is that he hears more than human passion in music. Or to put it more accurately, the things he feels as he listens—the dank chill of an underground prison, an arid desert floor, shady groves—defy any direct imitation. Rousseau concludes that the composer "substitutes the elusive image of the object for that of the movements its presence excites in the heart of the observer." That phrase should prompt a double take: music as the imitation of images of movements brought on by objects? Or again: "he will not directly represent things but will excite the same movements in the soul that one feels in seeing them."[28] Is there anything left of musical imitation in these descriptions?

Catherine Kintzler writes that Rousseau completely recasts the classical doctrine of imitation in this passage even while retaining its fundamental vocabulary.[29] Fair enough, though a more prosaic way of putting it might be that Rousseau, who summarized his life work as well as any with the phrase "I felt before I thought," simply sensed more in music than he could explain within the common frame of understanding and was not terribly eager to work out intellectually why this was so.

Diderot took another route in explaining how music could imitate human passion. The key for him was in hieroglyphs, distinctive melodic emblems that worked in much the same way that rhythmic cadence or the sheer sound of words adds sensuous depth to poetry. The examples Diderot provides of hieroglyphs are meticulous and, one must say, extraordinarily cerebral. One illustration employs a five-measure passage set to Virgil's text at the moment of Dido's death: in it, Diderot identifies a descending half step as the hieroglyph of Dido fainting, the interval of a tritone as that of Dido pulling herself up on one elbow, a half step up as her wavering gaze, a melodic descent as her last breath, and so on.[30]

Diderot thus succeeds in showing how melody "imitates" emotions in a way that goes beyond merely reproducing the sounds of the human voice. But if Rousseau's adherence to the terms of imitation produced some difficulties for coherence, Diderot's hieroglyphs provide dubious descriptions of how anyone actually listened. Is this why Diderot seems to soft-pedal the theory even as he presents it? Reading hieroglyphs is complicated and requires extreme concentration, he writes, and even then they are "so faint and fugitive that it is easy to lose them or mis-interpret them."[31]

Although for different reasons, both Diderot and Rousseau were backed into awkward explanations as they tried to cast their own experience in the dominant terms of aesthetic understanding. That they both stayed within the general paradigm of imitation illustrates its hold over their generation. That paradigm was in part linguistic, constructed in terms crystallized by Boileau ("Rien n'est beau que la vrai") and burnished by a half-century of elaboration and application, from Fénelon to Voltaire.[32] As Diderot and Jaucourt illustrate in their *Encyclopédie* articles "Imitation" and "Imitation (Poésie, Rhétor.),"the word was still the touchstone not just of music but of painting and poetry in the middle of the century.[33]

We sense Rousseau pressing up against the constraints of this language in his works on music, pushing the words beyond their logical limits. But the paradigm was also constructed from the music Rousseau and Diderot heard, music whose most salient expressive feature was imitation. Even as their analyses went beyond the directly imitative, Rousseau and Diderot found their points of reference in musical characteristics that seemed to confirm the truth that great art was fundamentally mimetic. Before another way of hearing would be thinkable—and therefore fully experienced—both the language of aesthetics and style of musical composition would have to change.

The conception of musical expression that shaped eighteenth-century listeners' musical accounts grew directly from the sounds of Lully and his rough contemporaries Campra, Destouches, Marais, and Delalande. The music of these composers established a framework for musical meaning in the minds of listeners, tacitly setting out the parameters of music's perceived powers. Rameau broke from that tradition in many important respects, and it is clear that his own views of musical expression were vastly more encompassing than those of any of his French predecessors. The important point here, however, is that spectators could approach and ultimately accustom themselves to the music of Rameau with the aesthetic expectations Lully and his immediate successors nourished largely intact. Despite its innovations Rameau's music confirmed spectators' beliefs that expression was imitation.

Given Lully's relatively simple orchestration and restricted harmonic scope, it is not surprising that French spectators discounted harmony as potentially expressive: Lully's instrumental writing leaves the burden of dramatic expression to the text. His orchestration is uncomplicated and in general exhibits little variety from one scene to the next. With notable exceptions, Lully seldom exploited the particular characteristics of individual instruments: oboes, flutes, violins, and trumpets often play the same lines. There are few wide leaps in his string parts, and virtuosic passages are rare.[34] During recitatives and airs there is very little instrumental embellishment and virtually no harmonic complexity to distract from the text. The cello plays a simple support, occasionally moving up and down stepwise, while the keyboard plays basic chords. Dissonances are brief, and instrumental movement independent of the vocal lines is virtually nonexistent.[35] In large choral scenes in which the full orchestra plays, the accompaniment almost always doubles the homophonic choral parts.

But it would be wrong to suppose that Lully was unwilling to write dramatic expression into the music. Lully frequently gives musical renderings of individual words by manipulating the prosody in a manner obvious even to an untrained ear. Virtually all the text of lyric works not only by Lully but by the other French composers through Rameau is set syllabically—that is, with each syllable given a single note, rather like early medieval chant. This made music a slave to poetry in a most literal way, for it means that instead of following a regular meter the melody shifts from one meter to another to follow the rhythm of the text. It also erodes any clear distinction between recitative and air, a characteristic that invariably confounded foreign visitors to the Opéra.[36]

Any deviation from such syllabic regularity draws instant attention to itself. For eighteenth-century ears it would be heard as a deliberate marker of expression. Composers from Lully to Rameau distinguished the same group of words in this way: *voler* (to fly), *lancer* (to throw), *enchaîner* (to enchain, as in "love enchains my soul"), *soupir* (to sigh), *triompher* (to triumph), *murmurer* (to murmur, as in a stream), *ondes* (waves), *tonnerre* (thunder), *ramage* (the warbling of birds), *gloire* (glory), and *victoire* (victory). These words are set to brief melismas, two- to four-measure passages of slurred notes sung on a single syllable. The compositional practice was so embedded that there was scarcely a melismatic passage in fifty years of French opera that did not emphasize a word from this group or its circles of associations.

Word painting operated in one of several ways depending upon the word. *Soupir* and *ramage* permit a rough musical imitation of what the words actually signify. Hence in the second act of *Omphale* (1701) by Destouches a descending melisma consisting of an eighth note, two sixteenths, and a quarter prepared by a flickering ornament occurs on the second syllable of *soupir*.[37] (Dubos must have known the work, and he may well have been thinking of this passage when he asserted that music could imitate the sounds of human passion.) Imitations of birds abound in eighteenth-century opera; one especially elaborate soprano solo, with trills and turns in the flute accompaniment, appears in *Les Éléments*.[38]

A second, more abstract form of imitation occurs on such words as *ondes, murmurer, voler, lancer,* and *enchaîner*. In these cases the melody gives a rendering that might be described as conceptual. The melody shoots up on *volez* in the second *Entrée* of Campra's *Les Fêtes vénitiennes* (1710), for instance, and a long, undulating phrase rises and falls on the word *ondes* in Aeolus' air from Lully's *Alceste*.[39] (See Example 1.) Most intriguing is the frequent appearance of the word *enchaîner* in these texts, predominantly though not uniquely used to describe love. It was of course a staple in the vocabulary of *galanterie*, but its particular emphasis through melismas creates insinuating, inextricable, ensnarling images wholly absent in the text.

It is difficult to imagine how a melody might paint such words as *triompher, gloire,* or *victoire*, and in fact there is no characteristic movement these melismas take to suggest that composers had any more precise motive in mind than simply to draw attention to the words with a punctuated phrase or flourish. The emphasis gives the words a small jolt of excitement, which, taken alone, accentuates the concept in a dramatic if imprecise way. But if eighteenth-century spectators heard "imitations" of birds, sighs, waves, and chains, it seems probable that some would draw the conclusion that these melismas were the attempted musical painting of glory or victory, whether successful or not. Judged from the perspective created by hearing abundant bird calls and sighs—that the only expression was in imitation—these latter instances likely appeared to test the outer limits of the art, attempts to imitate the things that have no sound. Maybe this was behind Rousseau's strange assertion that music "paints everything, even those things that are only visible."[40] What seems certain, and of extreme importance as a foundation of aesthetic expectations among eighteenth-century spectators, is that this most remarkable and enduring compositional technique of the first half of the century firmly tied musical expression to language. It would be many years before music was freed.

Other orchestral effects employed by Lully and fully exploited by his successors helped to establish the paradigm of imitation among listeners. The Olympian story lines—not to mention the prodigious stage machinery—made it difficult for librettists to resist including a tempest or two in their plots, and composers took the opportunity to narrate the storms with descriptive music. In the first act of *Alceste* Lully depicts

Example 1. Word painting from *Alceste*, Jean-Baptiste Lully.

a storm with rapidly ascending and descending scales in the violins; sixteenth-note whirlwinds depict a tempest in the prologue to *Cadmus et Hermione*.[41] The real pathbreaker in depicting the weather was Marin Marais, who composed a storm for *Alcyone* (1706) that raged on for over a hundred measures with drums rumbling and strings and oboes screeching out notes in the high end of their range. The storm made the opera's reputation. *Alcyone* was revived five times between its premiere and 1771, the storm was excerpted for special performances, and a dozen works with storms appeared on the Opéra stage in less than ten years.[42]

There are, finally, the battle scenes, in which composers quickened the rhythm into crisp patterns of an eighth and two sixteenth notes and scored fanfares for the brass. The first act of Lully's *Thésée* begins with a grand combat in which soldiers cry out "Avançons! Avançons! Frappons! Perçons!" to a background of drums and trumpets.[43] There is a similar battle scene in *Alceste*. One of the most riveting moments in *Issé* by Destouches comes near the start when Hercules fights a dragon as a nymph sings "What frightful noise!" and the orchestra plays fanfares and battle charges.[44]

Whether in word painting or orchestral imitation, most stage works in the first half of the century were susceptible to a literal reading that apparently worked against other ways of hearing. In so successfully tying their music to the text composers tied their own hands: for how could you *not* evoke images—wild images beyond all intention and expectation—once you had conditioned audiences to hear birds, storms, and battles? Before long spectators would be insisting they heard cyclops, titans, invalids coughing up phlegm, hornets, honeybees, and who knows what else.

In Lully we sense an effort to render more abstract, nonimitative emotional states: the gentle lapping motif that accompanies Renaud's sleep in *Armide* might be heard as imitating water, but we also derive from it a sense of peace and tranquillity.[45] There are similarly stirring sleep scenes in *Atys, Roland*, Desmarets's *Circé*, Marais's *Ariane et Bacchus*, and Montéclair's *Jephté*. The expanding scope and role of the orchestra among Lully's successors points to a greater psychological intent in their compositions.[46] We hear this psychological dimension because we have a conceptual space for it, having experienced music that so clearly operates on this level and possessing a vocabulary to describe its expression apart from imitation. That space had yet to appear for most mid-eighteenth-century listeners. Its absence, in fact, illuminates the peculiar fate of Rameau's operas in the eighteenth century: initially resisted, gradually assimilated, and at last embraced as the voice of French opera—and all for artistic reasons Rameau himself considered secondary.

When they first heard it, French spectators were shocked by the music of Rameau. "There's enough music in this opera to make ten!" exclaimed André Campra on hearing *Hippolyte et Aricie*.[47] Far and away the greatest innovator since Lully, Rameau filled his operas with thickly scored accompaniments and used dissonances and modulations that were without precedent. Solo instruments play lines that never appear in the vocal parts, and in contrast to the homophonic ensemble singing of Lully's works Rameau's duets and choruses are frequently polyphonic.[48] Rameau uses chromaticism in his harmonies and employs a wider range of keys than his predecessors.

Eighteenth-century listeners regularly criticized Rameau for writing accompaniments that distracted from the text. One claimed that Rameau, "like an idiot," had "sacrificed the librettist to his own musical pride."[49] Rousseau wrote that he "made his accompaniments so confused, so overcharged, so incessant, that the head can hardly tolerate the continuous din of the . . . instruments."[50] Others, such as Jean-Marie Clément, mocked him for his accompaniments, which they said were "too scientific, . . . too labored, recherché." Another critic rhymed:

> To judge our modern music
> I have a simple plan:
> If beauty is a theorem
> Rameau's a brilliant man.
>
> But if, by chance, pure nature
> Guides beauty as its rule,
> Then art must strive to paint it,
> And Rameau's an utter fool.[51]

One listener claimed he had been "racked, flayed, dislocated" by the accompaniment to *Les Indes galantes*. "The music is a perpetual witchery; nature has no share in it. Nothing is more craggy and scabrous. . . . Its airs are fit to stir up the bemused nerves of a paralytic."[52]

But the crucial point was that with time eighteenth-century listeners accepted Rameau's work as expressive in the Lullian terms they had come to expect. Its dense novelty may have been a jumble, but it still had recognizable features. Listeners seized upon Rameau's imitations, both intended and imagined, and ignored or complained about the rest. There were certainly enough musical imitations in Rameau's *tragédies-lyriques* and *opéras-ballets* to confirm listeners' basic expectations for expressiveness.[53] As Theseus sings to Neptune in *Hippolyte et Aricie* the accompaniment surges in ascending and descending scales whose long mellifluous lines evoke the rolling motion of waves. Piccolos playing in thirds with dotted rhythms and trills imitate the songs of birds in *Les Indes galantes*, and a shepherdess sings a virtuosic solo with a flute accompaniment whose trills and ornaments imitate nightingales in *Hippolyte et Aricie*.[54] The ferocity of Rameau's storms well exceeds those of Marais and his imitators, and *Les Indes galantes* contains the musical depiction of an erupting volcano.[55] (See Examples 2 and 3.)

Example 2. Nightingales from *Hippolyte et Aricie*, Jean-Philippe Rameau.

Example 3. Rameau's depiction of a volcano erupting, from *Les Indes galantes*.

Rameau was convinced that the orchestra could convey emotional states, and he experimented with ways to express these moods in music. "The expression of feeling requires a change of key," he wrote to a correspondent, "whereas the painting of images and the imitation of different sounds does not need it. . . . The wind will remain in the same mood . . . as long as the same key persists."[56] In his *Treatise on Harmony* Rameau claimed that harmony could "unquestionably" excite different emotions, and he wrote elsewhere that harmony was in fact superior to melody in arousing passionate responses among listeners.[57]

To modern ears Rameau's music bears convincing testimony to these intentions. The tranquility of the sleep scene in *Dardanus*, the fierce fury of the descent to Hades or Télaire's intensely mournful "Tristes apprêts" in *Castor et Pollux*, and the calm despair of Theseus imploring Pluto in *Hippolyte et Aricie* are among the many instances of Rameau's success in expanding the dramatic possibilities of the orchestra without resorting to imitation.[58] Judging from the reactions of the first generation of French audiences to hear Rameau's harmonies, however, his particular intentions for emotional expression went largely unrecognized, so great was the tendency to identify an image in the tones.[59] As d'Aquin wrote in the *Siècle littéraire de Louis XV*, "M. Rameau is the most sublime painter of our century."[60] To listen for and find musical images seems to have eclipsed other ways of hearing, even as Rameau attempted to press his audiences beyond the accustomed storm scenes, birds, and battles.

When expression is defined in terms of imitation, musical experience involves more the outer than the inner person, more the senses than the soul. To recognize musical imitations was largely an intellectual activity, even if the presumed imitations were bizarre: if the image was clear, then others should also be able to hear it. Recognition was not interpretation. A tableau of sounds painted clearly enough for all to identify contains no intimate knowledge. There is little mention of subjective, inner musical meaning in the musical accounts of spectators from the first three-quarters of the eighteenth century.

There was a rough convergence between views of musical expression and aristocratic social dynamics. Convinced that music dazzled the senses with its flourishes and occupied the mind with its images, spectators found that they could divide their attention between the stage and the hall without compromising the experience. An attentive, absorbed public was so foreign to the idea of opera that events which later audiences would condemn as distracting filled eighteenth-century per-

formances without great complaint. By discouraging undivided attentiveness, in fact, the reigning social expectations may well have preoccupied audiences to such an extent that other ways of perceiving
music—ways that required more focused and engaged listening—were
effectively not possible.

Like musical cannon blasts or thunderbolts, the decorations on the
stage and fashions in the first boxes touched the senses more than the
soul. "We are besieged from all sides at the Opéra, and there is no way
for us to defend ourselves," wrote Rémond de Saint-Mard. "Our eyes
are seduced, our ears are flattered at every instant, and from it all a kind
of enchantment forms." [61] Aesthetically as well as socially the Opéra was
a house of pleasure. If the music brought agreeable sensations or compelling images, you listened; if not, you could always talk or survey the
scene. "Let's take it for what it is: a marvelous journey where people
love each other, hate each other, caress each other, and beat each other
all so very pleasantly." [62] For deep emotion audiences went to the
Comédie. But for magnificence, enchantment, and a little mischief, they
went to the Opéra.

PART TWO

A Sensitive Public

Ours will be described as a century of profound science and philosophy, rich in discoveries and full of power and reason. The spirit of the Nation seems to be in a blessed crisis: vibrant, widespread enlightenment has made every man feel he can be better. One inquires, acts, invents, reforms. . . . I see in each class a wish to be useful, to succeed, to enlarge its ideas, its learning, its pleasures, which can only work to universal advantage, for this is how all will grow, prosper, and improve themselves. Let us therefore try, if possible, to improve this great spectacle as well.

> Pierre Augustin Caron de Beaumarchais,
> Introduction to his libretto for Salieri's
> *Tarare* (1784)

3

Tears and the
New Attentiveness

What most impressed Nicolas Karamzin when he arrived at the Paris Opéra during his Grand Tour of the West was the beautiful blond stranger in his box who was wearing red roses. Flirtatious, though a touch formal, she led their conversation from travel to music to love, pausing now and again to inhale the roses. When the curtain rose and flooded the hall with light from the stage the spectators broke into applause. "The men are pleased with the light," she explained, "but we fear it. Just see, for example, how suddenly the young lady opposite us has grown pale!" Karamzin examined the hall in the better light and began to comment on the women, but soon the music of Gluck's *Orphée et Eurydice* filled his attention. Before long, all he could think of was Rousseau: word had it that he wept the first time he heard the work. Karamzin began to understand the effect, and he listened more intently. All thoughts of the spectators around him had vanished.[1]

On first glance, the audience Karamzin observed might have looked substantially similar to the public from forty years before. The maréchal de Noailles, the duc d'Orléans, and the prince de Conti still sat in the boxes adjoining the stage—now variously called *baignoires, entre-colonnes,* and *crachoirs*—and new boxes of distinction called *timbales* flanked the orchestra pit, placing their renters the maréchal de Soubise

---

Part opening illustration: Moreau le Jeune, *Les Adieux*, 1777. Photograph courtesy of the Bibliothèque Forney.

and the duc de Luxembourg in prominent view as well.[2] As before, the first-level boxes were filled with counts and countesses, princes and dukes. Men still milled about in the parterre below, and, as before, occasional shouts of derision pierced the air.

But if the Opéra of the 1770s and 1780s was still the rendezvous of the rich, their experience there was in certain respects vastly different from what it was before. Despite the presence of princes near the stage, the precise map of social hierarchy maintained earlier by subscribers and free entries had now lost all its focus. Substantial numbers of non-nobles sat in the first boxes, and some—such as the art collector Dubreuil, an early supporter of Greuze, whose apartment on the rue Montmartre was filled with marbles, bronzes, and rare furniture—could even afford to rent the boxes on the stage.[3]

Some of the most powerful aristocrats took out boxes decidedly less visible than the first-level seats so prized earlier in the century. Perhaps it was Marie Antoinette's decision to move her royal box from the first to the second level that prompted Mme de Genlis, M. le duc de Biron, and the comte d'Artois to maintain boxes there as well. (Artois's box directly faced the queen's from across the hall, a place reserved for the king in earlier theaters—by now it was whispered that Artois had usurped his older brother's royal bed, too.)[4]

But it seems less clear why other notables of the Old Regime sought boxes yet higher and less visible, especially as the upper regions were sure to contain commoners—and perhaps worse. The duc d'Aumont and the prince de Condé both maintained boxes on the third level in the 1789–90 operatic season, an area "decent men" had been warned to avoid twenty-five years earlier.[5] Higher still in the fourth, fifth, and sixth levels sat Chancellor Maupeou, who inflamed opponents of absolutism in 1770 by exiling the parlements, the architect Lenoir, and the renowned chemist Antoine Laurent de Lavoisier.[6]

For spectators surveying the boxes of the hall, this mosaic of courtier, prince, courtesan, and commoner was surely striking—and perhaps disorienting for the old timers who had grown up in theaters segregated by status. In many cases the arrangement dispersed bankers and lawyers from the Third Estate among aristocratic subscribers, but with the high nobility now scattered throughout the hall the clash in status was sometimes flagrant. On the same level with the queen and her lover, for example, sat Mlle Dervieux, an actress saluted by the *Correspondance littéraire* for earning handsome incomes hosting "salons" where gentlemen dined, played cards, and threw dice (a far cry from the urbane gatherings of Mme de Geoffrin and Julie de Lespinasse, to be sure).[7] Between the third-row boxes of the prince de Conti and the prince des Deux-Ponts sat the former opera *danseuse* Mlle Renard, also grown wealthy through her charms, and her husband, Charles Böhmer, the humiliated court jeweler who first created the infamous diamond necklace.[8] Spectators looking to the highest boxes in 1786 might as easily see the duc d'Orléans (should he choose to sit here rather than in his box on the stage) as Mirabeau, the dissolute aristocrat who would soon turn revolutionary.[9]

If the highest elites of aristocratic society had scrambled the map of social power by choice in the last years of the Old Regime, the king himself upset the pattern further by neglect. Still in the habit of granting free entries to the opera as an act of royal munificence, the king maintained until the late 1780s the practice of specifying where his guests were to sit. Thus in 1775 royal architects and court advisers sat in the amphitheater, while pages from princely households and various inspectors and record keepers were directed to the parterre or paradise.[10]

Starting in 1787, however, the king simply sent opera administrators the names of persons to be admitted, with only the rarest mention of location. By now the lists were a major headache for the Opéra's administrators, whose complaints about the revenue they cost did little good: at any given performance up to three hundred spectators would compete with one another (and conceivably with regular ticket holders slow to find their seats) for the best vacant places.[11] Confirming one's artistic impressions in the responses of the powerful, already made difficult by the aristocratic migration, was further complicated by the king's indifference to seating.

Of course the Opéra was a still a prime spot to see and be seen—a habit Grimm sadly termed a "sickness without a cure"—but the high nobility's dispersal throughout the theater pointed to a contrary urge. By the 1770s there was growing interest in the artistic elements of the spectacle.[12] More and more, spectators were favoring the seats that faced the stage over those along the sides of the hall, "where there is no illusion," as one spectator wrote, "and one clearly sees the lights that produce sunrise and sunset."[13] And the acoustics were better in the theater's upper levels than in the lower boxes, where a slight echo made the singers sound like they were inside a barrel.[14]

The artistic considerations of sight lines and sound were a growing preoccupation among spectators in the closing decades of the century. The immediate cause of discussion about optimal theatrical design was a series of fires that kept architects busy designing and redesigning halls. In 1761 a fire at the Palais Royal destroyed the old rectangular opera hall that had served the Académie Royale de Musique for the previous eighty years. The company took up temporary residence in a hall at the Tuileries Palace as a new hall was built over the ruins of the old one. Opening in 1770, this second Palais Royal theater caught fire in 1781. A site on the outskirts of Paris near the Porte Saint-Martin was chosen for the fourth hall in twenty years.[15]

The fires occasioned near-continuous discussion in royal memoirs, pamphlets, and newspapers concerning theater layout and design. In his 1782 *Essai sur l'architecture théâtrale*, Pierre Patte summarized the position of many over the previous twenty years when he wrote that theaters must meet the demands "of seeing well and hearing well."[16] For one royal architect who contributed ideas for the 1770 Palais Royal construction, this imperative meant turning the partitions between the boxes toward the stage and eliminating the onstage boxes altogether. The dramatic "unity of place," he argued, was severely compromised by spectators sitting alongside the performers.[17]

Another architectural memoir suggested more modest changes in the boxes on the stage: reduce their number from six to two, move them farther downstage, and widen the available space on the stage by making them more shallow. Not only would the change reduce the number of spectators on the stage, the author argued; it would give the orchestra a better sound by permitting the double basses to sit on a slightly elevated platform. (A perennial problem at the Opéra had been the muffled sound of the low strings, but to seat them above the other players would obstruct the view of spectators in forestage boxes with the double basses' long necks.)[18] Charles-Nicolas Cochin made his case for heightened dramatic experience by proposing a theater in the shape of a flattened ellipse, with the back wall pulled considerably closer to the stage.[19] Others seized the occasion to lobby for seats in the parterre, which would "contribute to the tranquillity of the spectacle" without necessarily sacrificing revenue.[20]

Not all of the recommendations found their way into the new theaters, since most of the proposed aesthetic improvements came at the cost of the Opéra's social amenities. Despite efforts by planners from the first fire in 1761 until the completion of the Théâtre de la Porte Saint-Martin, the boxes remained on the stage—"marks of distinction," as one architect put it, that neither the blinding stage lights and poor views suffered by their renters nor the dramatic distractions they proved for the others would compromise.[21]

As for the proposal to free up space on the stage and raise the double basses, an anonymous message jotted in the margin of the memo reminded the architect of certain realities: "The expedient of depriving Monseigneur le prince de Conti and M. le duc d'Aumont of their large boxes and their view of the stage . . . seems to me the least practicable thing in the world. . . . The work and disorder resulting from these changes would accomplish nothing more than to disturb the established order. Do you think, for example, that M. le prince de Soubise would agree to a *baignoire* moved back by even 30 centimeters?"[22]

The press had the last word on these vaunted forestage boxes. When the new hall opened in 1770 with the boxes as conspicuous as ever, the slighted (and still muffled) double basses were moved to where the harpsichord had formerly stood, effectively obstructing the view of the prince de Conti: "Excellent reason," reported the *Correspondance littéraire*, "to go without a harpsichord in an orchestra!"[23]

But if the boxes of distinction stayed and the parterre remained without seats, there were other architectural improvements undertaken for the sake of art. A degree of privacy was lost in the 1770 hall when architects replaced all but a few of the ceiling-high partitions separating the boxes with breast-level dividers. While the change no doubt disappointed some by opening up what had been marvelously private salons, others welcomed the destruction of "this multitude of little cells . . . as detrimental to seeing as to the sound."[24] The change eliminated the beehive-like appearance of the theater and gave the impression of long, continuous balconies. In the 1781 hall the shortened partitions were at last turned to face the stage (see Figure 4).[25]

As with the increasingly heterogeneous placement of the spectators, the architecture of these theaters in the 1770s and 1780s showed signs of growing independence from the customs and hierarchies of the court, still a strong presence at mid-century. A most obvious change at the Théâtre de la Porte Saint-Martin was the replacement of the royal fleur-de-lys motif with vaguely national emblems. The columns that framed the stage and separated the second boxes were decorated with pikes and fasces with ribbons and golden helmets in their molding. The band just below the fourth boxes bore gilded eagles with their wings spread and their talons clenching national banners. Emblazoned throughout the theater were Gallic cocks trailing scarves from their wings.[26]

The former ostentation was toned down a shade in the two new theaters. The interiors of all the boxes in the Théâtre de la Porte Saint-Martin were decorated, democratically, in identical fashion: blue fabric embroidered with gold arabesques and garlands.[27] Apollo still chased

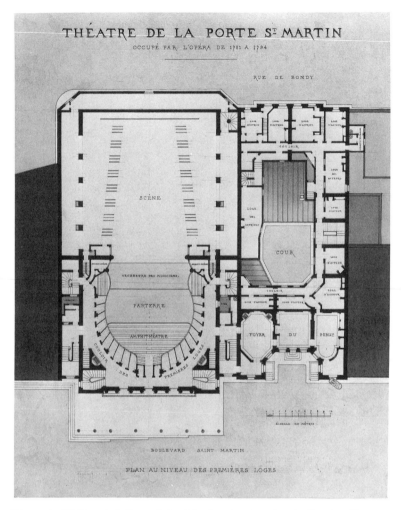

Figure 4. Théâtre de la Porte Saint-Martin: plan showing the first-level boxes. Photograph courtesy of Bibliothèque de l'Opéra.

Envy and Ignorance across the sky-blue ceiling of the 1770 hall, but by 1781 the heavens were empty save some scattered flowers.[28] Both the 1770 and the 1781 halls had rounded rather than rectangular interiors, a shape that permitted "more equality in the placement of spectators," in the words of one architect, and their deeper boxes suited those "who wish to go to the spectacle without being seen."[29] Some carried the rhetoric of equality further still. Even with the lower partitions between boxes, a journalist writing for the *Journal de musique* complained that the dividers broke up the ideal unity of audiences. "Tear down these partitions that turn our boxes into confessionals," he urged. "I know very well that you have erected them for the sake of utility and decency and to be assured of subscribers, but you should have sensed that a national spectacle cannot be formed from a multitude of boudoirs." [30] That sort of language continued to corrode Louis XIV's glorious ideal of the Opéra as the spectacle of the king.

The lights flickered during performances, so those who wished to pass their time watching others still could. Since the early 1770s, in fact, a new arrangement of footlights that burned some eight hundred separate flames, as well as new fixtures near to the ceiling with shiny reflecting plates, brought more light to the hall than the hanging chandeliers had provided before. [31] Still the place to parade fashions and frills—such as the outrageous wigs and "allegorical" hats so much in fashion in 1775—the Opéra maintained its many distractions. During one performance a few misfits in the parterre made sure the whole hall noticed one unlucky woman whose wig was taller than the door to her box. Stooping awkwardly, she finally managed to enter, though the wig was knocked sideways in the maneuver. "The whole assembly watched what was happening and began laughing and clapping their hands, until at last the beautiful lady was obliged to leave, returning only after having sacrificed her majestic plumage." [32] Such antics of the parterre continued to draw "low chuckles" from the subscribers above in the boxes. [33] The parterre was particularly cruel toward the end of Sophie Arnault's long career: at her lines "You burn with impatience that I go" in the title role of Gluck's *Iphigénie en Aulide* the parterre broke into applause. [34] And there persisted the more commonplace distraction of noise from below, which occasionally rose to levels that kept listeners from "seizing the nuances of the music." [35]

But despite such remnants of earlier rowdiness, spectators in the 1770s reported something new in the behavior of audiences: genuine attentiveness. "One sees for the first time a musical tragedy heard with sustained attention from start to finish," wrote a journalist in the late 1770s. [36] "An extreme and uninterrupted attentiveness," the *Mercure* noted, describing a premiere in 1779, "the strongest emotions visible on every face . . . prolonged by enthusiasm one moment and cut short the next for fear of losing a word or a note of music: such were the signs of interest and approval." [37] Still another journal singled out pockets of spectators in the theater who "do not permit themselves the slightest movement during the performance." [38]

Listeners were also beginning to complain about the distractions of others: one spectator wrote to the editor of the *Calendrier musical universel* in 1789 to complain of the "out-of-date beauties" who so annoyingly bragged about their land in Brittany through Gluck's *Alceste*.[39] J. H. Marchand, sensing the shift, went on the offensive: "Do you believe, Mesdames, that the state interests itself in facilitating your little whims? One doesn't go out in public to have a *tête-à-tête*."[40] The inconceivable in 1750—that the spectators might not be a necessary part of the spectacle, that chatter and appointments need not be accepted as normal—was now conceivable.

There was a more dramatic sign that audiences were paying closer attention to the musical drama: they wept, loudly and openly.

In the seventeenth century La Bruyère had written of the "disgrace" of crying in the theater, and tears were scarcely possible amid the diversion and frivolity of opera during the middle years of the eighteenth century.[41] With relative suddenness, however, spectators in the 1770s began to sob. The *Journal de politique et de littérature* reported that for the first time operas were heard "with an ever-growing interest and with tears shed as far as the backstage wings." Another observer said he was surprised to see "men without virtue and women without morals" bursting into tears during performances. One listener composed a poem that appeared in the *Journal de Paris* expressing his bewilderment that anyone could muster enough presence of mind to judge the music critically. "Whether for or against *Armide*, write on," he said. "As for me, I'll simply cry."[42]

Listeners identified their urge to cry with Christoph Willibald von Gluck, the German who took Paris by storm with the premiere of his *Iphigénie en Aulide* in 1774. "Opera had always brought boredom and melancholy to me," the playwright and prodigious observer of society Louis-Sebastien Mercier admitted in his *Tableau de Paris*. "I considered this a place where I would be constantly indifferent and never moved. Then Gluck came, and I now know the charms of music. . . . I have at last felt myself shedding tears as I never before have in this place of enchantment."[43] Hearing of the marvelous powers of Gluck, an aging Jean-Jacques Rousseau returned to the site of his public humiliation twenty years earlier to hear his music, an experience that prompted him to take back his taunt that the French tongue was unsuitable for great music. "Monsieur le Chevalier," he wrote to Gluck, "I have just left a rehearsal of your opera *Iphigénie* and am enchanted! You have accomplished what I had believed until now was impossible." When Rousseau left a performance of Gluck's *Orphée et Eurydice* with tears streaming down his face and a spectator asked him his opinion of the work, all he could do was mutter Orpheus' tragic lament from the opera: "J'ai perdu mon Eurydice! [I've lost my Eurydice!]"[44]

Tears, in fact, were among the less dramatic responses to Gluck. What later generations might have called hysteria—more humanely called a *bouleversement* by these sensitive spectators—occasionally seized women and the young during performances. When the tearful Alcestis appeared onstage with her children during the Paris premiere of *Alceste* in 1776, a boy caused a minor stir by loudly pleading with his father to take him home and never bring him back. As Charon beckoned Alcestis to the underworld during the same opera several performances later, three girls suddenly cried out, "Oh Mama! This is too painful!" A "young and charming girl" lost consciousness after suffering several convulsions during the fourth performance of *Armide*. Other spectators dragged her from her box, and she was eventually revived.[45]

One extraordinary letter narrates the thrill of being gripped by Gluck. The opera was *Alceste*, and the correspondent—who signs the letter Pauline de R***—relates that she had already discovered "the strongest and most intimate impressions" in Gluck's music before this particular encounter. Young in age and sentiment, Pauline writes,

I took care to close myself up within my box. I listened to this new work with profound attention. Soon they came to the beautiful march of the priests of Apollo in the first act. From the first measures I was seized by such a strong feeling of awe, and felt within me so intensely that religious impulse that penetrates those who attend the ceremonies of a revered and august religion, that without even knowing it I fell to my knees in my box and stayed in this position, suppliant and with my hands clasped, until the end of the piece.[46]

Gluck's arrival on the Parisian musical scene in 1774 was revolutionary. Interest in opera had flagged substantially since the War of the Bouffons had polarized audiences in the mid-1750s. A dearth of young talent and growing boredom with Rameau made the 1760s particularly lean years for the institution. Reverting to its traditional formula for making money, the Opéra mounted more ballets than ever in these years and refurbished the ancient classics of Lully, Campra, and Destouches, but even so it stayed alive only through the support of the state. The 1762 union of the Opéra-Comique and Comédie-Italienne and their attractive productions of light and lively comic operas didn't help matters.[47] By the early 1760s even the machines had grown stale: the *Correspondance littéraire* claimed that the public no longer had a taste for the "monotony and platitudes" of the Opéra, and on the eve of Gluck's arrival it mourned that "the *Opéra français* . . . no longer knows which wood to use to make its arrows."[48]

This manifest public indifference before Gluck's arrival made his triumph all the more dramatic. "In Paris, they are thinking and dreaming of nothing but music," a journal trumpeted three weeks after the premiere of *Iphigénie en Aulide.* "It is the subject of all our disputes and discussions, the soul of our suppers."[49] Other victories soon followed. Later in the same year the Opéra staged a French version of Gluck's *Orfeo ed Euridice* (1762), and audiences received the work ecstatically. In 1776 *Alceste* appeared in a French translation of Calzabigi's original Italian libretto.[50]

But no revolutionary is without his enemies, and Gluck certainly had his. On one side were the voices of tradition who objected that Gluck had effectively eliminated the true glory of opera—the ballets—and on the other were supporters of the new Italian school of Piccinni, Sacchini, and Jomelli, whose works were drawing crowds to the Opéra Comique. The French traditionalists quickly lost the field as the musical discourse shifted to whether Gluck's or the Italian style was better. For two years the dispute between Gluckists and Italianists kept to a low simmer. But when Niccolò Piccinni, the Italianists' great hope, arrived in 1776, war broke out. Mlle Levasseur as Alcestis sang her celebrated line, "These strains tear at my heart" in a performance several weeks after Piccinni's arrival, and a spectator in the hall shouted out, "And you, mademoiselle, you've torn at my ears!" A listener near him shot back, "And so much the better, too, if it means you'll get new ones!"[51] The hall erupted into hoots and cries, and the War of the Gluckists and Piccinnists—a conflict that would generate close to a thousand pages of pamphlets—was underway.

Word quickly spread through literary circles that the man to insult Levasseur had been Marmontel, the playwright, and her defender the abbé Arnauld. Polite society was shocked. It was one thing if offensive calls bubbled up anonymously from the parterre, but for two members of the Académie Française—and both contributors to the *Encyclopédie* to boot—to trade barbs in public was a disgrace! Soon thereafter an unsigned article in the *Feuille de soir*—rumor had it that Arnauld himself wrote the piece—reported that Gluck and Piccinni were both planning to set Quinault's seventeenth-century libretto of *Roland* to music: it wickedly concluded that the result would be *Orlando* and *Orlandino*, "respectively."[52]

From there the quarrel grew personal. Marmontel let drop in a salon that he considered Arnauld "a tramp and a fool for allowing himself such base and mean-spirited sarcasm," and a Gluckist replied by circulating a pithy poem:

> Old Marmontel, so slow, so thick, so dull,
> Can only bellow when he speaks his mind.
> He judges music like he's deaf
> And speaks of painting like he's blind.[53]

Laharpe, Ginguené, and d'Alembert joined Marmontel in writing pamphlets for Piccinni. Suard, Coquéau, and Bailli du Rollet countered with tracts for Gluck. "One no longer asks 'Is he a Jansenist, is he a Molinist, a philosophe, or deist?' One asks, 'Is he a Gluckist or Piccinnist?' " wrote the *Correspondance littéraire*. "The answer to this question determines all."[54] The marquis Caraccioli, ambassador from Naples and naturally a Piccinnist, grew so agitated during a performance of Gluck's *Iphigénie en Aulide* that he jumped out of his seat and shouted "It's the devil's music!"—a reaction so roundly jeered by the other spectators that the ambassador eventually left the theater.[55]

Even the queen scored a hit in the quarrel. When Piccinni, rumored to have been invited to Paris by the king's mistress Mme du Barry, gave the customary concert of operatic excerpts at Versailles, Marie Antoinette insisted that he accompany her at the harpsichord in her favorite arias, producing the score of Gluck's *Alceste* for him to play! It was perhaps no hyperbole when Laharpe announced that the *querelle* had become "an affair of state."[56]

There were ostensible musical reasons for the quarrel. In his last operas—those the French public heard—Gluck undertook to reform the dominant Italian style to intensify musical passion. Working with his Italian librettist Ranieri Calzabigi, Gluck developed a dramatic ideal as far from the traditional operatic plots with their lofty Olympian *fêtes* and thinly veiled analogies of the king as from the love intrigues and sugary lessons in virtue that filled the action of newer comic operas. Gluck and Calzabigi attempted to increase the dramatic intensity of opera by eliminating superfluous subplots and drawing the chief elements in broad, simple strokes. "Gluck hated those meek political, philosophical and moral views of Metastasio," wrote Calzabigi, referring to the preeminent librettist of Italian opera at the time, "his metaphors, his garrulous little passions, his geometrically devised word-plays."[57]

At the same time and for similar dramatic reasons, Gluck reduced the differences separating recitative and aria and eliminated or reduced the introductory ritornello before arias. What lover in the heat of passion waits patiently through a long orchestral introduction? Abandoning the pervasive da capo aria form, the structure in which the first part of the aria is repeated after a middle section, Gluck created a taut dramatic web that propelled listeners forward and offered them little respite in the way of instrumental interludes and repetitions. Finally, Gluck replaced the florid Italianate trills and runs with an overall melodic simplicity that he believed more nearly suited the musical expression of passion.[58]

The Piccinnists attacked Gluck on virtually every aspect of his reforms. Some denied altogether that true tragedy could be set to music, asserting that the result would inevitably be a weird bastard child, "a sort of monster set between opera and tragedy" that fell short of both. The Piccinnists claimed that Gluck's effort to simplify melodies succeeded only in making them boring or bizarre; and they found his recitatives needlessly long and too heavily scored.[59] Predictably, the Gluckists countered each point: there was no better testimony to Gluck's tragic effect than the tearful reactions of audiences, they said; his melodies and harmonies touched the "intimate relation between our sentiments and our sensations"; and far from being a distraction the accompaniments themselves are "complete tableaux." Echoing Gluck's own ideas, his supporters charged that Italian music "sacrificed verisimilitude and dramatic interest to the pleasure of hearing a brilliant voice toy with a syllable."[60]

Whatever the *gens de lettres* thought, however, Gluck carried the affections of the public. The sheer quantity of Gluck's work in the repertory before Piccinni's *Roland* premiered in 1778 had made a successful challenge by any rival, however gifted, nearly impossible. By spring 1777 spectators could see Gluck's *Iphigénie en Aulide, Orphée et Eurydice*, and *Alceste* all in the same week if they wished. Gluck's popularity boosted the revenues of the Opéra to unprecedented levels: in the 1777–78 season the Opéra nearly doubled its receipts from the 1750–51 season, with average monthly revenues outstripping the earlier totals by more than 15,000 livres.[61]

But Gluck's arrival in Paris before Piccinni does not entirely explain his immense success. His ideals, both dramatic and musical, nourished the new style for feeling that had swept through the beau monde a decade earlier. Readers of *La Nouvelle Héloïse*, available in Paris in 1761, wrote letters to Rousseau describing the very responses Gluck would evoke at the Opéra: "What attention, I hardly breathe, I scarcely inhale, . . . tears of tenderness stream down my cheeks," wrote one reader.[62] Parisians sighed with nostalgia reading the third-century Gaelic bard Ossian, whose verses appeared there in 1760, and they flocked to the salons of 1761 and 1765 to see works of Greuze. When Goethe's *Werther* appeared in French in 1776 the translator appended an emotional dedication urging the "sensitive and courageous" to read the book but warning off the "cold and level-headed."[63] The modern style of art seemed so personal, so exposed, and the public responded like a voyeur, vicariously tasting the ecstasies and feeling all their shame, trembling at the maledictions, shivering at the reconciliations, always watching and gratefully weeping when they glimpsed their own reflection. Even Ossian was eerily resonant to readers of the 1770s—and for good reason, as the poetry was in fact forged by their contemporary James Macpherson.

These were the years of sensibility in France, when to feel at all was to feel passionately, and to show it in public de rigueur. Tears, *sanglots*, crises, palpitations, *bouleversements*, convulsions, and *frissons* of every sort agitated hearts in the 1770s (often with uncanny regularity, as with one acquaintance of Mme de Genlis who managed to have a fainting spell from an excess of sensibility twice weekly, just after guests had arrived for her salon).[64] To open the soul to delicious sentiments was for these cultivated aristocrats the meaning of Rousseau's challenge to live simply and honestly, and Gluck more than any other composer encouraged precisely this.

Gluck may have encouraged crying but he certainly didn't cause it. The elites of French society were already primed to swoon and sob by the contagious *sensibilité* they saw all around them. In the 1770s, sobbing was only one of the possible behaviors for assembled audiences. The right question is therefore not how Gluck's works in the abstract might produce tears—for the behavioral responses of audiences are always social acts shaped by historical contingencies—but what it was about Gluck that provoked this particular response as opposed to others that were also available to audiences.

Part of Gluck's wide appeal to the sensitive lay in his librettists' treatment of traditional plots. As with Lully, he chose subjects for his Paris operas based upon legends or classical myths. Gluck's operas, however, have little dramatic relief in ballets or lightheartedness. Gluck's works are the musical embodiment of the same late-century spirit of neoclassicism that animated the paintings of David and the architecture of Ledoux, and as such they attain a level of directness and intensity not approached by the earlier *tragédies-lyriques*.[65] Passion in Gluck is deadly serious.

It is true that none of Gluck's operas is a tragedy in the classic sense: a sudden twist at the end—typically a god's intervention—averts the impending disaster.[66] But up until their final, liberating moments, gloom pervades Gluck's dramas. His oeuvre is filled with psychological pain. Where Lully treated Euripides' *Alceste* as a celebration of love's charms, the action of Gluck's *Alceste* is darkened from the outset by the imminent self-sacrifice of the heroine. His Alcestis sings of her "despair, torments, bitter sadness" when she learns her husband, Admetus, lies gravely ill. As she embraces her sons she sees his image in them, and she nobly sings in solitude that to die for a loved one is "natural virtue."[67] There are no gallant suitors or coquettish attendants in this *Alceste*; the love it contains is neither "*doux*" nor "*charmant*."

Yet the intensity of Gluck's dramas does not lie in a fatal choice of flawed characters or a blood debt incurred by earlier generations. The passion of Gluck is strikingly domestic, as if the tortured families of Greuze had all been recast in antiquity. Alcestis' anguish is maternal. Orpheus' tragedy is the death of his wife. *Iphigénie en Tauride* turns on Orestes' fraternal friendship with Pylades and his love for a long-lost sister. And *Iphigénie en Aulide* tugs at every strand of familial sentiment, setting up Agamemnon as a blessed father and happy spouse, Clytemnestra as a devoted mother and wife, and Iphigenia as an innocent bride-to-be before, inevitably, Artemis reminds Agamemnon of the terms for going off to war. From the opening moments of the opera the audience is aware of Artemis' bloody demand, which makes each new expression of family bliss all the more excruciating.

Despite Piccinni's clear musical differences with Gluck, the characters in his most popular works also suffer in love. *Roland*, for example, begins with Angélique singing of a "funeste amour" for a man she must soon exile, while Roland's first series of arias announce his own vain love for the queen.[68] *Didon*, which ends with the suicide of the central character, seldom digresses from the theme of love's fatal passion. Dido's farewell to Aeneas at the end of the second act was "so painfully true that it caused all the spectators to shed tears," while Piccinni's *Iphigénie en Tauride* (1781), with its heavy emphasis on the friendship of Pylades and Orestes, brought "tears at every moment."[69] The crest of sensibility carried Rousseau to posthumous vindication at the Opéra, as his *Devin du village*, a tuneful little opera he wrote in 1753 about a pair of suffering lovers, grew to be one of the most popular companion pieces to Gluck's tragedies of the 1770s and 1780s.[70] Sacchini's *Oedipe à Colonne*, which opened in 1786 and remained popular well into the Revolution, "disposed spectators to tenderness" with its depiction of family anguish, remorse, and sadness.[71] Even *Tarare* (1787), an eclectic and somewhat eccentric collaboration of Beaumarchais and Salieri that told the story of an oriental palace coup, minimized the spectacle for the sake of *sensibilité*. (The work, incidentally, made Salieri a household name among French audiences while Mozart was still politely ignored there.)

By the time the War of the Gluckists and Piccinnists had died down in the mid-1780s, most Piccinnists had reversed themselves at least on the issue of plot and were now calling for genuine tragedy. "Experience has proven," as Beaumarchais wrote in his preface to *Tarare*, "that for all that one resolves dramatically by waving a wand or having the gods intervene, [such effects] always leave the heart empty."[72] Of course these sentimental themes were the avant-garde, and there remained as well at the opera more traditional *pastorales* and ballets. By 1780, however, the public showed a clear preference for the "serious" musical dramas over the "extravagante coquetterie" of such works as *Des Caprices de Galathée*, *Calypso et Télémaque*, and *Diane et Endymion*—the latter famous for its scenes with deer and dogs on the stage.[73]

Neither seventeenth century nor wholly Greek, the passions that animated the Opéra in the 1770s and 1780s were, to judge by the reactions of Gluck's audiences, strangely familiar. Their enormous popularity is a window on the evolving temperament of France's elites as they grew more domestic, more attuned to the needs and tensions of the household, more bourgeois, one might even say.

But if Gluck's efforts to unify the notoriously loose dramatic action of lyric works suited the sensibilities of audiences, they did not please the ballet corps. Although Gluck included ballets in his operas, their drastically reduced number brought threats and protests from the dancers. Yet when Gluck relented in 1777 and inserted an extended dance sequence between the second and third acts of *Alceste* (this despite earlier avowals that he would do nothing of the kind), the public booed and the dancers had trouble finishing the scene. The incident was the talk of dinners throughout Paris, signaling as it did the "most glorious triumph of music over dance"; the *Almanach des spectacles* announced that "nothing proves more clearly that the system of [dramatic] unity . . . is founded in reason."[74] Not that this meant spectators had suddenly grown chaste in their tastes; by all accounts the *filles d'op-*

éra were just as *recherchées* as they had been before. But, one spectator wrote, "this throng of little creatures [who] tease my imagination and arouse my senses . . . interrupts the interest of the spectacle by exhibiting their beautiful arms and sending knowing glances to spectators in the *petites loges.*"[75]

The evolving taste of late-century audiences was equally at odds with traditional stage effects, which were also, strictly speaking, peripheral to the psychological import of the drama. Laughter echoed through the hall during Gluck's *Armide* when two demons made their exit through a door cut in wooden clouds that rose from the stage, and the "monsters, flights, and machines" in Philidor's *Persée* were roundly judged to have made a "ridiculous effect."[76] The convergence of spectators' tastes and Gluck's reforms was beginning to bring an overall sobriety to decor and plots. The descent of Artemis from the clouds was the sole reason for criticizing Gluck's *Iphigénie en Tauride*, according to one review. "The more pomp and show a spectacle has, the less it moves us if it lacks the coherence and verity it should have."[77]

As with changes in architecture and seating, the appearance of sensibility among audiences and plots separated the king from his Académie. With Gluck's triumphs the aging classics of mid-century and before were at last laid aside.[78] After the revolution of Gluck few (if any) spectators identified the "exact image of the King"—the phrase used earlier in the century by the *Mercure de France*—in mythic allegory.

The political effects of sensibility stemmed from its promotion of a popular taste whose points of reference were wholly outside the Court's view of the world. Dramatic *sensibilité* urged spectators to confirm the truth of the stories in their own emotions at least as much as in the judgments of the esteemed. It necessarily made the experience more personal, elevating the natural over the artificial and validating the truth of immediate feeling over the whims of opinion. Even if the audience seemed to cry on cue, the very pretense of personal affect presented itself as a good deal more subjective in response than had the reactions of audiences thirty years earlier.

Of course spectators still applauded Marie Antoinette when she appeared at the Opéra; and if she was present when *Iphigénie en Tauride* was performed, audiences would shower the lines, "Chantons, célébrons notre reine" with loud ovations.[79] Because the plots themselves no longer systematically celebrated the monarchy, however, such popular tributes to the king or queen would continue only as long as the royal family remained both visible and popular. And with a king who preferred hunting to attending the opera this meant the monarchy's reputation there rested on the queen's popularity—an increasingly shaky foundation in the 1780s. Neither Louis XIV nor Louis XV had so recklessly neglected his night at the opera. As the highest nobility receded from view and the king's real and symbolic presence disappeared in so many ways, art and artists became prime beneficiaries of the public's esteem. At the end of *Tarare* at its premiere it was not a prince in attendance whom the audience demanded to see but Beaumarchais and Salieri, an act, according to press accounts, that "has not been part of the practice of this theater." Audiences had also begun applauding during the music to show their approval and cheering for arias to be repeated.[80]

Naturally there were still traces of the old etiquette, where one deferred to the *grands* before risking one's own judgment. The baronne d'Oberkirch, for example, describes escorting the duchesse de Bourbon to the Opéra and watching the parterre savagely heckle a singer who had replaced an ailing lead at the last moment. When the singer stopped himself and walked downstage to protest that he was doing his best, the duchess rose to her feet to support him, whereupon the parterre applauded first the duchess and then the singer, and the performance resumed to overall contentment.[81] Spectators also kept to their earlier habit of censuring those who overstepped the unspoken rules of behavior: when the mistress of the duc de Bouillon, a Mlle Laguerre, appeared at Piccinni's *Iphigénie en Tauride* "drunk as a bacchante," the public "whistled, jeered, stamped their feet, and cried out that she should be sent directly to the Fort-l'Evêque prison."[82]

But audiences now paid at least as much attention to the performance as to the notables in the boxes, and the judgments they formed more likely drew as much upon their own passionate responses as upon the responses of the highly-born. "Why do you not judge for yourself, sir," reads a pamphlet from the War of the Gluckists and Piccinnists; "why submit your own judgments and sensations to the opinion of several persons who very often have neither the knowledge nor the sentiments of the truly beautiful in Art?" Sensibility did much to upset the secure *bienséance* of imitation in the theater: "Abandon yourself to your own impressions, and not to borrowed opinions; judge this music . . . without listening to pedants, those cold of heart, and all other assassins of the arts who wish to make the artist follow the path of an artisan."[83] It was no less than the ambassador of Naples, one should remember, whom the spectators evicted for his judgment on Gluck.

By the eve of the Revolution the dynamic of evaluating musical drama was substantially different from that of 1750. Artistic merit was no longer assumed synonymous with what the powerful thought. With spectators unable to find the *grands* in their most visible places and skeptical of their opinions, attentive now to the drama on the stage more than to the spectacle of the hall, and willing above all to feel the sublime effects of sensitive plots, artistic judgment was disassociated from personality. Hence a critical, unitary, anonymous standard emerged to dominate descriptions of musical judgment. "The men of taste," reports the *Almanach musical* in reference to a new production, "who stand in the parterre of the Opéra and who in their reactions determine the judgments of the people in the boxes, applauded almost all parts of this performance."[84]

4

Concerts in the Old Regime

At the same time French audiences were rediscovering opera in the 1770s they were taking their first, tentative steps toward public concerts. Although the administration of the Opéra tried to prevent the appearance of new concert societies—as always, they feared for their revenues—the 1770s and 1780s witnessed the birth of several important series devoted to the regular performance of instrumental and vocal works. Although not fully public, these performances nevertheless formed an essential part of the musical experience of French audiences.

The concert societies that appeared late in the century supplemented the *concert spirituel*, an institution of long standing that had provided sacred music in regular concerts. Founded in 1725 by Anne-Danican Philidor with the blessing of the Opéra administration, the *concert spirituel* was initially intended to provide inspirational music to Parisians on days the Opéra was closed. In its first two years this amounted to roughly thirty-five days a year and included Annunciation, Ascension, Pentecost, All-Saints' Day, and the three weeks of Easter. The initial success of the *concert spirituel* was so great that in 1727 Philidor obtained permission to offer a series of regular concerts beyond the holiday performances; these took place twice a week in winter and once weekly in summer.[1]

The original purpose of the *concert spirituel* was to provide an uplifting spectacle for Parisians while the stage of the Opéra was dark, so spectators to the two were largely the same. The scent of wealth certainly was. In 1762, the least expensive seats cost 3 livres, 1 livre more than admission to the parterre at the Opéra; the best seats cost 6. The concerts took place in a room decorated "like a magnificent salon" at the Tuileries palace, the Salle des Suisses, where an orchestra of forty and a regular chorus of fifty-three performed on a platform surrounded on three sides by an amphitheater with benches.[2]

A typical program at the *concert spirituel* mixed symphonies, concertos, and sonatas with vocal oratorios and motets. Chamber works by Tartini and Vivaldi (his *Spring* from *The Four Seasons* was especially popular), sonatas by Telemann, Leclair, Handel, and Couperin, and motets by Campra, Delalande, and Mondonville commonly appeared in programs there.[3] The series generally kept to its mission until its demise during the Revolution by providing explicitly sacred choral music set to Latin texts, a practice about which certain spectators complained on the grounds that they couldn't understand the words.

Its instrumental repertories late in the century grew increasingly eclectic: in 1785 one could as easily hear a Haydn symphony performed by the regular orchestra as displays of questionable virtuosity by touring child prodigies, composers attached to the courts of foreign princes, or nervous amateurs playing in public for the first time.[4] A small notice in the *Almanach musical* in May 1780 announces a concert beginning with a symphony "del Signor Amadeo Mozartz," although by and large the audiences here preferred the symphonies of Gossec and the *symphonies concertantes* of Giovanni Viotti and Étienne Ozi.[5] In general the *concert spirituel* performed more Italian and German than French music.[6]

Just how spiritual was the *concert spirituel*? Not very, to hear audiences describe it. The *Annonces, affiches et avis divers* cynically declared that the series was neither uplifting for audiences nor profitable for new talent but existed simply "to help an infinite number of persons carry the weight of their idleness and fill the void caused by the absence of other spectacles."[7] Surely the newspaper was exaggerating, but others also observed that the performances contained only the merest hint of spirituality. One reason might have been that most of its performers came from the Opéra. A spectator (protesting too much?) cautioned that the singers were a "swarm of nymphettes" who dress "in the most immodest clothing with their throats entirely naked, . . . hoping to reap fruit from the sentiments they inspire."[8]

It seems likely that elites came here neither expecting nor experiencing particularly profound sentiments. In his *Mémoires* the prince de Montbarey describes spending all evening gambling at the Palais Royal with his uncle before taking a carriage to the *concert spirituel*, "since it was Good Friday." By the baronne d'Oberkirch's reckoning the music was "too noisy, too confused, and the singers did not know how to project their parts." Just as at the Opéra at mid-century, *petits-maîtres* acted as self-appointed arbiters of good taste at the *concert spirituel*, clapping and shouting "C'est superbe!" or "C'est détestable!"[9]

The only other place to hear instrumental and chamber music until late in the century was in the homes of patrons. In the Old Regime an array of noble households sponsored concerts of all types and levels. Among the patrons Mozart mentions were the duc d'Aumont, the duc d'Aiguillon, and the maréchal de Noailles. Such settings provided the perfect mix of informality and ceremony to give composers and performers a chance to air works before they appeared in public. The baron de Bagge hosted musical evenings each Friday "where one debuts before appearing at the *concert spirituel*."[10] Grétry performed music from his opera *Les Mariages samnites* before more than two hundred "persons of the first rank" at the *hôtel* of the prince de Conti in 1768, and Sacchini, Viotti, and Martini all performed at the musical soirées of the young painter Elisabeth Vigée Le Brun.[11] The German traveler Nemeitz, realizing the potential for unknown composers, advised young musicians to come seek their fortunes in Paris: the *hôtels* of French patrons, he wrote, "give entrance to the *grand monde*, and you can attend the best concerts, every day, in full liberty."[12]

By far the best-known musical patron in eighteenth-century France was Alexandre-Jean-Joseph Le Riche de La Popelinière, a wealthy tax farmer as famous for his private concerts in a large *hôtel* across from the Bibliothèque du Roi as for his romantic humiliations. Unfortunately the two were never far apart. Having taken a mistress from the ranks of the Opéra, like many others, La Popelinière was rather less discrete than most, and when his renewal as farmer-general came due Louis XV directed Cardinal Fleury to remind him of his Christian duties. ("Monsieur," Fleury wrote to him, "the King's goodness is not reserved for those who live in public scandal, as you yourself do with Mademoiselle Deshayes.")[13] Mademoiselle Deshayes became Madame La Popelinière, and the farmer-general was renewed.

But this was only the beginning of the gossip. An anonymous letter informed La Popelinière of what his guests had whispered for several months: that his wife was still acting like Mlle Deshayes. The rumors continued for six months, until La Popelinière discovered the door cut in the back of his wife's fireplace.[14] La Popelinière had the *hôtel* demolished and moved his wife, and the concerts, to an isolated mansion on the outskirts of Paris in Passy.

La Popelinière's musicians probably took secret joy in the contretemps, since the move allowed the concerts to continue in even greater sumptuousness. Jean-Philippe Rameau, Johann Stamitz, and the young François-Joseph Gossec all performed their own music at Passy with an orchestra whose members lived in the mansion, rehearsing in the mornings and performing in the evenings. On weekends La Popelinière invited "illustrious names, distinguished talents, enchanting beauties, grand seigneurs, poets, painters, musicians, and actors" for superb meals and full concerts.[15] Seated amidst paintings by Van Loo and de la Tour his guests heard symphonies and solos before their premiere at the *concert spirituel*. Mme de Genlis remembers spending Sundays during her childhood at Passy, with a musical mass in the morning, lunch in the company of foreign ambassadors and their wives, an orchestral concert before dinner, and chamber music after.[16]

La Popelinière's patronage grew yet more lavish once he'd sent his wife away for good. An armoire in her bedroom, he discovered, hid a secret passageway large enough for a man to sit in comfortably.[17]

Although a crucial support for composers and musicians, these essentially private concerts reached only a relative handful of French listeners, limited as they were to invitees of the hosts. In the early 1770s a new approach to concerts emerged, and, if not entirely public, they departed significantly enough from the earlier form to increase the number and diversity of spectators. The first of these "concerts abonnés"—subscription concerts—was the Concert des Amateurs, founded by Gossec in 1769. Held in a room at the Hôtel de Soubise large enough to seat six hundred, the series offered twelve weekly concerts each season and employed an unusually large orchestra. The string section alone had forty violins, twelve cellos, and eight double basses. From the start the concerts were successful enough to make the Académie Royale de Musique object that they infringed upon its monopoly over all public vocal and instrumental performances; for a time the series was in danger of "being suppressed like a court of parlement," as Grimm irreverently observed.[18] The society took refuge behind the sponsorship of the prince de Soubise, but another fledgling series that lacked similar protection, the Concert des Abonnés, closed under the pressure of the Opéra—a remaining sign of the absolutist power that the institution still exercised.[19]

The Concert des Amateurs was as famous for its subscribers—"the best and most brilliant company of Paris"—as for its superior orchestra.[20] "This is one of the pleasures of society," wrote Laharpe of the concerts, "that one finds only in a great capital like Paris."[21] The orchestra was professional, but talented amateurs occasionally appeared there before audiences, as the *homme de lettres* and violinist Michel de Chabanon did in 1775. Soloists from the other Paris spectacles, both instrumentalists and vocalists, also performed at the Concert des Amateurs "for a certain fee, which is always on the account of the associates." Associates, or paying members, underwrote the concerts. Each associate held a group of tickets, which he could distribute to whomever he pleased.[22] For twelve years until 1781 the society flourished, meeting first on Monday nights and later on Wednesdays.

Franz Joseph Haydn is responsible for much of the posthumous reputation of the second major semipublic orchestral series in late eighteenth-century Paris. Shortly after the demise of the Concert des Amateurs, the Concert de la Loge Olympique was inaugurated under the guidance of the farmer-general La Haye and the royal *intendant* Claude-François-Marie Rigoley, comte d'Ogny.[23] The series functioned under the auspices of the freemasons. Banking on Haydn's popularity at the *concert spirituel*, d'Ogny commissioned six symphonies from him for the new society. The orchestra received such acclaim with these "Paris" symphonies (Nos. 82–87) that d'Ogny soon commissioned three more; Haydn obliged with two, Nos. 90 and 91.[24]

"As with other clubs," reads a popular guide to Paris from 1787 under the entry "Concert de la Loge Olympique," "this society, at No. 65 in the Palais Royal, is composed of persons whose merit commends them; their number is not limited, but no one will be admitted before the age of majority."[25] A musical association based upon "merit" was certainly a self-conscious departure from both the patronage system and organizations in which "associates" supported performers. Like a host of other scientific clubs and reading societies now beginning to appear, the Concert de la Loge Olympique did not exclude members of the Third Estate. And, in association with the "Loge d'Adoption," the Concert welcomed women as well.[26]

"Merit" in the guidebook's description referred primarily to membership in the Masonic lodge—the Loge de la Parfaite Estime et Société Olympique—that sponsored the concert series.[27] All members of the Concert de la Loge Olympique had to be affiliated with a chapter of the freemasons, and the names of all potential subscribers were submitted to a vote by members before they were admitted.[28] In 1785, 300 men and 102 women belonged to the Concert de la Loge Olympique; in 1788 the numbers stood at 357 and 231.[29] Names on the 1788 roll were overwhelmingly but not exclusively aristocratic: several bankers, a physician, and a printer were members of the lodge, and listed among its "free associates" were the musicians Méhul, Dalyrac, Philidor, and Garat. In 1788 the orchestra of the Concert de la Loge Olympique was large—74 members, only 4 fewer than that of the Opéra that year—and it had a chorus of 16. Although the Österreich Freimaurerlogen claimed that only freemasons could play in the orchestra, only 12 of its members were also listed as brothers of the Loge de la Parfaite Estime.[30] The quality of the orchestra was probably a few notches above amateur status and something short of professional; 8 of its members also played in the Opéra orchestra.[31] The concerts showed every indication of continuing, but the Revolution cut them short.

The same casual detachment of mid-century operagoers characterized concert audiences of the 1750s and 1760s, the largest number of which, according to Ancelet's *Observations sur la musique* (1757), were "idle persons . . . who come only to amuse themselves, gossip or make themselves seen."[32] What more telling example than the experience of the seven-year-old Mozart, who was paraded from one salon to the next in 1763 like a child conjurer? After he played several selections at one gathering the guests cheerfully covered his hands with a kerchief to see if he could play them again. (He could.) Friedrich Grimm then dashed off a melody to see if Wolfgang could fill in the bass. (He could.) An amateur singer challenged him to accompany her as she sang a melody he had never heard; his accompaniment to the first verse was understandably tentative, but to make amends Mozart proceeded to play ten more, each with a different set of harmonies, and would have played another twenty if the guests had not made him stop.[33] But judging from Michel Barthélémy Ollivier's painting, neither wit nor mischief particularly engaged Mozart's listeners when he played at the prince de Conti's: the prince himself has turned his back to the musicians, and the rest of the guests seem to be listening with half an ear as they eat. One dog does seem to show genuine interest (see Figure 5).

At twenty-two, on his next trip to Paris, Mozart was less patient. After waiting in an ice-cold room over an hour to perform a concert at the duchesse de Chabot's, Mozart was led into a salon where the guests were busily making sketches of one another. "At last, . . . I played on that miserable, wretched pianoforte!" Mozart relates to his father. "But what vexed me most of all was that Madame and all her gentlemen never interrupted their drawing for a moment, but went on intently, so that I had to play to the chairs, tables and walls. Under these detestable con-

Figure 5. Michel Barthélémy Ollivier, *Le Thé à l'anglaise au Temple dans le salon des Quatre Glaces chez le prince de Conti*, 1766. Chateau de Versailles. Photograph courtesy of Giraudon/Art Resource, NY.

ditions I lost my patience. I therefore began to play the Fischer variations and after playing half of them I stood up. Whereupon I received a shower of éloges."[34] To imagine audiences at concerts in the Old Regime as deeply attentive and silent is anachronistic. Elisabeth Vigée Le Brun acknowledges that in addition to being drawn by the music, her guests came to her musical evenings "to find each other"; and even at Passy La Popelinière employed his orchestra to provide background for his lavish meals as often as he sponsored full-fledged concerts.[35]

To be sure, the intimate setting of Old Regime concerts probably made it more difficult to ignore the music than at the Opéra. Nevertheless, in *Le Concert*, an engraving by Augustin de Saint-Aubin, spectators merrily turn their backs to the musicians, talk in groups of twos or threes, and discreetly sniff snuff (as the lady to the left of the musician rifling through his music seems to be doing) during the performance (see Figure 6).[36] Similarly the "concert" in Duquevauviller's *L'Assemblée au concert*—with the pitiful musicians tucked away in the corner—seems wholly secondary to the other pleasures at hand (see Figure 7). Chamber music apparently enhanced conversation as effectively as opera could.

In the larger concert societies of the 1770s and 1780s, however, the music competed successfully with the company for attention. In 1784 the audience "listened with a silence of pleasure and admiration" to motets by Gossec; the following year they "seemed to feel deeply the effects of the harmony and the beautiful expression" of two vocal oratorios.[37] A 1785 listing of musicians observed that the symphonies of Jean-Baptiste Davaux were heard with attention and "applauded with transport."[38] Sensibility made its inroads here, too. Tears interrupted the performance of a symphony by the late Simon Le Duc at the Hôtel de Soubise, where Le Duc had been the principal conductor: "Moved by the emotions the Adagio produced, the performers remembered the loss of their friend, under whose direction they were accustomed to playing, and they had to stop to wipe away their tears."[39]

But even at the larger societies spectators sometimes chattered during the music. Some composers began their symphonies with a loud *coup d'archet*, a practice presumably begun for the same reasons overtures at the Opéra started that way—to silence the crowd. Only the genius of Mozart, who by the mid-1770s had come to know well the special behavior of Paris audiences, could craft a symphony that at once delighted and mocked his listeners. His Symphony No. 31 (K. 300a/297), one of two originally commissioned by the *concert spirituel* in 1778, is a virtual dialogue with the inconstant audience, who might weep, or talk, or clap during performances. If the spectators then were too enthralled to see they were being toyed with, listeners today are too serious to get the joke.

Mozart's "Paris" Symphony begins with the expected attack. ("What a fuss the oxen here make of this trick!" he wrote to his father.) The last movement alternates quirkily between the very soft and the very loud: at its unexpectedly quiet opening spectators called out "Shh!!" to silence the audience, so that as soon as there was silence the orchestra burst out in *forte*, just as Mozart had planned. The surprise produced a cascade of gleeful applause. But Mozart was happiest with a theme he inserted into the first movement with the express purpose of eliciting applause. The theme appears just before the development and again at the end of the movement, and, as Mozart predicted, the audience

Figure 6. Augustin de Saint-Aubin, *Le Concert*. Engraving. Photograph courtesy of the Bibliothèque Nationale.

Figure 7. Duquevauviller, *L'Assemblée au concert*. Engraving. Photograph courtesy of the Bibliothèque Nationale.

Example 4. Excerpt from Symphony No. 31, Wolfgang Amadeus Mozart.

greeted it with delight. "There was a tremendous burst of applause," Mozart relates, "but as I knew, when I wrote it, what kind of an effect it would produce, I repeated it again at the end—when there were shouts of 'Da Capo.' "[40] The theme is one of the most banal in all of Mozart (see Example 4).[41] Revenge, perhaps, for having to play for the chairs, tables, and walls?

5

Harmony's Passions
and the Public

A new way of listening was emerging at the end of the Old Regime, one more attuned to sentiments and emotions in the music and more engaged aesthetically than mid-century audiences had described. Pauline de R*** fell on her knees after having discovered in Gluck's music "a new language"; others were silent and attentive "for fear of losing the precious union between the chords and the ideas they express." People now were just as taken with the passions of the music as with the drama of the text. "We haven't said anything about the lyrics of *Iphigénie*," reads a review not long after the premiere of *Iphigénie en Aulide*, "because no one talks about them. The music absorbs all the attention of the spectators; none remains for the poem."[1] Accustomed modes of listening seemed inadequate to apprehend the new music, and the bemused, self-absorbed accounts from the late *ancien régime* convey just how disorienting the experience must have been.

The most conspicuous sign of an expansion in the horizon of perceived musical meaning underway in the 1770s is the number of spectators who now described being drawn to harmony, the musical element derided earlier in the century as empty arithmetic when its imitations were not clear. A polemicist on the side of Gluck during the pamphlet war claimed his accompaniments literally fleshed out the libretto's passions: his harmonies were the arms, hands, eyes, and face of the text's sentiments, whereas the relation of accompaniments to texts in other composers' operas more nearly resembled a valet tagging alongside his master—a patronizing retelling of the noble old cliché about music being a servant to the text.[2] Another spectator, writing that the "principal subject of operas was the music rather than the text," claimed that listeners were wrong to seek musical expression in the singing, since it is "in the orchestra alone that true expression comes." [3]

To recognize the orchestral harmonies as legitimately expressive apart from the text at once changed the subject of expression and the means by which it was conveyed. To assert that music was expressive in ways other than imitation meant that its content went beyond audible, natural sounds. For these sensitive spectators the new field of expression was the passions. [4] Writing that music need not be "nature's slave" to be natural, C. P. Coquéau asserted that music properly approached "the heart and the imagination and not servile imitation." [5] Audiences chose evocative terms for this new musical content they discerned. The overture to *Iphigénie en Aulide* variously announced "religious," "warlike," and "pathetic" action; that of *Alceste* was full of "sighs," "sobs," "tears." [6] In a letter published in the *Gazette de littérature* a listener exhorted other spectators to "pay attention to the harmony that laments beneath the words sung on a single tone." "What cries!" he wrote. "What tears!" [7] In *Iphigénie en Tauride*, an orchestral passage in which the Furies pursue Orestes expressed "the agitation and remorse" of Orestes and his "attacks of despair." [8]

This was the primary reason spectators gave to explain the powerful emotional effects of the operas of Gluck. The epidemic of sensibility among musical audiences was more than a response to the emotional appeal of the plots. It was a reaction to the music itself. The revolution of Gluck forged a new way of listening among French audiences and in so doing facilitated aesthetic responses of a depth and intensity inconceivable to earlier generations of listeners. Accounts from the 1770s and 1780s describe harmony as recreating passions that libretti merely narrated; the difference between harmony and text seemed nothing less than the difference between experience and observation. Hence the explosive effect of Gluck: long accustomed to bird calls and babbling brooks, spectators now heard powerful sentiments.

One extraordinary pamphlet from the quarrel between Gluckistes and Piccinnistes vividly describes the newly perceived power of harmony. The author seems the perfect representative of this late-century change, for he is careful to identify himself with the light moods of mid-century opera goers: before Gluck he went to the Opéra to "amuse" himself and viewed the extent of music's powers in "pleasantly flattering the ears and bringing joy and pleasure to the spirit." That paradigm began to crack as soon as the overture began. The opera was *Alceste*, and in its overture he heard the expression of "sobs, sad and doleful cries."

"My soul was touched," he writes. "Already it was prepared for some deadly event." The action continued, and he soon realized that tears were streaming down his face. "It was for me a veritable revolution. . . . I successively felt the sweetest and the most violent emotions. Those around me were no less calm, and indeed it was the same for the majority of spectators."[9]

Yet if spectators of the period spoke of a wide range of musical expression there was one important point they shared with listeners from the 1750s, who had insisted that music painted sounds and images. They believed that instrumental music without a clear and discernible subject was artistically inferior, sterile at best and nonsensical at worst. Although more subjective by nature, the emotions music conveyed still had to be readily perceptible if the music was to be considered expressive. This seems a logical holdover from the earlier assumptions even as new aesthetic criteria took their place. A kind of literalism remained, with its content merely shifted from the imitable to the emotional.

A critic thus claimed that even if the words were omitted from a particular passage of Piccinni's *Adèle de Ponthieu* one could guess its emotional content from the harmonies.[10] Later listeners would find this logic hard to grasp, convinced of the incommensurability of all things emotional. To assume that harmonies conveyed a single sentiment, as many late-eighteenth-century listeners did, was to be locked into a literalism that led to some rather startling perceptions. But for many in this generation there couldn't be anything more obvious. "One can cite an infinite number of examples where the meaning is singularly clear. . . . Listen to the Sonata No. 5, Op. 5, of Boccherini, and you will feel all the changes of a woman who alternately demands and employs gentleness and reproach. One almost feels like setting words to it; a hundred times performed, it always offers the same meaning and the same image. . . . As for me, I consider music perfect only if it tells me something I can hear."[11]

Musical perception does not evolve monolithically. To sketch its contours by reference to those landmark composers who brought about change risks creating a false impression of immediate ruptures and discontinuities—that, say, after the first Gluck premiere the entire French public stopped listening for images and started listening for emotions. This did not happen. When, why, and whether individual listeners moved beyond hearing sounds and images to hearing emotions depended upon a whole range of variables particular to the person. The most we can do is to situate roughly the collective change by illuminating as lucidly as possible what made individual change conceptually possible. (And, alas, we must periodically remind ourselves, however reluctantly, of that great silent swath among audiences who didn't write, seldom spoke, and probably never thought systematically about how they listened.)

In reality the perceptual changes occurred unevenly. Descriptions employing the earlier mimetic terms persisted into the nineteenth century. At the *concert spirituel* the public applauded the line "Judex crederis esse venturus" from Gossec's *Te Deum*, which, according to the *Almanach musical*, "offered a somber and terrible imitation . . . of the end of the world, painted quite vigorously."[12] The critic for the *Journal de Paris* heard familiar sounds in Gossec's *Messe des morts* and identified in them "the shaking of the earth and the overturning of nature."[13] Sometimes spectators employed both views to describe the same piece, as one who praised Gossec's *Nativité* in a letter to the *Mercure* for its "surprising effects of harmony" and for its imitations of nightingales and thunder.[14] Although admirers of Gluck tended to discount the value of imitations—contending that the musical evocation of passion was vastly superior to musical imitation—there was no logical reason to keep listeners from employing both systems of reference simultaneously.

This was how a musician in the court of the prince de Condé explained music to his patron.[15] In a handwritten manuscript dedicated to the prince, Ducharger leads Condé through a detailed discussion of several instrumental works, describing their meaning at every turn. The best-known piece he describes is Vivaldi's *Spring* from *The Four Seasons*. It "represents" the season, Ducharger writes, by a choir of birds who accompany the "God of song" (presumably the solo violin playing above the ensemble). One hears a brook, he continues, which gushes over pebbles and forms a pleasant gurgling. A breeze rustles leaves in the trees, a sudden storm interrupts the calm, the bucolic peace gradually returns.

From these sounds and images Ducharger derives less concrete, though no less literal, tableaux. "To render the illusion yet more perfect, the author, through the sweetness of sounds, transports us to groves, he leads us from field to field, guides us through valleys, and shows us shepherds dancing on verdant fields or perhaps among bursting flowers to the sound of a pan-pipe." Finally, Ducharger claims that the music conveys sentiment, asserting that hatred, despair, worry, and inner agitation are all within the scope of its expression.[16]

Spectators' enthusiasm for instrumental works had its limits. The ornamented concertos of Locatelli and Tartini remained too mathematical and dry, too "learned" for most spectators' tastes. The *Mercure* explained an overall public indifference to Mozart's symphonies and sonatas by their difficulty: it was "that kind of music that can interest the intellect without ever penetrating to the heart."[17] There is no question that had the music of J. S. Bach been known in eighteenth-century France—as it was only fragments of his keyboard music circulated there, and this only among a tiny number of musicians late in the century—it would have been promptly dismissed as arid and empty. When Jean-Joseph Rodolphe ended one of his motets with a fugue the French press denounced it as "a genre of music worthy of the Goths."[18] As Ducharger wrote to his patron prince: "If music has no other object than that of running through modulations, now *piano*, now *forte*, through *crescendi* and *rinforzandi*, it signifies nothing: these are merely nuanced noises, suitable only as exercises for instrumentalists."[19]

The discovery of an additional, more emotional stratum of musical expression encouraged spectators to turn inward to feel the passions the music evoked. This articulated a shift in aesthetic orientation, from the objective recognition of sounds to a more subjective experience of empathetic response. According to B.-G.-D. de Lacépède, whose *La Poétique de la musique* appeared in 1785, the "profound affections" and "melancholy sentiments" that harmony arouses virtually compelled listeners to examine their innermost feelings with "candor of spirit." "All that saddens us, all that awakens somber thoughts in us, all that gives birth to profound affections carries the soul naturally to fold back upon itself, to contemplate and judge itself," he writes.[20] A popular guide to musicians that also appeared in 1785 employs the same language of the soul to describe Gluck: "In touching situations, he moves and carries away the soul."[21]

A listener more engaged emotionally was a listener less distracted socially. This was at least how the *Almanach musical* explained the growing calm that characterized audiences toward the end of the century. Not all spectators were silent, it acknowledged, but those who were seemed "intoxicated" with passions provoked by harmonies, their souls "penetrated intimately with the feelings music brings." For them the least noise "could distract them from the pleasure they find in the musical expression of a tender and delicate feeling."[22] To hear sentiments instead of storms and birds in the orchestra made listening with divided attention more difficult. It was easy to forget about the beautiful blond next to you with the roses on her chest.

This is where the ideological ramifications bound up with changes in listening begin to show. In much the same way that sensibility in plots affected dramatic judgment, the new emotional sensitivity to musical expression defined personal, natural passion as the essence of musical expression, thereby implicitly denying—or at the very least complicating—the courtly advice to watch the grandees before responding. As Lacépède wrote in 1785, "only the virtuous man will be able to taste the tender emotions true music inspires without uneasiness; only he can feel pleasure in the feeling it brings."[23] This view was a far cry from Jacques Lacombe's 1758 description of aesthetic experience, a description fully informed by courtly etiquette. "The politeness the arts have brought . . . has sometimes covered vice with a veil of virtue, but this necessity, even when it has forced fiends to hide their character, constitutes its praise. . . . For as men touch one another only on the surface, everything will remain in order if one can compel those who are born ridiculous to be so only within themselves."[24] Taste was no longer a function of birth or rank. It depended upon goodness.

At the same time, however, the new musical perceptions implied a shared experience entirely absent from descriptions thirty years before. Because emotion was now the essence of musical expression, listeners described it as a unifying fluid that flowed through all who could feel. A supporter of Gluck, for example, claimed to speak for all spectators "who possess sensibility" when he detailed the emotions he felt listening to his music: "All [are] affected in the same way in the same places in the music."[25] Such sympathetic solidarity was appropriate to the cultural force of sensibility, which embraced in sentimental fraternity not just the parterre with the forestage boxes but peasant girls with the queen. If greater calm, deeper engagement, and more focused attentiveness mark an increased subjectivity, *sensibilité* kept the experience from becoming radically different from one spectator to the next. We mustn't forget all those spectators who showed their profound individual emotions by crying, all at the same time.

With *sensibilité* so strong a cultural current in the late eighteenth century it would be tempting to attribute the revolution in musical expectations to cultural influences alone. The disposition to be moved predated Gluck and no doubt raised sensitivities in a general way. But audiences were very clearly responding to and describing *musical* innovations that caused them to expand the categories of perceived musical meaning. Most noticeable for eighteenth-century spectators was

Gluck's general omission of musical imitations and word painting. Their accounts do not mention nightingales, earthquakes, or surging oceans for the simple reason that Gluck employed that particular convention of French opera only on rare occasions.[26] Opportunities that Lully, Rameau, and any number of other French composers exploited for programmatic effects—the garden scene of Renaud's sleep in *Armide*, for example, or Orpheus' mention of birds and rivers in the Elysian Fields in *Orphée et Eurydice*—are devoid of all obvious imitation in Gluck.

Gluck's highest musical aim in his operas was to create moods and capture emotions, a goal he articulated in the celebrated preface to *Alceste* in which he laid out his differences with Metastasian *opera seria* point by point. "I have striven to restrict music to its true office of serving poetry by means of expression and by following the situations of the story, without interrupting the action or stifling it with a useless superfluity of ornaments," Gluck wrote; "and I believed that it should do this . . . by a well-assorted contrast of light and shade, which serves to animate the figures without altering their contours."[27] The claim merely to serve poetry, though sincere, was overly modest; in Gluck the servant has at least as many privileges as his master.

Gluck achieved this "contrast of light and shade" by pairing each emotional nuance of the text with a distinct musical style in the orchestra. The changes are frequent and unmistakable. *Armide*, for example, begins with Phonice and Sidonie singing of youth and pleasure to a lilting melody. The instant Phonice mentions war, the meter changes from three to four, the accompaniment shifts from F major to D minor, and the mood suddenly seems overshadowed by trouble. (Here Gluck refrains from all drum rolls and fanfares.) The key and character again change to create a resolutely martial mood when Armida enters and names the enemy soldier Renauld.[28] Although they are perfectly integrated and make eminent musical sense, there is nothing subtle about these changes: they would stand out to any spectator, musically trained or untrained, who listened attentively. The same is true of the great second-act aria in which Armida confronts Renauld as he sleeps. Gluck divides the music into three distinct sections by varying the tempo, meter, and key to suit Armida's murderous vengeance, the crippling sympathy that overtakes her when she sees Renauld's face, and her hurried invocation of spirits to strengthen her resolve.

This is how Gluck amplified each emotional shading in the text, and it is characteristic of all his French operas. In *Alceste*, a separate musical style accompanies each emotion of the heroine's opening aria as she offers fitful prayers for mercy from the gods, reflects upon her love for her husband the king, and sings of her children. The aria begins with a respectful moderato ("Great gods at least relax the harshness"), changes meter to become more urgent ("and have pity for my great misfortune"), and ends with a passionate allegro ("Only a wife and mother could know my despair, my torments, my bitter pain"). The harmonies of this third section grow yet more ominous when Alcestis mentions her children, as a descending chromatic sequence leads into a brief segment in the minor mode (see Example 5).[29]

As if to make the point indubitable that musical expression is more than a text or its melody, Gluck sometimes wrote unremarkable melodies above more passionate passages or unexpected harmonies. The raging tumult of the orchestra in Thoas' aria "Dark thoughts and evil terrors assail my soul" in *Iphigénie en Tauride* accompanies the simplest of melodies, and in *Alceste* a chorus of shades from the underworld declaim a single note for fifteen measures while the underlying harmonies twist and turn in lugubrious succession (see Example 6).[30]

Perhaps the most telling case of Gluck's intentions to *convey* rather than *depict* comes in the second act of *Iphigénie en Tauride*. Orestes, terrorized by the Furies for having killed his mother, Clytemnestra, cries out in remorse for the gods to crush him as the orchestra plays a turbulent, agitated accompaniment. Collapsing in his own shame, Orestes at length begins to regain his bearings, announcing finally that peace has returned to his heart. But the music is far from serene with its forceful syncopation, which effectively contradicts Orestes' words. "Le calme rentre dans mon coeur!" is a lie exposed by the orchestra.[31]

Gluck's innovations prompted audiences to transcend the imitative model of listening through the right combination of familiarity and innovation. Neither wholly alien to reigning expectations nor squarely within them, Gluck's music was familiar enough for French audiences to grasp and take seriously while novel enough to enlarge their accustomed ways of listening. Neither the music of Piccinni nor that of the most popular eighteenth-century symphonists could have produced such far-reaching perceptual change; if anything, they perpetuated the traditional ways of listening.[32]

Rameau, of course, had tried and failed to make his audiences hear the kinds of emotions Gluck conveyed through his harmonies, probably because in giving spectators what they already expected to hear with programmatic orchestral passages Rameau drew their attention away from more subtle expression. As long as there was a surfeit of images to

Example 5. Alcestis' opening aria from *Alceste*, Christophe Willibald Gluck.

Example 5. *Continued.*

Et sur l'ex-cès de mon mal - heur Je - tez un regard pi-toy-a - ble, Et _ sur l'ex-cès _ de _
mon mal - heur Je - tez un re - gard_____ pitoy-
a - - - ble!
Rien n'é - ga - le mon déses-poir, Mes tour-ments, ma dou-

Example 6. The chorus of shades from Gluck's *Alceste*.

contemplate, listeners were unlikely to delve more deeply. Gluck's innovations were of such importance because they blocked off the old familiar route of imitation while opening up an attractive new avenue of emotion. Judged by the box office, Gluck won the war against Piccinni, which shows that his music spoke the language of the French. By the end of the war he had also enlarged their vocabulary.[33]

From a twittering audience to a weeping audience, from watching the grandees to seeking the heart's reasons, from sounds to moods and images to emotions, from an assortment of opinions to an appeal to taste, from a series of *petites sociétés* to a theater unified by sentiment: the Opéra's administrators, sensing though not fully understanding the new atmosphere, rightly described the changes of the 1770s as a "revolution" in the history of the Académie Royale de Musique.

What the directors saw was an audience that displayed unprecedented attention and appreciation, a "Nation" eager to applaud and be moved.[34] What they could not have observed were the implications of this revolution they described. In the changes in seating and sociability, in taste and in etiquette, the tool of critical judgment emerged to challenge the former ways of evaluating musical worth. By 1780 individuals *qua* individuals formed and announced their own musical judgments with a legitimacy gained only through the transformations in sociability and musical sensibility of the previous twenty years.

This construction of individual experience at the Opéra, coupled with the corresponding sense of unity through sentiment, gave birth to the notion of a single musical public, which claimed in its public opinion to speak for a singular taste superior to arbitrary opinions. It represents, on the one hand, a conceptual space for individuals to formulate their own personal responses and, on the other, a collectivity conceived in terms apart from the earlier unity gained through the symbolic presence of the king. Groping to describe this new collective spirit among audiences in a way that would avoid the corporate connotations of a spectacle unified by courtly conceptions, observers referred to the Opéra as a national spectacle and its audiences as a nation.

Cultural and intellectual historians have identified the 1770s and 1780s in France as the crucial period for the emergence of a public sphere of judgment implicitly opposed to the authority of the crown.[35] Keith Michael Baker writes that in the context of absolutist politics, public opinion was a tribunal that claimed to arbitrate rationally the divisive and contested political claims that had come to characterize Old

Regime France.[36] It asserted a single "voix publique," as both Baker and Mona Ozouf have observed, that was far from Rousseau's descriptions of changeable, arbitrary opinions incubated in cliques and announced by the esteemed.[37] Baker argues that the emergence of the concept of public opinion was a political invention—a rhetorical category deployed to assert an open, consensual politics—rather than a direct reflection of sociological change.

But if various political groups in the final years of the Old Regime competed to claim that this concept spoke for their own political interests, it is also true that certain actual conditions prevailed to permit the emergence and growth of the concept. Jürgen Habermas describes the growth of such potential places of opinion in eighteenth-century salons, cafés, clubs, reading societies, and theaters.[38] The rise of critical political, literary, and artistic journalistic styles, Habermas argues—and a burgeoning press both legitimate and clandestine—at once articulated ideas formulated in these relatively circumscribed spheres and diffused them throughout society, rendering opinion public.[39]

Public opinion also carried a strong collective claim that distinguished it from absolutist conceptions of society: its very nature challenged the view of society as a series of particularistic groups unified by the public person of the king. Louis XIV summarized best that latter ideal when he declared that "the nation is not a separate body, it dwells entirely within the person of the King."[40] The public was its own nation, a republic of letters. Its identity didn't so much reject the monarchy as see its corporatist vision of society as irrelevant. Asserting itself as a judge of politics and taste against the arbitrary authority of fashion, dogma, or tradition, the public claimed an authority apart from all established arbiters, intellectual as well as institutional, of absolutism.

Like public opinion in political discourse, the musical public effectively challenged traditional absolutist patterns of judgment by offering a third source of musical arbitration apart from both the king and the opinions of disconnected groups. "Only the public can judge in the last analysis," a supporter of Gluck wrote in 1777. "It may require some time to prepare itself initially, . . . but it ultimately renders justice over the ignorant and especially the charlatans." Addressing Piccinni's supporters directly, the spectator referred contemptuously to the earlier conception of audiences: "Be content, gentlemen, to tyrannize your *petites sociétés* with the false wit of your so-called genius; be the oracle of busybodies. But be assured that the public has nothing to do with your opinion, and even less with your judgments and false erudition."[41]

Such was the force of an aesthetic that turned listeners simultaneously inward and toward other like-minded spectators (i.e., the virtuous ones, to recall Lacépède): "no judge other than the public should decide the merit of a piece designed to amuse and captivate it. This truth is indeed crucial, since failure has so often come to works thought excellent by pretended connoisseurs, men of taste, or theater directors."[42]

These terms also permeated talk about the nascent concert societies of the 1770s and 1780s. Supporters of the groups clearly viewed their purpose as something more than a pastime for the idle rich. When the Concert des Amateurs was dissolved in 1781 the *Almanach musical* expressed the hope that the musical library of the society could be passed on to groups offering "public" concerts, preferably at the expense of the state. The series at the Hôtel de Soubise, the journal continued in its best Enlightenment prose, had furthered "progress in knowledge" and "the development of all talents," propelling the "French Nation" to superiority in the arts.[43]

And this was the rationale Ducharger used to recommend a complete overhaul in the organization of concerts in France. In contrast to existing practices that exercise social discrimination in deciding who can and cannot attend, Ducharger writes, concerts should be open "to whoever can pay for his place." The goals of concert societies should be "the progress of music, the well-being of musicians, and the good of the public." In language that the French revolutionaries would soon repeat and try to realize, Ducharger spells out a vision of music for all citizens. "Concerts must in no way be private, but public: they contribute to the softening of manners, and it is unjust not to render them common to all the members of the state."[44]

The particular developments at the Opéra and in concerts of the 1770s and 1780s—the fires that forced new floor plans, the growing aesthetic interest that rearranged seating patterns, plots designed to move rather than enchant, a musical revolution that brought more engaged listening, and the greater subjectivity that necessarily followed—gave the musical public its particular personality. Not only did the emergent public space teach listeners to subvert earlier patterns of artistic judgment; in some respects, as with the spectator who exhorted his fellows to sound their own emotions and shun borrowed opinions, it defined the path that subversion would take. In the nexus of cultural influences that defined late eighteenth-century France, this decline of corporatist patterns of judgment at the opera resembled—and perhaps encouraged—the erosion of the cultural authority of absolutism in other domains as well.[45]

The tensions and contradictions created by appeals to public opinion ran through French political culture like fault lines in the waning years of the Old Regime. Spectators who invoked the authority of public taste could not have been ignorant of its wider resonances. Literary, artistic, and musical publics asserted their inclusive unity against the exclusive and fragmented corporate structures that still existed: the public "at large," although still legally divided into three estates, acted as a court of opinion set up to judge the crown.

Opera and concert audiences, too, spoke out for greater democratization and exhibited a sensibility that tended toward egalitarianism. But in reality the opera and concerts in the 1770s and 1780s remained almost exclusively the pleasure of a small elite.[46] This was precisely the kind of contradiction that led Marie-Joseph Chénier, in June 1789, to dream of a truly free theater, where "particular interests" would be destroyed before the "public interest" and drama would become "public instruction" for the "entire nation."[47] Here, as elsewhere, the momentum of reform would outstrip the hopes of even the most progressive dreamers.

PART THREE

The Exaltation of the Masses

Driven by national vanity, Antoinette brought the celebrated German [Gluck] to France, and he created dramatic music for us. In this she was unwise. For it is not at all inaccurate to say that the revolution accomplished in music shook the government: the chords awoke French generosity, and the energy that enlarged our souls at last burst out. The throne was shattered. And now the friends of liberty have used music in their turn, employing those same vibrant sounds this German composer produced.

Jean-Baptiste Leclerc, *Essai sur la propagation de musique en France* (1796)

6

Entertainment and
the Revolution

It was four years after the storming of the Bastille and just before the onset of the Terror, and spectators streamed through the doors of the new Théâtre National for its inaugural performance. On the program was a musical drama that promised close parallels with the current state of France, and, judging from the divided responses of spectators since 1789, its reception was sure to be contentious.

The moment, August 1793, was pregnant with change. Beginning with the beheading of the king in January, the year had witnessed more sweeping transformations in politics and culture than had occurred in the previous four years combined. War had been declared on England and Holland, and the *levée en masse* now swept citizen-soldiers together from every corner of the young Republic. The nation's representative body, the Convention, had been stormed by popular crowds enraged with its moderate members, and in a lurch to the left typical of a Revolution fueled increasingly by denunciation, Mme Roland, twenty-nine Girondin deputies, and two ministers were arrested. During the summer the Committee of Public Safety with Robespierre in command had emerged as the nerve center of the Revolution. By now the counter-revolutionary uprising in the Vendée had been raging for almost six months, and it was beginning to look like all-out civil war.

When the vast blue curtain rose for the first time at the Théâtre National—one of the many independent halls to sprout up after the gov-

Part-opening illustration: Detail of Charles Monnet, *Fédération générale des français au Champ de Mars, le 14 juillet 1790*. Engraving. Photograph courtesy of the Bibliothèque Nationale.

ernment abolished the Académie Royale's monopoly—the Revolution lay somewhere between pluralism and dictatorship. Each passing week brought it closer to the latter. By now, the Jacobins had made it clear that they intended the theater to be the nation's political classroom, and over the next ten months they would do all they could to realize their particular musical vision. Acting through decree and diktat with a force that surpassed even that of Louis XIV, the Jacobin leadership worked to remake audiences into a microcosm of the nation, unified in will and sentiment and aggressive in its enthusiasms. Private pleasures would vanish like mist, they were convinced, and every citizen would dance in common exaltation.

Opening night at the Théâtre National was heavy with the symbols of this uneasy passage to virtue. The theater and the performance alike held an anomalous mix of opulence and egalitarianism. Although plans for the new building had been completed long before anyone could have foreseen the radical turn the Revolution would take in 1793, its architects nevertheless departed from standard Old Regime assumptions in several important respects. Continuing the trend toward greater democratization, the architect Victor Louis designed a hall whose shape resembled a flattened horseshoe, which placed spectators sitting at the rear of the hall much closer to the stage than in the old rectangular halls (see Figure 8).[1] From floor to ceiling there were altogether five levels of benches and boxes. The partitions between boxes, as in the 1781 opera hall, were turned toward the stage. The theater did not originally contain seats in the parterre, but in 1794 the Committee of Public Safety ordered their installation for reasons they pointedly described as humanitarian.[2] ("One cannot conceive how, after the Revolution, there could still be French theaters with the audacity to pack spectators together and make them stand," one newspaper commented just before the seats were installed.)[3]

The feature most talked about in the revolutionary press was the absence of boxes alongside the stage. Never before had a major Paris theater sacrificed revenues for the sake of artistic illusion by depriving the well-to-do of their prestigious forestage boxes. It was a sign of the times. Instead of seeing the action framed by grotesquely illuminated faces, spectators now saw six stately columns adorned with emblems of Tragedy, Comedy, Music, and Dance.[4] The change at once elevated art and enhanced the actors' credibility: the innovation is "most remarkable," marveled the *Moniteur*. "With no one in boxes to mingle with the actors, the illusion is preserved."[5] The *Journal des spectacles* ap-

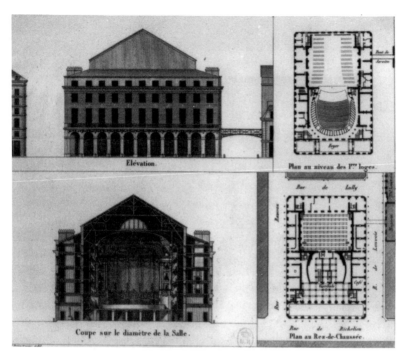

Figure 8. Théâtre des Arts: elevation, plan showing the first-level boxes, cutaway view of the hall, ground-floor plan. From Donnet, *Architectonographie des théâtres de Paris* (1821). Photograph courtesy of the Bibliothèque Nationale.

plauded the design on the grounds that "actors should be alone, so to speak, with the characters they portray."[6] On the proscenium a group of painted cherubs held a banner reading "To the Arts," another indication that architectural priorities had shifted from the patrons to the performance.[7] The Jacobin leadership evidently approved of these more popular touches: eight months after the Théâtre National opened, the Committee of Public Safety made it the official home of the Opéra, which was still performing in the hastily built structure at the Porte Saint-Martin.

On the program this opening night at the Théâtre National was *La Journée de Marathon*, a musical allegory of France's war effort set in ancient Greece. *La Journée de Marathon* ostensibly portrayed the defense of Athens against the invading Persians intent upon reinstating the tyrant-king Pisistratis. Spectators easily saw beyond the plot, however, to its intended parallels with the wars raging outside France and in the Vendée. "Tyranny destroyed, the family of the tyrant in foreign exile and leading numerous armies against Athens," the *Journal de Paris* summarized laconically, "partisans of ancient despotism scattered widely throughout various Greek towns looking to betray their home-land; . . . and in Athens itself, partisans trying to divide the people for their own gain."[8] *La Journée de Marathon* was the most recent produc-tion in a new style of drama that blurred the boundaries between fiction and reality. In the coming months audiences would see much more of the technique.

But if opening night prefigured the dramatic elements that would animate theater under the Terror, it also contained reminders of drama before the deluge. For apart from the austere columns framing the stage, the interior boasted an opulence far from republican simplicity. Citizens and sansculottes seated themselves in boxes swathed in fabrics of red and gold. A new system of lighting placed lamps behind diapha-nous clouds on the walls, bathing the hall in warm, diffuse light, an effect observers described as more magical and enchanting than in any previous hall.

The ceiling was a veritable Achilles' shield. In the cupola stood Comedy, with a mask and a bust of Molière, and Tragedy, with her red cloak and dagger. Music and Lyric Poetry held hands nearby; swans snuggled alongside Lully and Quinault, who were themselves surrounded by violins, flutes, horns, oboes, and drums suspended in the blue. Painting was cast as monkeys grasping brushes, Terpsichore touched a harp for Dance, and Mechanical Sciences dangled various in-struments to test the laws of gravity. *Trompe l'oeil* medallions appeared in every niche bearing the allegorical and the literal: Tragedy crowned Corneille with laurel leaves, Dance fluttered on butterflies' wings, satyrs trailed banners inscribed with antique verse, and Pastoral, Lyric, and Erotic Poetry each struck an appropriate pose.[9] This was hardly the spirit of Sparta.

At the opening, the closest the press came to outright criticism of this cloying abundance was an expression of utter exhaustion from identifying all the characters in its ceiling.[10] But soon the revolutionary aesthetic would denounce such froth as Old Regime decadence. When the Committee of Public Safety ordered renovation of the Comédie-Française in 1794, for instance, they gave explicit instructions on every-thing from its seating to its color scheme: the boxes were ripped out and an amphitheater installed, the ceiling was painted over in wide blue, white, and red stripes, and statues of Liberty and Equality were placed prominently in the niches.[11] The pace of events aged icons quickly.

The response of the audience on opening night expressed the transitional nature of the moment in another way. Clearly intended to arouse enthusiasm for the struggles both in and outside France, *La Journée de Marathon* produced more bewilderment than excitement. "*La Journée de Marathon* was received rather coldly," one newspaper reported. "Two days ago it was welcomed with a sort of coolness," another wrote.[12] At fault, apparently, was its dual agenda. For its critics, too close a correspondence between the stage and the street risked stripping the drama of its own internal dynamic. The analogies between the plot of *La Journée de Marathon* and France's current state were "superb," commented the *Journal des spectacles*, "but this is not sufficient for a play. There must be interest and action, without which the scene dies no matter how much heroism there is."[13]

Within weeks this lukewarm response would give way to fierce enthusiasm, as the slightest reference to the Revolution on the stage brought torrents of applause. Audiences had undeniably exhibited a gradual evolution of behavior and taste since the fall of the Bastille, but only with the onset of the Terror did they show the unanimity of response that Jacobin leaders urged. If there was a revolution in musical experience to match *the* Revolution it came now, in the autumn of 1793, rather than in 1789. But the nature and depth of this revolution are by no means certain: for with the fall of Robespierre spectators returned to their old tastes and habits virtually overnight, closing the parenthesis of exaltation. Eviscerated by Napoleon and excoriated by the Restoration, the Revolution ultimately left scarcely a trace on French musical experience.

In the summer of 1789 the Académie underwent a series of tremors touched off by Revolution—it was, after all, such a visible symbol of the aristocracy—but it survived them largely intact. Crowds furious over the dismissal of Necker rioted at the Porte Saint-Martin in early July and forced the Opéra to close for a week and a half.[14] On the fourteenth, before the Bastille was attacked, a mob invaded the Opéra in search of arms. All they turned up were a few dull swords, the director reported dutifully, "since the hatchets and clubs were made of cardboard."[15] And in August, having heard rumors of a plan to burn the Opéra and the Hôtel de Ville, Lafayette ordered increased protection of the theater, a task bravely undertaken by the dance corps.[16]

Apart from such crowd action, however, the Opéra in the early years of the Revolution differed little from before. In most cases, the promise (or threat) of sudden and radical change went unrealized. The convening of the Estates General, announced in August 1788, raised hopes throughout France, and here it was no different: performers sent in *cahiers* demanding the government do something to stop the parterre from insulting them and booing the works they didn't like. (Alas, the performers were in for a big surprise—revolutionary violence in the parterre made the earlier rowdiness look like petty salon squabbles by comparison.)[17]

Some took the establishment of the National Assembly as an occasion to demand reduced ticket prices; others called for seats in the pit.[18] One representative claimed (ironically?) that the Revolution's principles of human dignity required a new procedure for selling tickets on the day of a performance: "it is a fact that any man present when the Bastille was taken risked less injury than at the Opéra's ticket booth while buying places for the parterre on the opening nights of *Iphigénie*, *Alceste*, and even *Tarare*."[19]

For their part, supporters of the old order feared instant demise for the Opéra as aristocrats fled to other countries.[20] The emigration undoubtedly deprived the Opéra of a portion of its patrons, but numerous fixtures in the firmament of Old Regime France continued to shine there, a striking fact confirmed not only by subscribers' lists but also by press accounts of the persistent shouting matches and fistfights between royalists and revolutionaries during performances. The prince de Conti, Malesherbes, and the duchesse de Broglie all held boxes at the Opéra as late as 1792.[21] It is nonetheless true that the Opéra was much less an institution of elites after 1789; moreover, the Revolution quickly severed any remaining connections between visibility and social status, at least as the pattern had developed in the middle decades of the century. This was particularly the case in the post-1789 world-turned-upside-down, when not only the former carriers of status came under attack but the very concept was discredited: seating now seemed more random than ever.[22] The ambassador from Holland sat in a third-row box, and the ambassador from Venice was yet more anonymous on the benches of the balcony. How times had changed since mid-century, when diplomats watched from their boxes on the stage![23]

Renting boxes was still not the faceless business of acquiring seats on a first-come-first-served basis. Because the opera management had near total control over who sat where, most requests for a box were fawning, although some tried to intimidate. "Although I do not have the honor of being known by you, I take the liberty of appealing to your goodness to entreat you to grant me preference, if it be possible, for a fourth of a box at the Opéra," one potential subscriber wrote.[24] Another sent his "million million thanks" for receiving a desired seat.[25] Some viewed the arbitrary nature of the system, which operated halfway between the ordering principle of rank and a democratic distribution by order of request, as a clear threat to their traditional privileges. An aide to the duc d'Orléans, for instance, sent the opera a stinging letter when he was denied a box at the Opéra: "I will attempt to forget this blow," he wrote, "by persuading myself that the thirty or forty persons who have benefited from your distribution bear still more elevated titles than that of the chancellor to the duc d'Orléans."[26]

The lack of any clear order in seating continued to produce unlikely neighbors. Louis XV's last mistress and a close confidante of Marie Antoinette, Mme du Barry, watched the opera a matter of yards from "Le Père Duchesne."[27] Was it Jacques René Hébert who had signed the theater log that way? The imagination leaps at the possibility, since Hébert's pamphlets, emblazoned across the top with "Je suis le Père Duchesne, foutre!," lampooned the queen in rich scatological detail. (What did *he* shout in the direction of du Barry when they sang "Chantons, célébrons notre reine?") If ticket prices in the early phase of the Revolution still kept *le menu peuple* from attending regularly, spectators there nevertheless represented a broad spectrum of political opinion, ranging from the duc de Choiseuil, who served as a lookout in Louis XVI's failed flight to Varennes, to Louis Michel Lepelletier de Saint Fargeau, the aristocrat martyred for voting to condemn the king to death.[28]

There was one final sign, perhaps the most dramatic, that the Académie Royale was no longer the aristocratic pleasure dome it had once been. The stately mythologies that conveyed unmistakably noble grandeur now shared the stage with works more self-consciously popular—in some cases defiantly so.

Despite the boost the Gluck-Piccinni quarrel gave to attendance, the Académie Royale had still faced a formidable rival in the Comédie-Italienne, the third theater of the realm. Since 1762, when the theater merged with the rival Opéra-Comique de la Foire to form a single troupe, productions at the Comédie-Italienne had drawn a higher class of clientele than had the earlier boulevard shows with their broad slapstick and innuendo.[29]

The Italiens, as contemporaries sometimes called the theater, presented vaudeville, parody, picaresque plays, and *drame*, but its greatest attraction was the *comédie mêlée d'ariettes*, typically a farce with songs. Between 1760 and 1790 French composers working under Italian influence elevated the *comédie mêlée d'ariettes* from a farrago of improvised chatter and street tunes to an integrated, coherent form in its own right. *Opéra-comique* became synonymous with its masters Egido Duni (1708–75), Nicolas Dalyrac (1753–1809), François-André Philidor (1726–95), and André-Modeste Grétry (1741–1813). Particular traits varied according to the gifts of the composer, but its characteristic spoken recitative—progeny of the *comédie mêlée d'ariettes* and precursor to Beethoven's *Fidelio* and Bizet's *Carmen*—remained the identifying feature of comic opera performed at the Italiens.[30]

Too dependent upon the revenues it received from the troupe to consider suppressing it but smarting from the drain on spectators, the Opéra first met the challenge of comic opera by redefining the terms by which the Italiens could perform. The thirty-year privilege that opera administrators negotiated in 1780 hence forbade the theater from producing any Italian operas or *intermezzi*. It also forbade all parodies of the Opéra's own repertoire and prohibited any performance of comic operas on Tuesdays or Fridays, nights the Académie Royale counted on for its biggest crowds. The Opéra tightened its virtual monopoly on dance, too, by banning all ballets from the Italiens based on "historical" subjects.[31]

The restrictions actually helped the *comédie mêlée d'ariettes* by focusing the form more sharply. By the mid-1780s a distinctive, commercially potent musical genre reigned at the Comédie-Italienne, one written by French composers and performed by French actors with all the zest and patter of Italian *buffa*. Realizing that its attempt to choke the flow of audiences to the Italiens had backfired, the Opéra did what any business slipping to the competition would do. It brought the comic genre to its own stage. So *before* the Revolution, *before* a democratic politics defined the national agenda, and *before* the middle classes with their respectable tastes and restrained manners filed quietly into the comfortable seats of the parterre, the Académie Royale sponsored plots with bourgeois themes.

The first comic opera to appear at the Opéra was *Le Seigneur bienfaisant* by Étienne-Joseph Floquet (1748–85), a work remembered for its historic importance but musically unremarkable. *Colinette à la Cour* by André-Modeste Grétry seems to have misfired, too, when it premiered in early 1782; Grétry himself, not normally shy about relating his achievements, passes over the work in his memoirs with scarcely a word. But Grétry's next work for the Opéra, *La Caravane du Caire*, was an undeniable success, figuring continuously in the active repertory from its appearance in 1784 until 1791, and again from 1799 until 1829. "I saw that the public was tired of the tragedies that simply wouldn't leave the stage," Grétry wrote with obvious satisfaction. "And I heard numerous supporters of dance who were upset to see it reduced to a secondary and often pointless role in tragedies."[32] Grétry knew that *La Caravane* had inaugurated a new epoch at the Opéra.

The novelty of *La Caravane* was in its plot, although the score was certainly as skillful and expressive as any work new to the Opéra in the 1780s. The libretto was an odd mix of prurience and sentimentality, as though the scrappy new genre was having trouble hiding its circus origins under the fancy clothes. The combination was probably calculated to hit the high as well as the low. The "supporters of dance," after all, had vivid memories of what their art had been before Gluck's dour dramas swept the *filles d'opéra* into the wings.

The libretto of *La Caravane*—on which the comte de Provence, the future Louis XVIII, was said to have collaborated—sympathizes both with the pasha of Cairo, named Osman, who is in the mood to buy a slave girl, and with Saint Phar, a miserable French slave whose wife is for sale. "I have some spicy beauties, they're sure to stir your juices," the merchant Husca sings to Osman with a leer. Zélime's fate is sealed as soon as Osman sees her, but this isn't before Husca unveils his beauties to the pasha (and to the supporters of dance) in the celebrated "Cairo Bazaar" dance sequence. Who could have guessed that the storming of the Bastille was just four years off by listening to the randy song one French girl sings as she dances in front of Osman?

> We're each one born for slavery,
> And even kings wear chains;
> For such are humans' pains.
> . . . So out of all the masters
> Whose whims we might invoke,
> My pleasure stands with love's commands
> For that's the sweetest yoke.[33]

Alongside the salacious in *La Caravane du Caire* is the sensitive. That Grétry could combine the two musically, offering genuinely touching arias reminiscent of Gluck next to the raucous dance numbers, was surely what listeners found so engaging. "Oh, my Zélime!" Saint Phar sings, weeping in desperation as he watches his wife being sold to Osman. "I love you! Oh, my Zélime! I love you!"[34] Spectators no doubt saw the dénouement coming when a French officer roaming the seas in search of his lost son suddenly arrives: a sad aria extols the virtues of family love, Zélime appears one last time as Osman is preparing to take her home with him, she lets drop her husband's name. "Ô Ciel!" the father almost shouts to Osman. "Perhaps my son deserves death, but surely you see the tears of a father."[35]

The stroke was from the century's *comédies larmoyantes*, in which dramatic reunions and disguises revealed at the last moment provided a moving substitute in the bourgeois drama for deus ex machina resolutions; such would become the stock ending for comic operas over the next two decades.[36] Osman—and probably the audience, too—is so deeply moved by the father's tears and Zélime's entreaties that all lust evaporates, and the opera ends in a sentimental celebration of the couple's liberation: "A tender father, a husband so dear—blessed Saint Phar will dry your tear."[37]

In the 1770s and 1780s comic opera began to exercise its own influences over the perceptions of audiences and the techniques of young composers. The Comédie-Italienne premiered works that became classics in the new genre: *Richard, Coeur de lion* (Grétry, 1785), *Paul et Virginie* (Rodolphe Kreutzer, 1791), *Lodoïska* (Kreutzer, 1791), and *Stratonice* (Étienne-Nicolas Méhul, 1792) are only the more notable productions among numerous works to appear. The genre grew so popular, in fact, that a second company specializing in French comic opera opened a theater in 1791 on the rue Feydeau. The proximity of the Feydeau to the Salle Favart, the hall occupied by the Comédie-Italienne, no doubt exaggerated the inevitable rivalry, and the result was several sets of twins: the Feydeau's *Lodoïska* was by Luigi Cherubini (1791) and its *Paul et Virginie* was by Jean-François Le Sueur (1793); there were also duplicates of *Roméo et Juliette* and *La Caverne*.[38]

These innovations in plot and music changed for good what audiences saw at the Opéra, and the effects were only intensified under the democratic pressures of the Revolution. Grétry followed *La Caravane du Caire* there with *Panurge dans l'île des lanternes* (1785), a very simple love story that takes place on a fantasy island; Jean-Baptiste Lemoyne composed two *comédies-lyriques* for the Opéra, *Les Prétendus* (1789) and *Les Pommiers et le moulin* (1790), and his *Louis IX en Egypte* (1790), though not comic, portrayed recognizable characters in somewhat plausible settings. While *Didon*, the *Iphigénie* operas, and *Oedipe* all stayed in the repertoire of the Opéra in the early years of the Revolution, new works there steadily depopulated Olympus. Méhul's *Adrien*, written in 1790–91 but not performed until 1799, and his *Horatius Coclès* (1794) were set in Roman antiquity.

Less lofty than the *tragédies-lyriques* that had reigned at the Opéra for a century but tamer than the sidewalk burlesques that amused the popular classes, these *opéras-comiques*, *comédies-lyriques*, and *drames-*

lyriques subtly changed the relationship between spectator and performance by reducing the distance between actor and observer. By the 1790s the so-called comic operas were more often serious and sentimental than silly, and unlike in Gluck's day their psychological pain was seldom refracted through the distant mirror of mythology. The plot of *La Caverne* concerns a pitiful group of prisoners who nurse the hope that their kidnappers have not killed one of their friends; in *Lodoïska* a brutish landholder in Poland claims to be in love with a girl he has taken by force, and only a siege by invading Tartars saves her from his "marriage"; and Méhul's *Mélidore et Phrosine* (1794) is an unvarnished depiction of the murderous jealousy, implied to have stemmed from incest, of a man whose sister has declared her intention to marry.[39]

These melodramatic productions were a brutal recasting of the chaste *sensibilité* of the 1770s. They were a grittier version of Greuze, as if his characters had revealed their basest instincts before returning to virtue in a bitter trail of tears.[40] Nourished by the bloody events played out daily at the peak of the Revolution—its denunciations and summary judgments, its heroic sieges and miraculous rescues, the familiar slice of the national razor—this artistic formula would reap its own *fleurs du mal* in the grotesque exaggerations of romantic opera in the nineteenth century.

Given the route comic opera took to the Opéra, the Favart, and the Feydeau, this popular genre would likely have thrived even in the absence of a French Revolution that preached radically democratic principles and filled the theaters of high culture with popular audiences. That their content would have taken the violent turn it did while still entertaining spectators, however, seems doubtful. In 1793 revolutionary crowds circled the guillotine singing and dancing as it did its work. In 1793 a self-described sansculotte bragged that "fathers and mothers will be guillotined and assassinated and we'll sleep with their girls, and then we'll have women."[41] And in 1793 a journalist summarized the finale of Le Sueur's *La Caverne*: "The last scene is truly bloody; they fire off at least forty gunshots so close that it actually seems like they've split your skull. This was vigorously applauded."[42]

For spectators after 1789 attending the opera was politics by other means. Their heckling and harassment had roots in the Old Regime, but if the behavior was a continuation of earlier habits the mood was not. Old Regime unruliness in the theater had almost always contained a hint of play. The shouts and whistles of revolutionary audiences were more menacing. Arguments between spectators easily became brawls; seemingly innocent lines from operas could set off protest and counter-protest of such magnitude that the artists would have to stop singing. In a 1790 performance of *Iphigénie en Aulide* the duchesse de Biron provoked a near riot when she stood up and cheered at the lines, "Chantons, célébrons notre reine": half of the hall cried, "Bis! Bis!" and the other half whistled and hooted; her box was showered with fruit and vegetables, and by one account a knife was thrown. The singers repeated the chorus defiantly, and the duchess tossed a laurel wreath onto the stage.[43]

Piccinni's *Didon* invariably provoked battles inside the theater as royalists applauded lines that could be taken politically: "Kings, like gods, are above the law," drew a loud outburst when it was sung, as did the line, "It is for the gods to judge, and the subjects to obey."[44] By 1791 factions in theaters had taken to singing songs to show their political colors; most typically "Ça ira" was pitted against "Ô Richard, ô mon roi," an aria from Grétry's *Richard, Coeur de lion* that lamented the kidnapped King Richard I.[45] According to the *Chronique*, the opera *Didon* sometimes ended with the stage singing Piccinni and the parterre singing "Ça ira."[46]

The disorder touched other theaters, too. In 1791 an actor at the Italiens replaced the word "Richard" with "Louis" as he sang "Ô Richard, ô mon Roi" in a performance of *Richard, Coeur de lion*. The words ran:

> Oh Louis, oh my king!
> With our love we faithfully embrace you,
> And the law that's written on our hearts
> Dedicates us to serve your cause.

Applause erupted in the boxes, and sheets bearing the modified lines fluttered down to the stage. Cries of "Down with the traitors!" and "Burn their papers!" broke out from the parterre and the performers stopped singing. The orchestra, hoping to reconcile both factions in common patriotism, struck up "Ça ira," but only the intervention of the police could end the chaos.[47]

From this it was a short step to violence. When an actress looked directly at Marie Antoinette in her royal box at the Salle Favart in 1792 to sing the line, "I love my mistress tenderly. Oh, how I love my mistress!" spectators jumped onto the stage to silence her. Actors spilled out of the wings to protect her, and the stage turned into a massive free-for-all.[48] In the same year the lines "Il faut que le peuple soit éclairé mais non pas égaré [The people should be educated, not misled]" provoked a near riot at the Comédie-Italienne. The boxes burst into applause, the parterre responded with shouts and jeers, and the police were pelted with potatoes when they stepped onto the stage to restore order.[49] Similar scenes of chaos and violence reached such uncontrollable levels in early 1793 that the mayor of Paris temporarily closed all theaters.[50]

Tarare, the eclectic collaboration by Salieri and Beaumarchais that had premiered in 1787, provoked some of the most heated exchanges of the Revolution. The topical revisions Beaumarchais made for *Tarare*'s 1790 reprise at the Opéra brought boos from royalists and applause from patriots: the virtuous soldier Tarare, who replaces a tyrant as king of Asia, repeats his oath on an altar of liberty, he establishes marriage for priests and abolishes monastic vows for (Buddhist) monks, grants a divorce, and frees black slaves. By the third performance of the revised *Tarare* the combined chaos of protest and assent that greeted each contemporary allusion was so loud that the performers had difficulty hearing themselves.[51]

The message of the work was not entirely satisfying to those who sympathized with the more radical goals of the Revolution, however. The line "Respect for kings is our first obligation" invariably brought howls of indignation from spectators otherwise supportive and temporary applause from the rest. The *Chronique de Paris* called the line "unconstitutional," and one angry spectator published an open letter to Beaumarchais charging that if respect for kings were truly the first obligation the nation would be obliged "to burn the constitution, disband the National Assembly, and obey the whims of a tyrant."[52] Beaumarchais refused to change the line and remained vulnerable to both sides' attacks.

The potential violence of these and other scenes throughout the theaters in Paris was a bitter reminder that, far from inaugurating an era of peace and harmony, 14 July had unleashed a cycle of hatred and suspicion. In the spirit of freedom and fraternity, the National Assembly voted in 1791 to end all armed patrols inside the theater during performances and post a single unarmed civil guard, whose job it was to call in reinforcements whenever necessary.[53] In practice, a contingent of armed troops waited just outside the doors of theaters and were summoned inside regularly.

As a part of the same law the Assembly abolished all governmental censorship of dramatic content. Supporters of the measure praised it as the fruit of liberty, and Le Chapelier foresaw wide applications for civic education. Theaters would no longer devote themselves to frivolous pleasures, he said, but would "purify morals, give lessons in citizenship, [and] be schools of patriotism and virtue."[54] The idealism of the moment made audiences and government officials blind to the possibility that theaters might choose to perform inappropriate works: freedom couldn't possibly corrupt virtue.

Yet three years into the Revolution theaters continued to mount productions from the Old Regime, and tolerance was wearing thin among those who found their very presence an offense against revolutionary principles. The Opéra in particular had done little to adjust its repertoire to the changed political climate. Sacchini's *Oedipe à Colonne*, Piccinni's *Roland* and *Didon*, and the classics of Gluck all remained popular and in the active repertory. Ballets, particularly those choreographed by the opera's dance master, Pierre Gardel, were as popular as ever, and they were regularly given after full-length operas. And Gardel's *Télémaque dans l'île de Calypso*, his *Psyché* or *Mirza*—all popular productions with opera audiences in the early 1790s—could easily have passed for productions from fifty years earlier with their splendiferous costumes and machines.[55]

Those sympathetic to more radical goals of the Revolution worried that this traditional fare was impeding its progress. In the spring of 1792 the *Chronique* charged Grétry's *Richard, Coeur de lion*, Gluck's *Iphigénie en Aulide*, and Piccinni's *Didon* with eliciting "delirious applause of aristocrats"—"signs of revolt," it continued ominously, "and the wish to see France devastated by foreign armies."[56] Insisting that the classics should not be "distorted" by censorship (the concept conjured images of whim and high-handedness, certainly antithetical to liberty), the paper urged the production of explicitly patriotic operas and the discreet omission of any works apt to trouble true republicans.

At last, in October 1792, the Opéra responded to events by mounting its first patriotic spectacle, a "religious setting on the tune of the Marseillaise" scored by François-Joseph Gossec and choreographed by Gardel. The work, *L'Offrande à la Liberté*, was a brief patriotic sketch whose general contours would set the dramatic standards of revolutionary opera for the next two years. Stripped of any hint of plot, the work was pure commemoration. Dancers circled a statue of Liberty, a soloist announced the fall of the monarchy, and a chorus sang the "Marseillaise" as cannons and the tocsin sounded offstage. The piece ended in choreographed confusion as three hundred singers waving hats and flags sent French soldiers off to overthrow tyrants.[57] "Everyone flew into combat, waving armor, bonnets, and banners in the air," a spectator present writes. "This magical outburst was unlike all else; nothing was more skillfully combined than this disorder that so genuinely communicated the enthusiasm simulated on the stage to the hall." [58]

L'Offrande, which first appeared after the full-length opera *Corisande*, stayed in active production at the Opéra until the end of the Terror. At the same time, the theater gradually added longer and more fully developed patriotic scenes to its repertory. Ultimately these works would attempt to mirror the lives of citizens as closely as possible—with actors dressed in street clothes repeating excerpts from speeches already made and singing the songs sung by the people—but in these early patriotic productions some of the trappings of a hundred years of enchantment still lingered. *Le Triomphe de la République, ou le Camp de Grand-Pré* (Gossec, 1793) featured a general who sang his orders to the troops ("this long report does not and cannot produce any sort of effect when set to music," one journalist commented pedantically) and culminated with the goddess of Liberty descending from the ceiling by ropes to fraternize with the troops and sing of freedom. Dancers appeared on the stage in the national costumes of the world's free peoples, and soon the camp at Grand-Pré was filled with Greeks, Romans, Swiss, Dutch, and Americans dancing with the French army. [59]

Dramas set on the eve of great battles or in their midst grew very popular at the opera. In *La Prise de Toulon* (Lemière, 1793; Dalyrac, 1794) and *Le Siège de Thionville* (Jadin, 1793) performers hauled cannons onto the stage to fight mock battles punctuated with speeches and singing. The press now praised these more realistic works at the Opéra and other theaters for "augmenting theatrical illusion and eliminating from the stage the ridiculous machines and petty methods used there before." [60] But the inspiring verism was not without its costs. One theater director complained that the nightly explosions and thick smoke threatened to destroy his entire stock of stage furniture. [61]

Less destructive were reenactments of great moments and festivals of the Revolution. *La Réunion du dix août*, a 1793 work by Pierre-Louis Moline and Bernardo Porta and one of the longest-running patriotic pieces at the Opéra, consisted of static tableaux of the Revolution. The action opens at a dilapidated, post-1789 Bastille with a choir of citizens singing about their miraculous century. The president of the Convention, members of the Convention, and representatives of provincial assemblies enter and encircle a statue of Nature whose breasts shoot out arcs of water, and as the men drink deep draughts from a common cup the president pledges to live in Nature's simplicity. The citizens light a great bonfire of vanities—crowns, scepters, escutcheons—and move to the Champ de Mars to swear eternal faithfulness on the funerary urns of fallen martyrs.[62] This was roughly what had occurred at the actual festival. The Opéra recreated the Festival of Reason at Nôtre Dame in its production *La Fête de la Raison* in December 1793. Other Paris theaters staged versions of the Fête de l'Être Suprème and the Fête de l'Égalité at the same time.[63]

These celebrations of contemporary events matched on a grand scale what smaller musical theaters of Paris had begun to stage in more modest proportions earlier in the Revolution. Exploiting the relevance and immediacy inherent in comic opera, the Comédie-Italienne presented works whose action was drawn from the daily lives of good French citizens. *La Chêne patriotique*, an opéra-comique by Dalyrac produced at the Italiens four days before the Fête de la Fédération in 1790, aimed at presenting "a faithful portrait of what will occur all over France on 14 July."[64] Two young lovers, the son of a former seigneur "without prejudices" and the daughter of an honest villager, carve their initials onto a tree replanted in the village festival on the fourteenth. Just as the festival begins the initials are discovered. The fathers embrace, soldiers fire cannons, the civic oath is intoned, and everyone sings happy songs about fraternity among the orders.[65]

Les Rigueurs du cloître (Henri-Monton Berton, 1790), also at the Comédie-Italienne, used events of the Revolution—and the popularity of the dramatic rescue—to weave a clever story. The work tells of two lovers who are separated when the girl is forced into a convent against her will. The girl's hidden cache of love letters is discovered by her tyrannical abbess, who decrees that she will spend the rest of her days on rations of bread and water in the darkest cell of the compound. But hardly is the sentence pronounced when her lover bursts on the scene in his new National Guard uniform to announce the dissolution of monasteries and freedom for all inmates![66]

Accustomed to such stirring plots in theaters across Paris and now at the Opéra, and increasingly convinced that any remnants of culture from the Old Regime were obstacles to true regeneration, some by 1793 had started to rethink the value of any principle, even liberty, that permitted kings and princes to be celebrated in drama. Early in the year the Jacobin representative Jérôme Pétion warned of the perils of counter-revolutionary productions; hoping to avoid the term *censorship*, Pétion proposed that magistrates issue "invitations" to theaters expressing the "imprudence" of mounting certain works.[67] The method was used by the Committee of Public Instruction until August, but the persistence of productions from the Old Regime convinced the government that more urgent measures were needed. On 4 August 1793 the Convention passed a decree that effectively reimposed censorship in the name of public education by requiring all theaters to stage works "that retrace the glorious events of liberty" at least three times weekly, threatening to close any theater "tending to deprave the public spirit and reawaken the shameful superstition of monarchy."[68]

To avoid closure, theaters now had to send their scripts and scores to the Committee of Public Instruction before performances. If the script was unsuitable, theater directors made changes to salvage it; otherwise they canceled the performance. In *Le Déserteur* "le Roi passait [the king has passed]" became "le Loi passait [the law was passed]"; in *Tartuffe*, "nous vivons sous un prince ennemi de la fraude [we live under the prince, an enemy to fraud]" became "ils sont passés les jours consacrés à la fraude [they spent their days devoted to fraud]"; in *Le Cid* the king became a general leading a revolutionary brigade in Spain; and the action of *Alceste* was moved from the kingdom of Thessaly to a republic with military officers in command.[69] A new phase of revolutionary drama had begun.

7

Musical Experience of the Terror

In early 1794 a resident of Bordeaux was guillotined for having shouted out "Long live our noble King!" some months before. The charge of royalism was nothing new, but the circumstances certainly were. Arouch was an actor, and he had called out the words, just as the script instructed, during a performance of Pedro Calderón's *Life Is a Dream* at the Grand Théâtre. Angry spectators had denounced the company for the lines, the Military Commission of Bordeaux arrested all eighty-six members of its cast, and after a month of imprisonment and hearings it was determined who had spoken the phrase. All were eventually released except Arouch, who reportedly went to the scaffold desperately repeating, "But it was in my part!"[1]

Arouch was the only actor of the Revolution to pay the ultimate punishment for the crimes of his character, but he was not the only performer to be denounced by spectators demanding political purity on the stage. An officer on leave from Lyon was shocked to see actors depicting British aristocrats at the Comédie-Française in a 1793 production of *Pamela* and rushed from the hall to the Jacobin Club in mid-performance to denounce the cast as counter-revolutionaries. The aristocratic manners, black cockades, and lofty titles were offensive in their own right, he explained to the Jacobins, but an actor's plea for naive political pluralism—"The persecutors are the most guilty," his lines ran, "and the tolerant most forgivable"—was unbearable. (Several spectators had protested to the man without effect that the lines referred to *religious* and not political toleration.) The next day the theater was shut down and all its cast but three imprisoned as accused traitors, where the majority remained until the fall of Robespierre ten months later.[2]

These two incidents, though not musical in nature, illustrate the public mood in theaters as revolutionary politics grew more radical in 1793 and 1794. This mood also touched the music world. Those still performing in Paris when the guillotine started its work did everything they could to dissociate themselves from earlier aristocratic associations. When the *Gazette nationale* published a piece accusing the Opéra of being a "foyer of counter-revolution" in September 1793, musicians from the theater rushed to the Commune de Paris to say how unfair the charge was. To prove it they sang the "Marseillaise," publicly burned all documents they could find bearing the words "Académie Royale de Musique," and, for good measure, denounced the Opéra's directors Louis-Joseph Francoeur and Jacques Cellerier as traitors. Their performance was a success: the musicians were deemed patriots and Francoeur was arrested. (Cellerier managed to flee Paris.)[3]

The accusers of Arouch and the Comédie-Française clearly had in mind the sort of long, nefarious association between actors and elites that prompted the denunciation of the Opéra company. Robespierre, who happened to be present at the Jacobin Club the night Jullien de Carentin stormed in to denounce *Pamela*, improvised a speech condemning the Comédie as "a disgusting den of every sort of aristocrat" and demanded it be closed.[4] The radical *Feuille du salut public* gleefully reported the demise of the theater, "an impure seraglio," it wrote, where "Prussian and Austrian croaking had always dominated."[5] Likewise, the military commission that conducted the arrest and trial of the Bordeaux troupe announced in its report to the Interior Ministry that it had destroyed "a foyer of the aristocracy" and claimed that performers there had maintained "close relations with counter-revolutionaries and correspondence with émigrés."[6]

So when a spectator in late September 1793 denounced the Opéra cast during a performance of Sacchini's *Oedipe à Colonne* as shamefully glorifying "kings, princes, and the like," he explicitly linked it to the past: it was "time to forget these old mistakes of our fathers."[7] Under the combined popular and official pressure, *Roland, Iphigénie en Aulide*, and *Oedipe à Colonne* were withdrawn from the repertoire of the Opéra as offensive to most republicans and positively dangerous to the weak in spirit.[8]

These denunciations entailed more than criticism of traditional ties between actors and aristocrats. They suggest the fusion of perceptual categories, a collapse of dramatic fiction into political reality. As a result of their own understanding of the Revolution and its principles, coupled with a particular musical experience that new political works for the

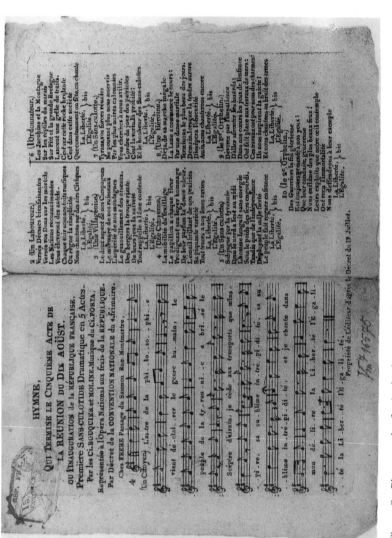

Figure 9. Photograph of a single-sheet song, the hymn ending the fifth act, assumed to have been distributed to spectators during performances of *La Réunion du dix août*. Photograph courtesy of the Bibliothèque Nationale.

stage seemed to produce, spectators during the Terror refused to suspend their disbelief for the sake of the drama. By the autumn of 1793 a triumphant Jacobin ideology had found its aesthetic embodiment in a fundamentally new set of artistic standards that purified plots and performers alike. Princes and secret conspirators weren't the only victims of censorship. The actors who portrayed them were also at risk. In the service of revolutionary fraternity, performer and spectator were united in the higher service of citizenship, and stage fiction effectively disappeared from the perceptions of the public.

The dramatic experience of transparency—transparency between stage and street, transparency among spectators, and transparency between the performer and his part—was the effect of two principal causes. On the one hand, the purging and retouching of repertoires to bring more revolutionary commemorations to the stage while eschewing all reminders of the impure past produced a different kind of engagement among audiences, one that demanded common exaltation beyond passive amusement. In some cases the methods that composers and librettists took to encourage solidarity between stage and spectator took novel forms. Single-sheet copies of the citizens' choruses that ended each act of *L'Offrande de la liberté*—hymns whose structure closely resembled the songs sung at festivals—were printed up, presumably so audiences could also join in the singing (see Figure 9). The presence of such sheets helps to explain accounts describing the robust singing of the audience during patriotic finales.

But more decisive, with the imposition of the Terror as "the order of the day" on 5 September 1793, there was now a way to enforce revolutionary consciousness. A "law of suspects" was voted, making denunciation simple and efficient. As the judicial system was reorganized to facilitate larger numbers of the accused, the number of arrests quickly leapfrogged over the executioners' ability to keep up. As the Revolution devoured first its enemies and then its children—Marie Antoinette, Mme Du Barry, Philippe Égalité, Brissot, Bailly, Barnave, Desmoulins, Danton—the prisons throughout Paris filled with men and women whose neighbors or family had denounced them, too, for sins against the Revolution.

When *La Journée de Marathon* reappeared in November and December after having foundered at the Théâtre National's opening in August, the reception was nothing short of ecstatic: the public cheered when the Athenians vowed to kill the usurper-king and reacted with "inexpressible transport" to the play's "analogies to [our own] liberty."[9]

Such responses stood in sharp contrast to the earlier, tepid reception of plots based upon political events. "Such a living tableau clings to none of the dramatic rules," wrote the *Abréviateur universel* in 1794 of *Toute la Grèce*, a historical piece whose heroes carried banners that read "Vive la République!" and "La Liberté ou la Mort!" and sang melodies modeled on the "Marseillaise"; "and this only proves that one can produce grand effects on the stage by explicitly renouncing all theatrical illusion."[10]

The changed public response was no doubt in part a reflection of the changing composition of audiences themselves, as sympathetic crowds filled the seats of royalists now less bold about coming to the theater to sing their songs and denounce change. But spectators also claimed to see their own lives authentically reflected in the dramas on stage. "Is there anyone in France or in Europe," a police spy wrote to his superior after seeing *Le Siège de Thionville*, "who still doubts how dear the Republic is to the French? They should hear the singing of the couplet that follows the news that there is no longer a king in France. At these words the hall, pierced by bravos, fell into a single burst of applause that was so loud that one would have thought the roof would rise into the heavens!"[11] The report ended with a phrase that must have made Interior Ministry officials reading it shudder with delight. In these productions the audience is "yet more citizen than spectator: everyone was an actor as the masculine voices of the hall supported those on the stage."[12]

During the Terror the gospel of the Revolution became the sole standard of public taste in the theater. With stage action justified inasmuch as its events and characters were recognizable, the definition of dramatic truth among audiences shifted from the plausible to the actual. The battles, festivals, and moral lessons from daily life taught audiences to equate fiction with falsehood, so that ultimately even productions without the objectionable cast of aristocrats were considered unacceptable if they were not "true." Such was the flaw of Dalyrac's *opéra-comique Merlin et Ugande*, according to the *Feuille du salut public*. Set in the time of Amadis de Gaul, it was a "fairy tale" that tried to please by illusion and fantasy instead of drawing analogies to the glorious present. "Why should we stay in the realm of dreams and trinkets," the newspaper asked, "when reality surrounds us? Why look outside ourselves for pleasure when the republican finds it within himself and in everything around him?"[13] *Révolutions de Paris*, employing the same reasoning, had nothing but praise for a new opera that was "without dances, without ballets, without love, without fairy scenes."[14]

In reducing the distance between art and life these works did not so much *represent*—understood in both senses as performance before passive observers and as actors expressing the will of the people in their stead—as encourage a radically democratic participation in the drama. By dressing in ordinary street clothes and singing the songs of the people, performers became citizens. The persona was the person. As the closing lines of *L'Heureuse décade* amiably stated in a direct address to the audience: "We wanted to offer some pleasant scenes for all good patriots with these couplets. If you have enjoyed yourself, applaud the author and the actor; they are all sansculottes." [15]

The incorporation of popular songs into the musical texture of these works also worked to reduce the distance between dramatic fiction and revolutionary reality: the overture to Rochefort's one-act opera *Toulon soumis* (1794) contains "La Marseillaise" and a snippet of the "Carmagnole"; later in the work the orchestra repeats "Ça ira" at great length to narrate the action; "La Marseillaise" ends the first act of *Le Siège de Thionville* (1793); and Gossec's *L'Offrande à la liberté* contains "Veillons au salut de l'Empire" and "La Marseillaise." [16]

If dressing actors in street clothes transformed performers into citizens, encouraging the audience to sing by distributing song sheets and lacing the performance with popular tunes transformed the citizens into performers. This was how drama without dramatic action so effectively inspired its revolutionary audiences. It made them recognize that the dramatic plot—that is, the work of the Revolution itself—was still unfinished after the final curtain. "We whipped the English buggers at Toulon," a teenager was heard saying after he saw *Le Prise de Toulon*, "but we'll whip 'em even better next spring when we go to London." [17] In this grand illusion to end all illusion the spectators became the spectacle, and the division between audience and actor was transcended in their common identity in the nation. During the Terror, revolutionary theater was *theatrum mundi*. Describing a performance of *Toute la Grèce*, a writer reported that "the spectators were themselves at one and the same time witnesses and actors; and when the Greek warriors on stage swore to conquer for their country's sake, the French soldiers in the audience reacted by declaring 'What they have sworn, we shall do.' " [18]

At its highest moments, musical experience of the Terror truly seemed to achieve the transparency that Rousseau had dreamed of in his *Lettre à M. d'Alembert* but thought impossible for the theater. The fault line of fiction that divided spectators from actors and made performance inauthentic, the weakened human bond as spectators forgot each other in a dim hall but found pity for unreal characters, the lack of moral instruction that produced sympathy for villains and a distaste for the upright: these obstacles to true communion of sentiment that Rousseau had outlined seemed to be overcome—willingly, even enthusiastically—in theaters during the Terror. "Let the spectators become an entertainment to themselves," Rousseau wrote. "Do it so that each sees and loves himself in the others so that all will be better united." [19]

The sentimental openness of transparency among audiences took on Rousseauvean political associations as well, for it implied the sacrifice of particular wills for the sake of the indivisible whole. Rousseau had warned in *The Social Contract* that to delegate the general will to representatives was to sacrifice one's own sovereignty, a notion the Jacobin Club used in May 1793 to encourage the popular uprising against Girondin members of the Convention. Now the source of power would be the popular *sections* that met in perpetuity. The haggling and compromise characteristic of representative bodies would give way to unanimous accord. What better place for viewing the unified nation than in the theater? How better could the sovereign people express its general will than in collective enthusiasm?

The evident success of achieving transparency between spectator and spectacle, and between audience and actor, saddled performers with the precarious burden of their roles. The category of character slipped from the minds of spectators who witnessed their own struggles and achievements before them. In a spectacle of common celebration the task of the citizens/actors was nothing other than to declare their own patriotic sentiments before others in public. It only followed that insufficient zeal was the fault of the citizen/actor. This was the reasoning that led one critic to charge that an actor in *Le Quaker en France* was not forceful enough in his defense of war against arguments for pacifism: "When one actor mentions peace, if another actor with him on the stage does not reply: 'No peace as long as our enemies are sullying our soil; no peace as long as there are still tyrants who haven't given homage to the Republic; no peace until the Republic is avenged,' then the actor is wrong and can be accused of being a moderate." [20] Patriots offstage, these actors were patriots onstage. Didn't it follow that aristocrats or British agents on the stage were aristocrats or British agents off the stage, too? This was the logic that doomed Arouch and the Comédie-Française.

Performers were particularly vulnerable during the Terror for a second reason, one that is closely tied to the Jacobin ideal of transparency that transformed performers into spectators and spectators into performers: because they had spent their lives perfecting the art of deception how could one be sure that actors sincerely felt the solidarity they seemed to share with the audience?[21] As François Furet has so perceptively discussed, an engine of Jacobin publicity was the drive to unmask, to denounce, to expose the hidden conspirators who disguised themselves as friends of the Revolution the better to subvert it.[22] Secret plots were, as Furet writes, the "antiprinciple" of the Revolution, and, like an episode of Rousseau's paranoia writ large, they seemed to loom ever larger as citizens opened their souls to the gaze of others.

As the Jacobin drive to unmask set the popular suspicion of deception on a hair trigger, the very talent that defined actors was suddenly politically threatening. "Only actors enjoy the surprising privilege of being perfect monarchists in the very bosom of the Republic," one spectator warned of the insidious gifts of deception performers possessed.[23] Similarly, just after the arrest of the Comédie-Française troupe, the *Feuille du salut public* charged that the theater was "a gathering place for criminals *disguised as decent folk*."[24]

Musical experience during the Terror was hence a curious coexistence of the all-embracing and exclusionary. Its own impulse to unmask was a condition of its fragile transparency. Just as revolutionary leaders, impelled by the threat of invasion by foreign armies and the paralyzing fear of internal enemies, increasingly relied upon purges and proscriptions to enforce the national unity, so, too, did spectators adhere to a mentality of coercion in the service of unified dramatic experience. A letter published in the *Journal des spectacles* demanded that theater directors be forced to stage revolutionary works: "I say *forced*, because republicanism is often a motive of exclusion."[25]

This was certainly the mentality—that plotters threatened to disrupt common exaltation by impugning the principles of the Republic—that led spectators to denounce "counter-revolutionaries" so zealously. Just as the Revolutionary Tribunal had only two possible verdicts to render to accused traitors, the guillotine or freedom, so did views of drama and opera contain a ruthless dichotomy. In its glowing review of *L'Heureuse décade*, the *Feuille du salut public* wrote, "In a time of revolution, everything that isn't *strongly for* is *against*; all it takes is some good sense to see the truth of this maxim."[26]

To suggest that fear of the guillotine was an element of the dramatic experience of the Terror—and by now the tool was so permanent a presence that it went by darkly endearing nicknames such as the "little window" and the "national razor"—doesn't necessarily question the sincerity of spectators' dramatic vision of transparency. If genuine revolutionary enthusiasm involved a willingness to denounce, the act of denunciation itself implied that no one, not even the accuser, was completely safe from scrutiny. As the director of the Lycée des Arts put it, pleading the innocence of *Adèle de Sacy*: "The good republican does not dread denunciations, for they are the touchstone of citizenship; but every denunciation must be examined, tested to its depths; this is the duty of surveillance, and it is only then that public esteem brings justice to the accuser."[27]

For audiences and artists who had gradually come to the ideal of transparency through their debates on censorship and their experiments in education through theater, the threat of the guillotine was simply the culmination of a natural chain of reasoning that led from suspicion to unmasking to purification. Viewed from the parterre, with spectators all around singing "La Marseillaise" and dancing to the "Carmagnole," the guillotine seemed less a tool of coercion than a necessary reminder. It guaranteed that this glorious, contagious display would keep within it a salutary dose of distrust, the needed glint of fear. It was undoubtedly with just such fear—overcompensating, vaguely accusing, and above all aggressively patriotic—that the director of the Lycée announced at the Jacobin Club that good republicans had nothing to fear.

Fueled by the spirit of purification that denounced all things not strongly for the Revolution as against it, the dramatic vision of the Terror was never stable, never satisfied with the state of public spirit, never convinced that there was a perfect identity of interests among citizens on the stage and in the audience. The moments of true unity seemed too brief, the state of permanent fusion between actor and audience remained just beyond reach. In early 1794, the very time when the number of "aristocrats" executed was highest, a police spy at the Opéra reported that the audience listened with its "typical" enthusiasm, yet he feared that the theater was still "an aristocratic foyer," "a rendezvous for men who want to speak freely."[28] Rumors circulated in the spring that nobles were hiding in the backstage areas of theaters, and in July the Commission of Public Instruction issued an alarming report that found theaters "still encumbered with the debris of former regimes, . . . with interests that no longer concern us, and with manners that are not ours."[29]

This late in the Terror, however, the problem was not aristocrats. It was representation. For despite the moments of unanimous exaltation, when performance seemed to give way to participation, in truth these scenes and reenactments remained representations: the street clothes, the speeches, the revolutionary songs were all coordinated trappings of an illusion of transparency. At times the illusion was strikingly successful, as the arrest of performers made abundantly clear. But as soon as the spectators stopped singing and the action continued on the stage without them, the chasm between actor and audience reopened and the specter of private experience reappeared. Ten months into the Terror the *Moniteur* found cause to worry that "certain frivolous people" in the audience could "escape the national movement by isolating themselves in the audience."[30]

Joseph Payan, secretary to the Commission of Public Instruction, grasped the maddening truth that any stage production, even if its subject were unimpeachably revolutionary, was ultimately inauthentic. No matter how much they resembled the spectators in the hall, performers recreated scenes that had already occurred. They were an elite who represented the experiences of the nation by proxy, a reality that no amount of popular singing and dancing could alter. The Rousseauvean political analogy rang false as Payan exposed the naivete in believing that reenactments and lessons in virtue could give mysterious birth to an indivisible general will. Writing on behalf of the commission less than a month before the fall of Robespierre, Payan vigorously attacked all stage recreations of great events: they were gross trivializations, he wrote, "masquerades [that will] become the festivals of preference for 'good society.' "[31] Only actual participation—that is, physical presence as the events unfolded—could solve the problem of representation. The end of this logic would be the elimination of all spectacles, a conclusion Payan broadly implied but left unstated.

The response of audiences between the autumn of 1793 and the death of Robespierre was the most visible aspect of musical experience during the Terror. Less visible were the speeches, essays, and books guiding official policy toward music during Jacobin rule. Intellectuals had been discussing the powers and role of music in revolution since 1789; by 1793 a coherent musical vision with clear ideological underpinnings had emerged. The terms of this radically democratic vision, in fact, would persist until late in the decade. A fundamental assumption was the necessary politicization of music: how could the art, these writers asked, be put to use by the government in the service of freedom? The question touched virtually every aspect of musical experience, from the logistics of performance to the nature of musical meaning to the degree of engagement among listeners.

The most systematic treatments of revolutionary musical experience appear in discussions of national festivals, the great outdoor commemorations of events, personalities, phases of life, and states of mind. Here the "dramatic" action was the people assembled, as if one enormous, invisible stage stretched beneath their feet. "In order to enjoy a festival it does not suffice simply to be a spectator, one must be an actor," one festival planner aptly wrote.[32] The festival formed "a single and unitary character," a "single and unitary spirit," a "single and unitary whole from all members of the state."[33] Their very publicity—they were typically held on the wide lawn of the Champs de Mars—made private experience next to impossible (see Figure 10). "If there were some individual or some class of citizen who wished to isolate itself in these festivities and hide," as Alexandre de Moy wrote, "this would be noted by the multitude and looked down upon by the totality."[34] There was a festival for youth and a festival for old age, a festival for virtue and one for morals. There were festivals for reason, liberty, enlightenment, and labor, of Continental Peace, of Terror, and of the Supreme Being.[35]

Music was a central element of festivals. As the *Journal de Paris* wrote, "Point de République sans fêtes nationales, point de fêtes nationales sans musique"—no Republic without national festivals, and no festivals without music.[36] Concerned that a single orchestra unfairly favored those close to it, some recommended that multiple orchestras be seated at equal distances throughout the crowds. Opoix, for instance, proposed that twelve orchestras with 12,000 choristers from all levels of society and regions of France perform at the Fête des Victoires in 1794. Merlin envisioned thirteen orchestras among the masses and devised a plan in which citizens would sing first in dialogue and then in unison to symbolize the emergence of a single will from its sundry parts: the resounding unison of this "universal choir," Merlin predicted, will "ravish souls with transports as yet unknown."[37]

The proposals of Opoix and Merlin were never attempted, but others that shared their vision were. In preparation for the Fête de l'Être Suprème, music teachers from the Institut National de Musique fanned out across Paris, violins in hand, to teach the city Gossec's "Hyme à

Figure 10. *Pacte fédérative des français le 14ᵉ juillet 1790*. Photograph courtesy of the Bibliothèque Nationale.

l'Être Suprême."[38] For another festival Méhul divided the crowd into four sections, and on a cue from the composer one sang the tonic, another the third, another the fifth, and the last the octave above, producing a glorious major chord sung by thousands. And late in the decade Méhul composed and executed a work requiring three orchestras spaced evenly throughout the masses.[39] The subtext was simple if unprecedented. In these times, all were performers. This was the musical expression of revolutionary democracy.

These public festivals combined the aesthetic of *sensibilité* with the politics of liberation. Their planners wanted to stir crowds in the same awesome ways Gluck had been able to do. In an essay on festivals dedicated to Robespierre and originally delivered before the Convention, Boissy d'Anglas wrote that citizens are most deeply moved when their passions are stirred: governments must therefore learn to deal in "all that can speak to the soul through the senses [and] please the mind in touching the heart."[40] Others used the language of sensibility to describe the effects of patriotic music in festivals. Edouard Lefebvre was

confident that even the coldest man could not avoid a "sense of enthusiasm," and La Revellière-Lépeaux asserted that "two or three thousand
spectators will feel the same sentiments and share the same pleasures at
the same time."[41]

In addition to radiating an overall spirit of sensitivity, these discussions carried aesthetic assumptions that grew directly from the perceptual changes Gluck initiated. P. C. F. Daunou asserted that music "cap-
tivates the mind, fills the imagination, agitates human passions."[42] For
Lamerville, music "takes possession of the soul rather than the senses."
"Music is not simply a song," he writes, "it is indeed a sentiment and a
thought."[43]

But if these legislators emphasized the emotional in music, their language also bears the unmistakable stamp of 1789. Those most strongly
moved will be the "free and virtuous men," Boissy declared; their pleasures will be shared, natural ties will be strengthened, and patriotism will
flare up.[44] Leclerc wrote that music would bring patience, discipline,
and courage, and the *Décade philosophique* wrote that music would inspire love of the Nation and respect for her laws.[45] Nicolas Framery formulated the most pointedly political set of musical effects: civic hymns
would "plant in the memory of the people patriotic sentiments, examples of virtue, and maxims of philosophy and reason."[46]

The potent combination of sensibility and political idealism appeared
in various forms throughout the decade, from misty embraces after
great speeches to the famous ardor of France's citizen-armies. One of
its more unexpected manifestations was the fascination for histories
recounting the miraculous effects of music in antiquity. The Athenian
lawgiver Solon inspired victory over the Megarans by singing a hundred-
verse elegy in the marketplace. Terpander emboldened soldiers march-
ing to battle by playing military airs on his flute. Timotheus aroused
Alexander the Great to such swift martial passion with music during a
feast that he leapt from the banquet table and began waving his sword
as if in battle; and miraculously he grew calm again the instant Timotheus changed tunes.[47]

Plutarch's descriptions of the effects of music seemed especially
tailored to the new republic's needs: "It was at once a magnificent and
a terrible sight to see them march on to the tune of their flutes, without
any disorder in their ranks, any discomposure in their minds, or change
in their countenances, calmly and cheerfully moving with the music to
the deadly fight. Men, in this temper, were not likely to be possessed

with fear or any transport of fury, but with the deliberate valour of hope and assurance, as if some divinity were attending and conducting them."[48]

Under the Old Regime such stories had been dismissed as myths. The chevalier de Méré, acknowledging that the Greeks were able "to touch the heart however they wished," was mystified by the effect. It must have been through "violence, or a spell whose secret has not come down to us."[49] But after the musical experience of the 1770s and 1780s such reactions could no longer be ruled out. Who hadn't seen women kneeling and men sobbing at the Opéra? If entertainment could produce such profound feeling, the possibilities for political lessons were staggering.

The task for the Revolution in recapturing music's ancient power, then, was twofold: preparing listeners properly to receive the higher message of music, and promoting the music best suited to instruct them. Each would naturally feed off the other. Pierre-Louis Ginguené, a founding member of the Institut, addressed the first point in a 1791 article on the effects of music upon listeners. Music was so powerful in antiquity, Ginguené wrote, because its citizens were so perfectly in tune with its simple accents. The chief reason Alexander lunged from the table waving his sword was his devotion to military matters. And *Salamis* impelled young Athenians to battle because they were already disposed to fight.[50] Ginguené's explanations offered a clear and convincing reading of these ancient stories from the perspective of the 1790s, with the implicit conclusion that modern nations would see the same effects if their citizens could only become as natural and virtuous as the Greeks.

Building on these early formulations of the potential powers of music, as well as upon the evidence of audiences dancing and singing in spectacles during the Terror, scientists in 1798 devised an experiment that seemed to confirm Ginguené's conclusions. Carefully isolating the variables governing musical response, professors from the newly created Conservatoire de Musique prepared a special concert to gauge the response of listeners "endowed with sentiment" and untouched by the Old Regime. The first requirement was easy enough but the second seemed impossible, short of recruiting children or beasts. On 29 May the musicians therefore met at the Jardin des Plantes to play a concert for the elephants, who had just arrived from India.

The *Décade philosophique* describes the experiment with scientific precision.[51] A door hid the musicians from the view of the elephants as they tuned their instruments, and Thompson, their keeper, kept them occupied by giving them little morsels "in order to heighten the effect of surprise." The door suddenly opened, and the musicians took up a trio for two violins and continuo.

Hardly had the first chords been heard when Hanz and Marguerite stopped eating; soon they ran to the site from where the sounds emanated. This trap door open above their heads, these instruments of strange forms whose extremities they could scarcely make out, these men who seemed suspended in air, the invisible harmony they tried to touch with their trunks, the silence of the spectators, the immobility of their carnac—everything at first seemed for them a subject of curiosity, surprise, and apprehension. They turned toward the trap door, directing their trunks toward the opening and raising themselves on their hind legs from time to time. They went to their carnac for reassuring pats, and, returning yet more anxious, they surveyed those present to see if they were being tricked. But these initial movements of apprehension gradually diminished as they saw that everything around them remained calm. Then, yielding to the sensations of the music without the slightest hint of fear, they at last shut out all sounds apart from the music.[52]

Next the orchestra played a dance air from *Iphigénie en Tauride* by Gluck, "music of a savage and strongly pronounced character." The movements of the elephants were abrupt and precipitous, "as if they were following the undulations of the melody and rhythm." They bit the bars of their cage and pressed up against the walls, shrieking and snorting, but when Thompson was asked if they were angry he replied: "Them, not mad."[53]

The observers noted other correlations between the music and the animals' behavior. The simple tune "Ô ma tendre musette" played on the solo bassoon softened and calmed them. The overture to Rousseau's *Le Devin du village* excited them to gaiety. The song "Charmante Gabrielle" plunged them into a sort of languor. Hanz showed "neither pain nor pleasure" listening to a symphony by Haydn.

The observers were most interested in the effect of martial music on the elephants. "Ça ira," the radical popular song, was their test case. Instantly the pair became livelier, and Marguerite, already softened by the solo bassoon, now "redoubled her solicitations." She "caressed" Hanz insistently and gave him gentle kicks from behind. Presently the Conservatoire's choir joined in with the words. Now Marguerite couldn't contain herself. She trotted back and forth in cadence, mingling her own blasts with the sound of the trumpets. Approaching

Hanz, her ears began to flap with great agitation as her "amorous trunk entreated him in all the sensitive areas of his body."[54] She fell to the ground in delirium, spreading her legs as she leaned back against the bars. "We heard her utter cries of desire from this position." But an instant later, "as if she had been ashamed of an act that had so many witnesses," she stood back up and resumed her nervous, cadenced trot.[55]

The experiment was a success. The swift and direct effect of music upon sensitive listeners uncorrupted by the monarchy was confirmed. A rough correlation between particular types of music and specific responses could now be made. Most important, the passionate impact of military music, just as the Greeks had chronicled, now seemed indubitable. The central lesson of the experiment was just what Ginguené had said earlier in the decade: music acts most strongly when listeners respond most naturally. The report offered a lofty conclusion: "Such is the empire of music over all beings endowed with life and with sentiment, that men may make use of it . . . to civilize themselves and regulate their morals."[56]

But the experiment held still greater discovery. Scientists, we are told, had long speculated upon the particular manner in which elephants consummated their "jouissances amoureuses," but no naturalist had actually seen it. Entering the animals' cage for feeding several nights after the concert, Thompson became the first man in the recorded history of science to observe the intimacies of elephants at close range. It was a triumph for science! (See Figure 11.) The article ends with a touching image.

One may believe that these first approaches were a consequence of the agitation and arousal music had created in them. It will therefore be wise to attempt a new experiment, but with a number of changes and at a time when they may enjoy a greater liberty in the park. . . . I would insist that the experiment take place on a beautiful night lit by the moon's gentle rays; that silence and absolute solitude seem to surround them; that they see neither the musicians nor the carnac himself; that no spoken voice strike their ears and the sole melody of songs and instruments be heard. Called back to their instinct, reawakened to their desires, assured of the security these acts require, and suspecting no snare or surprise, perhaps they would then abandon themselves to the vow of nature, as in the solitary fields of India.[57]

Unfortunately the young nation was less sensitive to music than elephants or Greeks, and the fault lay with the monarchy. Realizing the potentially upsetting effects of music, this conspiracy theory went,

Figure 11. J. P. Houël, *Les Eléphants représentés dans l'instant de premières caresses qu'ils se sont faites après qu'on leur a fait entendre de la musique.* Engraving. Houël was present at the experiment at the Jardin des Plantes. Photograph courtesy of the Bibliothèque Centrale du Museum d'Histoire Naturelle.

the French kings had deliberately corrupted it, weakened its powers, masked it with pettiness and frivolity so that audiences would view it as nothing more than entertainment. It was a policy, in one official's view, that "carefully hid from the people the relations between the arts and virtue."[58] The complicitous monarchy fed a vicious circle of artistic impotence: an emasculated art weakened taste, which in turn demanded more frivolity. By overthrowing the monarchy the Revolution had already begun to prepare citizens for their civic education. The special revolutionary songs, speech, clothes, and calendars would continue the process.[59] It would just take time.

The second task in reviving the ancient powers of music, the official promotion of properly revolutionary music, required a more directed effort. In 1792 the Commune authorized the establishment of a national school from a military band formed earlier by Bernard Sarrette, the École Gratuite de Musique de la Garde Nationale Parisienne. The school employed 70 musicians as teachers to instruct 120 students in music theory and instrumental performance.[60] In November of the following year the Convention changed the school's name to Institut

National de Musique and authorized funding to expand its teaching staff to 115 musicians and its enrollment to 600. In July of 1795 the Institut became the Conservatoire.

In each of its incarnations, the mission of the school was to train composers and performers in music to instruct the nation. Professors and students alike wrote hymns for marriage ceremonies, funerals, celebrations of youth, old age, and agriculture. They wrote hymns to commemorate French military victories, hymns dedicated to Rousseau and Voltaire, and hymns to mourn the death of war heroes.[61] They worked on the grand scale—among their duties was the planning and execution of music at national festivals—as well as the intimate, writing simple songs to be sung in the family.

They also wrote music for the war. Students went directly from the École Gratuite de Musique, a report filed with the Convention reads, to the battlefield, where they inspired French armies throughout Europe. "It was from the École de Musique that our civic songs, disseminated from one end of France to the other, went into foreign lands, even into the tents of the enemy to disturb the rest of despots in league against the Republic. The École de Musique inspired solemn and glorious hymns that our warriors sang on the mountains of Argonne, in the plains of Jemappes and of Fleuris, and as they forced a passage through the Alps and the Pyrenees."[62]

For those citizens who could not come to the national festivals, these patriotic hymns and marches were sent out in mass mailings across France. Responding to a 1794 proposal by Bernard Sarrette and its favorable recommendation by the Commission of Public Instruction, the Convention approved the publication and distribution of a periodical containing music composed by the artists of the Institut for civic occasions. The report of the Commission of Public Instruction to the Convention viewed the mission of the enterprise as disseminating music "most proper to the solemnity of national festivals, for the maintenance of public spirit, the awakening of patriotism, and the useful employment of periodic days of rest."[63]

The first issue of the monthly periodical appeared in April 1794, in the midst of the Terror. About sixty pages long, it contained an instrumental overture, a hymn to Voltaire, a military march, a patriotic romance on the death of the folk hero Bara, and a martial song celebrating the success of the nation's armies. Copies were sent to the 550 districts of France and distributed through the local communes. The Committee of Public Safety oversaw the distribution of 12,000 copies to French troops abroad and at sea. This widespread distribution of the *Ouvrage périodique de chansons et romances civiques* continued monthly until the summer of 1795.

The effort to publish and distribute revolutionary music on a massive scale, although short-lived, was in many ways the culmination of the Revolution's musical vision. It embodied the ideals of fraternity by encouraging communal singing and relied upon the view that music could move listeners in emotional and politically specific ways. Members of the Committee of Public Safety signed a letter endorsing the project that mentioned virtually every element of revolutionary musical experience. "It will ameliorate the public spirit by the propagation of republican hymns and songs, excite the courage of the defenders of the fatherland, and furnish both a principal ornament for civic festivals . . . and a means to exert influence very effectively over their moral effect."[64]

Although pronouncements on music and musical experience came from all periods of the Revolution by writers with differing political views, it was the Terror that turned their logic to its most potent effects. Spectators transformed into actors, a spectacle in celebration of itself as the nation, the eradication of private sentiments for a higher unity in identical experience, powerful music mass-produced and mailed to the tiniest towns and out across the battlefield—these goals, discussed by thinkers both before and after the Terror, were most nearly realized in the period of Jacobin ascendancy. The most obvious explanation is of course the cruelly efficient mechanism of enforcement between autumn 1793 and summer 1794, but resorting to the guillotine alone to explain the musical experience of the Terror risks obscuring the ideological consistency of revolutionary musical experience.

The revolutionary view of musical experience, proclaimed to be at the same time profoundly inward and shared, was deeply shaped by the Jacobin idea of liberty. Drawing from Rousseau's provocative assertion in *The Social Contract* that individuals must sacrifice all personal rights to the social body, Jacobinism defined and circumscribed the liberty of individuals within the higher interests of the social compact.[65] This "positive" liberty was a freedom *to*—a freedom to develop the manifold potential of human nature as defined by the revolutionaries—more than a freedom *from* governmental restraints or intrusions.[66] Establishing the habits of a new nation in fact turned the one to use by the other: restraints and intrusions would complete the formation of republicans. Saint-Just's simple phrase gives chilling clarity to this Jacobin idea of liberty. It was what allowed the legislator "to make men what he wants them to be."[67] For Marat, it was "a new order [built] by the sole force of philosophy."[68]

The revolutionary experience of music hence assumed a place in the Jacobin catalogue of rituals and habits designed to recover a true, essential human nature—the "one morality, one single conscience" Robespierre claimed existed for all humans.[69] To sing and dance with citizen-actors on the stage, glory in the sound of surrounding orchestras at national festivals, intone hymns with family or neighbors beside the hearth or in the fields, or rush into the heart of battle intoxicated by throbbing military marches was to participate directly in the general will. As defined by its leaders, musical experience in the Year II embodied a coherent political vision.

But was it a coherent *aesthetic* vision? Would the public truly sense sentiments identical to the feelings of thousands of others during festivals and concerts? Certainly the fraternal vision was similar to earlier, prerevolutionary claims that all listeners felt the same sentiments at identical points in the music. But by the mid-1780s some listeners (like Lacépède) were writing that registering the full emotional impact of harmony necessarily turned listeners inward to sound their own subjective passions. If true, this assessment threatened the entire revolutionary vision of music with a crippling dilemma: strong emotional responses might indeed come from rich instrumental writing (as the example of Gluck had showed), but such music risked provoking a hundred different responses in a hundred different listeners. Its alternative was no less troubling: simplifying music for the sake of unanimous, fraternal experience would weaken its emotional force.

No author of the revolutionary decade understood this logic better than Jean-Baptiste Leclerc. Leclerc, a deputy to the Convention who survived the Terror to sit on the Council of Five Hundred, detailed his views on music and its uses in *Essai sur la propagation de la musique en France* and *Rapport sur l'établissement d'écoles spéciales de musique*. Leclerc shared the view that music possessed the power to make all minds one in the nation—it produced "simultaneous and unanimous affections among the masses," he wrote—but he worried more than others about the effects of music whose emotional content was ambiguous or unsteady.[70]

For Leclerc the content of symphonic works in particular was too vague to produce the close-ranked community of citizens the Revolution demanded. Most symphonies conveyed only "calm or agitation, joy

or sadness"—mere generalities, Leclerc claimed, that demanded interpretation. But interpretation risked individual responses that might very
well be at odds with one another. "Ask ten people the meaning of a
Haydn symphony and you'll get ten different replies—I've tried this experiment myself."[71] This interpretive factionalism was a great enough
obstacle to solidarity to justify banning symphonic works from all national events. "Following Plato's example," he wrote, "we will exclude
purely instrumental music; unless the melodies were originally composed with words that carry a moral or political message, we will not
permit them to be played as marches by the national guard at the head
of military batallions or as dance tunes at public festivals."[72]

Leclerc's reasoning has a clarity not found in the plans of those who
imagined among audiences intense emotional engagement and unanimity of feeling. Seeing the two fundamentally incompatible, Leclerc
opted for solidarity over sensibility, reasoning that to sacrifice emotional
complexity in music was a small cost for the larger gain in fraternity.
Leclerc's books are soberly realistic, refusing the rhetoric of sensibility
other writers from the decade employed. Ultimately, however, they
were accurate in a way Leclerc dreaded most, for without the centralized
apparatus of the Terror to control what was performed, harmonically
complex music—music without "a moral or political message"—
assumed an increasingly prominent place in French musical life. As a
consequence musical experience, to the dismay of former Jacobins, grew
ever more subjective and interior.

8

Musical Expression
and Jacobin Ideology

Despite the extraordinary change in the music audiences heard from 1789 to 1799, the way they heard it remained constant. The particular language they used to describe their musical impressions varied, growing more or less politicized at certain moments, but a fundamental consistency stretching back to the time of Gluck prevailed. What had been miraculous and rare in 1775 was now commonplace. Music played an essential dramatic role in opera apart from the libretti and stage action. These terms dominated popular musical perceptions throughout the Revolution, even as the works audiences viewed moved from entertainment to civic instruction.

A 1790 letter to the *Moniteur* from an admirer of Zingarelli's opera *Antigone* was typical in its claim that the overture conveyed the sentiments of Antigone, which, it said, displayed both reverence for her departed brother and love for her sister.[1] Likewise, the overture to Méhul's *Horatius Coclès* bore an expression "perfectly analogous to the characters and situations" of the opera.[2] The *Feuille du salut public* praised Le Sueur's comic opera *Paul et Virginie* in a similar vein, commenting that music was "an expressive language, the only one, perhaps, capable of painting the passions without diluting them."[3]

As with earlier listeners, revolutionary audiences reacted to feeling in the music with feeling of their own, a kind of sympathetic stirring of emotion by emotion. As one journalist put it, Rousseau's *Devin du village* "always goes straight to the soul."[4] Nor was it only the operas and *opéras-comiques* of established composers that stirred passions during the Revolution. Mme Julien de la Drome described attending a session of the National Assembly that featured "warrior music" and a procession of citizens armed with an assortment of pikes and pitchforks. "All types of sentiments pass through the soul by degree: valor, pity, admiration, joy, pleasure, pain."[5]

Listeners during the Revolution continued to consider harmony a decisive—and at times deeply moving—element of musical expression. Méhul's accompaniments in *Mélidore et Phrosine* were such that "even if one did not hear the actor on stage one would still find in the orchestra the sentiment he [the actor] wants to convey and even the way in which he should express it."[6] According to the playwright J. N. Bouilly, the "epoch-making" music of Méhul's *Euphrosine, ou le tyran corrigé* contained "an accurate and appropriate accent for each character." Bouilly describes the "electric, irresistible force" that ran through the revolutionary spectators during one prolonged scene of jealousy. As Bouilly tells it, the force of the scene and the shock of the music sent him tumbling backwards, right onto the lap of Méhul himself who was seated behind him. "'Excuse me!' I said to him with an unnatural voice and in a state of nervous excitation impossible to control. 'I would never have believed that music could come so close to our being. Please forgive me! I don't even know where I am.'"[7]

Le Sueur, described by contemporaries as a master of painting moods and sentiments, received praise for supplying the singers with sentiments through harmonies in the music. "It isn't only in the melody that one should seek the expressive truth that distinguishes the works of citizen Le Sueur," one reviewer wrote; "one finds it in the orchestra."[8] The compliment no doubt made Le Sueur proud: in a pamphlet entitled *Exposé d'une musique une, imitative et particulière à chaque solemnité* (1787) Le Sueur stated his view that emotional expression—which he believed could reveal even the thoughts of a silent character—was the work of the orchestra.[9]

But if audiences recognized the emotional capacity of harmony they still believed that harmonies without discernible emotion were faulty. Spectators at the opening performances of Méhul's *Alonzo et Cora*, for instance, found his harmonies too rich—they were "often too noisy, sometimes monotonous, and little varied in effects"—and a critic claimed that Kreutzer's *Lodoïska* was "filled with noise where he ought to have painted the passions."[10] Appreciating harmony for its own sake—for purely musical meaning not conceived in emotional or programmatic terms—was still outside the horizon of possible musical experience. Music *depicted* according to these listeners. It *painted, conveyed,* or *related.* But audiences had yet to learn that it also might *suggest, evoke,* or follow its own wordless, imageless logic.

If anything, the musical descriptions of revolutionary audiences are more concrete than those of audiences who preceded them. A lively interlude was not merely joyful, it expressed *republican* joy. Doleful chords did not convey simple sadness, but the sadness of citizens mourning sons and brothers sacrificed for the *patrie.* Was this specificity an answer to the government's calls to share private pleasures, a way of fixing and labeling dangerously abstract emotions to make them more intelligible? The sources shed little light on the question. What distinguished republican joy from any other sort of joy was probably not entirely clear in listeners' minds, either. As one newspaper elusively (and awkwardly) wrote of an outdoor concert two weeks before the fall of Robespierre: "with attentive ear, each shared the emotions that the harmony of this imposing music made to pass in all souls." [11] No precisions, no clarifications, no further comment.

Nevertheless, the musical emotions described are of such clarity and distinctness that, if felt, they could indeed be shared by whole roomfuls of republicans. Here is a listener's account of the oratorio *La Prise de la Bastille* after its first performance in July 1790: "With its lightness of touch the overture paints the tranquillity of people who have placed their confidence in a well-beloved minister [Necker]; the mood is disturbed by the unexpected announcement that the minister has been sent into exile; soon bells imitating the tocsin are heard as the music grows more agitated; drums and tympani imitate perfectly . . . the musketeers' shots and cannon blasts, and an utter explosion from the organ and the whole orchestra expresses the fall of the Bastille's drawbridge." [12]

With such a title it is likely that the overture contained some rough approximations of just these effects (the score by Marc-Antoine Désaugiers has since been lost), but the description also demonstrates the willingness of listeners to locate political meaning in music during the Revolution. The momentous events that revolutionary music commemorated clearly held irresistible powers of suggestion and colored musical impressions. The music for the apotheosis at the Panthéon of Marat expressed "tranquil immortality" by one listener's lights. [13] Gossec's *Marche lugubre,* played in the cortege of Mirabeau, was "religious" and "funereal," its silences were "truly the silence of the tomb"; the music was "so sad and funereal that it made all who were present shed tears." [14] And the hymn of the Festival of the Law, like the law itself, was "at once religious and triumphant." [15] Political passions were contagious during the Revolution.

Such descriptions must have pleased the officials who monitored progress in the public spirit. They are as explicit in perceived meaning as at any time before or since. But from the perspective of the structure of listening—the manner in which listeners went about deciphering, classifying, and assimilating sound—there is nothing revolutionary here. The nature of perceived musical expression remained the same as before, even if the tocsin was an imitation not previously heard, or contentment with Necker an emotion not previously named.

What *was* different was a novel cultural context that gave tangible references to those expecting to hear images and sentiments, and a determined effort from above to tie that context to the act of listening. Spectators had always been susceptible to opera titles and plot summaries as they claimed to hear the blacksmith's hammer in Rameau or boiling rage in Gluck. To couple music with the events of the Revolution, whether in patriotic reenactments onstage or in large-scale commemorations out-of-doors, merely enhanced their suggestibility. Members of the Commission Temporaire des Arts might have intended to sound revolutionary when they boasted that organ music will serve "to paint the sentiments of free men and to paint above all the fury we are preparing for tyrants," but the perceptual categories of such saber-rattling came straight from the Old Regime. [16]

There is fascinating evidence that some listeners followed the same logic that led Leclerc to denounce purely instrumental music for political reasons. Significantly, these reports come in the early months of the Thermidorean regime and voice the fears held by Jacobin sympathizers that the Thermidoreans were out to overturn the whole revolutionary project.

Four months after the fall of Robespierre the Théâtre Feydeau gave a concert that featured vocal and instrumental works. For one staunch republican present the evening was a mockery of everything he had learned about music during the Revolution. First, the songs were in Italian, which deprived them of any practical value to French audiences. Worse, the featured selection was a symphony. "Tell me what the author wanted to paint in the symphony that starts with the kettledrums making a horrible racket and continues with tender, languorous phrases only to be interrupted by more beating and by meaningless chords." [17] For this listener the symphony was a manifest failure because it had no social use. There was no other criterion. "Can a republican spend four hours at a spectacle that teaches the mind nothing and does not move the soul?—Oh! for spectacles to be useful in a republic men must be instructed in the art of declamation and sing good songs; they must relate interesting facts, whether about war or about love, through simple but expressive tunes." [18]

The same discomfort this republican felt over symphonic music surfaced the following January when the Convention marked the second anniversary of the execution of the king with a concert by the Institut de Musique in the Convention's Great Hall. The orchestra had hardly begun when a delegate leapt to his feet and interrupted the playing. "I demand to know if you are celebrating the death of the tyrant," he shouted. "Are you for him or against him?" Murmurs rose from the others, but he continued. "I don't think that any of my colleagues can doubt whether I am against the king or against the people. I only want to know if these musicians intended to mourn the death of the tyrant or celebrate the anniversary of that day in the piece they were playing." [19]

Such was the risk of music without a clear message, the very ambiguity Leclerc feared from orchestral music. But whereas Leclerc was afraid that ambiguous chords might disrupt the solidarity of response, this delegate voiced a stronger critique. Without words to prove its political purity, music was suspect. What if it was a crypto-royalist dirge? What if the musicians were in on the secret and deviously mocking everyone present? This was the familiar Jacobin fear of conspiracy, which equated privacy with sedition, transposed into music. Just as the secretive citizen was suspect, so, too was symphonic music at all subtle or complex. Its meaning was obscured by shifting colors, subjective sentiments, changing moods. For minds obsessed with ideological purity the ambiguity of symphonic music was intolerable.

Despite the explicitly political images and emotions listeners heard in an overcharged moment, therefore, the logic of the French Revolution resisted the kind of subtle harmonic writing listeners before 1789 had come to accept. At best useless and at worst fractious and even seditious, instrumental music—like the citizens themselves—had to prove publicly its good intentions. With music the proof was a text, a title, or an aggressively martial mood. The situation might have been different if these listeners could have dismissed all instrumental music without recognizable imitations as empty arithmetic, as French audiences fifty years earlier had done, but the changes in musical perception during the previous two decades made that step backward impossible. Now music could carry sentiments, and in a Revolution sentiments are either pure or treasonous ("everything that isn't *strongly for* is *against*"). With the changes in perception sowed by Gluck and reaped by revolutionaries, music lost its political innocence.

Musically, the revolutionary period produced no single master whose style dominated all the rest. The greatest innovators were the leaders in *opéra-comique*—Dalyrac, Grétry, Cherubini, Méhul. Their "revolution" in music, if the term is not too strong to describe their gradual elevation of the *comédie mêlée d'ariettes* to the level of elite art, came well before the taking of the Bastille. Their works from the seminal year 1789 are little different from those of 1787, or 1791. But the Revolution was not without its consequences for melody, harmony, and methods of orchestration; its impact upon composition simply came later, during the period of Jacobin ascendancy. The artistic response to this most radical political phase of the Revolution, discernible in the music composed for the theater as well as for the open-air festivals, corresponds in clear ways to the ideological orientation of the government. While the fact is not in itself terribly surprising, the result was. For while revolutionaries in 1793 and 1794 did all they could to enforce the "irrevocable condemnation" that 1789 pronounced upon the past (the phrase was Michelet's), the ironic result in music was to revive styles from the past—styles, moreover, that composers had long since abandoned.

Imitations of natural phenomena, mimetic renderings of battles, and the types of word paintings Lully and his successors employed are scattered throughout in musical works of the 1780s and 1790s. There are musical thunderstorms in Cherubini's *Elisa* (1794) and *Médée* (1797) and in Méhul's *Mélidore et Phrosine*. In Grétry's *La Caravane du Caire* flutes trill and flutter while the pasha's harem keeper sings about butterflies. And the Polish lord in Cherubini's *Lodoïska* receives orchestral support in angry flourishes when he sings the words "tremblez audacieux" during a blazing aria in the second act. These devices remained in composers' expressive vocabularies to be used for special or startling effects and would persist throughout the nineteenth (and twentieth) centuries.

But these orchestral scores reveal a much broader concern among composers for rendering psychological states. Increasingly composers went beyond exercises in musical literalism to capture more elusive and changeable moods. André-Modeste Grétry was explicit on this point in his *Mémoires*. To hear "physical effects such as rain, wind, hail, birds' songs, earthquakes, and the like is like seeing a bust painted or clothed—you retreat in horror, because nature is rendered too slavishly."[20]

Grétry devotes a sizable part of his 1789 memoirs to the question of how a composer conveys emotional states and whether there are limits to the range of moods capable of being rendered. He was particularly expansive on this latter point, insisting that "every passion and every character" had its own unique quality that a skilled composer could convey.[21] The sheer quantity of emotions Grétry lists points to the exuberance he and other French composers must have felt as they cast the emotions of ordinary mortals into a musical mold until now reserved for gods and goddesses. Grétry writes, perhaps with reason, that composers of *tragédies-lyriques* had explored only a narrow slice of possible musical emotions, as the passions of characters in the genre could never be gross or ignoble.[22]

Grétry was sure that music could depict the ostentatious man—"a certain harmonic richness and melodic poverty"—or the hypochondriac—"a heavy, melancholic music . . . the darkest tones, . . . long and sudden silences."[23] The jealous lover should sing chromatically, "which is both sad and sinister"; the feeling of maternal love in music is a tune at once romantic, pious, and mysterious. The accents of a well-disciplined man are "uniform, exacting, and mannered," while impetuous movements express moral vice.[24] Grétry's treatment of emotions capable of musical depiction stretches to fill an entire volume, encompassing the predictable (happiness, sadness, madness), the creative (indolence, impudence, stubbornness), and the frankly incredible (hypocrisy, flattery, the spirit of intrigue among valets).

Although Grétry explicitly describes this approach as painting the passions, he denies that it is akin to imitating their sounds—copying a sigh with a slurred descending motif, for example, or approximating a laugh with little explosions. Instead of "rendering the thing directly," he writes, it is an "indirect imitation," a way of "expressing the sensations" that arise from a particular passion.[25] Grétry was vague about exactly what the "sensations" arising from a passion consisted of, but he was emphatic in his conviction that the essence of orchestral writing lay in the expression of psychological states. Superior music "is always associated with a sentiment or a passion, which has its distinct accents and movements."[26]

At the same time Grétry realized that the experience of instrumental music was necessarily subjective. "Let us add that often the vague effects of instrumental music act only relatively upon the constitution of the individual who receives them. It is the cloud that floats through the sky: the soldier sees the face of battle in it, and the village girl sees her sweetheart's flock."[27] This was a lucid reading of the logic of musical experience. Hearing emotions in the music implied an engaged, creative subjectivity.

The musical output of Grétry and his contemporaries echoes these artistic aims. Beginning with Dalyrac's efforts in the 1760s and 1770s to fill out the sketchy accompaniments of the *comédie mêlée d'ariettes*, composers such as Philidor, Grétry, Cherubini, and Méhul steadily expanded the role and scope of the orchestra in comic opera. By the 1790s comic operas often boasted forces as large as a full-scale *tragédie-lyrique*, and their orchestration often rivaled works by Gluck and Sacchini in sophistication and complexity. The structure Cherubini employed in his overtures that begin with slow introductions, for example, reflects his cultivation of Haydn's symphonic movements as models, and the individuation and alternation of solo lines in the orchestral texture seems Haydnesque as well.[28] (Cherubini, as one contemporary related the story, was "completely astonished and entranced, even pale and almost petrified" when he heard his first Haydn symphony at the *concert spirituel* in Paris.)[29] Whereas Gluck generally kept to his pledge to subordinate the orchestra to the text, the music of these composers asserts dramatic claims independent of the text.

The spoken recitative remained standard for comic operas composed for the Comédie-Italienne and the Feydeau, while those prepared for the Opéra contained sung recitatives accompanied either by continuo or larger orchestral forces. In both instances composers advanced the dramatic action of the plot in either a single aria or a succession of arias stitched together without the interruption of recitative. At its best this created a dramatic impulsion that fixed the attention of spectators with a different musical style for each new revelation.

The finale of the second act of Méhul's *Mélidore et Phrosine* contains this sort of succession in events and emotions, conveyed through arias, without interruptions. So unfolds the secret marriage of the eponymous lovers in a cave on an isolated isle, the unfocused rage of the incestuous brother Jule, a chorus of sailors warning ominously of bad weather ahead, and the departure of Jule and his sister Phrosine from the island. One event moves seamlessly to the next as the music moves from allegro, to adagio poco andante, to allegretto, to andante grazioso, with each separate tempo reflecting the rapidly shifting moods. Tonal variety contributes to the drama as well, as the sequence moves through A major, A minor, F major, and B-flat major.

There are other instances of composers relying on the orchestra to convey information about their characters. Méhul supplements the jealousy of the tyrant in *Euphrosine, ou le tyran corrigé* with sudden crescendi and decrescendi as the comtesse d'Arles, a kind of Iago manquée, stirs up his suspicions. When Coradin's rage at last boils over Méhul fills the texture with hurtling sixteenths spilling forth furiously.[30]

An even more prominent use of the orchestra to convey dramatic content occurs in a strange and effective sequence near the start of the third act of Méhul's *Mélidore et Phrosine*, as the solitary Mélidore paces the shore of their island-rendezvous for some sign of Phrosine's arrival. By turns confident, fearful for Phrosine's safety, and maddened by her brothers' obstructions, Mélidore speaks his thoughts aloud ("Never was a night so dark," "How can I desire and fear at the same time?," "Rare, priceless child!," etc.).

Between each spoken line Méhul interposes short orchestral passages of various lengths and moods that provide a musical articulation of Mélidore's thoughts before he utters them. A gentle melody in 6/8 precedes his statement that "all of nature is asleep"; a heavily accented, three-measure burst precedes the words "Cruel brothers!"; a phrase that begins with a loud, rhythmic motif but suddenly slows and grows quiet precedes Mélidore's realization that the stars have disappeared; and so on.[31] With so concentrated a display of contrasting passions and so clear a match between their verbal and musical articulation, audiences of *Mélidore et Phrosine* heard not only insubstantial emotions in the music but even the flickering uncertainty when sudden fear turns resolve into a shadow of itself (see Example 7).

A notable development in French operatic writing of the 1780s and early 1790s was the greater use of counterpoint in orchestral and vocal parts. The application was splendidly suited to the melodrama of plots and the polarized passions that fueled them. Dramatically these works thrived on conflict, not stasis or accord. Many of the ensembles therefore combine passions in raging opposition to one another. To render the conflict composers set one phrase against another, often giving each character different words to sing.

Example 7. Mélidore's monologue from *Mélidore et Phrosine*, Étienne-Nicolas Méhul.

Example 7. *Continued.*

A six-part ensemble embraces five distinct sentiments in the finale of the first act of Méhul's *Euphrosine, ou le tyran corrigé* as the headstrong Euphrosine announces her intention to tame Coradin by marrying him. "Be fearful of enraging him, my very blood freezes," sings the tyrant's valet, and Coradin himself puffs and blusters: "Dread my anger; great God what audacity!" The comtesse d'Arles does what she can to provoke

him, singing, "Avenge yourself, seigneur, strike hard, punish her bold-
ness," while Euphrosine's two terrified sisters ask her, "Euphrosine,
what are you doing?" Euphrosine's voice soars above the chaos in supreme self-confidence: "Your threats amuse me; . . . Coradin will be my
spouse" (see Example 8).[32]

In a superb depiction of opposed wills in a duet from *Mélidore et
Phrosine* Méhul conveys the delight and hatred that each character pro-
nounces, shifting with lightning quickness from sustained major tones
to frenzied chromatic runs in triplets.[33] Cherubini's early Italian training in counterpoint is particularly evident in his ensembles, which depict
the intense conflict of his characters in webs of interlocking parts. The
dense textures produced by the clash of texts and thick braid of melodies
can be seen in an ensemble near the end of *Lodoïska*, where Cherubini
juxtaposes love and rage (see Example 9).[34]

A very different style came to dominate operatic writing during the
Terror, for both practical and ideological reasons. The style, characterized by overall simplicity, would prevail as long as Robespierre stayed in
power. The orchestral parts are always secondary to the voice lines in
these works, often doubling them. Harmonic variety is significantly reduced, both in terms of key changes within acts and of the accompaniments to given arias.

But their most striking aspect concerns the chorus, which now assumes primary importance with its civic oaths, threats against the
enemy, and rousing send-offs to soldiers. In autumn 1793 polyphony
virtually disappeared from choral writing in an abrupt departure from
trends of the previous fifteen years. The choruses of *Toute la Grèce*
(Lemoyne), which premiered in early January 1794 with the Committee
of Public Safety in firm command of the government, are homophonic
virtually throughout.[35] Apart from very occasional rhythmic divergence,
the three parts of the opening chorus, "We gladly prepare our arms to
overturn the foe," move together; women and girls sing farewells to
soldiers in two-part harmony with words and rhythms that line up exactly; a three-part chorus of warriors sings, "Far from knowing terror
ourselves, we strike it into the hearts of others"; and so on.[36]

With one three-page section an exception, all the choruses in *La
Réunion du dix août* (Porta, April 1794) are also homophonic. With its
identical rhythms the singing is hymnic, particularly in the more pastoral
settings. "Nature at last unites us, oh tender and generous friends,"
a simple two-part chorus goes. "Let our voices repeat it together:
through equality our hearts are united!"[37] And Méhul's *Horatius*

Example 8. Ensemble from Méhul's *Euphrosine, ou le tyran corrigé.*

Example 8. *Continued.*

Coclès, which first appeared at the Opéra in February 1794, employs a severe and simple musical style utterly stripped of the kind of expression that results from independently moving ensemble lines (see Example 10).[38] These features contrast sharply with the musical style of *Le Siège de Thionville* (Jadin), which premiered just two months before the onset of the Terror. *Le Siège* contains the sort of polyphony that typified the *opéras-comiques* of the period: the chorus, "Death, yes death a thousand times before suffering infamy," contains four independently moving parts, for example.[39] There is also a significant amount of independent instrumental movement in the orchestra parts.

The dramatic structure of these revolutionary works is partly responsible for the sudden simplification of their musical texture. They were celebratory and didactic; they defied the canons of suspense and high conflict in order to present a citizenry united to overturn the past. If the knotted melodrama of *opéra-comique*—its fierce tyrants, headstrong virgins, and families with unspeakable secrets—could best be captured through complex ensemble writing, the replacement of plot with fes-

Example 9. Four-part polyphony from *Lodoïska*, Luigi Cherubini.

Example 9. *Continued.*

tivity took away the dramatic rationale for polyphony. But beyond this the cultural climate of Jacobinism worked against polyphony, for polyphony implied a divided social body. Dramatically, it signified protagonists at cross purposes; experientially, it made transparency between stage and spectator difficult; and musically, it promoted dangerously

Example 10. Homophonic choral singing from the finale of Méhul's *Horatius Coclès*.

Example 10. *Continued.*

personal experience. In short, polyphony was the musical equivalent of dissent.[40]

These were the musical consequences of a political fact of life during the Terror, the victory of equality over liberty. At least in the musical sphere, the ideological imperatives for change turned back the clock. Homophonic choral writing, predictable harmonies, and eminently singable melodies were the musical ingredients—all of them musically conservative—for revolutionary equality. The culmination of this logic would be to claim that the more ordinary the composer, the better his music, which is exactly what Nicolas Framery said. The hymns with the profoundest effects upon listeners, Framery insisted, were those composed by amateur musicians.[41] This was how a Revolution determined to erase the past and begin all things anew could produce music with such a profoundly divided soul, revolutionary in form—the huge choruses, the heavy percussion and brass, the multiple orchestras—but reactionary in style.

Thermidor and the Return of Entertainment

Louis-Sebastien Mercier, an indefatigable chronicler of Parisian vanities, marked the fall of Robespierre in his characteristic fashion by publishing a book. A section in his *Nouveau Paris* describes the arts after the Terror. "Luxury emerged from the smoking ruins more stunning than ever. The culture of the fine arts has recaptured all its luster, and, whatever one might say, letters suffered an eclipse that was merely passing. Spectacles have recovered their pomp, and fashions are again what people idolize the most."[1] By Mercier's reckoning the previous five years of upheaval left barely a trace on the arts and their public.

The extravagance of society's collective sigh of relief when the guillotine fell silent took many forms. There were the many public balls, some conventional and some grotesque, such as the *bal des pendus* for relatives of the decapitated where a thin red ribbon tied round the neck was obligatory. There were the extravagant coiffures, cropped close in the back as for the guillotine or laced with ribbons and ornaments. There were the disruptions of the *jeunesse dorée*, the dandified delinquents who made a pastime of taunting former Jacobins. And there were the provocative clothes and gestures: the *incroyable* with his oversized hat and suit wide at the shoulders and tight at the ankles, the *merveilleuse* with her audacious *décolleté*, the *femmes grecques* who wore transparent muslin dresses and sometimes no top at all.[2]

As speculators snatched up the former lands of aristocrats and the church and war contractors turned handsome profits by supplying the armies, a new aristocracy of wealth eager to show off its fortunes appeared in Paris. The private ostentation of the Old Regime gave way to public display. In the topsy-turvy universe after Thermidor, when national heroes became traitors overnight and inequities forever abolished sprang up more glaring than ever, even the most solemn transactions of the Revolution were appropriated as fads. A M. Ruggieri hosted a "grand Fête extraordinaire" in his salons on the rue Lazare that featured "pantomimes of combat, of the death and funeral of Marlborough, superb illuminations, and fireworks."[3]

The unanimity of audiences during the Terror quickly fell apart with Robespierre's execution in late July 1794, to be replaced in theaters by a rowdy mélange of ex-revolutionaries, ex-nobles, and *nouveaux riches.* One incredulous spectator at the Feydeau less than six months after the end of the Terror described women in diamonds, rubies, silk tunics, and serpentine wigs. "My eyes were . . . overwhelmed by the light in the hall and the luster of the ladies, and I was surprised by the muscadin faces of the men," he wrote. "It appeared to be a spectacle from monarchical times! I must have dreamed the Revolution!"[4] The Feydeau, which increasingly specialized in Italian works, quickly became the preferred theater for the new regime of ostentation. The society sheet *La Sentinelle* reports the fashion of coming directly from the racetrack at Longchamps, preferably with a layer of its "noble dust" on one's riding clothes. "It isn't the concert that has occasioned all of this," another newspaper commented, "for however grand the talent is, the people hardly listen. The women are concerned only with making themselves noticed."[5]

This abrupt intrusion of extravagance was discernible in other theaters, too. A police agent in 1795 claimed that the foyers were filled with a new class of spectators—"royal thieves," he called them, whose politics were reactionary and business in the war unsavory.[6] The *jeunesse dorée* in their colored ribbons and waxed collars reinforced the impression as they shattered commemorative busts on the stage of the Favart and the Feydeau and humiliated singers who had acted in revolutionary spectacles in earlier years at the Opéra. When François Laïs first appeared after 9 Thermidor, the date of Robespierre's fall, to sing the title role in Grétry's *Panurge dans l'île des lanternes,* youths in the parterre extracted their revenge for his earlier roles in *scènes patriotiques* by stopping the performance with raucous shouts of "On your knees! On your knees!" and forcing Laïs to sing the counter-revolutionary "Réveil du peuple."[7]

But if it is true that spectators opposed to the Revolution's egalitarianism now seemed to set the terms for performers and response, they did not have a monopoly on public manifestations. Some spectators still came to the theater wearing the Phrygian cap of the sansculottes or with a tricolor cocade tucked into a pocket, and they made their disapproval of the others well known.[8] Nor did they let the antics of the *jeunesse dorée* go unchallenged. By the summer of 1795 singing wars between "La Marseillaise" and "Réveil du peuple" often sparked brawls that could grow serious enough to suspend the performance.[9]

The return of political division and contest to musical audiences was a mark of the political pluralism that returned to French society after the Terror. The unsteady government of the Directory in fact had as difficult a time maintaining order inside theaters as it did securing its own rule against threats from the left and the right. Having received a fright from the royalist coup attempt in September 1795, which claimed 1,400 lives in street fighting, and sensing renascent royalist sympathies among audiences, the government swiftly ordered the performance of songs "dear to republicans" in all the major theaters of Paris.[10]

The decree succeeded only in providing the *jeunesse dorée* and their allies a fresh target for derision. Spectators at the Opéra showered "ironic applause" on the word "oppresseur" in the "Chant du départ," they exited noisily at the singing of "La Marseillaise," and at the Vaudeville two prostitutes were arrested for greeting patriotic songs with "indecent gestures." Singers quickly learned that the only way to avoid public humiliation for obeying the decree was to deliver as cold and lifeless a performance as possible.[11] Only in late 1796 did police agents monitoring Parisian theaters begin to see general calm returning to audiences. The audiences of national festivals also showed notably less patriotic exuberance and fraternal unity after Thermidor. One observer contrasted the 1790 Fête de la Fédération, where "universal joy" had reigned, with the festivals of 1796, which were "colorful in effect, agreeable for the eye, but . . . without any effect on the soul."[12] "Boredom hovers over the whole expanse of the Champ de Mars," wrote another observer in the same year. "One notices . . . contagious yawns that pass successively from one spectator to the next."[13] The patriotic spark had gone out.

Old repertoires returned to the musical stage soon after Thermidor, and with them came all the pomp and artifice the Revolution had tried to suppress. The Opéra with its decorations and dances had "everything that could dazzle the eyes," one spectator wrote. "There is nothing more perfect than the rapid, fleeting, quick scene changes; the meteors, the apparitions, the disappearance of divinities into the clouds or in chariots are all full of truth and of colorful effects."[14] "As for the Opéra," wrote the *Décade philosophique*, "it is a spectacle made entirely for the eyes and the ears and, in this respect, the choice of music by Gluck and a ballet from *Psyché* could not have been better."[15] The last five years of the century saw few new productions at the Opéra or the Favart as both rode largely on the success of works dropped in 1793–94.[16] The Feydeau, meantime, distinguished itself by inviting foreign virtuosi and offering concerts as well as staged productions.

With the old repertoires came the former enthusiasm for fantasy and fiction in plots, another mark of the decisive break in musical experience after the Terror. Gluck's *Iphigénie en Tauride* returned with its kings and priestesses two months after 9 Thermidor and was deliriously applauded. When Sacchini's *Oedipe à Colonne* reappeared at the Opéra the following February one happy spectator wrote to a newspaper to say that he considered it unworthy of republicanism to have banished from the stage kings who had lived and died a thousand years before.[17] "The great masters have reappeared on the French stage," the *Moniteur* summarized simply, and the *Journal des théâtres* appealed to theater directors in the name of "taste, love for the arts and . . . even liberty" to replace the patriotic productions with former *chefs-d'oeuvre*.[18]

Spectators welcomed the return to more intricate orchestral writing after the conservative musical style of the Terror. A reviewer of the opera *Sapho* (Padre Martini) writing in late 1794 was grateful to hear "dramatic" music again, "of which sensitive listeners have been deprived for so long."[19] Grétry was more blunt, writing to a friend in 1796 that theaters were no longer playing revolutionary music, "which is to say the noise of dogs."[20]

On the whole, works with contemporary references disappeared, although those with allusions to the foreign wars could still generate enthusiasm. *Les Epreuves du républicain*, whose plot was loosely constructed around several unnamed battles with the British, was "applauded with transport" at the Opéra-Comique. *Encore une victoire*, a work by Kreutzer and Dantilly that also appeared at the Opéra-Comique, portrayed the French victories in Brabant and Liège.

Yet despite the persistence of scattered works with contemporary allusions, the public now abandoned dramatic standards refined during the Terror. After its disappearance from newspaper critiques and letters from spectators during the Terror, when revolutionary truth alone legitimated works, the criterion of autonomous dramatic interest returned to prominence. Despite the massive public repudiation of Robespierre after his execution, for instance, the explicit similarities between a virtuous Greek tyrannicide and the Convention's arrest of

Robespierre in the opera *Timoléon* were received coolly. "The author . . . has sacrificed dramatic perfection for a pressing obligation to depict the violent death of an ambitious man . . . who aspired to supreme authority," explained one account.[21]

Another spectator, saying that he was tired of seeing contemporary political references in dramatic works, was more direct. Writing a matter of weeks after the execution of Robespierre in response to *La Chute du dernier tyran, ou la Journée du 9 Thermidor*, he attacked the habit of turning actual events into "operas, vaudevilles, dramas, and scenic trifles" and saw in such *pièces de circonstance* a "true decline of the art."[22] Perhaps the most eloquent evidence of a return to dramatic standards from before the Terror was a rhapsodic letter the *Moniteur* published from a man moved beyond words by the Cinderella story. "Return to nature," he pleaded. "I cried; but my tears were not drawn out painfully; they flowed naturally, I shed them with pleasure."[23]

What accounts for the swift disappearance of the earlier common celebration and the resounding rejection of plots that fused dramatic action and reality? The dismantling of the Terror and the collective relief no doubt goes far in explaining the new tone in accounts of audiences. There was a clear sense after Thermidor that the dramatic arts could once again follow their own relatively autonomous path of development, influenced by, but not identical with, politics.

The return of dramatic distance after Thermidor was also a sign that audiences no longer viewed themselves as "actors," nor the actors as "citizens," in the spectacle of the Revolution. Thermidor, and the manifest acceptance of its legitimacy by the public in and out of theaters, effectively changed the relationship between the people and the government. By imposing its own authority over that of the revolutionary sections and committees, the Convention successfully substituted the principle of representation for the immanent and indivisible sovereignty of the "nation assembled." To recognize the Convention's authority was to recognize the state and society as separate entities and to reject the former politicization of every aspect of private life. Spectators no longer fused their personal fears and ideals with those of the actors on the stage because the theater for them had ceased to be a microcosm of national will.

The general calm that had begun to prevail during performances by 1796 is a sign of this gradual depoliticization of personal experience. If some regretted the lack of patriotism it seemed to represent, others recognized that it also meant blood was no longer being shed nor performers arrested as a result of political passions. "The general sentiment appeared to be overall contentment," reads a description of the audience in a public festival in 1796. "No enthusiasm, but the forgetting of positions, the forgetting of parties, abandonment to pleasure, simple and frank happiness. Let us repeat this, it is a good thing that all enthusiasm is absent today: in 1790, every person was an actor for the public interest, we were making a constitution, a revolution; we needed enthusiasm. But today, the revolution and constitution are accomplished. It is up to the government to tend to our affairs, and the public spirit cannot show it better than by enjoying the pleasures offered it with confidence and security."[24]

As for ways of hearing and describing music, audiences after Thermidor kept to the same general terminology they had employed during the Terror and before. The willingness to seek emotional expression continued to lead listeners to credit a greater dramatic capacity to harmony, a process that was well underway before 1789 and continued into the nineteenth century. The orchestral expression of Cherubini's *Lodoïska* seemed so great to one listener in late 1794 that it almost made the plot and action secondary: it was "a concert with pantomime scattered throughout."[25] The judgment probably valued instrumental music more than most spectators were inclined to do, but it clearly points toward what would increasingly hold true for audiences.

Surveying the dress, taste, ways of hearing, and styles of describing music after the fall of Robespierre, one is tempted to concur with the *Vedette*, which wrote in 1795, "such is Paris—revolutions change nothing."[26] By most accounts the behavior, repertoires, and aesthetic expectations of audiences in 1795 were not much different from what they had been in 1789. But even as Thermidor ushered in a new ostentation, other aspects of musical experience of the Terror remained. The intense, immediate experience of music under the Terror taught audiences to seize contemporary references with an acuity altogether different from the vague equation some spectators had made between kings and the gods in the early eighteenth century. Even as post-Thermidorean audiences rejected the facile imitations of daily scenes, the revolutionary habit of finding analogies to the present persisted. When the Treaty of Campo Formio was concluded late in the decade, spectators at the Opéra responded by showering applause on lines with the slightest reference to peace.[27] And when the French won at Marengo an actor announced the news from the stage—just after the defeat of the Saracens in *Armide*. Such a blend of fact and fantasy was on an entirely different plane than Lully's allegorical prologues.[28]

This new attention to contemporary relevance and the willingness of audiences to applaud military references in particular were not lost on the young General Bonaparte, who was occasionally spotted in Paris theaters in the late 1790s. A new class of notables eager to display their wealth, audiences hostile to revolutionary excesses but favorable to military glory, citizens less distracted by the event and more attracted to the stage: the Opéra would be a fertile ground for the sort of revolutionary fulfillment Bonaparte promised when he staged his coup on 18 Brumaire 1799. The only question was whether the Revolution would survive its protector.

PART FOUR

Respectability
and the Bourgeoisie

It used to be that no one paid any attention to the harmonious sounds of amateur societies. Gossip, politics, debate, whist, dice, cards—it all took place at the same time as a quartet or a symphony. . . . [Now there is silence] during the arias, the string quartets, and even the piano sonatas.

Castil-Blaze, *De l'Opéra en France* (1820)

9

Napoleon's Show

On Christmas Eve, 1800, the Opéra offered a program that set the upper crust of Napoleonic society abuzz with excitement. Banking on the growing popularity of concert music and the particular success of Haydn's symphonies, the theater doubled its orchestra and put its chorus through extra rehearsals for a single performance of Haydn's oratorio *The Creation*. Bonaparte was expected, and the combined thrill of a new work by Haydn and Bonaparte's promised attendance seemed, as one spectator wrote, to make the very diamonds on the ladies' shoulders dance with delight.[1]

The audience responded with immediate applause to Haydn's evocation of primordial chaos, the brilliant burst of light that answers God's command, and the tearing orchestral storms that erupt when the heavens and firmament separate. Bonaparte had still not arrived when the angels sang of the beasts of the earth and the fowl of the air, but few found cause for concern. He often appeared late for performances, and at any rate the spectators were preoccupied with the music, which furnished a catalogue of sounds and images from nature. But latecomers brought terrible news, and even as the music played the story raced from one listener to the next. The din grew steadily. The orchestra now noticed and the conductor looked over one shoulder, then the other unsteadily. Bonaparte had been assassinated!

Since his days as general in the Italian campaign Bonaparte made a

Part-opening illustration: Detail of Henry Emy, *Une Loge aux Italiens*. Musée Carnavalet. © 1993 ARS, New York/SPADEM, Paris.

point of appearing regularly at the Opéra, and he was always late. Initially he seemed embarrassed about the rounds of applause and scattered shouts of "Vive Bonaparte!" that greeted his arrival and momentarily covered the music. "If I had known these boxes were so exposed I would never have come here," he told a companion during one noisy ovation.[2] The first consul quickly learned to project a more confident persona from his box. Appearing during the last scene of an opera by Gluck in 1801, he kept to the front of the box until the curtain came down, no doubt wearing the same "theater smile, where you show your teeth but the eyes don't smile" that Stendhal recalled seeing when Bonaparte saluted crowds at the Tuileries.[3]

Often audiences knew when Napoleon was expected, thanks to a tidy system whereby his secretaries would alert the Opéra management, who in turn notified the press.[4] Spectators responded with practiced zeal. As the performance began the audience would eye the box at the front of the hall and to the left while still trying to keep some sense of the action on the stage. A door would open, a burst of applause would shoot through the theater, and Napoleon would suddenly be standing at the edge of his box, waving with supreme satisfaction.

His appearance roused spectators from the bored and baffled state that a watered-down version of Mozart's *The Magic Flute* had produced, and at a performance of Le Sueur's *Les Prétendus* spectators seemed "less interested in the delightful spectacle that had drawn them there than in the pleasure of seeing again the sovereign and his worthy company."[5] The ovation for Bonaparte was sometimes prolonged enough to force the singers to break character and join in the applause, and when the imperial family appeared at the premiere of Cherubini's *Les Abencérages* the ballet corps ran back onto the stage to perform a special sequence that Bonaparte had missed by arriving late.[6]

For as rousing as his dramatic entrances were—at least until the spell of bad luck that began with Moscow took away some of the spark—Napoleon's appearances at the Opéra were just short of routine. He appeared after Wagram and Jéna, he presented Marie-Louise after having packed off a barren Josephine, he basked in the celebration after the birth of his son the King of Rome. Just after the duc d'Enghien's execution on trumped-up charges of treason Napoleon appeared in a chasseur's uniform, appropriately solemn, and received a spirited welcome. During his rule Napoleon attended the Paris Opéra twenty-six times, by far more visits per season than Louis XV, Louis XVI, or any other nineteenth-century head of state.[7]

He also appeared, eventually, on that fateful night of Haydn's *Creation*—but not before half the hall assumed he was dead. According to the story circulating among spectators, a bomb had hit the consul's carriage in the rue Saint-Nicaise, there were casualties, and the condition of Bonaparte and his family was unknown. As they would later learn, the bomb demolished the carriage behind Bonaparte's, damaging close to fifty buildings and killing or injuring scores of people. But that was no reason to miss the show. When Bonaparte stepped into his box, unharmed and apparently unruffled, the outburst of relief and horror was so great that the musicians stopped playing, the curtain came down, and the shaken spectators went home.[8]

Bonaparte's determination to hear Haydn was heroic by any reckoning, but especially so given his general indifference to German music (and a fair amount of French, too). He preferred the Italians and was passionate about Paisiello and Zingarelli, whose music he would sometimes listen to at the Tuileries until after midnight. Napoleon made time for music, but the ideal setting was in his own salons, away from the public clamor and distractions of the Opéra. His favorite was an Italian castrato named Crescentini.[9] But Bonaparte kept these details private. If he could be a revolutionary among revolutionaries, a Muslim among Egyptians, and a Catholic before the pope, he could surely become an operagoer among the leisure class. This was another case of his famous "flexibility," his knack for taking on the colors of those around him the better to dominate them. *Paris vaut bien un opéra.*

Judging by what they saw as they sat in the revolutionary-era opera hall on the rue de Richelieu, spectators had every reason to believe that not only Bonaparte but members of his family and his cabinet, too, were all devoted melomanes. The Paris opera hall still kept the lights up during performances—by one description the hall was bright enough "to read in every corner"—and as a consequence spectators were always mindful of the ring of governmental officials surrounding them.[10] During the Consulate, Lucien Bonaparte held three of the ground-level boxes that now ran along the perimeter of the parterre, an arrangement made possible only with the recent addition of seats there. Foreign Minister Talleyrand held a box on the first level; just above him was Second Consul Cambacérès. Third Consul Charles-François Lebrun sat in the box next to Cambacérès's, and not far from them were Minister of Police Fouché, Interior Minister Chaptal, and Minister of War Administration Dejean. Bonaparte himself reserved three boxes next to the stage on the far left, on both the floor and the first levels. These had been the places of royalty in the Old Regime. Perhaps wishing to hold himself at an arm's length from the king's public image, Bonaparte took the queen's place.[11]

The same pattern prevailed after Napoleon crowned himself emperor: the minister of police, the arch-chancellor of the Empire, the arch-treasurer, ambassadors, customs officials, and military officers crisscrossed the hall in a visible cordon of power. Still on the far left at the front of the hall—and now with boxes on the floor, the first and the second levels—was Napoleon, inscribed as "His Majesty" on subscription rolls.[12] The illuminated infrastructure was reminiscent of Louis XV, who had regularly filled out the hall by granting free places to his own administrators and bureaucrats, but there was one important difference. Louis XV had specified that his royal functionaries sit in the dark and unseen amphitheater to leave the first-tier boxes clear for high nobility. To seat members of the regime and officers of the military in these places, as Napoleon did, was to replace the mercurial power of personality with the strong arm of governmental office. It replaced the person with the position. Old Regime audiences had perfected the art of observing the first-level boxes to discern which arias to praise and which to damn. Napoleon's audiences probably felt themselves more observed than observers.[13]

The methods of renting boxes and the habits of their renters had changed in important ways since the last years of the Old Regime. The procedure was now entirely first-come, first-served. Although the accustomed places of Napoleon and his close circle generally stayed the same season after season—anyone requesting the far left-hand box on the first level would have been politely turned away—even these government officials had to send representatives to the Opéra at the end of each rental period to place themselves on the rolls.[14] Yet this equality of opportunity in subscriptions, a legal equality suited to the new age, did not result in a particularly diverse group of subscribers. Prices were back up after the state-supported performances of the Revolution, and attending the Opéra had again acquired the aura of wealth and prestige that enveloped the institution for most of the eighteenth century. In 1810 the least expensive tickets were in the parterre and the fourth-level amphitheater at 3 francs, 60 centimes; from there the prices went up to 4.50 for most seats in the fourth and fifth levels, 6 for most in the third, 8 for most seats in the second- and ground-level boxes, and 10 for all first-level boxes.[15]

"It is indispensable for a man of fashion to appear at the Opéra on Fridays," advises a guide to the new century. Regular opera goers already knew this. Sundays at the Opéra were poorly attended, and Tuesdays were popular though uneven, as the management sometimes inserted understudies in principal roles.[16] Yet even for those fashionable spectators who came every Friday the hall had a feel far different from what eighteenth-century subscribers knew. Where the trend in the eighteenth century was toward greater numbers of subscribers—so many citizens reserving their weekly plot of prestige—the preference under Napoleon was to purchase tickets by the performance. In the 1788 season 369 individuals rented boxes at the Opéra; in 1809 the number was 53, and in 1812 it had fallen to 26, a figure that included 13 governmental officials.[17] Between 1785 and 1789 the Opéra brought in 1,539,564 francs through subscriptions; from 1806 to 1810 subscriptions totaled just 640,908.[18]

In terms of experience these figures meant that the spectators were reshuffled weekly. Only a few boxes now radiated an accustomed personality. A large percentage of these regular renters not formally a member of the government were nevertheless tied to the new regime in some way. Of the roughly forty subscribers in 1809 not in Napoleon's cabinet, of his immediate family, or in the diplomatic corps, seven had been newly ennobled by Napoleon and four others would be within the next two years.[19] Such were the fixed points of reference for Napoleonic opera goers, the pillars of order at the post-revolutionary Opéra: ministers, police officials, distinguished officers from the revolutionary wars, notables who owed their prominence to the State, and the extended family of the emperor.

Bonaparte also put his stamp on the theater in more subtle ways. An 1811 renovation of the hall added crowns, stars, and bees to the mythological deities painted on the ceiling, symbols all related to the emperor in one way or another. The renovation also changed the overall color scheme of the hall from the blues, reds, and golds that had been there since the Revolution. Now the front of the boxes and balconies were white with gold trim, and the fabric lining the boxes' interiors was green.[20] Deliberate or not, the new decor recalled the day of Napoleon's coronation through the image emblazoned onto French minds by Jacques-Louis David: the same color scheme prevails in David's *Consecration of Napoleon I*, unveiled in the Salon of 1808, where crowns, stars, and even a few bees on the capes of Josephine and Napoleon are visible.

The renovation was intended to revive the hall's prerevolutionary luster, but already an important change was underway in theater design that would rule out a full return to Old Regime luxury. Theaters should be comfortable and decorated in the best possible taste, wrote a participant in the remodeling, "but we also need to remind ourselves that people don't come day after day to see the hall; they come to see the spectacle."[21] Unlike the architectural improvements proposed and vetoed for fear of offending the powerful in the Old Regime, this attitude was to prevail among the press, the public, and the theater managers in the nineteenth century.

Napoleon had a clear vision of the audience he wanted at the Opéra: orderly, fashionable, and above all in unified adoration of His Majesty. In the early years of the regime spectators could be as boorish and unruly as in the most obstreperous moments of the Old Regime. During an 1805 performance thieves shouted "Fire!" and took advantage of the ensuing panic to steal spectators' valuables. Just before another performance a loud argument between a couple already in their places caused a minor hubbub when the man slapped the woman. The police instantly appeared, he bolted, and the chase careened through the crowd and up to the third-level corridors, where the man made a swashbuckling escape by grabbing the curtain-cords and swinging out an open window.[22]

More often the distraction was the steady hum of conversation. "During a pleasing solo by Rode, to which they give not the slightest attention, they praise another one by Baillot," a new newspaper dedicated to music complained. To the majority of spectators at the Opéra, the paper continued, the chief difference between a chorus and a solo was how loudly they could talk.[23] One listener described how a neighbor had spoiled a performance of Catel's *Les Bayadères*: the man surveyed the dancers one by one to conclude salaciously that a better title would be *Les Nymphes de l'Opéra*.[24] And an English visitor was surprised to see the audience "talking, laughing, and exchanging compliments," doors opening and closing, spectators coming and going while the orchestra played or the chorus sang.[25]

And despite its improvements, the hall had annoyances of its own. A fourth balcony several yards shallower than the third proved too great a temptation for misfits in the audience, who on occasion would "spit and throw garbage" on the heads of those below.[26] Not even the state boxes on the second level were spared humiliating surprises. The comte de Daigrefeuille, guest of Consul Cambacérès, fainted and Cambacérès burst out of the box coughing and sputtering during a performance when the stove used to heat the corridors disgorged a thick cloud of disgusting fumes.[27] An orderly musical experience was still some years off.

Of more immediate concern to the government was a different sort of outburst that occasionally interrupted performances: anti-governmental sloganeering. A police agent on duty at the Opéra reported in 1800 that the sort of *esprit de parti* that divided audiences during the Revolution still existed. Notably, some spectators cheered obnoxiously when lines in the libretto could make a political point with a forced double entendre, just as opponents of Jacobinism had done during the Directory at "Tremblez tyrants" in "La Marseillaise." The report noted, however, that these "hateful applications" seemed to diminish as the government's power grew.[28]

The state was apparently coming to the same conclusion. Although the Opéra's armed guards were gone by 1804, their duties were not neglected. As a confidential report addressed to the Interior Ministry stated, "police surveillance has replaced it."[29] The principal tool of Napoleon's inconspicuous observers scattered among the spectators was intimidation. Hardly had the banker Defly taken off his coat and hat in his box at the start of a performance in 1804 when three representatives from the Prefecture of Police "invited" him to join them outside. Their interrogation lasted for several hours, and Defly was ultimately released. He was never told why he had been detained.[30] But the government had its reasons, or so it imagined. Four years earlier police agents learned of a plan to kill Bonaparte at the Opéra, and they arrested the four conspirators quickly and quietly while *Les Horaces* by Bernardo Porta played. They were executed the following day.[31]

Occasionally the state asserted itself for petty reasons, but whether trifling or grave its interventions all made the same point. Someone was watching. When a woman "not particularly well dressed" appeared at the ticket window, it was State Councillor Roederer who refused her entrance; only after long protests from her companions was she permitted to enter, but her seat was selected for her.[32] The ceremonial presence of ministers and officers was the velvet glove, and the secret police who emerged from the shadows to reprove or harass the iron fist, a combination that brought marvelous results to this regime built on bayonets. By 1805 reports from surveillance officers at the Opéra routinely ended by noting that order reigned both inside and outside the theater during performances.

But the police were not the only ones trying to bring order during performances. Audiences themselves—critics, journalists, ordinary

spectators—were increasingly bothered by the distractions of late arri-
vals, early exits, and the maddening, perpetual chatter. They framed
their complaints in terms of proper manners. In 1802 the *Décade
philosophique* advised its readers that it was impolite to talk, yawn,
sneeze, cough, or "blow one's nose to shake the windows" while music
was playing.[33] Louis-Damien Emeric's 1819 manual of *politesse* echoed
this exasperation. "Don't you hear the others all around you calling out,
'Quiet over there!' and even some who say, 'Leave! You're interrupting
the spectacle'?"[34]

Emeric frames his indignation in terms of the public, a collective conscience, he implied, that wagged a finger and clucked its tongue whenever a spectator raised his voice. "What! you are angry that others no
longer allow you the liberty to scandalize the public? But this is inconceivable; I wonder if I am truly in the midst of a civilized country when
I see such little respect among those who compose it."[35] This, too, was
the tone struck by the listener who endured his neighbor's inventory of
dancers in *Les Bayadères*. "From now on I intend to sit far away from
those in blond perukes, and hope to have neighbors who show a little
more respect for the precepts of Pythagoras, of which the first is
SILENCE!"[36]

Spectators also describe an artistic interest at times strong enough
to compel attraction apart from the precepts of etiquette books. The
English visitor who was so annoyed by the doors opening and closing
noted that a soprano or flute solo brought instantaneous silence: "those
who *are* restrained by good manners, and those who *are not* equally
join in silent admiration, and the mouth, unconsciously half opened,
expressed the pleasure which is thus received."[37] When Jean-Victor
Moreau, general of the French armies in the German campaigns, appeared in the first-level boxes in 1803 for a new opera by Paisiello, a
handful of admirers in the sold-out hall waved, called out, and tried
to raise an ovation. "But this did not succeed in attracting attention,"
the surveillance officer on duty reported, "and not much more was
said."[38] And far from using their boxes as salons, some women were said
to escape the "cold etiquette" of social appointments in *le monde* by
withdrawing to the "liberty" of their loge: "at such moments these
women exist only in antiquity, and their sole intimates are Hermione,
Andromaque, and Iphegenia."[39]

Increased interest in the opera surfaced in other telling ways, too,
as details that earlier audiences had accepted without comment now
seemed to be glaring artistic impediments. Some complained that the

light in the hall was too strong, that scenes set in the darkest night were as bright as day. Others found the practice of placing the chorus in lines on either side of the stage stiff and unreal, as the singers bade heroes to love or dance or vanquish the foe from the same stony position. They called the habit of keeping the curtain raised from start to finish ludicrous, especially when, as in the first act of *Fernand Cortez*, a scene ended dramatically. At one moment the besieged Aztecs huddled in fear around their king as conquistadors swore allegiance to their flag, and at the next a jumble of singers, dancers, and stage hands hurried off pellmell into the wings.[40]

Reports of Napoleonic audiences sketch an assemblage without particular coherence. They comprised dissatisfied revolutionaries, self-satisfied notables, nostalgic aristocrats, and imperial cabinet ministers who had earned their stripes as republicans. Musical experience in the first fifteen years of the century was an incongruous patchwork whose squares were particular moments of the past half century. The citizens now seemed less inclined to watch the boxes, but they invariably cheered the emperor whenever he appeared. They were bothered by the distractions but bored by the productions. And their behavior was an odd mix of snobbery and egalitarianism, as quick to damn the rural upstart as the noble in his powdered wig. In Napoleon's spectacle Old Regime insouciance shared the hall with an end-of-century attentiveness, and both were occasionally lit by bolts of enthusiasm that seemed straight from the Revolution. It was just what the emperor wanted.

Napoleon's task at the opera—no less than in French society at large—was to unite and pacify an impossibly polarized and heterogeneous public of ex-revolutionaries, new notables, and returned émigrés. Here his celebrated ability to mask the police state with a cloak of Roman grandeur was most potent. Through a careful combination of censorship and state patronage, the regime created an operatic style that simultaneously appropriated revolutionary forms and recreated the pomp of aristocratic pleasures. The result was a unique combination of revolution and reaction, a musical hybrid that could appeal as easily to new wealth as to old nobility. It was a fitting symbol of a regime that legitimated itself by claiming to guard against the dual threats of unbridled Jacobinism and counter-revolution. The scheme had devastating success, artistically as well as politically. Many of the operas and ballets that flourished in the Consulat and Empire were both dazzling and patriotic. But if these works were built on the two bases of pomp and *patrie* they had a single apex, so that whatever its motive and wherever its appearance, the applause redounded on the emperor in his box, smiling with his teeth.

The atmosphere of ostentation that returned to the Opéra with Thermidor remained, and it was no doubt this conservative cachet that spared the institution when an 1804 decree forced twenty-five other theaters in Paris to shut down immediately.[41] If it escaped closing, however, it did not avoid strict supervision by the government. "Theaters have too strong an influence upon *moeurs*, upon education, and upon the public mood not to devote to them the attention of the government," State Councillor Roederer decreed in a characteristic use of benevolent rhetoric for restrictive ends.[42]

Starting in 1800, the minister of police approved all ballets before they were danced at the Opéra, a task Fouché undoubtedly undertook with some relish given the reputation of the *danseuses*.[43] (Fouché had come a long way since his bloody "pacification" of Lyon during an anti-Jacobin uprising in 1793, a career path he probably pondered now and again as he watched the ballerinas.) Soon thereafter a decree was issued that limited all dance at the Opéra to the "noble and gracious genre"; it further specified that the subject of all operas performed there be drawn from "mythology or history," with their principal characters "gods, kings, or heroes." The same decree required comic operas with spoken recitative to play at the Opéra-Comique and Italian-language works to be given at a new theater that went by the name Opéra-Buffa.[44] A complicated screening system involving the Prefect of Paris and the Ministry of Police was established to review all new works submitted to the Opéra.[45]

A work might make its way past all the committees and still be vetoed by Napoleon, however, who reserved the right to demand changes in a libretto or cancel a performance altogether. Outraged to learn that Le Sueur's *La Mort d'Adam* would present a religious text on the same stage that offered *Les Bayadères* and *Les Sabines*, Napoleon wrote an angry letter to the opera's directors: "From now on, I will see that no opera is given without my orders."[46] On another occasion he wrote to his Interior minister that he had read some "very bad verses" from the Opéra and emphatically directed him to convey his displeasure to the administration.[47]

By requiring the plots and characters to be mythological or historical, the Napoleonic directives effectively precluded a return to the revolutionary portrayals of contemporary scenes. At the same time, the emphasis on dance and pomp effectively worked against the intensely emotional experiences of Gluck's audiences. Men weeping and children screaming out in terror were not Napoleon's image of a stalwart nation. Not that the music of Gluck could have achieved its former effects, anyway. When a revival of *Iphigénie en Aulide* was attempted a journalist explained the public's indifference by commenting, "Gluck is dead, and his music is sick."[48] "The music of *Alceste* puts the pretty women and clever men straight to sleep," another spectator wrote in 1809; "so in order to avoid this soporific, most don't arrive until the beginning of the ballet."[49]

The guidelines tapped a popular taste for a return to the rococo reminiscent of the mid-eighteenth century. A pastiche called *Dance-Mania—Dansomanie*—dominated the stage for several seasons running, its title an accurate description of an earlier public passion lately rediscovered. *Psyché*, a three-act ballet by Gardel that premiered in 1790, was in the active repertory until 1829. It was presented more times at the Opéra than any work by Gluck, Rameau, or Lully, with 1,161 performances.[50] A self-proclaimed "man of the world," asserting that a pretty dancer "pleases less by her art than by her charms," declared that a good ballet could make an opera succeed even if the music were poor.[51] Now whenever Gluck's works were performed additional music was inserted to produce longer ballets, a measure he had explicitly forbidden.[52] "No one goes to the Opéra to hear beautiful music," one reviewer wrote, trying to account for the sparse attendance at a performance of Sacchini's *Oedipe à Colonne*.[53] "You see people turning their backs to the singers and the orchestra to talk about business or the gossip of the day," G. A. Villoteau wrote, "but they make the greatest effort to maintain absolute silence during the dance, when they're all eyes and ears."[54]

The opening decade of the nineteenth century was the time Mozart's operas first appeared with any regularity at the Opéra—if the bastardized, bowdlerized works that went under his name can at all be called Mozartian. *The Magic Flute* first appeared in 1801, adapted for its French audience by the Opéra's director Morel de Chefdeville and the Czech composer Lachnith. The pair took out whole scenes, added fragments from *Don Giovanni* and *The Marriage of Figaro* and even inserted extracts from popular Haydn symphonies. The work, sung in French, was rebaptized *Les Mystères d'Isis*.

Morel made the story more explicitly Egyptian and less Masonic, consulting histories of ancient rites of initiation. Tamino became Isménor and Papageno Bochoris; a magic lyre replaced the latter's flute. Pamina's name remained but she gained a servant, Mona. Capitalizing on the Opéra's tradition of spectacle, the revised tale has Isménor save

Pamina from drowning in a churning sea as the opera ends. Louis Spohr saw *Les Mystères d'Isis* during a visit to Paris and deplored the mutilation. But Morel and Lachnith knew their audiences. Of all new operas to appear in the first decade of the nineteenth century *Les Mystères d'Isis* was among the most popular, with forty-nine performances in its first two years of production alone, a total that the genuine article could not have approached with French audiences of the time.[55]

Mozart's *Don Giovanni*, its libretto rewritten by Baillot and Thuring and its music rearranged by Kalkbrenner, was also dismembered to suit Parisian tastes, although here the results were somewhat less successful. Despite the addition of Vesuvius erupting at the end of the opera and substantial transformations of the plot, too much Mozart survived. There is "too much music in *Don Juan*," the *Journal des débats* declared; "the ensemble pieces are so numerous, so full, and so loud that the spectators find themselves crushed under the weight of harmony."[56] The failure of Kalkbrenner's Mozart did not deter later arrangers from launching projects to improve *Don Giovanni*. In the late 1820s the critic, translator, and sometime-composer Castil-Blaze reworked the ending of the opera, adding text from Molière's *Don Juan* and composing a new "landscape-of-Hell symphony" for a final ballet featuring the don in the underworld.[57]

The most popular works of the Consulat and Empire were packed with unabashed extravagance. The single most performed opera in the first fifteen years of the century was *Fernand Cortez* (1809) by Gaspare Spontini (1774–1851), a work loosely based upon the Aztec conquest and made unforgettable by the fourteen horses it required. Despite the inevitable stable jokes, the work remained in the repertoire until 1839.[58] Jean-François Le Sueur's *Ossian, ou les bardes* (1804) also pleased, particularly in its fourth-act dream sequence that was executed from behind a light gauze cloth stretched across a portion of the stage. Clouds floated in and a castle appeared in the sky, virgins danced and strewed flowers, a tomb materialized, and weeping maidens gathered while harpists in flowing robes gently strummed.[59] "Of all the solemn nuisances we pay to see at the Opéra," a hardened critic for the *Courrier de l'Europe* wrote, "none is a more spectacular nuisance than *Les Bardes*."[60]

Uninspiring Gluck, unrecognizable Mozart, and an abundance of works whose special effects were easily as interesting as the music—it is tempting to explain such exquisite ennui at the Opéra by resorting to commonplaces about a population exhausted by revolution and war and seeking relief in mindless entertainment. In fact there is some truth to the cliché. As the "Compte général de la situation morale et politique du Département de la Seine" reported to the Police ministry, comedies were now vastly preferable to tragedies among French audiences, "who have wept over misfortunes that were not imaginary" and to whom the Revolution "daily exposed the most bloody tragedies."[61]

But this return to hollow magnificence also seems to have been encouraged by the government, whose commissions, awards, and censorship policies emphasized the showy over the sublime. The Decennial Prize in 1810 for the best opera since 1799 went to Spontini's *La Vestale*, a work widely known to have been Josephine's favorite. The work, which enjoyed a run of over two hundred performances, was an extravagant production portraying the improbable love story of a Roman vestal virgin named Julia who allows the eternal flame to go out while trysting with her lover Licinius. In the best baroque tradition, a thunderbolt reignites the flame just as Julia is about to be interred alive. All is forgiven, and the whole stage bursts out in song and dance as the opera ends.[62]

Such works probably appealed to the emergent notability's sense of what opera should be. A good portion of the new elites who filled the hall—military men, speculators, hardworking bachelors from the provinces—had probably never gone to the opera before. As for the returning nobility, they likely sensed in the works some grandeur of the Old Regime minus the lugubriousness of Gluck. But pomp was only half the equation. Underlying the overwhelming extravagance of such productions was a technique straight from the Revolution: transparent reference to the present couched in settings from the past. This was the master stroke of Napoleonic administration, for it represents the appropriation of a highly successful revolutionary form for less-than-revolutionary purposes. What better way to cause spectators to forget the revolutionary scenes at the Opéra than to use their forms to support the new regime?

The strategy was most successful in *Le Triomphe de Trajan*, a monumental work by Louis-Luc Loiseau de Persuis, commissioned by the government in 1807 to celebrate the Battle of Jena. No one claimed its interest was chiefly musical. It loaded the stage with six hundred Roman soldiers, a forest of gleaming swords and spears, triumphal arches, thirteen live horses, and an enormous chariot for the emperor Trajan. The effect was numbing. "We worry that after growing used to so much luxury our eyes might begin to disregard the modest productions that characterize most of our operas," reads a review in the *Courrier de l'Europe*.[63]

But if the setting was the heroic past, the spectators quickly realized that the content was contemporary. Trajan is the liberating conqueror, the clement ruler who showers the vanquished with acts of mercy. Spectators recognized its allusions to Jena and thundered out their approval, especially when the consul Licinius praises the emperor as "the greatest of all humans, the brilliant model for heroes and king," and the people sing that "the titles of Prince and Father have long been given him by our love."[64] Press accounts of *La Triomphe* echoed those describing the patriotic scenes a decade and a half earlier. *La Triomphe de Trajan* was "a truly national festival," one synopsis read, where the nation "rejoiced in recognizing the hero it admires daily in the guise of the greatest prince of antiquity."[65]

A long letter published in the *Courrier de l'Europe* the week of the work's premiere gives the firsthand impressions of one spectator's gradual recognition that *La Triomphe de Trajan* is about French, not Roman, armies. The letter is signed by a M. Le Franc, who describes himself as a humble citizen of Romoratin and a member of the Agricultural Society of Melun. When the curtain rises Le Franc's senses begin to swim, and he turns to his neighbor to ask if these aren't Roman soldiers who fill the stage and Roman monuments they seem to be dedicating. Le Franc is astonished to hear his neighbor reply that the soldiers on the left are Prussian and those on the right French. "He even went so far as to say that Trajan was a French prince," Le Franc reports. "At that moment I was sure I had goofed, that my neighbor was a provincial like myself, and that maybe he wasn't even a member of an agricultural society."[66]

But the realization slowly dawns on Le Franc that the work is an elaborate allegory of the victory at Jena.[67]

I do not know what sort of revolution gently worked itself inside of me, but at every moment my ideas seemed to change, and I gradually found myself in the midst of familiar events. . . . Dear editor, I cannot describe to you what I felt at the sight of the triumphal chariot. Never have my eyes, my ears, my soul been more deeply moved. I followed every scene with a kind of intoxication, and at the dénouement . . . I grabbed the hand of my neighbor and said to him, "Yes, yes, monsieur, we *are* in Prussia; I can see the French, I can see the Prussians, and I even recognize Trajan. But Trajan himself would be lucky to count among his actions such a heroic gesture."[68]

This is a rare glimpse of the powerful effects produced by *Trajan*'s skillful combination of ostentation and allegory. But the letter's clear ideological message (not to mention the little ironic smirk it wears) arouses suspicion. What better preparation for audiences than a description of the work's true message from a wide-eyed farmer? Letters in the Opéra's archives from the Interior Ministry—some requesting press notices of an imminent appearance of Napoleon, others specifying works to be performed—betray the nature of the government's "attention": each note ends reminding the management that "the desires [of the emperor] are orders."[69]

But whether the letter was actually by Le Franc or a fabrication of the government, the larger motivation behind *Le Triomphe de Trajan* is clear. The work commandeered the tradition of allegorical pieces from the Revolution, with the signal difference that *La Triomphe* elevated one man and not the sovereign people. The audience was no longer one with the actors and action on the stage. To be sure the spectacle pleased them with its pageantry and craven flattery and, if the night was right, the emperor himself in attendance. But in the process it redefined the revolutionary associations, at once providing an illusion of continuity with the Revolution and eclipsing the citizens from the spectacle.

Other works followed the same dynamic. The ballet *La Fête de Mars* (1808, Kreutzer and Gardel) allegorically reenacted events from Brumaire to the Austrian campaign, telling, in the words of its composer, how Mars brought peace to a nation whose priests, elites, men of commerce, and farmers had turned against one another in civil war. Kreutzer's opéra-ballet *Le Triomphe du mois de mars* (1811) mythologized the King of Rome on the occasion of his birth ("Achilles' son is born! Mars is triumphant! . . . How glorious to see the birth of the greatest Caesar's son!").[70] Writing of Paisiello's *Proserpine* a censor recognized Bonaparte as "the destroyer of factions" and "the peaceful conciliator."[71] There were also lines in the more popular works clearly meant to flatter Napoleon. "Triumph! Victory! Mexico falls beneath our blows," sings the chorus near the end of *Fernand Cortez*. "Children of glory, this world is ours! Who can stop the victor in his infinite course, who can resist genius when it commands courage?"[72] During Licinius' triumphal entry in the first act of *La Vestale* the chorus hails the general as "the judge of the world" for bringing peace through conquest. *Ossian* ends with a chorus celebrating their leader's renown, which reverberates throughout the universe. (In case the connection was unclear, Le Sueur repeated the phrase in his dedication, where he relates having modeled his Ossian after Napoleon, "whose glory fills the very globe we walk on—or I could even say the universe: is that too presumptuous?")[73]

So it was not surprising that audiences were not wholly absorbed in the drama. Even the most polished compositions contained elements that worked at dramatic cross-purposes. Works from the Revolution had already shown that commemoration discourages plot development, but whereas revolutionary artists eventually did the logical thing and gave up on plot, Napoleonic artists tried to graft present-minded celebration onto the traditional stock of an autonomous fiction. The consequence was a flaccid dramatic construction that regularly left loose ends dangling and disappointed with inappropriately happy endings. The finale of *Fernand Cortez*, which Napoleon explicitly commissioned to coincide with his conquest of Spain, is grossly improbable: Cortez courteously excuses himself before Montezuma, claiming "it is only your friendship that I wish to conquer"; meantime the Mexicans happily welcome the reign of "pleasure and the arts."[74] (The Spanish in *Fernand Cortez* were all too noble in the view of the minister of police, who recommended that the premiere be postponed until after Napoleon's Spanish expedition. Such were the drawbacks of allegory.)[75]

Similarly, the librettist Étienne de Jouy all but apologized for the vapid deus ex machina lightning stroke that relights the eternal flame at the close of *La Vestale*, arguing that while dramatic plausibility might have had Julia buried alive, Paris audiences were not accustomed to such horrors.[76] More to the point, a tragic ending would have kept the glorious conqueror and his destined wife from swearing their eternal love on a sacred altar—and, after all, Josephine had favored Spontini since long before he wrote the opera.[77]

In a virtuosic performance of his own at the opera, Napoleon replayed Brumaire. Preserving enough of the trappings of revolutionary drama to retain its spirit and rekindle its enthusiasm, he usurped the popular sovereignty it proclaimed. "I am not an intriguer; you know me," Bonaparte declared on the morrow of his coup against the Directory; "I believe I have given enough proofs of my devotion to my *patrie*. . . . The sovereignty of the people, liberty, equality, these sacred foundations of the constitution, still remain: they must be saved."[78] To revolutionary sympathizers in operatic audiences (at least early in the regime) Napoleon was the savior of the Revolution, an embodiment of the people who linked the action on the stage to the accomplishments of the nation. To aristocrats and spectators with noble ambitions he was the prince come to receive the tributes of his grateful subjects. And in both cases, the enthusiasm could only enhance the regime's stability. As Trajan sings in his triumphal return to Rome: "Your tributes enrich these altars only for the sake of the State, and for its august grandeur."[79]

It worked to Napoleon's further acclaim that the public was not terribly engaged by the drama or moved by the music. Fortunately the music of Rossini and Scribe's riveting libretti were still a generation away.

For as effective as the strategy was of mixing Old Regime richness with revolutionary forms, however, its overall neglect of explicit dramatic appeal proved limiting. *Le Triomphe de Trajan* stayed in the active repertoire for as long as Napoleon remained in power, and four years after its premiere reviews still reported enthusiastic audiences applauding its heroic allegories.[80] But one has the sense that as the memory of Jena gave way to the horrors of Moscow, *Le Triomphe* became as empty dramatically as the other works from the past that audiences found so boring. The problem with commemoration is that the applause, too, can become a ritual.

Is this what explains the strange decision in programming made by the Opéra's directors just after Napoleon's abdication? The date is 1814, and the Allied rulers appear before a cheering audience. The management takes from its repertoire what it thinks will be a fitting tribute and announces the imminent performance of . . . *La Triomphe de Trajan*. The audience does not object but Alexander does, so at the last moment *La Vestale* is staged—with sets and costumes from *La Triomphe!*[81]

Maybe this was the revenge of the Revolution itself. Stripped of its raison d'être, contemporaneity, revolutionary form was as empty to nineteenth-century spectators as were the fanciful mythologies of the Old Regime. By the time of his fall, Napoleon had worn out the Revolution.

10

The Théâtre Italien
and Its Elites

Given the success earlier governments had had in enhancing their reputations from the stage, it seemed natural that Charles X should also be feted with an opera for his 1824 coronation. The logical place was the Théâtre Italien, home to the Parisian glitterati of the 1820s and the undisputed leader in operatic quality. Having tottered on the edge of insolvency for the first fifteen years of the century, the institution had now come into its own, and no other Paris theater could approach either the receipts or the enthusiasm it generated. On the program was Rossini's *Il viaggio a Reims*, a circumstantial piece like those Napoleon had used so effectively in the best days of his reign. The theater's regulars awaited the premiere with the same eager nervousness with which they had greeted *Il barbiere di Siviglia* and *Semiramide*, and Rossini did not disappoint them. But Charles did, and his thoroughly unnecessary stumble across the threshold of his rule was somehow appropriate. It was a bad start for this unregenerate Bourbon who tried to make like the Revolution had never happened.[1]

Hardly had the opera begun when Charles began to fidget. He blankly scanned the spectators, inspected the ceiling, located the gas outlets for the lights one by one, shifted, whispered to his entourage, and, after all that, let out a loud sigh when the duchesse de Berry showed him in the libretto that the opera was only one-third finished. Charles found nothing of interest in the spectacle that had delighted his most notable subjects three nights a week for the better part of ten years, and they noticed.[2]

Charles might have done more that night for the sake of his reputation, but the truth of the matter was that the king was out of place

at the Théâtre Italien. The public—and not necessarily its most famous members, either—set the tone here. That tone was a sort of
formal informality that minded its manners while still leaving room for
spontaneity.

More fitting was Balzac's visit to the Théâtre Italien in 1822. He
arrived drunk but insists that it was not on account of the seventeen
bottles of wine he and Eugène Sue had consumed during dinner.
Rather, it was the two cigars Sue offered him after dinner. Balzac finds
his seat, though the steps of the theater feel soft and the faces of the
spectators seem cloudy and indistinct. The overture to Rossini's *La
gazza ladra* puts him into ecstasies; he tosses his head back, and golden
trombones, the heaving bows of violins and violas, clarinets, and trumpets sweep past his vision. Everywhere he looks he sees lace and feathers.
"This man smells of wine!" a woman seated behind him in the balcony
says loudly enough to rouse him, and Balzac, momentarily indignant
("Non, madame, répondis-je, je sens la musique"), leaves his seat to
find the box of a duchess. The opera ends, and Balzac is still searching
through the maze of corridors for the right door, occasionally peeping
into their tiny windows as (he tells himself) lovers also do. The crush of
exiting spectators pins him against a wall, feathers and lace brush past
him from all sides, Rossini says several witty things when he passes (Balzac forgets them), he extends his arm to a duchess or a ticket girl, he
isn't sure which, and his coach carries him home still swimming in
music.[3]

The Théâtre Italien had already suffered several false starts before it
rose to glory in the 1820s. It opened in 1801 as the Opéra Buffa. France
occupied much of Italy at the time, and Napoleon, more clever in almost
every way than Charles X, demonstrated his fondness for Italian music
by exposing his subjects to its wonders. A group of Italian singers was
assembled, a theater secured, and performances in Italian began. The
most popular composers were Cimarosa, Paër, and Paisiello; Cimarosa's
Il matrimonio segreto and Paisiello's *Il barbiere di Siviglia* were especially successful. The high ticket prices and exotic sound of Italian
quickly established what would be a permanent feeling of exclusivity
associated with the theater. "Our Opéra Buffa has become the rendezvous of the most delicate ears and most distinguished society in the capital," the *Courrier de l'Europe* proudly announced in 1807.[4] But its exclusivity did not ensure solvency: it suspended productions twice in
1803, once in 1804, and again in 1818; during its first twenty years it
moved locations five times.[5]

The Théâtre Italien was the first Paris theater to present Mozart's

Italian operas in the original version. *Le nozze di Figaro* opened in 1807, *Così fan tutte* in 1809, *Don Giovanni* in 1811, and *La clemenza di Tito* in 1816. Predictably, the press attacked the music as too complex; at one performance of *Le nozze* several wags shouted out "Piano l'orchestre," and the second performance of *Don Giovanni* played to a half-empty hall.[6] Although the theater's directors valiantly revived Mozart's operas throughout the 1810s and into the 1820s they earned only modest success. For the time Mozart stood a better chance of succeeding in the stripped-down versions the Opéra gave.[7]

The composer who made the Théâtre Italien the crown jewel of Restoration society was Gioacchino Rossini. By the mid-1820s its audiences were mad for his music, and during a handful of golden years it seemed that the flow of his Parisian premieres might go on forever. *L'italiana in Algeri* premiered in 1817, and *L'inganno felice* and *Il barbiere di Siviglia* appeared in 1819. *Il turco in Italia* and *Torvaldo e Dorliska* premiered in 1820, *La pietra del paragone, Otello*, and *La gazza ladra* in 1821, *Tancredi, Mosè in Egitto*, and *Cenerentola* in 1822, *Semiramide* in 1825, and *Zelmira* in 1826.[8] In 1822, 119 of the 154 performances at the theater featured Rossini's work; in 1825, 129 of its 174 performances were by him.[9] Starting in 1826 Rossini's works began appearing at the Opéra as well.

Rossini, who arrived in Paris in 1823, enjoyed near-cult status in the late Restoration. Brilliant conversationalist, famous gourmand, facile composer who by reputation could hold up his end of a salon conversation while composing an aria, Rossini sparkled with *sprezzatura* even as the style of the *artiste* was shifting to earnest solemnity. Orchestras serenaded him at his window, the vaudeville paid its own tribute by way of parody (the Gymnase staged a farce with characters called Biffsteakini and Trombonini), street songs cited him, restaurants honored him with banquets. ("We are unwell," his wife wrote to a friend. "It is from eating too much. The maestro and I live to eat.")[10] His Saturday night soirées—the house packed and overflowing onto the sidewalk—were most recherchées: when he came back to Paris in 1843 after several years' absence, 2,000 people signed a two-month waiting list to visit him.[11] Stendhal contributed his extravagant, often-quoted tribute: "Napoleon is dead, but a new conqueror has already shown himself to the world, and from Moscow to Naples, from London to Vienna, from Paris to Calcutta, his name is on every tongue."[12]

But not all tongues spoke praise. To his opponents, Rossini was an interloper and an opportunist. He was a none-too-diligent overeater, they said, whose prolific output depended upon self-borrowings and plagiarisms. Worse, he was Italian, and defenders of the French tradition sprang up to attack him (despite the fact that French music over the previous century and a half had regularly drawn from Italian sources). The *Quotidienne* claimed that only a tiny fraction of listeners were Rossinistes, while "the public has shown itself truly national" by seeing the ridiculousness of a composer who spent as much time in restaurants as in theaters. The Conservatoire was whispered to have been behind an effort to thwart him. One anonymous pamphleteer, tongue in cheek no more than halfway, called him the antichrist.[13]

But the Opéra was impotent to challenge him, a fact that severely compromised the national attacks on Rossini. During the first few years of the Restoration the Opéra sustained its earlier momentum and enthusiasm, but by the 1820s its successes were largely atavisms. Incredibly, *Le Triomphe de Trajan* stayed in the repertoire and was given whenever Louis XVIII attended, although that was rare.[14] *Pélage, ou le roi et la paix* and *Les Dieux rivaux* were allegories akin to the works commissioned by Napoleon, the one telling of the return to the Spanish throne of the Austrian leader Pelayo in 717 after a long exile and the other celebrating the duc de Berry's marriage. But Napoleon's interventionist style and his habit of appearing at the Opéra frequently—both crucial to the success of his musical politics—were unpalatable to Restoration monarchs, so the formulaic allegories that appeared with dull regularity failed to rouse any sustained enthusiasm. The ballet *Blanche de Provence, ou la cour des fées* (1821; a pastiche with music by Berton, Boieldieu, Chambine, Kreutzer, and Païs and text by Rauché and Théaulon) celebrated the birth of the posthumous son of the duc de Berry; *François Ier à Chambord* (1830; music by Ginestet and text by Moline de Saint Yon and Fangeroux) celebrated the comte de Chambord; and *Vendôme en Espagne* (1823; music by Auber and Hérold and text by Mennechet and Empis) celebrated the entry of the French army into Spain. Whatever rough historical accuracy was aimed at in such earlier works as *La Vestale* or *Fernand Cortez* was lost in these works. *Pharamond*, which celebrated the enthronement of Charles X, was set among the Gauls and the Romans with prominent views of the Tuileries.[15]

Lacking fresher works of more enduring appeal, the Opéra dusted off its old productions of Gluck, Grétry, and Sacchini. Even Rousseau's *Le Devin du village* reappeared. But to a public still without a sense of reverence for a musical canon, the resurrection of Old Regime works was an admission of profound weakness at the Académie Royale.[16]

(François-Joseph Fétis would be one of the first to promote self-consciously "historical" programs in France with his "Concerts Historiques" beginning in 1832.) Sopie Leo, friend of Chopin and acute observer of the Restoration musical scene, sketched a pitiful portrait of a company filled with aging, toothless singers whose exhausted voices made listeners cringe.[17] "The theater is intended more for the eyes than for the ears," a visitor wrote with evident generosity; another found there "something of the Old Regime, something antediluvian."[18]

It was no wonder that Charles X chose the Théâtre Italien over the Opéra to celebrate his accession. The institution of national honor was at death's doorstep. As the *Pandore* wrote in 1824, the Opéra was "a poor invalid, who raises himself from his bed, makes an effort to speak, falls back, struggles, lifts himself again, and continues so, languishing between life and death."[19] To believe Stendhal, charting the relative stock of the two theaters was as easy as finding a twenty-year-old in touch with "our new ways," a reference to the changed face of social life since the Revolution: "as soon as the name Rossini is mentioned . . . they mock the esteemed admirers of Gluck and Grétry."[20]

The sad fact was that the Opéra had become little more than a tourist attraction. Without a clear artistic direction, the Opéra had slowly lost regular subscribers, the backbone of its audiences throughout the eighteenth century. Whereas 369 different subscribers took out boxes at the Opéra in 1788, it had 66 regular renters in 1819; the following year the number fell to 38.[21] The bulk of audiences and income thus shifted to single-ticket buyers, a transient public that, according to contemporaries, consisted largely of out-of-towners.[22] "The audience at the Opéra has constant turnover; if one exempts a few immovable regulars in the balconies and two or three dozen powdered wigs who sleep in the orchestra-level seats, one never sees a core of intrepid spectators there."[23] Stendhal claimed that the Opéra attracted the inferior classes, provincials, tasteless spendthrifts, a handful of Englishmen, and pleasure seekers who came only to watch the dancers.[24] Receipts attest to the Opéra's lethargy and the transience of its audiences: in 1820 door receipts accounted for 90 percent of its revenues from audiences, and its total annual receipts from audiences during the decade fell roughly 100,000 francs short of receipts at the Théâtre Italien during the early 1820s.[25]

The Opéra's decrepitude only intensified Rossini's success at the Théâtre Italien. When his work was performed the main floor and balcony would fill long before the curtain rose at 7 : 30, and scalpers could clear 3 francs on every ticket.[26] The crowd at the Théâtre Italien was the cream of Parisian society, and since the Revolution that elite had broadened to include not just the aristocracy by birth but those ennobled by Napoleon and an increasingly prominent *haute bourgeoisie* of wealth. Heinrich Heine caught the right tone of inclusive exclusivity when he wrote, "The elite of the *beau monde* that distinguishes itself by rank, by education, by birth, by fashion, and by laziness have all taken refuge at the Opéra Italien, this oasis for music."[27] Stendhal dedicated his *Life of Rossini* to the worldly man who had been there at least two hundred times; one of his friends claimed that works performed there achieved their fullest powers over the imagination only when heard twenty or thirty times. Balzac wrote that he attended as often as twice weekly.[28]

Tickets for a performance at the Théâtre Italien in 1826 ranged from 2 to 10 francs, as expensive as the Opéra at the high end and only slightly less so at the low end.[29] As a consequence there was plenty of lace and feathers to be seen. Castil-Blaze described the theater as the musical equivalent of the fancy balls once again in fashion, with "all of elegant society . . . [in attendance] in its richest apparel," and Gabriel Fictor rated possessing a box at the theater on par with riding in the Bois de Boulogne and attending the sermons of Fayet or Bonnevie.[30] Administrative ordinances forbade all servants from entering the hall and restricted the interior guard to the foyer and corridors unless summoned inside, though even there they were seldom needed.[31] "Thanks to the composition of the public that attends, . . ." reads an internal memorandum from the theater, "use of the Commissaire de Police is utterly unnecessary."[32]

Although the number of subscribers at the Théâtre Italien could not approach that of the Opéra at the end of the Old Regime, its 112 renters in 1821 represented by far the largest regular musical audience of any theater in Paris during the Restoration.[33] There was no clear pattern to the seating at the Théâtre Italien, either by governmental position in the Napoleonic manner or by birth. Individual tickets were sold and boxes rented by the laws of the market. Seventy-five years earlier prestige brought visibility at the Opéra; now wealth alone brought visibility, and with it came prestige. Nathan-Mayer Rothschild, the banker whom the Austrian emperor had recently made a baron, watched from a first-level box. Nearby sat a diplomat in the service of Russia, Charles-André Pozzo di Borgo, a cosmopolite of Corsican stock whose hatred for Napoleon led him to fight variously alongside the British, the Austrians, and the Prussians before settling in Russia. Talleyrand (who also knew something about political survival) held a box at the Théâtre Italien. Other notables occupied prominent places: the duc d'Orléans (the future Louis-Philippe) regularly kept a box there; the count de Noailles, incarnated this generation as an elected member of the Chamber of Deputies from Corèze, rented a box on the third level. Prince Metternich of Austria purchased the right of "grande entrée," which meant he could enter performances whenever he wished to join others in their boxes.[34]

Just as visible if not always as noticeable were scores of comparatively anonymous subscribers who surrounded the notables on every level and in every corner of the theater. Journalists, composers, and novelists sat among the individual ticket holders in the stalls along the balconies, the place Balzac briefly visited during his enchanted evening (see Figure 12). Both the Favart, which was home to the singers from 1815 to 1818 and again from 1825 to 1838, and the Louvois, which hosted them from 1818 to 1825, tampered with the seating to increase their capacities and revenues, but some open-balcony seating always remained. The artists, actors, and critics who received free entries sat in the second or third balconies, the galleries, or in the floor seats.[35] According to the comtesse d'Agoult, the balconies also contained girls from the Faubourg Saint-Germain, whose well-to-do families preferred this to other theaters because "Italian singers were not excommunicated, and no one could understand the words of their libretto."[36]

By the 1820s names without titles or aristocratic prefixes appeared in the administrative registers for even the most expensive places. M. Beauman, M. Gatry, M. Bocher, Mme Davilliers, M. Perius, Mme Turette, M. Valentin, Mme Dupuy—for every aristocrat, ancient or newly ennobled, there was a wealthy bourgeois renting a box at the Théâtre Italien, proud, no doubt, that success in commerce, real estate, or the judiciary could buy such eminence.[37] Eugène de Rastignac, dazzled by his first visit to the theater in Le Père Goriot, expressed the kind of admiring envy that the Beaumans and Gatrys probably lived to hear. "Yesterday evening Rossini's The Barber of Seville was at the Théâtre des Italiens. . . . Good Lord, how nice it would be to have one's box there!"[38]

This was the future of Parisian musical audiences: hardworking spectators known more by generalizations than by personalities. They were elites, to be sure (ticket prices hardly permitted otherwise), but elites of a new stamp who resisted ostentation and drawing attention to themselves in public places. The short three- or six-month contracts for rent-

Figure 12. Gustave Doré, *L'Opéra Italien*. Photograph courtesy of the Bibliothèque Nationale.

ing boxes nourished the sense of disconnectedness and unfamiliarity among audiences, since no particular care was taken to assign subscribers the same box for successive subscriptions. Moreover, the theaters that were home to the company during the Restoration boosted their revenues by squeezing in as many spectators as possible, a move that could only add to the relative anonymity of the experience. The old Palais Royal opera hall had seated roughly 1,300, and the 1793 Théâtre des Arts 1,750; the Favart, by contrast, could hold 1,900 at peak capacity (see Figure 13).[39] These factors urged patrons silently and subtly to focus on the stage and not on the boxes.

Nevertheless there persisted some of the socializing that had made musical experience in the eighteenth century so resemble a salon. Gas lighting now supplemented the candles and oil lamps, illuminating audiences yet more brilliantly after its more or less successful introduction at the Opéra in 1822. (During the first few years minor explosions from different parts of the opera hall peppered performances, and spectators frequently complained about the terrible stench that hung in the air.)

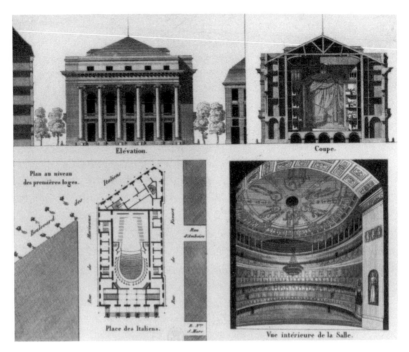

Figure 13. Théâtre Favart: elevation, cutaway view, plan showing the first-level boxes, interior view of the hall. From Donnet, *Architectonographie des théâtres de Paris* (1821). Photograph courtesy of the Bibliothèque Nationale.

While gas lamps were employed to brighten and dim the stage to suit the scenes, they stayed up during performances; one spectator observed with apparent satisfaction that the gas lights at last eliminated the theater's dark spots.[40] In *The Red and the Black* Mathilde is sickened to find a stack of letters from Mme de Fervaques to Julien, and she convinces her mother to go to the theater on an unaccustomed night in to see if Julien might appear in the maréchale's box. He does, but when he sees Mathilde's tears glistening in the light he immediately rushes to her box.[41] (Note the brightness of the chandelier in Figure 14.) Stendhal doesn't say, but they were both probably cursing the lights that night.

Restoration audiences at the theater were orderly, if ambulatory. One visitor said that silence there was "de rigueur"—"the loss of a note . . . is a public calamity"—but he added that the habitués sought out one another during performances.[42] Another noted that the greatest silence preceded the overture and reigned during arias but that during the recitatives spectators would quietly talk among themselves and move from box to box.[43] Such reports reveal much about what held the attention

Figure 14. Eugène Lami, *Intérieur du Théâtre Italien (Ovation d'un acteur)*. Photograph courtesy of the Bibliothèque Nationale.

of audiences at the theater, since the arias of Rossini are filled with vocal fireworks. "The public at the Théâtre Italien brings to the spectacle a disposition most agreeable to musicians," the *Journal des débats* reported. "They know how to listen, and in music above all one shouldn't judge before one listens."[44] But the public also liked to talk about what they heard. The cavatina "Bel raggio lusinghier" from *Semiramide*, sung by the French soprano Joséphine Mainvielle-Fodor in this enclave of Italians, was followed by several minutes of excited chatter. "Each spectator wanted to share his opinion with his neighbor."[45]

The public was agreeable to musicians in another way. It was, by operatic standards, exceptionally polite. The *Globe* observed that a series of inept scenic effects in Rossini's *Mosè in Egitto* would have produced robust whistling in any other hall "less aristocratic and less attuned to etiquette."[46] Stendhal relates that a particularly poor performance of Rossini's *Donna del lago* richly deserved whistling but did not receive it from the public: "it is too polite for that."[47]

Much breathless commotion came from the parterre and the balconies, where the Théâtre Italien's celebrated dilettanti sat. These were the *mélomanes*—the music maniacs—who hardly seemed to notice the broad mocking they suffered from the press and other spectators. Spiritual heirs to the *petits-maîtres* and *incroyables* of the eighteenth century, precursors to the yellow-gloved partisans of Hugo in his battles against the classicists, the dilettanti were the wealthy set's version of *bohème*. For them the Théâtre Italien was a haven for eccentricity within the bosom of privilege (see Figure 15). Already in 1810 a kernel of devotees attracted attention with their odd habits. They were like "fugitives from Charenton":[48] their muscles swelled, they made grimaces as they listened or screwed up their faces in contortions, crying out "Oh how lovely!" "Oh how divine!" with such force that they sometimes covered the singers.[49]

The glory days of the dilettanti were the 1820s, when they occupied large tracts of the parterre and formed small congregations in rented boxes. To Joseph d'Ortigue, who wrote a book in praise of *dilettantisme*, they represented an elite, the true connoisseurs, who understood music that was too difficult for the ordinary spectator. "Rossini's music is far from being suited for everyone," he claimed. "One must already be somewhat dilettante, somewhat civilized to appreciate it." While the "people" might retain a tune from Mozart, Méhul, or Grétry, only the "semi-learned" fully understand Rossini.[50] According to the *Pandore*, the parterre was "a true revolutionary tribunal" that showed no mercy to those it condemned.[51] To sympathizers the ecstasies of the dilettanti were evidence of genuine turbulence in the soul. Their whole body was a quivering tympanum, a "musical organ that stretches from head to toe."[52]

The dilettanti knew only two states, gushing enthusiasm or utter silence. Once arias were underway, they managed to "keep themselves from saying a single word that could cause them to lose a measure."[53] Stendhal, who considered himself a dilettante, describes the response of his friends with almost embarrassing immediacy.

Lost in his private and ecstatic universe of contemplation, anger and impatience are the only reactions that he is likely to manifest towards the importunate intrusions of *other people*—towards anyone who is rash enough to come between him and the rapture of his soul. . . . His mouth will gape half-open, and every feature will bear traces of intolerable exhaustion—or rather, will seem utterly drained of the last thin drop of vitality; his eyes alone may give some insight into the fiery recesses of his soul, and even then, should anybody chance to advise him of the fact, he will bury his head in his hands, so desperate is his contempt for *other people*.

In these moments, Stendhal writes, the dilettante is in such a state that "the most prosaic happenings in all the world—say, a dog run over by a

Figure 15. *Les Dilettanti à l'Opéra Buffa*. Musée Carnavalet. © 1993 ARS, New York/SPADEM, Paris.

cab in the rue de Richelieu—are transmuted into great tragedies of Destiny and mysteries of the heart."[54] Only an initiate could get away with such bathos. But Stendhal was nothing if not effusive when the topic was Italian opera. "Rossini has a duet in *Armide* that'll give you a ten-day erection," he wrote to Adolphe de Mareste. "If your bladder can stand it, go listen to it."[55]

Another self-described dilettante was Théophile Dondey, a poet who took the pseudonym Philothée O'Neddy. O'Neddy's "Dandyisme" is a vaporous hymn to music, testimony that the birth of romanticism was not without its labor pains. Music brings O'Neddy "a thousand confused thoughts, like flaming punch full to the rim of its bowl." It was "the rending of the clouds' curtain, where the livid hand of the gnome of storms designs a sulfurous delta with thunder." O'Neddy has fantasies of paying the ultimate tribute to music at the Théâtre Italien. His poem ends in a rapturous climax.

> Golden angel, harmony! Your nimbus always rains
> Sweet peace into my mind's domains!
> Oh harmony, harmony! Love, potent and intense,
> Attuned to all your miracles, within my blood ferments!
> If life's cruel blows should make me ere decide
> To seek the calm embrace of suicide,
> My artistic exaltation will make my death's location
> The Italian Opera.
> As the trills of oboes and the sound of strings
> Accompany the singer as he sings
> And the dilettante's contentment clearly shows,
> I'll close myself within my private loge.
> With stoic eye turned toward the sounding spaces
> I'll fall asleep within the drugged embraces
> Of a hundred drops of opium sublime.
> Music, my Egyptian girl voluptuous and rare,
> You spread your feast before my sweet despair.[56]

Some spectators made fun of the dilettanti. They claimed that their histrionics had little to do with music and everything to do with fashion. A new, serious-minded periodical, the *Revue musicale*, was particularly harsh, painting the dilettanti as a blind pack that senselessly idolized first one singer and then another. They loved the sound of their own applause when the famous singers sang but seemed indecisive and ill at ease before a new performer: "not knowing if he should applaud, he quickly turns to a neighbor, sounds out his opinion on the person . . .

and if he finds some evidence of knowledge he promptly takes up the same view; if the neighbor does not seem any more knowledgeable than he, on the other hand, the question circulates until it finds some enlightened listener, who then decides."[57]

When the dilettanti gave a cool reception to Niedermeyer's *Casa nel bosca* at the Théâtre Italien, the *Revue musicale* claimed it had proof of the group's fickle nature. Had they known Niedermeyer was a protégé of Rossini, it wrote, they would have showered it with applause instead of sitting through it with sour looks on their faces. It is "open season" at the Théâtre Italien when a composer is unknown. "In these circumstances one must rely on one's own taste, on one's own judgment, without the authority of a name as security against exposing oneself. And how unpleasant that is!"[58] "The dilettanti are a funny lot," the paper wrote in another issue. "They seem incapable of judging individually what's good and bad; someone has to give them a lesson before they let their enthusiasm loose."[59]

The disdain showed toward the dilettanti reveals a tension at the theater. Rossini drew the engaged attention of spectators and often prompted spontaneous and apparently genuine outbursts. At the same time, however, the grip of "respectable" behavior tightened, and the acceptable range and manner of displaying emotion were narrowed. The *Revue musicale* may have been right in what it said about the herd spirit of the dilettanti, but the dismissive tone of the newspaper conveyed an additional message, one consistent with earlier denunciations of rural visitors to Paris theaters. The tone was censorious and superior, even sarcastic. "This isn't done," it seemed to say; "good society doesn't act this way." In absolute terms, the only thing that separated the dilettanti's raptures from the tears of sensitive souls in the 1770s was the response of other spectators. Increasingly, responses that drew attention to themselves would be frowned upon by the emergent code of respectability. Audiences did not shrink meekly into silence from self-doubt. Rather, they convinced themselves that propriety demanded self-control and, when necessary, outright confrontation with those whose gauche behavior deserved correction.

Stendhal approved of the whispers after major arias, yet he sensed an encroaching conformity in the public's hesitancy to whistle or laugh. He feared a future where every listener would suppress his pleasure and displeasure "solely to seem 'de bon ton' in the eyes of the four-hundred and ninety-nine others."[60] Even as he chronicled its lively audiences—

where drunken authors and breathless lovers slipped from their seats in mid-performance and the flamboyant impulsively gushed out praise— Stendhal foresaw a future of rigid, expressionless listeners at the Théâtre Italien. "What will result from this scrupulous silence and continuous attention?" he asked. "That fewer people will enjoy themselves."[61] If we call him prescient, then it was a prescience that extended well beyond his time and into our own.

11

The Birth of Public Concerts

One of the most musically significant institutional changes the Revolution brought was to break the monopoly the Académie Royale held over performances. With the gradual return to political calm after Thermidor came a growing confidence in public pleasures, and lyrical and dramatic performances blossomed in the new freedom. Some in Paris stressed the political nature of this artistic renaissance; for the Paris correspondent of the *Allegemeine musikalische Zeitung*, the arts could again exert their influence because the "wounds" of "vandalism" had now begun to heal.[1]

But the birth of public concerts reflected a new economic reality, too. Those few who possessed the kind of wealth that had sponsored musical dinners à la Pouplinière or private salon performances as at the Hôtel de Soubise did not generally share the Old Regime's taste for ostentatious consumption. Once private, festivity was now a public good. The slightly startled tone of one description of post-revolutionary concert life underscores the shift: "It is a truly flattering encouragement for our artists to have theaters at their disposal where they may submit their talents to the judgment of the public."[2]

Between Thermidor and 1805 three major concert societies formed to offer regular performances. While the comparatively small public for instrumental music through the 1810s made the business of concerts uncertain, these early series were decisive in carving out a space, aesthetically and socially, for what would ultimately be a vibrant concert scene in Paris. If judged by their ability to draw consistently large audiences, the success of concert societies in the early 1800s was modest.

But for a public who still had its doubts about the viability of music without dramatic action even this hesitant beginning was a new departure.

The first regular concert series in post-Thermidorian Paris was the Concert de la Rue Cléry. Also known as the Concert des Amateurs, the series opened in 1798 and offered a season of twelve concerts of both vocal and instrumental music. By 1803 its annual offerings had doubled. Admission was limited to subscribers, although those holding annual subscription passes could lend their cards to acquaintances if they were unable to attend a particular concert. A very respectable 600 subscribers joined in the first season. The price of subscribing for a single season was 48 francs for men, 36 francs for women, and half-price for children under fifteen.[3]

With its eighty players the orchestra was the largest in French musical history, and its public called it one of Europe's most polished. The *Allegemeine musikalische Zeitung* wrote that it was "the world's best in instrumental music and the finest in France in vocal performance," noting that the conductor led the group without stamping his foot or rapping a music stand with a bow.[4] Its audiences, too, were praised in superlatives. "The most enlightened music lovers, people of taste and the prettiest women (although they are sometimes indifferent to the beauties of a Haydn symphony) are all swept up in the enthusiasm."[5] The author of a small book on Paris credited the music of the series with easing the tensions of the Revolution. "There, all rivalries, party spirit, and animosities cease," he wrote. "One thinks only of art, one is committed solely to its progress."[6]

To a music lover, the charge of indifference to Haydn was serious, for he was the reigning master of all instrumental concerts. The French reception of Hadyn, widely noted but never satisfactorily explained, is nothing short of astounding.[7] For the first fifteen years of the nineteenth century, few concert programs were without at least one of Haydn's symphonies, and often two appeared in a single evening. Haydn is the "prince of instrumental music," wrote the *Journal des débats* in 1808. "He reigns without rivals in all our orchestras: no one contests the superiority of his talent in this genre." The *Tablettes de Polymnie* observed that Haydn was the only composer to possess "the rare privilege of always captivating spectators," and the *Correspondance des amateurs musiciens* called his music "the true model for every aspect of the art."[8] His symphonic music even turned up in ballets and operatic pastiches at the Opéra, where the troupe danced to snippets of his symphonies in

Le Volage fixé (1805), *Persée et Andromaque* (1810), and *L'Heureux retour* (1815).[9] In 1801 the Institut de France elected Haydn to associate membership, and in 1805 the Conservatoire honored him with a monument.[10]

Haydn was certainly the preferred composer at the Concert des Amateurs, and his symphonies soon became a particular speciality of the orchestra. The program typically contained two of his symphonies, one at the beginning and one at the end. Symphonies No. 103, "The Drum Roll," and No. 100, "The Military," were in greatest demand.[11] Sitting below a portrait of the composer, which hung in the hall on the rue de Cléry, spectators dizzy with delight forced the orchestra to repeat sections by thundering out applause between movements. Their enthusiasm was rapturous when Prince Esterhazy, Haydn's patron, came to a concert in 1803 and positively giddy when Haydn himself appeared there during a turn through Paris in 1802.[12]

Between the Haydn symphonies that framed their programs like bookends, the orchestra of the Concert des Amateurs performed works representing a wide range of genres. A typical program—this one was from an early-February concert in 1804—might contain as well an aria from *The Creation*, a *symphonie concertante* by Devienne for oboe, flute, bassoon, and horn, a vocal trio from Cherubini's *Hôtellerie portugaise*, and an aria from *Ariodant* by Méhul.[13] With the exception of a chamber series that played only string quartets and quintets, concerts in Paris would continue to follow this same eclectic and highly varied programming throughout the Empire and Restoration.

Sitting through a public concert without dramatic action to fix one's attention could be challenging for even the most devoted listeners, for many still considered instrumental music difficult by definition. Warning that a program of exclusively "learned" music or even virtuosic playing condemned the vast majority of listeners to "enforced boredom," Fortia de Piles declared in 1812 that "the true merit of a concert is variety."[14] Even the *Correspondance des professeurs et amateurs de musique*, which did all it could to encourage Parisian musical culture, observed that a concert was "a particular sort of spectacle that offers no dramatic interest as in tragedies, comedies, or paintings."[15] Some concert performers, such as a Mme Sassi, apparently trying to compensate for a public still learning to listen, appeared in full costume to sing an operatic excerpt.[16]

Performances by the Concert des Amateurs were held in an amphitheater not particularly appropriate for concerts. The seating was cramped and the acoustics concussive, but on good nights when the hall was filled, as one listener wrote, the public "muffles the sound sufficiently to keep spectators from going deaf."[17] Spectators arrived hours early to assure themselves a place; because there was only one exit the crush of people leaving the hall at the end of concerts was fierce.[18] But when the management proposed moving the series to a more attractive hall the musical press responded with nostalgia for the hall's quirks and inconveniences—almost as though its crude interior had kept away all but the true music lover. "The great silence that prevailed there, the scrupulous attention we gave to every piece and to the least musical phrase, and the resulting perfection have made them [the subscribers] worry that it would be completely different in a regular performance hall. There, every piece would be interrupted by the arrival and exit of the spectators, the opening and shutting of doors to the boxes would diminish or certainly change the musical effect so justly praised at the Cléry hall, and every spectator in the boxes would come more to show themselves than to listen or let others listen to the concert."[19]

This was a sensitive reading of the effects of a hall's ambience upon crowds and their behavior. And, at least initially, the fears of a fancier hall attracting a different sort of spectator were well founded. The Concert des Amateurs moved to a more comfortable concert hall on the rue de la Victoire furnished with boxes in February 1805, and for the first few concerts latecomers raised a commotion finding their seats. The press reported an overall coolness that fell far short of the excitement of the Cléry concerts. Gradually the listeners grew accustomed to the hall, however, and the press reported with relief that most spectators now arrived before the first symphony. As before, the lusty applause of the public routinely forced the orchestra to repeat movements.[20]

Yet despite the initial enthusiasm the series abruptly stopped after its first season in the new hall on account of a "lack of subscribers." The change from the first season seven years before with its 600 members was striking, and the cause was an element new to concert life now that the Old Regime's monopolies and patrons no longer existed—competition. Already musical audiences were beginning to segment themselves according to taste, and by mid-century the clientele of each concert and opera hall would have its own particular personality. But for the moment the aficionados of instrumental music were too few to support competing concert series.

In 1803, two years before the Concert des Amateurs folded, a new series began to offer regular public instrumental concerts. Founded by thirteen professional musicians, the Concerts rue Grenelle aimed at establishing a musical academy where skilled performances would alternate with amateur music-making. It offered two three-hour public performances weekly, with a symphony by Haydn on each concert. Two additional days were designated for performances by women, although spectators were limited to the families of performers, "in order to avoid embarrassment."[21] In addition to providing an abundant source of accessible instrumental music, the Concerts rue Grenelle regularly read through the new work of young composers who wished to hear their compositions before submitting them to public performance. As with the Concert des Amateurs, critics lavished praise on the orchestra of the Concerts rue Grenelle. At the start of the series, a journalist declared the group unmatched.[22] But the series shared the fate of the Concert des Amateurs, also for lack of sufficient subscribers, and at the end of the 1804 season it effectively folded, although several abortive attempts were undertaken to revive it over the next decade.[23]

A third major concert series that began in the first decade of the nineteenth century ultimately overtook the Concert des Amateurs and Concerts rue Grenelle in reputation and influence, the regular public performances, or Exercices, of students of the recently formed Conservatoire. Its official sanction from the government—not to mention its funding—was probably what allowed the series to survive in the still-small market for public concerts. The original purpose of the Conservatoire—martial music for festivals and wars—had by now been replaced by compositional instruction and training "to bring students to perfection in performance."[24]

The first public concert of the Exercices was 21 November 1801. After its initial 1801–2 season, held in the future home of the Concert des Amateurs on the rue de la Victoire, the Exercices moved to the rue Bergère. The Exercices had the right combination of virtuosity and unpolished enthusiasm to win audiences (professors were scattered throughout the orchestra). It was the latter that won over the critic for *Journal de Paris*. "I admit . . . that one can hear elsewhere as much precision, purity, and unity; but where else can one find such warmth of young blood, such youthful verve? They are radiant with fervor; their love for their art is a cult, and one knows how vibrant, ardent, enthusiastic youth's devotion can be."[25] The public apparently shared the sentiments: in 1807 receipts totaled 9,807 francs; in 1811 the figure stood at 15,949 francs; and in 1813 the Exercices brought in 24,627 francs.[26]

Haydn was the most popular composer among audiences of the Ex-

ercices. In the 144 concerts given between 1800 and 1815, his symphonies were played 119 times; until 1807 every concert opened with a
symphony by Haydn, and the practice continued for the majority of
concerts well into the 1810s.[27] "The Haydn symphony is ordinarily
the work that generates the greatest pleasure in a concert," wrote the
Journal de l'empire. "Those who come only for his music lose virtually
nothing—and sometimes even gain something—in leaving immediately after the symphony."[28] This was the apogee of Haydn's fame in
France. Enthusiastic parents watching every breath and bowstroke of
some young player and connoisseurs sizing up the sound of the ensemble never seemed to tire of him in the first dozen years of the
century. "Admiration and gratitude are inseparable from the name of
J. Haydn," enthused one musical review.[29] "This is not the kind of
music that makes you say, 'Sonate que me veux-tu?' " wrote the *Gazette
de France* about the symphonies, which, it reported, seized the attention of "the least experienced listeners as well as the most demanding
experts."[30]

The monumental success of Haydn in France throughout the early
years of the century stands in sharp contrast to the generally indifferent
reception of Mozart—and indeed any other representative of the Germanic symphonic style—in France. Mozart's work was certainly known
in France, and his name was "respectfully mentioned" by the cogno-
scenti. But, as the *Allegemeine musikalische Zeitung* continued, his symphonies were "rarely played and even more rarely understood."[31] An
1811 concert review in the *Journal de l'empire* reflects the widespread
bewilderment that the French public felt in the early nineteenth century
over the symphonies of Mozart. "I don't know what fantasy led the
orchestra to give the G minor symphony of Mozart, unless its intention
was to prove to the public how superior Haydn is to Mozart in the symphonic genre."[32]

During the nineteenth century Mozart would never gain the mythic
status in France that Haydn held during the Consulate and Empire, or
which Beethoven would achieve in the 1830s. By 1815, however, and
after Haydn's symphonies had dominated repertories for twenty years,
Mozart's works began to appear with some regularity on programs of
the Exercices.[33] In contrast to the coverage of Haydn's popularity, however, few newspapers reported the response of audiences to Mozart's
symphonies, an omission that suggests something less than whole-
hearted support. The critic for the *Journal des débats,* though speaking
of *Don Giovanni,* may well have put his finger on the same stumbling

block that prevented others from appreciating Mozart. "We have too much taste to put up with this complication of parts; we prefer that which is natural, simple, and touching." [34]

Alongside Haydn and the occasional Mozart, audiences of the Exercices heard overtures, *symphonies-concertantes*, and vocal excerpts from dramatic works. The string concerti of Viotti were performed there often, and Catel, Berton, and Boieldieu appeared with some regularity. One of the most popular French composers was Étienne-Nicolas Méhul, whose overture to *Le Jeune Henri* enjoyed such popularity that it sometimes appeared in successive weekly performances. [35] The work depicted a hunting scene: its opening andante suggests a sunrise in the forest, horns mark the arrival of the hunters through a sustained crescendo from pianissimo to fortissimo, a sharp kettledrum blow signals the kill, and the overture ends with a brief doloroso and final triumphant shouts of the hunters. [36]

The audience of the Exercices came to listen. Was it the silence of proud parents? The press read it as a tribute to the quality of playing. "At the bigger concerts one assembles in elaborate elegance, one gossips, and one listens to music as something superfluous; the true friend of art, however, will desire more pleasure from the student concerts of the Conservatoire where one meets only those who understand and love music and enjoy it wholeheartedly." [37] Of course there were cynics who maintained that the concerts' greatest attraction was the jewelry on display. One such observation came from the 1812 *Reflections of a Man of the World*, which declared confidently that a marionette show would draw the same crowds the Exercices attracted if the same beautiful women attended: "very few are there for the music." [38] But these judgments were rare. Although still small, the concert public in the Consulate and Empire already showed an attentiveness to the music that would emerge with such unanimity elsewhere in the late 1820s and 1830s.

The regular Exercices ended with the Bourbon Restoration. Mistrustful of the Conservatoire for its revolutionary origins, the new regime moved swiftly to eviscerate the institution. In 1815 the monarchy dismissed the founder and director of the Conservatoire, an aged Bernard Sarrette, whose past revolutionary associations made him a highly visible target. In the next year many other respected teachers, including Gossec and Catel, were released. A new school of music, the École Royale de Chant, was formed and staffed, which effectively terminated the Conservatoire as a vital element in French musical culture.

François Perne, the new director of the École Royale, recommended the Exercices be replaced with annual or biannual performances of instrumental, vocal, and dramatic works. Complaining of "too many symphonists," Perne instituted concerts with fragments of comic opera and spoken dramatic excerpts interspersed with instrumental music. He further declared his hope that as many members of the court would attend the performances as possible, so that the performances would acquire the reputation of pleasing "la bonne société." "Charmed to find themselves gathered together, these spectators will come to regard the Exercices as their own concert and will as a consequence only praise them."[39] There was one Exercice performance in 1817, one in 1818, two in 1819, and none in 1820. Altogether there were nineteen performances by the École Royale de Chant between 1815 and 1830, compared to 144 Exercices during the period 1800–15.[40]

One surviving sign of life was a series of public chamber concerts organized by virtuoso violinist and composer Pierre-Marie Baillot in 1814, which continued throughout the Restoration. In the early years Baillot offered a dozen performances a year in a hall that held 150 spectators. These programs typically began with a quartet by Boccherini and ended with a work by Baillot himself; chamber works by Haydn and Mozart and the Op. 18 quartets of Beethoven also appeared regularly.[41] No one could doubt the enthusiasm of Baillot's audiences. For some the sign of his success was the "religious respect" that inevitably prevailed—"even the ladies hold their tongue."[42] But the reverence did not spell utter silence. By the late 1820s the custom was to clap and call out while the music played, so that for the length of the concert, by one account, "the enthusiasm never ceased bursting out from every part of the hall."[43]

Baillot's following points to the emergent segmentation of audiences that was beginning to define the Parisian theatrical landscape, a specialization defined not only by taste but by status. Baillot's audiences during the Restoration were not "gens du monde," to employ the terms of one sympathetic listener, who went on to suppose that if these urban style setters only knew the pleasures of listening to the chamber masterpieces of Mozart, Haydn, and Beethoven they, too, would come en masse. "But the *gens du monde* only know and understand theater music; all the rest, however perfect it is, hardly seems to merit the name for them."[44]

The writer probably had the Théâtre Italien in mind when he mentioned "theater music"—or at least the music most closely associated with that theater, that of Rossini, which by now was appearing in performances all over Paris. With Rossini's stunning success arrangements of his works appeared for every conceivable combination of voices and instruments. By the late 1820s Rossini monopolized both public and private performances. One despairing critic claimed that by 1827 Rossini had forced Gluck, Mozart, Paisiello, Cimarosa, and Cherubini off concert programs, that a listener might hear one of his arias thirty or forty times in a single winter, and that even the exquisite ears of the dilettanti were beginning to grow dull. "Fontenelle cried, 'Sonata, what do you want?' I say, 'Sonata, where are you?' "[45]

12

In Search of
Harmony's Sentiments

Two themes dominated musical impressions in the first decade of the nineteenth century: that the greatest challenge in listening was in coming to terms with the instrumental music of burgeoning public concerts, and that the act of listening was an exercise in decipherment to find the meaning intended by the composer. Both were consistent with the structures of musical perception that prevailed during the Revolution. Listeners who kept a finger on the musical pulse of Paris just after the Revolution knew that instrumental concerts were entering mainstream cultural life, and to read their accounts of the concerts is to see just how difficult and foreign much of this music was. The listeners approached instrumental music as though they were at the theater, attuned to a supposed emotional or programmatic message of the pieces. They sometimes dreamed up little narratives to explain the mood, a method that worked for some pieces but not for all. One writer hailed a concerto by Viotti for its depiction of an abandoned lover in despair, for instance, while another damned an overture as "scientific" and beyond most ordinary listeners, who "like to recognize what the composer wanted to express."[1]

Into the 1810s, as numerous spectators' accounts attest, music that resisted any simple reading appeared in the concert repertoires.[2] The social history of concert life, together with the increasing internationalization of repertoires, would steadily erode this practice of listening as decipherment. The evolution of compositional techniques ensured that works heard in concerts and at the Opéra in the first twenty years of the century were of a nature ultimately incompatible with the reigning demand for a clear painting of human moods. Listeners recognized this. The moment represents a recalibration of attitudes in order to grasp music just beyond the border of sense, and a corresponding expansion in the horizon of aesthetic experience. The period 1800–1820 is thus a time of transition in aesthetic sensibility, when musical descriptions show that the urge to affix emotions to sounds was beginning to give way to a more romantic approach that refused to assign any determinate meaning whatever to music. Of course the timing and pace of this change varied from listener to listener; nevertheless, written accounts suggest that a number of them were consciously reconsidering basic assumptions of the previous generation. Concert and operatic repertoires provide the key to explaining this transition.

In the first ten years of the century musical descriptions gave a straightforward and familiar account of listening. G. A. Villoteau, whose 1807 treatise on aesthetics concentrated on the connections between music and language, wrote that musical expression "exists essentially in the melodious imitation of our passions."[3] Quatremière de Quincy, describing an essentially similar process, pointed to the subjectivity that musical experience entailed: "The magical power of the musical art forces us . . . to translate fugitive sounds into images and through innumerable other transpositions to complete within ourselves the effects of an imitation."[4] Others listed the images they imagined. The critic Castil-Blaze describes listening intently to the overture of a new opera to discern "what the author wanted to paint." Was it murderous passion about to strew the stage with blood? A fire? A rebellion? A battle? Listening within the framework that sought a single, objective musical meaning for each passage, Castil-Blaze writes with a musical innocence that would seem hopelessly naive to listeners a generation later. "The curtain rises, lightning pierces a cloud, and I am completely surprised not to have realized that the composer wanted to paint a storm."[5]

One listener's guessing game was another's exasperation. Harmony's new inroads into concert and operatic repertoires, a spectator wrote in a letter to the *Journal de l'empire*, has done nothing but prove its impotence. "I don't know if these laments are the passion of a lover's heart or a physical pain; if it's the soul or the body that suffers; if the sighs I hear announce the tears of betrayed love, some pain I don't perceive, or tears shed on a tomb."[6] The position pointed to the Achilles' heel of instrumental music in the minds of those who sought precise emotions as they listened: not all works would—or could—succeed in conveying an unambiguous mood. The trouble with the music that now filled concert programs, the correspondent concluded, was that either the mind reeled in a kaleidoscope of images or turned away bored from the Babel of notes.

This attitude goes far in explaining the extraordinary popularity of Haydn in France and the exceptionally slow start for Mozart.[7] Indeed Haydn's popular success—a success the *Journal des débats* insisted was earned without the pressure of "fanatics from the schools"—helps to explain the rapid rise of concerts in these years. For Haydn appealed even to those who believed that harmony was incapable of genuine expression.[8]

Simply stated, Haydn knew the secret of planting images and emotions in his music for his audiences to discover, or so audiences insisted. Listening to Haydn was like attending the opera. "One often forgets that these are mere instruments that produce such magical effects on the soul and intoxicate it with sweet sensations. One feels transported to the stage; it is as though one is watching a lyric spectacle where all the human passions are painted with this account of truth that, uniquely, can produce such strong emotions."[9] In his *Life of Haydn*, Stendhal imagines concerts in theaters where scenery corresponding to the "principal thought" of each work would be mounted on the stage as the music played. Stendhal cites a movement for which the image of a calm sea beneath a vast, clear sky would be appropriate.[10]

That the programmatic elements of Haydn's music attracted French listeners in the early years of public concerts is abundantly clear in their reaction to Haydn's *The Creation*, one of the most programmatic of all the composer's works. Based on the first two chapters of Genesis, *The Creation* is a musical rendering of the first six days of the world. In the oratorio Haydn employs patently imitative devices and a finely honed manipulation of moods to evoke animals and natural phenomena. The opening orchestral prelude portrays primordial chaos. Rhythmically irregular, harmonically unpredictable, and melodically disconnected, it suggests a churning, formless mass. ("You have doubtless noticed how I avoided the resolutions which one would have most expected," Haydn reportedly told an associate about the prelude. "The reason is that nothing has yet assumed form.")[11] Haydn continues his programmatic depictions throughout the work, distinguishing wind from clouds, thunder from hail, and rain from snow. In an aria about birds he evokes turtledoves with a playful melody of bassoons in thirds and imitates nightingales with a darting flute solo filled with trills.

The more ambitious evocations of the work touch more abstract

Example 11. "Vom tiefsten Meeresgrund wälzet sich Leviathan," from *The Creation*, Franz Joseph Haydn.

ideas—the grandeur of a lion, a coursing tiger, oxen grazing serenely in meadows, insects. The most compelling musical renderings in *The Creation* are not the mimetic depictions of birds, wind, and rain but those passages that create a feeling appropriate to the subject. Beneath the words "Vom tiefsten Meeresgrund wälzet sich Leviathan [From the deepest ocean bed Leviathan rolls up]" surges a ponderous double bass solo with a dainty ornamentation that approaches the ridiculous. (Are the grace notes of the passage a musical joke on the near pun *waltzen* [waltzes]/*wältzen* [rolls up]? See Example 11.)

"*The Creation* is the most beautiful subject upon which a poet and a musician may exercise their descriptive talent," a critic proclaimed after its Paris premiere. "For they are obliged, so to speak, to make nature pass in review. They must imitate all things, paint all things, from the sun and stars to the lowliest insect."[12] For this reviewer each object mentioned demanded a musical depiction, but it was far from certain whether music could meet the challenges of the text. "Haydn *did* paint, at least as far as the limits of his art allowed him. But I would ask those who went into ecstasies over the accuracy with which he imitated the bound of the horse, the agility of the stag, the roar of the lion, etc.: seriously, could you have guessed what these chords which seem so full of meaning expressed if the poet had not indicated the musician's intention? This is not at all a criticism of the composer; his art does not permit him to do any better."[13]

Music was a limited, earth-bound art, in other words, and Haydn did as well as any could. Others were less accommodating and pronounced Haydn guilty of hubris. "Haydn tried to roll back the boundaries of his art," wrote the *Journal de l'empire*; "he aspired to describe what cannot be described with music. His *Creation* is a piece of musical chaos."[14] (In his scorn the critic stumbled onto a line of logic that would lead the next generation to the infinite vistas of romantic musical experience, noting that the work achieved "several admirable harmonic effects while seeking tableaux that harmony cannot render.")[15] Whether successful in its intentions or not, Haydn's *The Creation* was recognized by the musically literate of the 1810s as a work at the apex of the art. It exhausted the signifying powers of harmonic music, whose sine qua non was programmatic, emotional, or "atmospheric" fidelity.

It goes without saying that a composer's expressive intentions do not always correspond with how his work is heard, but Haydn's own statements concerning musical expression lend a certain legitimacy to French responses from the period. It is evident that Haydn sometimes composed with extramusical associations in mind, even when he wrote so-called absolute music. Haydn explained that he had often "portrayed moral characters/characteristics [moralische Charaktere geschildert habe]" in his symphonies, citing one whose "dominant idea" was a dialogue between God and an unrepentant sinner.[16]

Although Haydn claimed that he rarely depicted specific images (thus departing from certain French perceptions of his work, as well as Grétry's goals), he affirmed a general association of ideas with instrumental music by the approval both explicit and tacit he gave to the subtitles attached to his symphonies. Haydn himself affixed the title "Le Midi" to his Symphony No. 7; Nos. 6 and 8 were soon called "Le Matin" and "Le Soir." He accepted the title "Laudon," the name of an Austrian field marshal, for his Symphony No. 69 ("the word 'Laudon' will aid the sale [of the keyboard arrangement] more than any ten finales," he wrote), and he apparently listed the nickname "Military" for No. 100 in his London notebook after audiences coined the tag. Some of the other nicknames—"Passione" (No. 26), "Alleluia" (No. 30), "Feuer" (No. 59), "Surprise" (No. 94)—flourished in Haydn's time but were not directly acknowledged by him; the rest came from other countries or were nineteenth-century creations.[17]

Of all Haydn's symphonies, Nos. 100 ("Military") and 103 ("Drum Roll") were the most popular among French concertgoers. This is hardly surprising. The "Military" is one of the most evocative of a particular, describable mood: its first movement has a distinctly martial theme, a solo trumpet sounds a fanfare for battle in the second movement, and in the last movement the bass drum and cymbals keep up a foursquare cadence. Symphony No. 103, the "Drum Roll," is more novel than strictly descriptive. It begins with an extended tympani roll that returns later in the movement. In the second movement Haydn makes use of eastern European folk tunes.

There were other popular Haydn symphonies in which French audiences could visualize concrete scenes or contemplate particular emotions. The subtitle "Clock" was first attached to Symphony No. 101 in 1798, when the Viennese publisher Johann Traeg published a piano reduction of its second movement and called it "Rondo—Die Uhr."[18] The designation derives from the "tick-tock" repetition of the second movement. Symphony No. 73, "La Chasse" ("Hunt") conjures a hunting scene in its last movement: violins hurtle through passages in aggressive virtuosic playing while the full orchestra maintains a driving, galloping rhythm. Even those French listeners who may not have known that Haydn took the clarion hunting-horn call of the symphony note for note from de Changran's *Manuel du chasseur* (Paris, 1780) could have clearly identified the spirit of the hunt in the music.

Several of Haydn's Paris symphonies written in the 1780s for the Concert de la Loge Olympique were soon given French subtitles to identify their presumed subjects. The oboe's impertinent pecking in the first movement of Haydn's Symphony No. 83 earned the work the title "La Poule" ("Hen"). Its numerical predecessor (actually composed after No. 83) has received what must certainly be the oddest designation for a symphony, "L'Ours" ("Bear"). (The bagpipe dance of the last movement was said to evoke visions of a dancing bear—surely a measure of the tenacity of the view that images could unlock difficult instrumental music.) Spectators had a different image to embroider when they listened to the Symphony No. 85, which was also composed for the Concert de la Loge Olympique. Marie Antoinette, who was present at its premiere in 1787, declared it her favorite of Haydn's works, and the symphony soon became known as "La Reine de France" ("The Queen of France"). The symphony probably brought a host of associations for its French listeners, as Haydn built the second movement around the French folk tune "La Gentille et jeune Lisette."

Haydn was the most popular composer during the first years of public concerts in France because his music best addressed the aesthetic expectations of French listeners. The programmatic, emotionally tangible nature of his symphonies kept them from foundering on the reef of abstraction at a time when a sizable portion of the public still declared abstract harmonies impenetrable. The image of Marie Antoinette as evoked by "La Gentille Lisette," or the thought of a hunt, a hen, a battle, or a bear gave the elusive sounds form. One author wrote that "La Reine de France" as a title was a way of "sharing a thought that brings glory to our land"; it allowed listeners to follow "the development of the action that is given to us."[19]

In comparison to the genial, eloquent Haydn, Mozart was positively gothic. When his symphonies were first performed in France, listeners complained that they couldn't see the subject. "The Symphony in C [No. 41, the 'Jupiter'] offers such harmonic riches," a review from 1810 reads, "and its effects are so scientifically complicated that it is only with a fatiguing attention that one arrives at following the details of the orchestra and forming an idea from the many tableaux of just what the composer wanted to draw."[20] Another newspaper observed that even the most experienced listeners had difficulty "deciphering" Mozart's symphonies.[21] The G-minor symphony (No. 40) was to another reviewer "nothing but a vain bundle of difficult harmony, without motif, melody, or life."[22] And the *Mercure de France* summarized Mozart's faults with devastating economy: he "passes continually from one idea to the next . . . mechanically piling effects upon effects."[23] The quip that there was "too much music" in Mozart's works was repeated elsewhere, but the history of listening in France made it particularly potent there.

The compositional style of early nineteenth-century French opera reinforced these *idées reçues* of musical expression. Spontini's efforts fall short of the majesty of Gluck, to be sure, but his intentions for musical expression were similar. Richard Wagner recognized him as Gluck's greatest successor in realizing the "opera-cantata."[24] Like Gluck,

Spontini attempted to create a sustained musical drama broken up nei-ther by *secco* recitative nor by grand arias that ended with crashing fi-nality. *Fernand Cortez, La Vestale*, and *Olympie* spin a continuous thread of music, as accompanied recitative moves seamlessly into aria and one scene moves quickly to the next. The end of *La Vestale* is typical. Licin-ius pleads for Julia's life, Julia steps into her sepulcher, a storm breaks out and lightning ignites the flame, Julia reappears, and the couple is happily united—all in a single musical moment. To hold all the requisite emotions within a single gesture, Spontini, like Gluck, crafted a distinct musical style to match each psychological mood.

More than any lyric composer for the French stage before him, Spontini relied upon shifts in tempo to convey changes in mood. His scores provide minute instructions for conductors and performers: "en-liven without changing the tempo," "rapidly and with fire," "slow down imperceptibly," "speed up imperceptibly."[25] In a brief duet that occupies scarcely five pages in the original score of *Fernand Cortez* there are no fewer than three different metronomic markings to follow, each tailored to the particular sentiment of the text.[26] Coupled with frequent changes in key and orchestral color, such flexibility gave the music a living, breathing quality. A duet between the Aztec Amazily—who has fallen in love with Cortez and accepts Christianity—and her brother Télasco changes key four times to reflect the emotions of the text. A raging Télasco begins in C minor as he abandons Amazily to the ven-geance of the "God of Mexico." The key shifts abruptly to F major, and Amazily prays for the "God of Cortez" to soften her brother. Télasco relents for a moment, and as the key changes to A-flat major he gently pleads with her to come home. Vengeance quickly returns in C minor as Télasco repeats his early rejection of Amazily, but when she quietly prays that her love might somehow save her brother and her country the to-nality of C major struggles weakly against all the raging sixteenth notes. The tonality remains, albeit unsteadily, until the end. The duet cannot in honesty be called a masterpiece of expression, as the key changes are unprepared and sometimes jarring, but the intent is unmistakable: each emotion demands its own music (see Example 12).[27]

In his Cornell University lectures in the late 1930s Edward J. Dent called Spontini the greatest producer of "characteristic" music, by which he meant that Spontini best conveyed the feeling appropriate to whatever group dominated a scene—gypsies, sailors, huntsmen, and the like.[28] Indeed *Fernand Cortez* is filled with military marches, and *La Vestale* is suffused with an affecting lyricism. But other composers

Example 12. Duet between Amazily and Télasco from *Fernand Cortez,* Gaspare Spontini.

Example 12. *Continued.*

of the Empire just as surely attempted to convey moods through their music. Le Sueur read widely hoping to intuit the music of ancient peoples for his operas. *Ossian* has a melodic and rhythmic strangeness, especially in the dances, that Le Sueur thought appropriate to third-century Caledonians and Scandinavians. The "Scandinavian Death Song" in the first act is constructed around an awkward motif, and a later sequence of dances has a modal, vaguely Scottish sound (see Example 13).[29] Le Sueur appended the score of *La Mort d'Adam* with learned speculations on "antique harmony" and wrote what he believed to be ancient Hebrew melodies and rhythms.[30]

This was the expressive vocabulary that composers had employed since the time of Gluck. While they probably confirmed the aesthetic expectations spectators had held since before the Revolution and shaped the views of those who were discovering opera for the first time, their sometimes weak exposition—within libretti that were weaker still—was not always compelling enough to hold the undivided attention of the public, particularly with the spectacle on the stage and Napoleon's appearances in the hall. For those attuned to ideas and images in music, Haydn's expressive gifts were certainly greater. Accounts of attentiveness in the Conservatoire Exercices, the Concert des Amateurs, and the Concerts rue Grenelle bespeak an audience engaged aesthetically, "translat[ing] fugitive sounds into images," as one of them wrote. But strict correlations between attentiveness and the music, accurate to a point, must be resisted as complete in themselves. There was the creeping silence of etiquette, too. Some of those quiet spectators might have merely been keeping up appearances while they thought about dinner.

In these decades of growing specialization among the musical public, generalizing about any common musical experience becomes more and more difficult. But it seems clear that by the late 1820s descriptions of operatic and instrumental music were pointedly excluding the extra-musical. The change first struck François-Joseph Fétis in 1828, when he remarked that ten years earlier people spoke of music imitating "certain effects"—waves, storms, birds, etc.—or expressing the passions; moreover, they never stopped railing against "science" in music. Now they spoke only of orchestral forms, modulations, stretti, and the like.[31]

Of course the transformation from seeking passions and images to reading the language of tones was in some respects a gradual evolution. For if it was true early in the century that, as an observer wrote, "the great Haydn is the only composer to possess the rare privilege of always pleasing auditors," it was also the case that less evocative and program-

Example 13. "Scandinavian Death Song" from *Ossian, ou les bardes*, Jean-François Le Sueur.

Example 13. *Continued.*

matic works also appeared on programs—concerti by Viotti, Dussek, and Baillot, overtures by Boieldieu, Berton, Cherubini, and Méhul, solo works by Steibelt and Spohr.[32] Repeated exposure to these works, which resisted any simple programmatic reading, likely seduced by sheer familiarity. There was also the dogged presence of Mozart, whose symphonies and operas were roundly denounced in the first decade of the century yet remained just as surely on programs. Already in the 1810s some of the initial bemusement was giving way to interest, and by the 1820s Stendhal could claim that the true dilettante was as enamored with Mozart as with Rossini. And it is conceivable that once listeners were hooked by the supposed descriptions in Haydn they gradually moved beyond thinking of hunts, battles, and queens to focus on the purely musical logic.

But the force of Fétis's realization—and the precision of his dates—points to something more than accommodation by osmosis. The language of these new kinds of descriptions implied a clean break with past conceptions, an outright rejection of the idea that music necessarily had to project tangible passions. If exposure to composers considered less gifted than Haydn in painting images slowly subverted the scheme of deciphering music's message, then a single composer, one whom all of musical Paris had heard with numbing frequency, gave it the coup de grâce: Gioacchino Rossini. Fétis himself recognized this, writing in the same passage that Rossini taught listeners to use a purely musical vocabulary. Tantalizingly the name was dropped in passing, and Fétis gave no explanation.

The revolution of Rossini, which did more than anything else in France to break the perceived bond between musical meaning and determinate content, was in the pure musical virtuosity he summoned. In Rossini's Italian works, *buffa* as well as *seria*, it's the brilliance that leaves the strongest impression. Rossini's acrobatic demands—the turns and trills, the chromatic runs, the rapid-fire diction and intricately coordinated ensembles—are explosive. The vocal brilliance in Rossini does not so much embody the emotions of the drama as exist alongside them, at some moments coinciding in happy harmony, at others merely approximating, and at others destroying them completely. In the virtuosic passages Rossini's music goes far beyond merely enhancing the dramatic force of the text. It overwhelms it, and sometimes buries it in a blaze of fioritura.

The finale endings to an act, where he strings together a series of numbers uninterrupted by recitative, are excellent examples of Rossini's powers to fine-tune for maximum effect. Finales with the greatest musical complexity typically come at the end of the first act in two-act operas (and near the end in one-act operas), when the characters are the most deeply entangled in the inevitable imbroglio.[33] There is considerable musical variety in tempo and key in the finales, with a sustained musical logic of key and rhythm that drives through to the last number.[34] Just as a clever phrase or tune starts to wear thin from repetition—and Rossini's technique in such moments was to repeat lines relentlessly, both for comic effect and to build momentum—Rossini will shift keys, abruptly introduce a new rhythmic pattern, or crank up the tempo a few more notches. While these changes often accompany a new twist in the plot, they are sometimes placed for uniquely musical effect, as in the sudden modulation in Gaudenzio's early comic aria in *Signor Bruschino*.[35] Such transitions often bring a jolt of additional energy, with the cumulative effect a calculated tension that grows to the last moment of the act. Rossini's famous *crescendo tutti*—where the harmonic rhythm quickens, the instruments jump up to a higher register, additional players are added successively, and the general volume increases—often caps the climax by bringing the whole orchestra to a boil.

Often in the comedies Rossini, taking a page from commedia de-ll'arte buffoonery, indulges in silliness for the pure fun of it. In the finale to the first act of *L'italiana in Algeri*, the shipwrecked Isabella is delivered to the court of the lecherous and bumbling potentate Mustafa, where she encounters her long-lost lover—now Mustafa's slave—and Mustafa's newly discarded wife. Everyone wants someone else, and Isabella's impudence before Mustafa only compounds the chaos. The seven-part ensemble is barely controlled confusion at lightning speed. They're upside-down, they sing, they're in a shipwreck, there's a bell in one's head, a hammer in another's, a third hears a crow, another a cannon, and soon they're swapping patter that crackles with excitement: "din, din, din"; "crà, crà, crà"; "bum, bum, bum"; "tac tac tac tac tac tac tac"; "bum bum bum bum bum bum bum"; "crà crà crà crà crà crà crà"—on and on in glorious defiance of dramatic nuance or, by this point, singularity of character (see Example 14).[36] The music exists for its own sake, and in the thick of things it's impossible to think of anything but the pyrotechnics.

Yet more astonishing in the works heard at the Théâtre Italien are the solo passages. The most famous is of course Figaro's "Largo al factotum" ("Fi-garo, Fi-garo, Figaro") from *Il barbiere*, but show-stopping virtuosic parts appear in all his works: Isabella's sixteenth-note passages in "Pensa alla patria" from *L'Italiana*, for example; the runs, arpeggios, and turns of Semiramis' "Bel raggio lusinghier" from *Semiramide*; Amenaide's flying leaps in "Giusto Dio" from the second act of *Tancredi*; Desdemona's treacherous ascents in the second-act finale of *Otello*; and so on (see Example 15).[37] When performed well such passages provoked explosions from the hall, and those who rose to the challenge—Nourrit, Levasseur, Davide, Viardot, Sontag, Mainvielle-Fodor, Pasta, Mallibran—were instant celebrities.

The effects of Rossini's writing went well beyond admiring the virtuosic singers. The parts that sent singers straight into the stratosphere and barreling back down with the unstoppable momentum of a locomotive were pure fun to listen to—too much fun, in fact, to complain that Rossini lacked emotional nuance, or pictorial power, or whatever other categories earlier spectators had used to dismiss music. The old epithets for music with "too many notes"—scientific, mathematical, lifeless, and so on—dissolved in the glory of electrifying coloratura and bone-rattling rhythms. Music, for the first time in the history of French musical experience, aroused great emotion without conveying it. It created an effect without wrapping it in an image.

Rossini led Parisians the farthest distance possible from the austere aesthetic of Gluck, who had deliberately avoided, as he put it in the

Example 14. Excerpt from the Finale to Act I of *L'italiana in Algeri*, Gioacchino Rossini.

Example 14. *Continued.*

Example 15. Excerpt from "Pensa alla patria" from Rossini's *L'italiana in Algeri.*

Example 15. *Continued.*

preface to *Alceste*, "making displays of difficulty at the expense of clearness."[38] The Restoration historian Augustin Thierry described what amounted to the reverse of Gluck's credo in his harsh evaluation of Rossini. "Rossini has added nothing to the progress of music. Melody and harmony are squandered haphazardly and without discernment in order to amuse the ear, but also done in such a way that when the ear is amused the mind must withdraw so moral displeasure will not disturb the physical pleasure . . . [Rossini] does nothing with the principal passion. The scenes of confusion, surprise, noise, imbroglios—this is worthy of his verve. He didn't even bother to make Rosina and her lover love each other."[39]

Surely the judgment is wrong, at least in the absence of some strong qualifications. As Philip Gossett has written, Rossini often takes pains to capture the emotional nuances of a situation, emphasizing, for example, Angelina's confused naivete in *La cenerentola* with rapid declamation and spare orchestral parts, or, in a tenor aria (no. 14) in *Equivoco*, matching a dramatic structure of rage, suffering, and again rage with a musical structure of allegro, andante, and allegro.[40] But it is also true that the vocal and orchestral brilliance *does*, occasionally, set the wrong dramatic mood. In such places, as Thierry observed, to listen is to suspend dramatic associations. In the *seria* operas the music can sometimes sound a bit too merry (even when the theme is matricide, as in *Semiramide*). The *seria* libretti—*Semiramide, Tancredi, Otello, Mosè, Elisabetta*—demand sober music, and, as Winton Dean observes, Rossini's successes here are at best mixed.[41]

So what was winsome in the comedies struck French ears as shallow in the serious works. Joseph d'Ortigue ridiculed the "shocking contradictions between the expression and the subject" in Rossini's writing, and Stendhal, with no malice toward Mozart, wrote that "Rossini always amuses, Mozart never amuses." Beethoven reportedly quipped that Rossini should have stayed with comedies.[42] A similar slippage occasionally occurs between the musical character of overtures and the overall dramatic character of the plot. Even for those who know the bloody, incestuous tale of *Semiramide* the overture is a jolly affair, and the long crescendo that ends it almost always sets feet tapping and heads bobbing happily along. That Rossini used overtures written for one opera to open others suggests reduced concern for crafting a particular emotional valence for each overture: that of *La gazza ladra* was employed in *La cenerentola*; that of *La pietra del paragone* in *Tancredi*; that of *Aureliano in Palmira* first in *Elisabetta* and then in *Il barbiere*.[43]

Through their brilliant vocalism and orchestral effects, as well as the gulf that sometimes opened between musical and dramatic impact, Rossini's operas achieved, forcefully and decisively, what the concerts of the 1810s had begun to produce ever so tentatively. They made audiences listen to music, not as imitation or image or emotion, but as sheer music. In the breathless responses to Rossini from the Théâtre Italien come sustained discussions of music apart from any extramusical crutch, a sure sign that the works were transforming the way spectators listened. A critic for the *Journal des débats* writes:

I'll never forget the sensation I felt during the victorious, rapidly rising chromatic scale written by Rossini that ends the second act of *Otello*. All the most famous Desdemonas have cheated there before, but Mademoiselle Sontag sang it with such force and freedom that I bounced on my bench. From that moment I have possessed my complete *Otello.* Go ahead, criticize this singer on the rest of the role, say that she is inferior to her estimable challengers, fine. It doesn't matter. I have my chromatic scale.[44]

Although the singers received the greatest attention from audiences, the listeners also commented on Rossini's orchestral writing from a purely musical perspective. His use of harmony sounded exotic to French ears accustomed to the tamer progressions of such composers as Le Sueur, Gluck, Salieri, and Spontini. As one early supporter wrote in a tribute to Rossini, "however experienced the ear may be in seizing the nuances of harmony, it still needs to habituate itself to this sound." The spectator goes on to say that despite her best efforts she can appreciate neither the beginning of Rossini's operas nor the end; the mental exertion needed to make sense of the harmonies takes time, she relates, and yields only a certain amount of pleasure before the mind grows dull, irritated, and incapable of judging. "At that moment," she concludes, "you just have to leave the hall—you're dead."[45] These are the words of a reader struggling with a new expressive language, one that demanded comprehension on its own terms and required a fixed, focused attention.

The *crescendo tutti* also grabbed the attention of spectators with its insistent surge. "The orchestra's waves rise from sea level to the clouds, always accelerating their agitation, ever heightening their roar," a listener writes in a long, lyrical sentence; "pleasing chords follow harsh and lacerating chords, chords that move above an insistent, tenacious, even stubborn bass that stays on a single tone; the white and sparkling froth of the melody arrives at its zenith to proclaim its brilliant triumph, and the whole audience is animated, excited, carried away; a thunderbolt of applause answers the musical lightning, the dénouement, foreseen but always feted, of the *crescendo.*"[46]

Exposed to Rossini's techniques for a decade and more, in chamber concerts and on both major operatic stages, listeners learned the logic of pure music. They heard a master composer break the emotional link between musical feeling and precise dramatic mood forged by Gluck and burnished by Spontini, Le Sueur, and Catel. The music was so compelling, and so compellingly sung, that it gained a signifying logic of its own. Some of course dismissed Rossini as chaotic and soulless, but others said that his music changed even the way earlier compositions sounded. As the anonymous author of a pamphlet in praise of Rossini and his works "strong in harmony" wrote in 1821, "I'm not sure if it means an advancement or a decline in taste, but over the last several years our earlier works—those compositions whose only merit was their simple, true, direct melodies—have received nothing more than polite applause and the kind of success that is deeply troubling to the cashier."[47]

Runs were judged for the notes hit or missed, orchestral effects were anticipated and applauded, harmonies were penetrated with unprecedented effort not to find any presumed connection to the text but to understand their musical language. Ironically what some have called the dramatic weaknesses of Rossini—the periodic misalliance between sound and sentiment—redounded to the glory of the music. During the decade that Rossini ruled unchallenged there occurred in the minds of listeners a silent revolution that prepared them for the next musical titans to come: Beethoven, whom the public rejected earlier as incoherent only to be astonished now by his accessibility, and Meyerbeer, whose dense harmonies and blood-curdling plots aroused the bourgeois imagination.

13

The Social Roots of Silence

In *The Fall of Public Man* Richard Sennett provides a psychological explanation tied to urban growth and the rise of capitalism to account for the greater silence of audiences in mid-nineteenth-century theaters. Isolated from others by the city's segmentation into *quartiers*, Sennett argues, forced into public transactions as a consumer without the human contact of the market, afraid of exposing himself as gauche by a faux pas, the nineteenth-century bourgeois withdrew into unhappy passivity. For Sennett, the silence of the spectator was a sign of profound self-doubt, an indication that audiences were projecting their own emotional needs onto stage performers, who alone acted freely and showed feeling spontaneously in public. Critics flourished in this collective crisis of confidence, Sennett writes, because "the public was losing faith in its own capacity to judge."[1] At the center of silence was fear. "The mid-19th Century audience, at both concert and theater, worried about embarrassment, about being ashamed, about 'making fools of themselves' on terms and to a degree that would have been incomprehensible to the audiences of Voltaire's time, who were enjoying themselves thanks to the efforts of a high class of servants."[2]

Although noble titles flourished under Napoleon and two kings—David Higgs estimates that some 7,000 new titles of nobility were granted in these first three decades of the century—the economic changes upon which Sennett constructs his thesis make the period 1800–1830, rather than the decades after 1830, the time to map the emergent social psychology of the bourgeoisie.[3] It is true that the later July Monarchy, beginning in 1830, was the period of unrivaled bourgeois ascendancy in France, but it was during these thirty years that the bourgeoisie began to forge its orienting values. Sennett's portrait of a bourgeoisie wary of public spontaneity and conspicuousness jibes with spectators' accounts, but they also convey the image of a confident and proud, rather than skittish, bourgeoisie. The two aren't necessarily incompatible. To display proper manners confidently and knowingly went with success as its virtual companion; but the nature of that success also entailed caution, prudence, and, perhaps at the extreme, fear.

Equality before the law was the most enduring legacy of the French Revolution, and it was arguably the most essential feature of bourgeois self-conception. The Revolution's abolition of castes and the establishment of civil equality was, to the liberal historian Mignet, "without contradiction the most profound and complete change to renew the nature of civil society in France."[4] As enshrined in the Napoleonic *Code civil* and confirmed in the 1814 Charter, civil equality opened careers to talent and eliminated all juridical obstacles to social ascent.

Napoleon's establishment of his own "nobility" reinforced this principle of social advancement thorough merit. Following the same logic that borrowed revolutionary musical forms to protect against revolution, Napoleon's sweeping honorific system, with its princes, dukes, and barons, was a firewall against a return to royalism. A new nobility, as Cambécérès commented in 1807, was "the only means of wholly uprooting the old."[5] By the end of the Empire Napoleon had bestowed titles upon some 3,200 individuals, only 22.5 percent of whom had been nobles before 1789.[6] By forbidding the use of any title not granted by the regime, Napoleon effectively replaced the aristocracy of the Old Regime with his own hand-picked elite.

"I have permitted each to arrive anywhere, from everywhere," Napoleon boasted of his *noblesse*. "My act is popular because it consecrates equality from the very start: talent, courage, and wealth decide the rest."[7] None were more aware of this than the blood aristocrats, who saw the death of their own social eminence in the soldiers and self-made men who paraded their tastes and titles before them. "Fighting a rear-guard action in their salons," Louis Bergeron writes, "the survivors of 1789 were the first to proclaim that their rivals of 1808, despite somewhat vulgar appearances, were the great victors in a replacement of elites."[8]

This civic emphasis upon personal merit and wealth continued under the Bourbon Restoration, which recognized all imperial titles as legitimate and instituted an electoral system whereby only those with a specified minimum amount of land could vote. The electoral law particularly favored the nouveaux riches. Despite Louis XVIII's insistence that 1814 marked the nineteenth year of his regime—thus denying the Revolution and Empire in a single stroke—the king took his cue for staffing his administration from the changes of those last twenty years. "We have always sought to fill the functions of mayors [*maires*] and assistant mayors [*adjoints*] with what we formerly called the *haute bourgeoisie* of Paris: retired bankers, notaries, lawyers, and solicitors," a minister of the king wrote in 1821.[9] The tax rolls of 1820 show just how quickly society had changed since the Revolution: of the 1,967 most-taxed individuals, a social elite who had the privilege of voting twice, only seventy-two were nobles from the Old Regime.[10]

The outlines of a changed etiquette took shape as society's new notables began filling out audiences. Statistics tell what these spectators knew firsthand, many from their own experience—that with a taste for hard work, good business sense, and a bit of luck a man might rise from obscurity to wealth. Under the Restoration, a mere 20 percent of the richest bourgeois paying 1,000 francs or more in tax were descended from established notable families, a figure that shows the Restoration to have been more propitious than even the July Monarchy for dramatic social ascent.[11] While the new men took up the trappings of wealth— multiple residences, objets d'art, horses, personal libraries—they retained the spirit that earned them their prominence. At its core was a devotion to work and disdain for indolence. In her magisterial studies of the French bourgeoisie, Adeline Daumard concludes that the Restoration's notables were more likely imitated than imitators in their cautious habits of life; and contrary to a popular myth, returning émigrés were not blind to the changes since 1789, one of which was that wealth, not birth, meant power.[12]

Those who succeeded told themselves that anyone could, a view in part justified by the social transformations, but one that eventually took on the sound of a mantra. "The constitutional aristocracy . . . is composed of grand notabilities that support themselves with their fortune, whether they owe it to the heritage of their fathers, their work, or their talents," declared the *Constitutionnel*. "Anyone of the inferior classes who has intelligence and probity will enter with his family the ranks of the bourgeoisie," wrote the *Journal des débats*.[13] And the *Revue française* insisted that the bourgeoisie was "not a class closed at either end, organized as an aristocracy, and driven by a single interest."[14] So ran the great liberal credo, chanted with conviction by Guizot and his fellow *doctrinaires*, a tenet of faith for the successful and the merely hopeful. The Revolution had not done away with distinctions after all, but henceforth they would be rooted in capacities and abilities. The *doctrinaire* political vision of a superior ruling class drawn continuously from the polis encased an apt metaphor for the marketplace, too: from equality of opportunity would grow, naturally and beneficially, a new aristocracy.[15] "The characteristic of representative government," according to the *doctrinaire* duc de Broglie, "is in extracting from the nation an elite composed of the most enlightened, to bring them together at the summit of the social edifice, in a sacred place, inaccessible to the passions of the multitude, and to have them debate openly the interests of the state." [16]

A bourgeois self-conception suited to this climate of economic and political winnowing—a sort of happy proto-Darwinism oblivious to red tooth and claw—emerged from Restoration-era successes. Self-made, the bourgeois was convinced that personal qualities produced success. "I am a parvenu, . . . a soldier of '93," general de Pelleport proudly proclaimed on being made a baron of the Empire and peer of France. "I date only from myself." [17] But if the profits were large, the pretensions stayed modest. Ostentation, extravagance, resting on the fruits of one's labor without ploughing the returns back into the business made bad economic sense and, perhaps worse, reflected poorly on one's character. As de Tocqueville observed, the craving for material well-being among moderns was often coupled with the "private virtues" of family love, a sense of decorum, respect for religion, and moral rectitude.[18] Where earlier elites were assured of their status by birth, the bourgeois knew that his place was to be continually won and that negligence might bring a reversal of fortune. A ruined aristocrat was still an aristocrat; a ruined bourgeois was déclassé.[19]

Hence the vigilance. It was with good reason that one of Balzac's images for the bourgeois of Paris was the wheel of fortune that dealt out wealth one instant and disaster the next. "The bourgeoisie isn't a class, it's a position," cautioned the *Journal des débats*, "you acquire it, you lose it." The newspaper warned particularly against "vice, dissipation, and laziness." [20] In post-revolutionary France bourgeois propriety was perpetual, and perpetually on view, always proving itself in the street, in the law-courts, at the theater.

The golden rule of bourgeois decency was not to bother others. A civil regard for one's fellows took the place of the insolent neglect or disdainful charity that flourished naturally in the Old Regime. It would probably be unfair to suggest that every considerate spectator saw in his neighbor a potential client, but the possibility cannot be dismissed that correct demeanor in commercial transactions crept into the concert setting. Abel Goujon certainly believed that gross ambition among the powerful precluded proper manners, writing in his 1822 *Manual for the Man of Refinement* that "good society exists in the middle class [*classe mitoyenne*], whose spirit has not been stifled by servile work and whose heads have not been dazzled by ambitious ideas."[21]

Whatever the motive, etiquette books of the Restoration counseled a certain fastidiousness in order to avoid disturbing others during performances. Goujon wrote that it is the "highest breech of politeness" to hum with the music, beat the rhythm with one's head, hands, or feet, or otherwise "distract attention" from a concert. It was likewise unfitting to turn one's back to the stage, he wrote, to speak aloud while performers were on the stage or to offer a running commentary on the work or its execution. "Nothing is more unbearable for your neighbors, who have gone to the spectacle to watch the performance, not to hear ridiculous criticism."[22]

Hence a public by turns confident and cautious, proud of its regular spot in the theater and respectful by habit. But there was also an edge to the rhetoric of proper manners, a tone of aggressiveness that carried exclusionary connotations, both in the etiquette books and in their popular enforcement during the Empire and Restoration. The emergent code of silence during performances was more than an innocent and unreflective consequence of a certain work ethic. Audiences reasoned on some level that if politeness was necessary to succeed, its absence signaled inferiority. Policing manners thus became an act of self-reassurance. It confirmed one's social identity by noticing those who didn't measure up, whether through (choose your label) ignorance, laziness, bad upbringing, insensitivity, or overall dullness.

There is particular irony in proper bourgeois audiences using politeness as a club to pound away at the *gaucheries* of misfits. Note the language of one listener appalled by the talking that went on during performances: "For Heaven's sake, wait, you merciless blabbermouths, wait until the intermission to satisfy your terrible talkativeness. Wouldn't the slightest bit of education tell you that it shows the worst taste to talk aloud in a public place, where all attention should be directed toward the characters on the stage? Honestly, one would think you had lived your whole life in the woods, and that you found yourself in good company completely by accident."[23] This was the same outward indignation (but inwardly preening: "I know better than to do *that!*") that would later furrow brows at applause between movements.[24] It was apparently present during a recital by the violinist Lafont. "One-half of the hall acted as police, so to speak, and demanded silence."[25]

Edmond Goblot's 1925 essay *La Barrière et le niveau* treats this feature of bourgeois psychology brilliantly.[26] Goblot accurately characterizes the borders of the post-Revolutionary bourgeoisie as considerably less permeable than the *doctrinaire* mythos of the time proclaimed. But because its boundaries were unclear at both ends if judged strictly by wealth, bourgeois identity was in large part dependent upon confirmation by other members of the bourgeoisie. While the bourgeois viewed his class as egalitarian for those within it—the "level" of the essay's title—class identity implied boundaries to others, barriers that clearly marked the social terrain.

A distinctive set of behaviors emerged to help define and police those borders. (As Balzac observed rather less abstractly, "Savoir-vivre, elegant manners, an undefinable quality, these are the fruit of a thorough education and form the only barrier between a lazy man and a productive man.")[27] Politeness became central to the self-conception of the bourgeoisie, Goblot suggests, because it both leveled and excluded, maintaining equality within the class and refusing membership to those who failed to master its nuances. This duality reverberates through the pages of Restoration-era etiquette books. "In politeness, all men are equal," reads the title page of an 1828 handbook, which goes on to describe the appropriate manners for concerts. If you find yourself in an excruciating performance, it counsels, discreetly cover your face with your hands or a handkerchief to avoid showing discomfort.[28]

Politeness was no respecter of persons. It was anonymous and rule-bound where mid-eighteenth-century theater behavior had involved personality and imitation. Bourgeois politeness gave allegiance to an abstract ideal of decency. One author hit just the right tone of pious impartiality to damn all who had left a concert early. "We will permit ourselves no reflection on this conduct, which did not seem to us entirely keeping with the rules of decency."[29] With faceless rules of decency enforcing respectability, the "powdered wigs" who insisted upon talking at the Opéra—presumably aristocrats brought up in another time—were as little immune from bourgeois criticism as eccentric dilettanti like Théophile O'Neddy. The bourgeoisie, as Goblot writes, "disdains all forms of superiority that seem largely or uniquely based in advantages exterior to the person, whether in wealth or in the luxury of dress, an

Figure 16. Montand, *Un Concert à la chaussée d'Antin*. Musée Carnavalet.
© 1993 ARS, New York/SPADEM, Paris.

expression of wealth."[30] For as distinguished as the bourgeois considers
himself to be, he eyes others warily who stand out from the crowd.
Note, for example, the conformity in dress and behavior (with one mischievous exception on the far left) in *Un Concert à la chaussée d'Antin*
(Figure 16).[31]

Stendhal's fear that politeness would stifle spontaneous responses to
Rossini was soon borne out. The melomanes of later decades were *lions*,
the romantic men-about-town, sought after for their good looks, imitated for their fashions, but not for a moment considered eccentric. Increasingly in the 1830s spectators—including those most serious about
music—placed themselves within the secure borders of bourgeois identity. This was the paradox of bourgeois individualism, a predicament
that echoed beyond the concert hall and opera house. How could a society built upon the virtue of individualism breed conformity? Alexis de
Tocqueville, who understood his journey to America as a glimpse into
the future of European democracy, wrote that the principle of equality
rendered Americans at the same time more independent and more subject to conformity. Faced with a society of equals, the individual feels

Figure 17. Honoré Daumier, *Une Victime de la politesse.* Musée Carnavalet.
© 1993 ARS, New York/SPADEM, Paris.

slight and insignificant. "This very resemblance gives them almost un-
bounded confidence in the judgment of the public; for it would seem
probable that, as they are all endowed with equal means of judging, the
greater truth should go with the greater number." [32]

Bourgeois politeness: for audiences of the Empire and Restoration, it
was a source of status and a reminder of its fragility. But in the history
of listening it was more than this. In labeling a range of responses unacceptable, and defining when the acceptable ones could be expressed,
politeness directed musical responses inward, carving out for social rea-

sons a private sphere of feeling that in earlier generations had been public. Perhaps the emotions, now bottled up and interiorized on account of good manners, were no more intense than those felt by the sobbing public of the 1770s or the exultant audiences of the Revolution, but they were more personal and certainly seemed more subjective. The social elements of romantic musical experience—quite apart from its musical sources—were coming into place.

Bourgeois politeness had still another effect upon musical experience, one known chiefly by those who felt the social pressure without hearing the musical wealth. Politeness invented boredom. Happy were the days when you could mill about the parterre if the singing got monotonous, or visit the next box when you heard a good conversation, or continue with your parlor sketches as the musicians played from over in the corner. Now indignant spectators were bearing down sanctimoniously with all the weight of "propriety." Now they made you listen. Politeness may have created a private space for inner communion, but it also had its victims (see Figure 17).

PART FIVE

The Musical Experience
of Romanticism

We have long had artists of the first order in France;
we simply lacked listeners. Now we have them, or almost.

La France musicale, 17 January 1838

14

Operatic Rebirth and the Return of Grandeur

It seemed like all of Paris was present when Albéric Second took his seat at the Opéra. The overture to Rossini's *William Tell* had just ended, and Second was wondering only half facetiously if the roof would collapse from the roaring ovations. He looked around before the music started up again, trying to make out faces in the dimmed light across the vast hall—both the darkness and the size of the hall made it difficult. With some effort he recognized journalists, actors, stockbrokers, lawyers, and politicians. As far as he could tell the boxes were packed, and the parterre, the amphitheater, the orchestra, galleries, and balconies seemed to be overflowing. The curtain rose on a Swiss mountain village so stunning in illusion—two cozy chalets in the foreground and the Alps behind them, villagers in straw hats coming down from the hills, girls swinging wicker baskets filled with flowers, a peasant gliding across the lake in a skiff—that Second quickly forgot where he was.[1]

Since the 1830 Revolution the Opéra had come back to life. After limping through the 1810s and 1820s with a debt as intractable as the boredom, the Opéra suddenly turned around. Spectators tried to capture the feeling. Charles de Forster saw a buzzing, industrious beehive in his imagination whenever he took his seat before the music started, the parterre full and the people leaning forward and back in their seats, turning to one side and then the other to talk with excited animation.

Part-opening illustration: Detail of Honoré Daumier, *Le Banc des amateurs: Vue prise à l'Opéra*. Musée Carnavalet. © 1993 ARS, New York/SPADEM, Paris.

"The impatience is terrible! Then, suddenly, the three knocks are heard, a prolonged *shh*! runs through the hall, a magical silence follows. Habeneck raises his arms, and with the movement comes forth a wave of harmony that washes over this vast place, where thousands of receptive ears take in the rich sounds."[2]

It was natural to focus on the conductor, Habeneck, by now a celebrity with his dual posts at the Opéra and the Société des Concerts. There he was at the front of the hall, silhouetted against the stage lights, a violin in his left hand and the bow dancing above his head. He faced the singers—was practically under their noses at the edge of the stage—with his back to the orchestra, who sat facing him with their backs to the spectators. The system made imminently more sense than the earlier more obstreperous method of pounding out time with a stick. Credit went to the players, who were now good enough to keep together without the continuous thumping.[3]

The curtains and the lights added much to the theatrical illusion. After a decade and a half of refinements, engineers by the late 1830s controlled the gas lights with considerable skill. This meant not only some impressive sunsets on the stage but the ability to lower the houselights during performances. (The idea of dimming the lights for performance was still novel enough to cause a stir when Franz Liszt darkened the hall in 1837 for Beethoven's "Moonlight" Sonata.)[4] By the 1830s the curtain went up and down with each act, at last framing the dramatic action to make the fiction truly convincing.

Once the curtain was up and the action underway most spectators at the opera fell into rapt silence. "As the singing opened out wide and majestic, the interest grew," *L'Artiste* reported of Meyerbeer's *Robert le diable*, a work that premiered two years after Rossini's *William Tell*. "There was a silence, an attention, an amazement, an admiration, all of it interrupted by bravos at every instant. . . . Men, women, they all applauded, they were all drunk with enthusiasm."[5] For some it was the shredding vocal parts that riveted attention; others mentioned Meyerbeer's orchestral parts that stunned with their sheer weight; still others cited the romantic imagery of the sets with their caverns, cliffs, and gothic cathedrals. And then there was the chorus of debauched nuns who slid out of their habits to swivel and gyrate and guzzle down wine. This was Grand Opera, assured to widen the eyes and hasten the heartbeat of the bourgeoisie. French Grand Opera revolutionized the art by uniting drama, stage design, and music to create an aesthetic whole as potent as any the French lyric stage had seen. But of equal importance to the overall intoxication was its audience, a public primed to listen critically and watch with undivided attention. If Meyerbeer, his librettist Eugène Scribe, and the chief stage designer Pierre Cicéri were the musical mesmerists of the July Monarchy, their bourgeois audiences were ready to be entranced.

The surge in the Opéra's popularity after 1830 was no accident, however, no mysterious convergence of musical style and popular taste brought ineluctably together by the spirit of romanticism. After 1830 there was money to be made in opera, so the director who took the risk and invested the capital had an interest in knowing exactly what would attract the bourgeoisie.[6] Louis Véron, self-described bourgeois, director of the Opéra from 1831, physician, journalist, promoter, and businessman extraordinaire, sensed not only what the bourgeoise would like on the stage but what would make them comfortable in the hall. His tenure was short—four years—but the changes he brought were profound and lasting.

In retrospect Véron's investment seems failproof. The success of Rossini at the Théâtre Italien and Beethoven at the Société des Concerts, a symphonic society inaugurated in 1828, was evidence that the newly wealthy were willing to spend money on musical entertainment; moreover, it implied a taste for works significantly different from the ephemera that had held the Opéra stage for most of the 1820s. Yet the Opéra had considerable baggage the bourgeoisie might just as soon avoid. Véron was well aware of the aristocratic associations that had gotten a second wind (however weak) during the Restoration. An 1831 interview with a supporter of the deposed Bourbon branch of the monarchy and self-described spokesman for the aristocracy revealed the hostility still felt among the old habitués of the Opéra toward the nouveaux riches. The 1830 Revolution would do nothing to change audiences, the man insisted. Aristocrats would continue to occupy the most prominent places, no major family would boycott performances for political reasons, and above all "bankers, men of commerce, money makers, and notaries' wives" would not set the tone there. "You will replace us nowhere," he announced defiantly, "for though there is no longer a court you will still see us at the head of society."[7]

But the 1830s promised otherwise, and Véron knew it. (No one, as Philarète Chasles said, had "such a nose for the scent of profit, or such a greyhound speed for running it down.")[8] The government ministers kept insisting, after all, that 1830 had been a "bourgeois" revolution. Immediately upon assuming the directorship Véron lowered ticket prices and renovated the interior of the hall to attract audiences of greater frugality and less ostentation. At the high end of the scale, the price for a first-level box came down from 10 francs to 9, and the least expensive places—those on the highest balcony on either side—were reduced from 3 francs 60 to 2 francs 50. The gesture was probably more important symbolically than for its actual saving, which was negligible. The last time prices had come down at the Opéra was during the Revolution, thirty years before.[9] The bulk of the Opéra's audiences would still be those privileged members of society, the upper bourgeoisie, whose incomes could line life with comfort and pleasure.

Aware of the growing calm during performances around Paris, and as ever seeing a chance to increase profits, Véron decisively put an end to the practice of treating boxes as little salons by making most first- and second-level boxes smaller by two places, from six to four. The change at once increased the total number of boxes and reduced the price of subscribing, a modification intended, as Véron explained, to suit "the fortunes and the habits of economy of the new 'grand seigneurs' of the third estate who had replaced those of Charles X."[10] It would in addition make it more difficult to arrange chairs for guests who might drop in, although the question was largely moot since a new regulation requested spectators not to leave their seats once performances had begun.[11]

If the new arrangements helped to fix the attention of spectators on the stage by discouraging social calls, other improvements in the hall did their part by eliminating some of the unexpected nuisances that had emptied seats pell-mell in the past. Steam heat replaced the portable warmers whose fumes sent occupants tumbling out of boxes gasping for air twenty years before. The mini-explosions from gas lights in the hall were eliminated with refinements in the lighting system, and the administration even boasted in 1834 of new ventilation for the latrines.[12] In the early 1840s the management refurbished the seats in the hall, putting backs on the benches in the parterre, replacing any remaining hay stuffing with horsehair and exchanging the benches in the new galleries for armchairs.[13] Slowly the hall grew more comfortable (see Figure 18).

Véron added other touches in the 1831 renovation to give the hall a more popular feel. Since 1821, the year the company moved to the building on the rue Le Peletier, the interior colors had been as clean and dignified as the monarchy's white flag with fleur-de-lys: the first-level boxes were white with gold trim and the rest of the boxes were white with blue trim. Véron apparently wanted a different mood (again the national flag, this time that of the new regime, comes to mind), and the

Figure 18. Bertrand Ferdinand, *L'Opéra avant l'incendie*. Photograph
courtesy of the Bibliothèque de l'Opéra.

fronts of the boxes were painted red with their interiors a light blue.
"The result is not in the best taste, but it is rich," responded a critic of
the scheme in faintly patronizing tones.[14]

Véron's ceiling banished the mythological deities who had fluttered
above audiences since the first great hall in the Palais Royal. The new

design was more worldly and earthbound, one suited to the practical-minded age. Watching over the assembly now were symbols from Periclean Athens, Augustan Rome, Italy of the Renaissance, and France of the seventeenth century.[15] The *Revue musicale*, a pillar of the Parisian musical establishment, could not resist the double entendre. "It appears that this spectacle is about to become more popular."[16]

To the secretary of the Russian ambassador to France the hall was frankly disappointing. As he sat through an 1842 performance of Meyerbeer's *Les Huguenots*, the fifth man squeezed uncomfortably into a box for four, Victor de Balabine could only think of the lavish theaters in Saint Petersburg. His chair was "contemptible," the colors "sordid," the costumes rumpled, and the overall ambience dull.[17] It required backhanded reasoning, but Balabine's complaints were probably just the sort of thing that made Véron happy. He had not undertaken the improvements to please diplomats; he wanted to make the bourgeoisie feel at home. His instincts were confirmed by one Frenchman's assessment of the hall. "It is indifferent to the progress of music whether a hall is well—or poorly—decorated; it suffices merely if the singing there is fine, the orchestra is good, and the works are worthy."[18]

Judging from accounts and subscription records, Véron was remarkably successful in broadening the clientele of the Opéra. Some marked the change by noting that men "of every position and all ages" were dressed in black, that somber suit of bourgeois belonging.[19] The *Courrier des théâtres* announced that "all of Paris" was represented at the Opéra, and Frédéric Soulié wrote that the audience embraced everyone "from the peerage to the proletariat."[20] With the least expensive seat the rough equivalent of a worker's daily wage, the latter claim was likely an exaggeration, or at least an exception, but the heterogeneity of the bourgeoisie was nevertheless sufficient to produce some remarkable contrasts. When the ticket-jobbers who stood in line for hours to buy in bulk and sell at a profit had trouble selling out, they would sometimes swallow the loss and take their own family—an element the Opéra's regulars were unaccustomed to seeing there. "One is very surprised to see faces and apparel in the box of Mme la marquise de *** or Mme la comtesse Mondor that would not belong even to their chambermaids," sniffed one spectator.[21]

Opera had found its place in the ordered lives of the middle classes, or so went the rhetoric of the day. "The middle classes [*classes intermédiaires*] like this theater very much; it has their kind of music," a newspaper wrote after the July Revolution.[22] Another observed in the audience a mélange of "old names, new names and non-names."[23] Véron claimed that the Revolution made the Opéra the "Versailles" of the bourgeoisie.[24]

But were opera audiences a true mirror of the middle class? Subscription rolls reveal a majority of names without titles, on first glance a sure qualification for the middle-class designation. But the middle class was large, and the opera drew from its upper end. In the 1833–34 season, 65 percent of subscribers were members of the government, the liberal professions, high finance, or entrepreneurial commerce. Another 10 percent earned their incomes from investments in real estate or more liquid capital.[25] Individual ticket buyers are not included in these figures, and it is likely that the city's less well-to-do, when they appeared at the Opéra at all, accounted for an important part of these purchases. But subscribers provided the continuity and more permanent clientele, which, despite Véron's talk of giving the hall a more popular feel and the enthusiasm of the popular press to take up the claim, represented the highest stratum of the bourgeoisie.

There was in truth some slippage between how the Opéra presented itself and whom it actually attracted, though the illusion likely operated as well in the minds of the upper bourgeoisie who called themselves, following the watchwords of the new regime, solidly middle class. The underlying political messages of the operas they saw there, moreover, flattered just such an identity, the identity of the respectable middle, the *juste milieu*, neither royalist nor revolutionary, opposed to religious fanaticism while still vaguely believing, dedicated to honor, allied with order, suspicious of the masses.

They were solidly bourgeois in behavior. Opera audiences of the 1830s and 1840s came more to watch the spectacle on the stage than the spectacle of the boxes. The places most keenly sought were in the middle of the hall, a point amply made when Louis-Philippe chose the first-level box in the center and at the rear. (And why shouldn't the "citizen-king" have the best view of the stage?) Next to the royal box and with a view almost as good were the Rothschilds.[26]

Connoisseurs, artists, and journalists sat in the choice seats on the ground floor, and the true fanatics, this generation's version of the dilettanti, crowded into the "loge des lions" adjoining the stage to fawn and sway and throw out bouquets at every available opportunity (see Figure 19). But unlike the dilettanti of the Théâtre Italien, these melomanes were universally admired—"lionized," to use the anglophilic term of the day—in society and in the theater. They dressed in smart

Figure 19.   Gustave Doré, *La Fosse aux lions*. Photograph courtesy of the
Bibliothèque Forney.

suits and never let their enthusiasms overstep the acceptable. "They're
young, they're handsome, they're noble, rich, and clever. . . . This box
is five times favored of the gods." Respectability had co-opted the
eccentrics.[27]

Véron's brief tenure at the Opéra was responsible for institutionaliz-
ing another lasting fixture there—the claque, a professional, highly organized unit that guaranteed applause in all the critical places. Although
some had suspected hired hands to shore up a singer or a work as far
back as the late eighteenth century, it was Louis Véron who raised the
claque to an art. The presence of strategically situated bursts of passion
might spell the difference between failure and a profit. Ever the businessman, Véron hired Auguste Levasseur for a salary that approached
that of the principal singers to manage the operation. Auguste, as he was
known, studied the score of each new work, noting what sort of applause was needed where, attended rehearsals, and met regularly with
Véron to discuss tactics.[28] Auguste affected (and to be fair probably possessed) great musical discernment. "It is a pleasure to work for such a

composition," he wrote to one of Véron's successors after reviewing Meyerbeer's *Les Huguenots*. "We can 'do' all the arias and almost all the duets. I'll try to raise a triple salvo for the duet in the fourth act. I intend to cheer for the trio in the fifth act. As for the artists and the authors, I await the instructions of the administration."[29]

Auguste received as many as 300 tickets from the administration to "do" a particular performance, although on normal occasions the number was much lower. Over time an arrangement of Byzantine complexity came to govern distribution. The chief of the claque gave his veterans free tickets; these were the trusted soldiers—"intimates"— who had spent years in the ranks. "Washables" paid one-fourth to one-half the face value of a ticket and were usually well enough known by the chief to be relied upon to applaud. "Solitaries," claqueurs not sufficiently known to the chief to be completely trusted, paid the full price for a ticket but avoided standing in line; the solitary also paid the chief a deposit that would be returned at the close of the performance if he applauded satisfactorily.

Claqueurs were ingenious in their methods. The chief had two lieutenants, who each had four sublieutenants, and the sublieutenants had ten men under them. Auguste, sitting in an orchestra seat in the center, would tap his cane lightly on the floor to give the signal. His lieutenants would take up the gesture, and after them, their sublieutenants, and a cascade of approval would tumble forth from all sides.[30] The aggressive claqueur stamped and shouted "Bravo-o-o! Bravo-o-o!" or "Brava-a-a!" ("That is the scholar of the gang," Berlioz quipped; "he has kept company with Italians and can distinguish masculine from feminine.") The yellow-gloved claqueur drew attention by leaning out from his box and slowly, noiselessly, bringing his hands together. The violinist-claqueur tapped the back of his instrument with the wood of his bow. Others threw flowers, which some said were carried offstage and whisked back up to the box to be thrown a second and third time.[31] If all functioned smoothly the chief might be rewarded by composers or performers. Jules Lau, one of Auguste's successors, spoke particularly warmly of Scribe's and Auber's generosity.[32]

The public was aware of the claque and tolerated it with various degrees of patience. His was a biased view, but Jules Lau claimed that the applause of the claque was needed "to animate and encourage the actors, to warm up a sluggish audience, and to emphasize the most beautiful passages."[33] Théophile Gautier made essentially the same point although with greater detachment when he argued that the claqueur might well be guilty of protecting mediocrity but he also enlivened performances and encouraged the nervous young performers.[34] Improbable as it seems, the claque, at least under Auguste, upheld an image of judiciousness and politeness. Its members usually avoided confrontation and did what they could to fit into the audience, a task facilitated by the public's increasing heterogeneity. But their efforts to pass for regular spectators could be exasperating. One listener wrote to a newspaper to complain that the "true public" was no longer able to express its opinion.[35] It was as though the forces that made truly public judgment possible—legal equality, the end of personality setting taste, the rhetoric of popular fair-mindedness—created an opening for a clandestine pseudo-public to subvert the process.

Yet even the factitious applause of the claque—applause that complicates discerning just how popular the "popular" successes of Auber, Meyerbeer, and Halévy really were—worked to strengthen the rhetoric of public judgment. Although the truth was often different, the claque's ovations had all the marks of public approval; or perhaps, as Lau claimed, its ovations nudged the rest of the public into enthusiasm of their own. Accurate or not, the rhetoric of the public as a legitimate, unified authority in the theater remained. As Edouard Fétis wrote, "the public, guided by an instinct of good sense, knows very well what it likes. If works submitted to its judgment displease it, it knows to do the just thing."[36] The public remained a rich term in its theatrical usage, both embracing a socially heterogeneous collection of spectators and connoting a harmonious whole.

A telling incident in 1842 illustrates how fully the authority of public judgment, with its connotations of democratic consensus over deference to elites, influenced behavior and taste in the July Monarchy. Spectators knew that the forestage box on the right was rented by the king's son, the duc d'Orléans, but they seldom caught sight of him there. During a performance of Auber's *La Muette de Portici* spectators saw some movement in the shadows and felt sure they were about to see the duke's face. Instead, as *La France musicale* narrates, "a discreet hand arranged the curtains of the box in such a way that no one could see inside." The newspaper could only suppose that the duke listened "with transport" as the others had and concluded, significantly, that in applauding the artists he "contributed his own acclaim to the enlightened acclaim of the public."[37]

In the 1830s even the heir to the throne was courteous at the opera. No longer was it the place for boisterous nobles or spoiled lackeys.

These bourgeois audiences were exceedingly proper. "The behavior of the audience at the Opéra is calm and polite toward the artists as well as toward the works," reads a typical report.[38] Even when performers faltered, which was enough to bring howls in an earlier age, the public for the most part kept its consideration. A new singer wandered off-key during a performance and wrecked an ensemble sequence, yet "the habitual politeness of the public at the Opéra saved Mme Démeri from any energetic expressions of discontent."[39] There were still flashes of rowdiness, to be sure, as when Raguenot replaced Doultier as Masaniello unannounced in *La Muette de Portici*. Facing an obstreperously unhappy audience, Raguenot broke character to plead with them, an act they considered so audacious that they booed and hooted for ninety minutes, sparking seven arrests and twenty expulsions.[40]

But on the whole, calm prevailed. By now the silence of the spectators had several sources, from the concrete—the darkness of the hall, the awkwardness of sharing a box with strangers, the more comfortable seats (which M. A. Bazin said permitted you "to stretch out and sleep in comfort")—to the more ineffable sense of propriety.[41] There was also the overwhelming force of the performance. That was what audiences talked about most in the 1830s. "The public rush to see and hear this work will sustain it for a long time to come," wrote the *Revue musicale* on the premiere of *Robert le diable*, "for the story is fascinating, the spectacle is magnificent, the music, as with all things beautiful, can only gain by being heard often, and finally the execution offers perfection in the whole and in the details that crown the pleasure of sight and sound."[42] The *Revue des deux mondes*, writing of the same occasion, noted that there were surprisingly few lavish dresses but everywhere the "despairing bourgeoisie [*désespérante bourgeoisie*], . . . quite attentive and very moved."[43]

Which brings us to the nuns. French Grand Opera thrived on scenes that glued attention to the stage. It was filled with heart-stopping turns that danced on the edge of the permissible and numbing, unrelenting pomp. *La Muette* ends with the sweet, silent girl at the center of the story hurling herself, Tosca-like, into the mouth of a volcano. A fifth-act wedding celebration in *Les Huguenots* is cut short when the hero stumbles onto the stage dripping blood. In the climax of *La Juive* an old man reveals to the judge that the girl he has just sentenced to death, and who is now being lowered into a cauldron of boiling oil, is his own long-lost daughter.[44] Never had the opera stage seen such horror.

Nor had its long tradition of titillating dances quite prepared audi-

ences for the nuns in *Robert le diable*, the tale of a medieval knight torn
between the forces of good and evil. The ballet came in the third act,
when the satanic Bertram lures his son Robert into an abandoned,
moonlit cloister to let the ghosts of nuns unfaithful to their vows seduce
him. Mysterious music sounds and the sepulchral statues slowly begin
to move. Silent, white-clad dancers slip from between the tombs and let
their gowns fall from their shoulders. The *Revue des deux mondes* continues the narration. "Stirring the cold dust from the tombs, they suddenly throw themselves into delights from their past life; they dance like
bacchantes, they gamble like lords and drink like soldiers."[45] Robert
appears, and the nuns bring him cups brimming with wine, "exciting
his passions" (the stage directions indicate) with drunkenness, gambling, and lust. The seduction comes to a climax when their leader "allows herself to be ravished by Robert's kiss."[46] "That's vulgar," Felix
Mendelssohn wrote in a letter after seeing the scene.[47] Others had a
different view. As one French reviewer wrote: "What a pleasure to see
these lithe, loose women." (*Légère* was the single adjective employed, a
pun that holds both meanings.)[48]

French Grand Opera, which flourished from the late 1820s to the late
1830s, was romantic art par excellence, synthesizing stagecraft, drama,
and music into one colossal whole. Berlioz was ambivalent about its
Gargantuan scope, at once admiring Meyerbeer's dexterity and tiring of
his histrionics:

high c's from every type of chest, bass drums, snare drums, organs, military
bands, antique trumpets, tubas as big as locomotives' smokestacks, bells, cannons, horses, cardinals under a canopy, emperors covered with gold, queens
wearing tiaras, funerals, fêtes, weddings, and again the canopy, the canopy
beplumed and splendiferous, borne by four officers as in *Malbrouck*, jugglers,
skaters, choirboys, censers, monstrances, crosses, banners, processions, orgies of
priests and naked women, the bull Apis, and masses of oxen, screech-owls, bats,
the five-hundred fiends of hell, and what have you—the rocking of the heavens
and the end of the world, interspersed with a few dull cavatinas here and there
and a large claque thrown in.[49]

Above all, Grand Opera was spectacle, an updated mix of revolutionary-era scenes of masses crowding the stage and Napoleonic glitter.
Most of the stage machinery that had dangled deities from the rafters in
the eighteenth century was now gone, replaced by more realistic props
and costumes. Cherubini's *Ali-Baba* (1831) featured a great bazaar
scene with an exotic spread of merchandise and dress, and Auber's
Gustave III (1833) opened onto a set modeled after the great hall at

Versailles.[50] The scenic high point of *La Juive* (1835) by Halévy was indisputably when dignitaries of the Church and the Holy Roman Empire marched and rode horses past the Cathedral of Constance. The stage directions suggest that Berlioz's account wasn't far from the truth.

PROCESSION marches past during chorus: 1. The emperor's trumpeters, preceded by three mounted guards richly armed and equipped; 2. One banner-bearer; 3. Twenty cross-bow carriers; 4. One flag-bearer; 5. Two cardinals followed by two clergymen; 6. Two other cardinals followed by two clergymen; 7. One banner-bearer accompanied by bishops and masters of various trades; 8. One banner-bearer accompanied by two other bishops and several guild officials; 9. Three *échevins*; . . . 10. One-hundred soldiers richly armed and dressed in coats of mail and armor; 11. Six trumpeters (the instruments are decorated in richly emblazoned hoods) . . . ; 12. Six more trumpets; 13. Six flag-carriers; 14. Twenty cross-bow carriers; 15. Three cardinals followed by their pages and their clergymen; 16. CARDINAL BROGHY on horseback, under a magnificent canopy carried by four heralds (a fifth holds the horse's bridle); 17. Ten soldiers; 18. Three armed heralds on horseback; 19. Twenty pages of the emperor; 20. THE EMPEROR SIGISMOND in dazzling armor [on] a horse harnessed and in armor with all imaginable luxury.[51]

Louis Véron gave as good a description as any of the elements of Grand Opera when he listed its requisites like a grocery list: dramatic action in five acts exposing the passions of the human heart, historical interest, a large orchestra, plenteous decorations, and varied costumes. "The public awaits and demands great things of you," he crowed.[52]

Although Grand Opera flourished under Véron's stewardship, its tributaries ran back into the Restoration, drawing from musical styles of the Théâtre Italien, dramatic styles culled from melodrama, and techniques of painting and design refined in the boulevard theaters. Gioacchino Rossini's productions at the Opéra in the 1820s aroused the same musical excitement there that he had stirred up at the Théâtre Italien. Set amidst a tired repertoire of long-familiar works, Rossini's *Le Siège de Corinthe* (1826), *Moïse* (1827) and *Le Comte d'Ory* (1828) (adaptations of *Maometto Secondo, Mosè in Egitto*, and *Viaggio à Reims*) were a shot of adreneline to the sclerotic institution.

Guillaume Tell (1829), Rossini's last work before retiring from opera at the ripe old age of 37, was a synthesis of vocal brilliance and the kind of massive staging that would soon be synonymous with Grand Opera. Rossini toned down the *buffo* vocal acrobatics in these French works.[53] Moving away from the extended solo passages typical of his years at the Théâtre Italien, Rossini concentrated his forces in ensemble and choral numbers, setting quartets, quintets, or septets of principal singers against massed choruses, themselves divided into as many as seven parts. But enough of the Italian lyricism and powerful instrumentation remained to pull listeners out of the torpor that two decades of Spontini, Le Sueur, and Gluck redivivus had induced.

By setting individual accomplishments against a backdrop of national upheaval, *Guillaume Tell* and other Romantic operas simultaneously diminished the importance of particular heroes and elevated the people as a world historical force. "History is a novel whose author is the people," wrote Alfred de Vigny in an appendix to his *Cinq-Mars*, a sentiment that could easily serve as a tag for the plots of Grand Opera.[54] The group of brilliant young historians writing at the time, writers like Thiers, Guizot, and Barante, would not likely disagree. Nor would novelists like Merimée and Hugo, whose works cast lives and events within the collective passions of an epoch. The expanded musical and dramatic roles of the chorus was Grand Opera's way of portraying these monumental passions.

It quickly became apparent that Rossini would revitalize the institution. The vicomte Sosthène de la Rochefoucauld, the last superintendent of theaters of the Restoration, pronounced *Le Siège de Corinthe* a "veritable revolution in French opera" just after its 1826 premiere, and Adophe Adam, echoing his words, called it "the signal for the immense revolution which has been effected at this theater."[55] Rossini's music brought "good society," and that brought the crowds, a spectator reported. Another specifically credited him with advancing musical knowledge. "It is only since the performance of works by this great composer that there is singing at the Opéra, and it is only since there is singing that the musical intelligence of the spectators here has developed."[56] Those who had resisted the tide of *rossinisme* ten years earlier—the "ultra-recalcitrants," a critic called them—were swept away in this second Rossini wave. Just as he had done at the Théâtre Italien, Rossini transformed the landscape at the Opéra.

At the same time, the dramatist Eugène Scribe (1791–1861) and composer Daniel Auber (1782–1871) collaborated to transform a popular *opéra-comique* about a seventeenth-century uprising in Naples into a work suitable for the Opéra. *La Muette de Portici* was the result, which premiered in 1828 to great acclaim. Although *La Muette* was less powerful musically than the work of the mature Rossini, its grand views and skillful use of crowds were stunning. Pierre Cicéri, the Opéra's master of stagecraft, carefully recreated the Spanish viceroy's palace overlooking the Bay of Naples, and, for the first time ever on the stage of the

Opéra, the chorus moved dramatically to participate in the action as they sang.[57] The text was good and the music excellent, observed the *Revue musicale*, but the staging and sets, "the likes of which we've not seen before," received the greatest interest.[58]

Staging worthy of *La Muette* and music as powerful as Rossini's converged in the operas of Giacomo Meyerbeer, who set the standard for French Grand Opera of the 1830s and 1840s. He finished composing *Robert le diable*, a collaboration with Eugène Scribe, just before the July Revolution, and its premiere in 1831 was epochal. Meyerbeer and Scribe followed the same formula of massive staging, hair-raising dénouements, and powerful, percussive music to produce *Les Huguenots* in 1836, whose success was immediate and sustained. *La Juive* (1835) by Scribe and Jacques Fromentin Halévy (1799–1862) was in the same tradition and held immense appeal. Auber's *Le Philtre* (1831), set to a text by Scribe, was moderately successful; his *Le Dieu et la bayadère* (1830) and *Le Serment* (1832) somewhat less so. Halévy remained active with *Guido et Ginerva* (1836), *Le Drapier* (1840), *La Reine de Chypre* (1841), *Charles VI* (1843), and *Le Lazzarone* (1844).

If the plots of Grand Opera had something for everyone, so did the music, mixing folk song, full-throated hymns en masse, romances, *bel canto*, beer-hall songs, and church music. Meyerbeer defied all musical pedigree, the hybrid of Italian and German music, as Blaze de Bury insisted. Or perhaps he was the embodiment of neither, as Victor Planche held.[59] Immediately following a chorus of solemn religiousness reminiscent of the French baroque in *Les Huguenots* is a solo of Rossinian virtuosity, as Marguerite de Valois flutters up and down above a gracious women's trio.[60] *Robert*'s musical styles alternate quickly and freely, from swaggering Germanic drinking songs to ethereal choruses with heavenly harps and an organ; the changes were so fluent, in fact, that Schumann claimed they paraded listeners through the church and into the brothel.[61] Meyerbeer was a master of instrumentation. The orchestral timbres are chilling when Bertram summons the spirits of hell, a passage scored to a trio of trombones and an ophicleide (the intervals they play are strongly evocative of the statue's stentorian call to Don Giovanni), and the bassoons are ghoulish as the nuns begin to materialize.[62] Hector Berlioz called the English horn and harp accompaniment to the fourth-act cavatina from *Robert* especially affecting.

Most of all Meyerbeer excelled in writing music that overwhelmed with its mass. Although Meyerbeer managed to avoid the sort of popular caricature that Berlioz suffered for his weighty orchestrations, there are resemblances in the deadening force of the large-scale numbers. If the dramatic use of the chorus was the operatic embodiment of popular passions on the stage of history, massive orchestrations were a musical expression of their power. At climactic moments, particularly at the end of each act, Meyerbeer employs multiple-part choruses (and sometimes multiple choruses), soloists, and full orchestra to crushing, grand effect. At the end of Act Three of *Les Huguenots*, just as the Protestant Raoul is about to be cut down ignominiously on the banks of the Seine by a band of Catholics, the seven-part ensemble suddenly gives way to martial rhythms. Huguenot soldiers flood onto the stage and the orchestra's brass take up a phrase from "A Mighty Fortress Is Our God." The musical texture becomes thicker still when two nearby taverns empty and groups of students appear—some Catholic, some Protestant, all emboldened by beer—and a highly controlled, prodigiously heavy orchestration carries the rival masses as they hurl insults at the other.[63]

Grand Opera was also calculated to appeal to the public in explicitly political ways. For all their historical specificity the libretti carried contemporary political associations calibrated to confirm the convictions of the audience. *La Muette* set the tone in 1828 with a text fine-tuned to endorse a moderate social vision. That the 1830 revolution in Brussels reportedly started when singers and stagehands took to the streets singing the chorus "Amour sacré de la patrie" after a rehearsal of the opera has created an impression that the work was incendiary.[64] The image misrepresents the mood of the work and the response of the opera-going public in France. Perhaps the misunderstanding comes from assuming that the middle class audiences of the late 1820s and 1830s were angry and cantankerous and on the verge themselves of rushing out into the streets to overturn the status quo. In truth it is difficult to conceive of any audience—especially that of the 1820s and 1830s—being inspired to subversion by *La Muette de Portici*. The political content of *La Muette*, the first of several Grand Opera libretti to deliver this reassuring message to operatic audiences, was in its middle-of-the-road, *juste-milieu* message.

To be sure, *La Muette* portrayed political revolt from the perspective of the people. The deaf girl Fenella has been seduced by the Spanish viceroy's son, whom she publicly identifies as the guilty one just after his marriage. When the viceroy's soldiers attempt to seize her, Fenella's brother Masaniello explodes in rage, and his resistance emboldens the native population to rise up against the foreign occupation. But Scribe tempers the revolutionary message as soon as he delivers it. The aristocratic seducer is not a shameless Don Juan but expresses great remorse over the betrayal (moments before his wedding, no less!). His new wife Elvire forgives the transgression and even proposes bringing Fenella into the palace to live with them, a good intention the crowd mistakes for high-handed arrest. And Masaniello himself is deeply disturbed by the carnage unleashed by the crowd's revolutionary passions ("What horrible scenes this day of terror has brought," he sings when he sees mothers and infants slaughtered).[65] By the time a fisherman named Pietro accuses Masaniello of betraying the revolution and has him poisoned (invoking the Virgin Mary for help), Scribe's political message is clear: tyranny of either stripe, royalist or revolutionary, is shameful; there are good, if fallible, aristocrats just as there are decent commoners; however necessary, sudden political change is dangerous, so a prudent middle path is best.[66]

The view appealed to the political instincts of the Opéra's audiences. True, *La Muette, Guillaume Tell, Le Siège de Corinthe*, and *Les Huguenots* all elevated "the people" to heroic status, but "the people," at least when they were not duped by demagogues like Pietro, were a dam against revolutionary fanaticism. In *Les Huguenots* the cruelty of Protestant extremists during the wars of religion is portrayed just as vividly as that of the Catholics. Bloodthirsty monks seething with hatred pledge to carry off the Saint Bartholomew's Day massacre in an eerie reenactment of climactic moments from the revolutionary stage: kneeling, they swear on their weapons—weapons soon to be wet with "un sang impur"—while an unmistakable snatch of "La Marseillaise" sweeps by.[67] Schumann, missing the political point, was disgusted that Meyerbeer could not come up with anything more original than a "reworked *Marseillaise*."[68] Those among the audience more familiar with their own operatic history were more likely disgusted with revolutionary fanaticism, whether religious or republican.

Not all were happy with Grand Opera. More and more, spectators had their preferred theater and favorite musical style, so some of the harshest critics of Grand Opera were strong supporters of other forms of music. Some intellectuals and artists, like the critic Jules Janin, charged that the Opéra merely dressed up cheap tastes in shiny trappings and called it art; Delacroix marveled that so many should think that music, the most powerful of all arts, needed such pomp to support it. Castil-Blaze quipped that the Opéra was quickly becoming the spectacle of choice for "the young, the deaf, and the ignorant"; he was no doubt right to claim that without the show—"the decors, the costumes, the dressed-up horses, the velvet, the satin, the armor, and all the luxury of the setting"—much of the audience would be lost.[69]

The critiques held a grain of truth. Of course spectators were dazzled and attracted by the spectacle of Grand Opera. But audiences also said that the music itself was just as moving as the stage effects—a claim notably absent from audiences dazzled and attracted by the spectacle of Lully or Rameau in the mid-eighteenth century. Two years into the production of *Robert le diable*—a run that would ultimately exceed 500 performances—the *Revue musicale* wrote that the public considered the piece "a work of art." "The wealth and ingenuity of the sets have contributed to public enthusiasm, but it has been clear that this was only an accessory, that their real interest lay in Meyerbeer's score."[70]

Perhaps that was wishful thinking, as the *Revue musicale* consistently pitched its articles to a musically enlightened readership and generally resisted gimmicks, but others made the same point. "The music of *Robert le diable* raises a ruckus, but in the good sense of the word," wrote the considerably less highbrow *Courrier des théâtres*. "People are talking about it everywhere, from the salons to the shops."[71] The music of Grand Opera was difficult for these listeners, layered with its multiple choruses and dense textures. They acknowledged the challenge and listened all the more intently to comprehend it. As *Le Temps* advised of *La Juive*, "One should see this great work at least ten times to understand and savor it completely."[72]

Spectators listened to the wealth of harmony that flowed from the stage and gradually made sense of it. While a reigning etiquette of politeness enforced by encroaching conformity did its part to produce ever more restrained and outwardly attentive audiences, this purely musical element so entranced and captivated them that breaking the spell of the music with visits or discussions about other spectators was unthinkable. To listen with the attention these listeners claimed the music required was all-consuming. The silence that prevailed in the Opéra was the surest evidence.

15

Beethoven Triumphant

"Oh Beethoven! You were magnificent last night, when three thousand hearts and more beat to the harmony of your muse and every eye was fixed on your melancholy image!"[1] Not every spectator wrote such feverish lines to the master, but the sentiments of the letter—a note sent to the conductor Habeneck after he'd led a brilliant performance—were typical of the enthusiasm many felt. Beethoven was the grand conqueror of repertoires in the 1830s and 1840s, the revolutionary who sent a generation of listeners into ecstasy every time he was played. He was a despiser of men who redeemed mankind, they said, a half-divine, half-mad genius. "He is the man of our time," Delacroix remarked to George Sand as they left the concert hall; "he is romantic to the supreme degree."[2]

Nothing could have prepared audiences for the explosive impact of Beethoven's reappearance in 1828 after his fitful, irregular performance earlier. With Paris having passed the better part of twenty years without regular orchestral concerts, Charles X's administration authorized a 2,000-franc grant to the Conservatoire to begin a new series, adding, in the wooden language of government grants, its confidence that the money would bring the series "all possible brilliance."[3] The official tone missed the mood of the public by a mile. The *Revue musicale* reported that the enthusiasm of the listeners during the inaugural concert on 9 March was rapturous. The *Journal des débats* announced that the new series, the Société des Concerts, was no less than a musical revolution.[4]

Audiences confirmed the judgment. Beethoven's *Eroica* was repeated the following week, and the public filed out "in a kind of delirium," ecstatic and electrified, calling out "divine!" "delicious!" "superb!" They would linger in the hallways and lobby of the Conservatoire for an hour and longer after concerts. The unlucky ones without tickets offered as much as twice the regular price for a place. One spectator promised 3,000 francs if the orchestra would stay and play the whole program again.[5]

Such were the reports—overcharged with excitement and a bit bewildered by it all—that appeared after every concert that opening season of the Société des Concerts and for many seasons to come. François-Antoine Habeneck, the maestro who conducted clutching his violin, opened the third concert of the 1828 season with Beethoven's Fifth, whose first movement produced "a kind of stupor visible on every physiognomy" and elicited prolonged salvos of applause. (This, apparently, despite the fact that the nervous hornist botched the opening motif every time it came around to him.)[6] At a later concert, by popular demand, the orchestra played the Fifth Symphony in six movements—that is, with each of the last two repeated—establishing a precedent that would be repeated many times in succeeding years. Often the public would interrupt the music with applause. This is how spectators showed their delight the first time they heard the transition from the third to the fourth movements of the Fifth Symphony, as well as when they first heard the da capo return after the middle section in the scherzo of the Ninth.[7] As late as 1834, six years after the revelation of Beethoven, bemused journalists were still devoting large parts of their reviews to describing the ecstatic transports that erupted at the end of each movement. "This was not the light applause of etiquette," reads a typical review, "or of personal interest for the composer, or any other motive for applause other than the work itself."[8] Another reviewer announced dramatically that the spontaneous eruptions during the Fifth proved that humans are not the masters of their own emotions.[9]

One of the elements of surprise in Beethoven's success in 1828 involved the dismal memory listeners had of earlier performances. The Paris premiere of his First Symphony came in 1807 and was rejected virtually universally. It employed German barbarisms, the reviewers wrote, and grated on the ears while freezing the soul. The reception was the same when his works—usually the First or Second Symphony—appeared on Exercices programs once or twice a season during the Empire and early Restoration.[10] His ideas were "frenzied," his themes followed "grotesque paths," he prepared his public for soothing cadences only to shock them with monstrous surprises—"he seems to harbor doves and crocodiles at the same time."[11] When he died the little renown Beethoven enjoyed in Paris grew chiefly from the early quartets that appeared on the chamber music concerts of Pierre Baillot. His symphonies were still given with the greatest infrequency. The First had appeared last in 1819 and there was little interest in hearing it again; the Second aroused slightly more interest in 1821 when, according to Berlioz, the Allegretto from the Seventh was substituted for its slow movement.[12]

The instant and sustained success from 1828 was a bolt from clear skies that caught professional observers of music entirely by surprise. Unable to reconstruct their earlier objections, critics began pointing fingers. One blamed the carelessness of musicians for letting the masterpieces languish in libraries; another blamed the years of indifference upon ignorance and misunderstanding.[13] There was certainly no hesitation now, as a work by Beethoven figured in virtually every concert for the next twenty years. Undeterred by the hall's uncomfortable seats and stifling temperatures, spectators flocked to the Conservatoire on Sundays at two o'clock between February and May, where they sometimes heard two and occasionally three Beethoven symphonies on a single program. There were frilly Cupids on the ceiling and smiling Muses on the orange-red wall behind the players, but Beethoven apparently transfigured even the gaudiest decor (see Figure 20). "I often forget that the Conservatoire is not a church, that the hundred musicians in the Société des Concerts live scattered throughout the twenty arrondissements of Paris and not in a seminary, that they are not a college of priests gathered before us to perform a holy service each Sunday," wrote Hermione Quinet.[14]

By early in the 1832 season the society had performed all nine of the symphonies, and in the 200-odd concerts between 1828 and 1859 the series gave 280 performances of Beethoven, as compared with 58 for symphonies of Haydn and 37 for those of Mozart. If Beethoven was a barbarian in 1815 he was a liberator in 1830. François-Joseph Fétis may well have intended to draw musical comparisons when he wrote that Mozart was a suitor who seduces you and Beethoven a headstrong rogue who takes you by force, but the metaphor also rang true for what Beethoven had done to the repertoire.[15]

It was in part the excitement of contemporaneity that made the programs at the Conservatoire so electrifying. Excerpts from operas by Meyerbeer and Rossini frequently appeared alongside the Beethoven

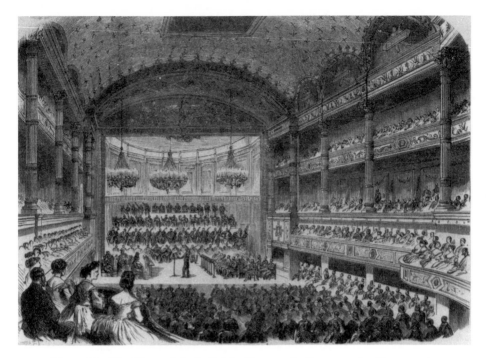

Figure 20. *Une Séance de la Société des Concerts du Conservatoire.* Photograph courtesy of the Bibliothèque de l'Opéra.

symphonies, as did works composed by local Parisian musicians. The program of the inaugural concert was typical, with the *Eroica*, a duet from Rossini's *Semiramide*, a solo for trumpet by Meifred, a concerto for violin by Rode, an unspecified aria by Rossini, and three works by Cherubini, with a chorus from his *Blanche de Provence*, the overture to *Abécérages*, and two sections from his Mass. Sometimes the small works were sandwiched between two halves of a Beethoven symphony, which was how the Ninth was first heard at the Société in 1832; at its second performance, the first three movements were separated from the choral movement by light popular romances and tunes by Weber and Rossini.[16] Audiences might as easily hear the Société's principal trumpeter there playing his own virtuosic concerto as Frédéric Chopin or Franz Liszt playing their compositions.[17]

Or Hector Berlioz, percussionist. Despite the harsh criticism in the press and stiff resistance among segments of the public, Habeneck occasionally put the music of Berlioz on the program at the Conservatoire.

Berlioz himself sometimes stood in at the tympani. Heinrich Heine, the poet and professional gadfly now in Parisian exile, remembers spotting Berlioz at the back of the orchestra during an 1832 performance with the Irish actress Harriet Smithson in attendance. The music was the *Symphonie fantastique*, composed at the peak of Berlioz's boiling passion for Harriet and whose program sketched the story of his love enlarged to grotesque proportions. "Berlioz did nothing to hide his constant gaze in her direction," Heine writes, "and every time he caught her eye he would strike the tympani as though in a great impulse of rage."[18] Harriet was swept away: she recognized herself and Berlioz, she wept, a meeting was arranged, they fell into a delirious romance, marriage followed.[19]

The image of Berlioz oblivious and an audience in awe was an apt symbol for musical experience in the 1830s and 1840s. It signified the bourgeoisie transfixed and silent before the Artist. Audiences at the Conservatoire concerts represented the elite of the Parisian population, and in many respects that elite had the same demographic composition as the crème de la crème of Restoration society. Subscription rolls show a fairly even distribution among members of the liberal professions and finance, entrepreneurial trades, and those with "neither employment nor profession," a designation that embraced both family wealth and income from real estate or other investments.[20] Spectators sporting a string of titles might be seen—seated in box 11 in the *premières* was M. le marquis de Louvois, Peer of France and Officer of the Royal Order of the Legion of Honor—but more numerous were the titles that turned the cogs of commerce and finance, non-noble by birth but wealthy to be sure—M. Coulomb, 60 Faubourg Poissonnière, banker; M. Morin, 8 rue Mont-Thabor, wine in bulk; M. Leloup, 37 rue de Verneuil, attorney; M. Lefebure, 42 rue de Clery, lace. The majority of addresses hailed from the neighborhood of the Chaussée d'Antin, a stylish area that held the same magical status for the early-nineteenth-century monied class that the Marais had held for aristocratic Paris of Mme de Sevigné.[21]

Like society itself, or at least those places where the comfortable came together, audiences at the Société were a harmonious mingling of old-style aristocrats and post-revolutionary notables who got their start during the Empire and Restoration. Most spectators at the Société probably thought of themselves as middle class—a designation that seemed to be on everyone's lips, especially since the 1830 revolution—but their level and source of income placed them firmly in the upper bourgeoisie.

Ticket prices at the Société, which ranged from 2 to 5 francs in 1828 and would later rise to 12 francs at the high end, effectively excluded most but the wealthiest of the middle classes.[22] With an average day's wage 2 francs for workers in the 1830s, Société audiences were by and large limited to the upper crust of French society.[23]

By all accounts these audiences gave the performers their full attention. Subscribers to the Société des Concerts had the reputation of being the most serious of all Paris audiences. One author gave a simple explanation: the symphonic form employed no outside ornaments to help it and consequently required the greatest attention.[24] Organizers of the series had intended to attract just such an audience and were careful to stress their aim of cultivating talent "for the sole interest of the art."[25] Whenever spectators acted otherwise they were chided. *La France musicale* for instance called the departure of some during the last movement of a Beethoven piano concerto "a veritable sacrilege, since it concerns a musical masterpiece." (They were trying to get to their coaches to beat the crowd: *plus ça change . . .*)[26] The Société concerts "are not a gathering place for chit-chat," wrote the critic Joseph d'Ortigue. "They are a sanctuary where writers, painters, and all serious artists come together."[27]

In fact all was not utter silence during performances at the Conservatoire, but the sounds from the hall were friendly. In addition to applauding during the music, spectators sometimes bubbled over with happy sighs and murmuring approval. A "light rustling, . . . unplanned and almost involuntary," coursed through the audience during the French premiere of Mendelssohn's Third Symphony at the Société.[28] Listeners listened visibly, their eyes closed or heads thrown back, drinking in the sounds with their whole being. Eugène Lami captured the mood of complete absorption that prevailed at the premiere of Beethoven's Seventh Symphony in a watercolor that shows just how serious the descriptions of rapture were (see Figure 21).[29]

The same palpable silence prevailed during a concert of piano trios performed by Franz Liszt, Chrétien Urhan, and Alexandre Batta. The fact seemed all the more incredible since half of Paris was sick with the flu. "They coughed plenty between movements, but their love of art was strong enough to repress all coughing . . . during the performance."[30] The trio brought the same effect several weeks later, when spectators stifled even their little sighs and murmurs "for fear of losing a single note." This was not a matter of mere fashion, at least in the eyes of the reviewer; fashion might make people attend and even ap-

Figure 21. Eugène Lami, *La Première audition de la Septième Symphonie de Beethoven*. Photograph courtesy of the Musée de la Musique, Conservatoire National Supérieur de Musique et de Danse de Paris.

plaud, but it could not entrance them: "It's unheard of!"[31] The critic for *La France musicale* took measure of the "religious attention" of a group of spectators at the Salle Saint Honoré and announced a new epoch.[32]

Habeneck's success with the Société des Concerts inspired a profusion of public concerts, and, unlike at the beginning of the century, instrumental music now had a solid core of listeners to support it. Instrumentalists throughout Paris seized their chance—they had a public. In 1829 Hippolyte Chélard founded the Athénée Musicale, which performed at the Hôtel de Ville until 1832. Between 1832 and 1839 Masson de Puyneuf conducted open-air concerts on the Champs-Elysées. The Union Musicale, founded in 1847, had as conductors the Saint-Simonian Félicien David and Hector Berlioz. Berlioz led the Société Philharmonique in 1850–51, and Segher conducted the Société de Sainte-Cécile from 1849 to 1856. There were also pedagogues such as François-Joseph Fétis, who undertook to educate the musical public in early music, launching a series of four "concerts historiques" in

1832, which featured the works of Josquin des Prez, Palestrina, Corelli, Handel, and Alessandro Scarlatti.[33]

In addition to these full-scale orchestral concerts chamber music also blossomed during the July Monarchy. In 1830 the violinist Pierre Baillot moved his regular performances of trios, quartets, and quintets—performances he had held steadfastly since 1814—to the great hall of the Hôtel de Ville to accommodate their surge in popularity. The hall seated seven hundred, and, judging from subscription lists, the upper middle classes dominated. Merchant, proprietor, attorney, deputy, author, stockbroker, dealer in wines, and banker appear in the category "occupation" on the society's subscription lists (along with a mischievous "gastronome").[34] The Baillot concerts typically contained the music of Mozart, Haydn, Boccherini, and Beethoven, and the response of audiences was a familiar sight to anyone who had been to the Société des Concerts. "This was more than mere admiration, and more even than enthusiasm: it was delirium."[35]

In the 1830s chamber music moved out of the salon and into the great performance spaces of piano makers. Jean Pape held regular concerts of vocal and instrumental concerts in his studios, including one massive performance of the Overture to *Don Giovanni* transcribed for three pianos, twelve hands.[36] And irregular public concerts for variegated groups sprouted up in other halls around Paris. Viewed from this perspective, Beethoven's revival was perhaps the first and most dramatic evidence of a new taste for pure music, but it was by no means unique. In 1838 *La France musicale* counted six hundred-odd concerts of one kind or another in Paris, a stunning growth from just ten years before, when the *Revue musicale* had mourned that "instrumental music . . . has virtually disappeared from France."[37] The comparison was morbid, but one writer likened the sudden spread of instrumental concerts to the cholera bacillus. Concerts were "swarming, teeming, surging with every step, under every form, in every dimension, of every color."[38] "Music is the new art of France," wrote Jules Janin. "It is our new passion, it is our daily study, it is our national pride."[39]

But it was not just the music that transfixed spectators of the July Monarchy, it was also the artist. This was the dawn of the great romantic legend of the artist-as-genius, divine or diabolical, who revealed glimpses of another world. If Rossini's music had turned voices into dynamos of virtuosity, the generation of composer-performers who came of age in the 1830s went one better by embodying the fire and living continuously in its heat. Since the Old Regime the performer's identity had undergone steady transformation in the minds of the public, as the old image of artisan in the service of prince or church gave way to artist answering to no one. A moment in 1790 crystallizes the transition, when the violinist Viotti agreed to give a private recital for eminent nobles on the condition that it be held in a modest fifth-floor apartment. "We've descended to their level long enough," Viotti reportedly said; "times have changed, and now they have to come up to ours."[40]

Answerable only to Art, holy and inviolate, the artist was at last free to feel pure inspiration unsullied by patrons' demands. It was time to make the wealthy come up to their level. But romantic freedom was never more than a step away from paralysis, tied as it was to the supreme commandment of originality. Hence the agony of creation, the imperative for individuality above everything else, and the sense of sin when artists betrayed Art for lower ends.[41] Liszt captured both sides of the equation with a rich metaphor: "[Artists are] predestined men—bound and chained—who have stolen the sacred flame from heaven."[42] The myth of the predestined, driven artist was especially potent among audiences, who were fed a diet of real artistic suffering that almost always contained a dose of hype. Audiences, and for that matter the artists themselves, could not always tell which was which in the passion of performance.

The artist whose genius seemed closest to divine madness was Niccolò Paganini, violin virtuoso and self-styled Faust of the popular press. Paganini's renown was enormous in France, extending beyond the regular concert and opera audiences. It was said that doormen feared dying without hearing him play; seigneurs and workers alike knew of his powers; mothers who had never been to the theater took their children to see him as *the* extraordinary event in their lives.[43] When vague rumors about gambling, women, and a criminal past surfaced in Paris, Paganini's very public response to the gossip turned his musical acclaim into a more potent *succès de scandale*. Paganini never lost the tone of outrage denying the rumors, but it's also true that the denials kept his name in the papers. In a letter to the influential *Revue musicale* he meticulously recounted the gossip, he insisted, the better to expose it as calumny: he had *not* been a prisoner in the Bastille, he had *not* killed a rival in the house of a mistress, Satan had *not* appeared next to him dressed in red on the stage in Vienna, he did *not* murder a curé in Milan for his money.[44]

The public in these early years of mass-circulation newspapers responded with that particular form of fascination that masquerades as umbrage. ("Il nous faut toujours ici un certain petit parfum de crime et de désespoir," as Alfred de Vigny wrote: we always want a little whiff of crime and despair.)[45] A letter appeared in the *Revue musicale* making no accusations but broadly hinting that Paganini had indeed been in prison. Lithographs of "Paganini en prison" soon appeared in print-shop windows. A physician contributed a lengthy physical description that accentuated the abnormal—the deathly pallor, the sharp nose, the spidery fingers and long, thin neck.[46] When in 1834 stories began circulating that Paganini had abducted a sixteen-year-old girl in London, the virtuoso again addressed readers in the French press. She was eighteen, not sixteen, he protested, and his intentions were honorable, since he planned to marry her.[47]

The newspaper-reading public didn't know all the details of the case, but they knew enough to take umbrage. Charlotte Watson, a gifted young singer from London, and her chaperone had accompanied Paganini in his travels off and on for at least two years before the incident. Paganini apparently convinced Charlotte that he was serious about marriage, and she slipped away from London alone. But her father got wind of the elopement and beat her to Boulogne, where he greeted her as she stepped off the steamer. The knot of outraged spectators gathered to watch reported seeing an enormous diamond tiara on the girl.[48]

Is it any wonder audiences flocked to hear Paganini play? (Twenty-five years later, just after publishing *Madame Bovary*, Flaubert would write, "Now I have been attacked by the government, by the priests, and by the newspapers. It's complete. Nothing is lacking for my triumph.")[49] Upon arriving in Paris in 1831 the Opéra engaged Paganini for ten concerts over five weeks; among his audiences were Théophile Gautier, Charles Nodier, Alfred de Musset, Eugène Delacroix, George Sand, Heinrich Heine, Liszt, Donizetti, Auber, and Rossini.[50] His performances produced a chilling sense that the man was not quite of this world. His feats were famous—the violin tuned up a half step to give it a frenetic, scrappy sound; his contorted posture, hunched over to one side with the right shoulder unnaturally high; bravura transcriptions that all but obliterated the original melody under a firestorm of notes; his ability to play entire pieces on the G string, all others having broken under the strain; the abrupt silences and looks of sharp pain; the moments when he would suddenly stop and piously cross himself; the pizzicati, double- and triple-stops, piercing harmonics, and grotesque imitations of dogs and cats.[51]

Listeners forgot about Mozart, Paisiello, Rossini, or whoever else's tunes Paganini improvised upon. It was all Paganini, passion incarnate, genius unchained. "There's sorcery in this fantastical talent; it's all supernatural," one listener wrote. "Yes, it's him, it's Mephistopheles," another vowed. "I saw him and heard him play the violin."[52] The tumult was so great as he played that the roar sometimes forced him to stop. After momentarily gathering his forces he would attack the strings with yet greater fury. "It would be impossible to describe the enthusiasm that seized the public when they heard this extraordinary man. It was delirium, frenzy. After lavishing applause on him during and after each piece, the listeners would not accept that he had finished. . . . A rumble began to spread throughout the hall, and you could hear shouts of surprise and pleasure from all sides. We simply couldn't believe what we had just heard."[53] Fétis struggled manfully against Paganini's hypnotic pull to conclude that he was "not touched," but Joseph d'Ortigue was totally overcome, avowing that Paganini had stripped him of his human shell and transported him to places no mortal had seen.[54] "His bow shimmers like a steel blade; his face is as pale as crime; his smile is beautiful, like Dante's Inferno; his violin cries like a woman," *L'Entracte* wrote. "[He's] Satan onstage, Satan knock-kneed, bandy-legged, double-jointed, twisted. . . . Fall to the knees of Satan and worship him."[55]

Personality thrust itself to center stage in the romantic decades. Now for the first time listeners started to believe that knowing the artists' personal lives could give an insight into their works. Was it because the sins and sorrows of genius, unequivocal signs of authentic individuality, proved an irresistible attraction to a public who gave lip service to the ideal even as encroaching conformity in dress and behavior seemed to deny it? What is sure is the striking regularity with which individuality was linked to artistry. "We cannot praise too highly this individuality formed entirely of itself," *La France musicale* wrote of Liszt, whose displays of passion in the early Paris performances were no less remarkable than Paganini's; he "has no imitators." "What speaks most for Liszt," wrote Heine, "is the respect with which even his enemies recognize his personal character."[56] Of Paganini, Castil-Blaze wrote, "He is not a violin player; he is an artist in the greatest sense of the word; one who creates, invents."[57] And of Hector Berlioz, a reviewer claimed that "The Ball" and "March to the Scaffold" from his *Symphonie fantastique* revealed a "vast imagination, . . . an individual countenance that goes beyond the ordinary forms of the art."[58]

The artist-as-iconoclast is a well-worn cliché of Romanticism, but seldom are the effects of that image upon the public considered, a public composed of so many stock traders, lawyers, bureaucrats, well-to-do merchants, who wouldn't dare risk dashing clothes or displays of passion. They just might have harbored a touch of jealous admiration for those who did.

In his life and work Hector Berlioz was the consummate romantic. His image as an individual who refused to play by anyone else's rules was only enhanced by the early institutional obstacles he encountered trying to have his music performed. His prickly passions that sometimes skirted the edge of insolence, like the rumors about Paganini, held a strong fascination in the bourgeois imagination. In 1825 Berlioz rented the church at Saint-Roch and engaged an orchestra with funds borrowed from a wealthy singer to perform his Mass. (With "the devout old ladies, the woman who rented the chairs, the holy-water man, the vergers, and all the gapers of the quarter declaring themselves well satisfied," Berlioz later wrote, "I had the simplicity to regard it a success.")[59] In 1828 Berlioz borrowed enough money to hire musicians and secure the hall of the Conservatoire for a performance that featured his *Scène héroïque*, the *Waverly* Overture, excerpts from *Les Francs-Juges*, the *Marche religieuse des mages*, and the "Credo" and "Resurrexit" from his *Messe solennelle*.[60] The premiere of the *Symphonie fantastique* in 1830 was sponsored by private funds, as were the premieres of the *King Lear* Overture, the symphony *Harold in Italy*, and *The Damnation of Faust*.[61]

Invariably Berlioz gave concerts the stamp of his own unique personality—a personality his friend Rouget de Lisle described as a volcano in continual eruption.[62] Berlioz's individuality constantly gave the Parisian caricaturists grist for the mill, as when he assembled 450 performers for a "Festival de M. Berlioz." ("The performance will end, by popular demand, with an ascent by M. Berlioz in a bass drum," smirked the *Charivari*.)[63] Another concert announced to begin at the Théâtre Italien at 7:00 P.M. started at 8:00 with dramatic readings by Harriet Smithson. The music began at 11:45 with the *Francs-Juges* Overture and continued with a performance by Franz Liszt that went until well past 1:00 in the morning.[64]

But beyond the prying fascination with artists' personal lives and the praise for their individuality, audiences looked to composer-performers for a higher message. They sought a share of whatever inspiration it was that produced these creations. The century seemed spiritually exhausted, sapped of its inner resources by two generations of revolution and warfare. The artist possessed an energy and vision that even the church seemed to have lost. For the Saint-Simonian Barthélemy-Prosper Enfantin the "new church" was the theater: "The Christian temples are deserted, the playhouses are filled with the faithful, the actor is taking the priest's place. . . . It is by the regenerated *actor* that the Christian will be saved."[65]

Intellectuals described the mood as sickness and abandonment. "We have lost our gods!" Michelet wrote in *Le Peuple*; yet more than ever humanity needs "a God . . . through whom men will recognize and love one another."[66] Expressing the *mal de siècle*, Alfred de Musset wrote that his "disgusted reason" could no longer believe but his heart was still unable to doubt. Sully-Prudhomme said that the doubt of his soul insulted the God of his desires.[67]

It didn't take announcements of malaise from the intellectuals to make spectators aware of severe social problems. The Lyon silk-workers' riots of 1831 quickly doused any notion that the Revolution of 1830 had, in the ringing pronouncement of Châteaubriand just after July, rendered the people peaceable: the street war between 10,000 National Guard troops and 15,000 workers produced 600 casualties before the fighting stopped.[68] Violence spread to Paris, and Daumier caught something of its disgusting pathos in his *Rue Transnonain* with its blood-soaked victim in nightshirt and cap in a heap at the foot of his bed. The large-scale violence was matched by the pitiful everyday sights. A critic for the *Globe*, a Saint-Simonian paper, described what all operagoers must have seen as they filed into the hall to revel in the richness of Grand Opera: the hungry and cold beggars huddled outside the theater. Perhaps their pain would "disturb the complacency of those who swoon with enthusiasm at the harmonious accents," he added pointedly.[69]

By 1830 music was in a position to answer this emptiness. The appearance of the predestined artist, a set of aesthetic expectations that now made abstract instrumental music accessible, and all the talk of promised redemption converged in the 1830s to create a musical experience that restored and healed, at least for those who felt the sickness and sought consolation. As *L'Artiste* wrote, "In our nineteenth century, a century that no longer believes anything, music has become a kind of religion, a last belief to which society is clinging with all its might, exhausted as it is by dogmas and words."[70] As with most religions, however, there was disagreement about what this one actually commanded.

16

The Musical Experience
of Romanticism

Romantic musical experience involved a new way of listening. To be sure, the physical features of theaters and concert halls and the larger patterns of bourgeois etiquette contributed to a more absorbed experience by focusing attention on the stage and reducing distractions. But behind the silence of operatic audiences, the galloping popularity of instrumental concerts, and the delirious enthusiasm for music in all venues was a changed structure of hearing.

At the heart of the new way of hearing was the liberation of music from language, a process well underway among spectators familiar with the music of Rossini and now encouraged by the programs at the Opéra and the Société des Concerts. If the Rossini-dominated decade of the 1820s was an apprenticeship in listening for the sheer thrill of the music, the 1830s was the time of mastering the new perspective, of exploring its implications and experimenting with ways of capturing and conveying music's meaning. Spectators describing the music of Beethoven and Meyerbeer asserted that listening was not an act of emotional decipherment; its expression did not depend upon identifying a mood, a familiar sound, or an image. The essence of music defied anything that specific. It was possibly even beyond words.

The widely read critic and musical educator François-Joseph Fétis pointed to the structure of this new way of listening in an 1831 essay. Past listeners have viewed the goal of music as "expressing the author's ideas or realizing sentiments or images," he wrote, citing as examples love, joy or sadness, the sounds of storms or battles, and the image of a sunrise. Instrumental music was independent of all this. "To say what

Haydn, Mozart, or Beethoven intended to paint or express in their admirable quartets, quintets, sonatas, or symphonies would not be easy."[1] Whereas twenty years before, musical imprecision was for most a sign of weak writing, the reverie it was now said to produce was a splendid voyage into the imagination. As M. P. Lahalle wrote in an essay on the nature of musical expression, "uncertain, indefinite qualities that are so harmful in virtually every other art are by contrast quite fitting to music."[2]

The extent of the change from listening for sounds, ideas, and emotions to listening for abstract meaning is most evident in the re-evaluation of Haydn in the 1830s and 1840s. Although his symphonies continued to enjoy respectable success in the shadow of Beethoven, their programmatic elements now seemed secondary and largely inessential to their true musical worth. "The merit of Haydn's work is not in the somewhat questionable accuracy of his imitation," reads an 1844 review of *The Creation*. "What we seek above all in music is the intrinsic value of its melodic conception and the wealth of its development, richness in instrumentation, a correct expression, and a powerful effect."[3] The journalist Alexis Azevedo wrote that *The Creation*'s thunder, rain, and hail could as easily be made by the sound-effects man at a common stage play. "From the point of view of music the result is *zero*, and just as childish as the first."[4] Azevedo denied that the opening of *The Creation* was a representation of chaos; its interest, rather, was purely musical, in the "uncertain, vague, and deceptive harmony."[5]

A similarly strong reaction against musical imitation appeared in popular French responses to the Sixth Symphony of Beethoven, the *Pastoral*. Beethoven wrote descriptive titles for each movement, which the Société des Concerts printed and distributed when it performed the work: "Awakening of happy feelings on arriving in the country; by the brook; joyous gathering of country folk, storm, shepherd's song; happy and thankful feelings after the storm."[6] The most explicitly programmatic of all of Beethoven's symphonies, this work contains the distinctive songs of the cuckoo, the quail, and the nightingale as well as a convincing evocation of a storm.

For one critic the work was "a sad parody" in which Beethoven had "prostituted his pen in the imitation of farmyard birds." Another accused him of triviality, and the *Journal des débats* said that the outmoded symphony would have been scarcely noticed had the composer not been Beethoven.[7] This was enthusiasm for absolute music with a vengeance. Apparently few detractors wanted to heed the advice of Berlioz, who recommended that those who blamed Beethoven for writing a program should simply listen to the work as a symphony "without a determinate subject."[8] As the influential critic Paul Scudo sternly wrote, "No, music is not intended to paint material sounds for the ear: it is the divine language of sentiment and imagination by which even those things that words are incapable of revealing are conveyed."[9]

Berlioz received his share of criticism in the same terms for his *Symphonie fantastique*, one of the most programmatic symphonies in the repertoire. At the work's early performances Berlioz distributed the febrile narrative of a murderous, opium-induced dream in which a lover kills his mistress and is punished by decapitation. Numerous correspondences exist between the text and the music: the frenetic waltz of a ball, the shepherds' *ranz des vaches*, distant thunder in the tympani, even a grotesque plink-plink-plink in the strings when the guillotine falls and the murderer's head presumably tumbles to the ground.[10] For this Berlioz's contemporaries called him a traditionalist who couldn't resist the tired tricks of the past (albeit a particularly noisy one).[11] One scathing review castigated Berlioz for "writing on the notice all that he wanted to paint" rather than leaving listeners to their own "vague and infinite reveries." "M. Berlioz wishes to be dramatic, and the title of this concert is the proof," another critic wrote. "But nothing is less dramatic than the material imitation of the things that are more likely to captivate us in nature."[12]

This shift in aesthetic presuppositions deprived listeners of any reliable way to discuss musical meaning, which is just what earlier generations believed they were doing when they spoke of chiseling sculptors in Rameau or angry women in Boccherini. As Fétis rightly observed, to express anything in words is to express an image, an imitation, an idea, or an emotion. To say what Haydn, Mozart, or Beethoven "expressed" would misrepresent the very nature of music. A critic for *L'Artiste* followed this path to its logical end, cautioning in an essay about Beethoven's Fifth Symphony that "to analyze a symphony . . . with words, with a pen, would be sheer madness. To convey to readers what one has heard, one is reduced to analogies and comparisons."[13]

The conclusion was insightful. If music and language were two different systems of expression, then words could grasp the intimations of music only by metaphor. Even then the fit was imperfect.[14] The best one could do was to create a kindred feeling by indirection. No poem could describe the Mozart Requiem, as George Sand wrote, because the arts "do not speak the same language [but] . . . are understood by mysterious analogies."[15] The abundance of metaphorical language in musical accounts from the 1830s and 1840s shows the logic working itself out in the efforts of ordinary spectators as they attempted to describe what, according to their own suppositions, could not be described. Hermione Quinet's description of the Allegretto from Beethoven's Seventh Symphony was typical:

Imagine an enormous cathedral of marvelous architecture. It is night. A pale stream of starlight falls through the windows. The stones begin to move. The souls of the dead leave their underground tombs. They whisper, and their obscure sounds grow more and more distinct as they advance toward the nave. They rise, they unfurl into the high galleries, they continue their funeral procession. Life comes back to them slowly. Suddenly it bursts into a fortissimo. Pizzicato fugues mark the irregular and urgent steps of these phantom people that have recovered their existence through the tender invocation of harmony.[16]

In a single paragraph François Stoepel gave a staggering succession of metaphors to evince in the reader his own sensations hearing Beethoven, who made him think of moons, meteors, stars, a magic garden, aeolien harps, white statues, tombstones, a castle on the edge of a still lake, invisible demons, a dank prison, and eternal Spring. "I am the toy of a thousand romantic dreams, I see stars of gold encircling my breast with a sparkling halo."[17]

This was the reenactment of sentiment, designed to recreate the feeling of a feeling. This vivid and poetic imagery dominates the accounts of listeners who tried to express the effects of Beethoven upon them. For one listener, the opening of the Ninth is Dante's dark wood or the moment of suffering when every man becomes a Job; for another, the beginning of the Fourth is a solitary walk after the death of a loved one; still another writes that his whole symphonic oeuvre is a world with savage lands and precipices, where night falls suddenly and terribly.[18] The scherzo of the Ninth "produces the effect" of a playful dance of girls on a beautiful summer's night on the prairie, and its first movement is like the trembling, buzzing whir of the world being born.[19]

A second effect of accepting absolute music as expressive without reference to a determinate subject was the interiorization of experience. With the liberation of musical meaning from words, experience necessarily became intensely subjective—more even than during the revolution of Gluck, when listeners sounded their own emotions to feel the full impact of passions inscribed in the music. Realizing that the elusive meaning of music was not reducible to anything so simple as a single emotion—or perhaps emotion at all—these listeners enclosed the act of listening in a private space closed off from community and inaccessible to language. The result was more than just a new rhetorical style of describing. This perception created a new experience, one deeper, more personal, more powerful.

Beyond the anecdotal evidence of deeply engaged audiences, there is a structural correlation between the belief that musical meaning surpasses words and absorbed listening. For earlier audiences, those seeking to pinpoint the precise sounds imitated or emotions conveyed, aesthetic experience had been first intellectual and then emotional, a process of "translat[ing] fugitive sounds into images . . . [and] complet[ing] within us the effect of an imitation," as Quatremère de Quincy had described it.[20] To reject images and imitations created the sense that the intellect was somehow not fully engaged when listening, that music touched a more elemental stratum. Adophe Guéroult, for instance, wrote that music was "a mysterious and invisible voice without form or figure that speaks to the soul without appearing to the senses"; Joseph d'Ortigue said that the musician addressed himself "more to the soul than to the ear."[21] Finding mental images impoverishing and language inadequate, listeners cast perceived musical content in spiritual terms, almost as though the musical tones were necessary but secondary to the ethereal, intuitive content they carried.

Of course this was not a monolithic process; listening for wordless content was not a great spirit that swept through all listeners at the same time. Moreover we must be sensitive to the possibility of imitation not just in behavior but in styles of description, too. To insist upon too rigid a correspondence between the perceived nature of expression and the degree of engagement while listening is misleading, both conceptually and historically. The point must stand properly qualified, but it still stands: for those who truly experienced music as they described, who resisted seeking concrete sounds and emotions as they listened, and who believed that the content they heard could only be conveyed indirectly, hearing meant total absorption.

This entailed greater participation on the part of listeners and greater attention during performances. It also convinced listeners that their own musical experience was unique. No one could possibly know what I feel, the reasoning went; even I can hardly express it to myself. An 1835 essay on Beethoven described a "poetic" attitude before music rather than one that was "technical" or "didactic," insisting that the act of listening was the interrogation of "the voice that responds from within." In a similar vein, Fétis rejected "programs" and "prescribed feelings" and argued that the actual sentiments stirred by music could not be communicated, "for out of a thousand individuals perhaps not one would feel the same as another."[22] The title character from Balzac's novella *Massimilla Doni* rehearses aloud the reasons for this subjectivity in listening: "The other arts impress definite creations on the mind, music is infinite in its creations. We are obliged to accept the poet's ideas, the painter's picture, the sculpture's statue; but each one of us interprets music according to the dictates of his sorrow or his joy, his hopes or his despair. While other arts circumscribe our thoughts, and direct them upon one definite object, music sets them loose upon all nature which it has the power to interpret to us."[23] Late-eighteenth- and early-nineteenth-century listeners, believing they had found objective images and emotions in the music, had claimed that all sensitive listeners could be united in common experience. Now every man was an island. "The immense superiority of music over the other arts is in the marvelous variety of feelings that strike each individual differently."[24] The once-common event of commenting upon the music from your opera box or while tea was being served, already weakened by a nineteenth-century code of behavior that called such chatter bad form, was further deprived of legitimacy by the belief that your own impressions were incommunicably unique.

Musical experience of the 1830s and 1840s bears all the marks of romanticism. Subjective, intuitive, and infused with mystical feeling, musical experience was undeniably romantic, if we take as a guide Baudelaire's definition of romanticism as a sense of profound inwardness—a "manner of feeling," as he writes, rather than a concern for subject or a search for eternal verities.[25] Moreover there are clear similarities between the descriptive styles of spectators and those of authors and artists associated with romanticism. E. T. A. Hoffmann called music the most genuinely romantic of all the arts, and Beethoven was for him "a purely romantic composer."[26] Balzac employed rich metaphors to convey the sense of Beethoven: in *Séraphita* he describes the symphonies as "a river of light" and "waves of flames"; and in a letter to an acquaintance he painted the Fifth as "fairies who flutter with womanly beauty and the diaphanous wings of angels."[27]

The similarities between spectators' experiences and descriptions from the pillars of French romanticism were not the result of romanticism "in the air," as some have suggested.[28] Nor was Beethoven's surprising success at the Société des Concerts, or the rapid rise of concert societies after 1830, primarily the consequence of audiences first reading romantic literature and imagining its ethereal phrases as they listened to music. The first complication for these explanations concerns dates. Hugo, Balzac, and Sand published their own responses to Beethoven well after sold-out audiences hailed him as a genius; Émile Deschamps's opening volley in the popular campaign for romanticism, his *Préface des études françaises et étrangères* (1828), came in the year that audiences had started to gather at the Conservatoire; E. T. A. Hoffmann began to appear in translation only in the following year; and romanticism gained institutional credibility in 1830, when Lamartine was elected to the Académie Française and Hugo's *Hernani* scored its triumph at the Théâtre Français. Finally, as James Smith Allen writes, the literature read by the French in the 1820s and 1830s generally lacks the dreamy sensibilities we commonly associate with romanticism and can be called romantic only from a formal point of view—that is, their verses were less rigid than before, the three unities were sometimes violated, and their narratives included more local color.[29]

But even putting aside the question of dates, there are more severe difficulties in explaining a shift in musical taste through a new *Zeitgeist*. Listeners of the early 1800s found Beethoven *musically* inapproachable. To French ears, his symphonies were filled with barbarous chords and incoherent progressions; they had no meaning. The symphonies fell into none of the categories of aesthetic understanding that French listeners of the time possessed to make sense of the music. They had no key to decode its language, no grammar to read its expression. In these circumstances no literary idea alone is sufficient to bring instant understanding, any more than a Russian with no English could read *Ulysses* in the original by imbibing the spirit of modernism.

The explanation for the similarity between the language of romanticism and the musical accounts of spectators lies in their common acceptance of absolute music on its own terms. Stripped of a language to convey the sense of an art better felt than thought about, and perceiving the experience above all to be intensely subjective, Balzac, Berlioz, Delacroix, and Sand, as well as ordinary listeners and critics, attempted to define an infinite realm of which instrumental music gave a glimpse. Necessarily they resorted to imprecision and metaphor. Romanticism does not account for the deeper aesthetic engagement of audiences and their acceptance of pure music; instead, what made that acceptance and the deeper engagement it produced possible, along with a host of other cultural patterns, accounts for romanticism.

In his characteristically brilliant and elusive study *The Idea of Absolute Music*, Carl Dahlhaus discusses the critical acceptance of absolute music. Speculating about nonmusical influences on musical experience, Dahlhaus writes: "Instrumental music's claim to being taken seriously as a manifestation of 'pure art,' rather than being dismissed as empty sound, was nourished by literary models that guided a new musical consciousness to its formulation, through which it was able to constitute itself as musical consciousness in the first place." [30]

"Literary models that guided a new musical consciousness to its formulation": this phrase is the starting point for understanding the similarities between the musical accounts of French spectators and the other, nonmusical preoccupations and themes that we associate with romanticism. As spectators began to approach harmony as an irreducibly meaningful medium, their experience necessarily grew more subjective and its description more indirect than for contemporaries of Rameau or Gluck. The style and wording of these accounts, however, were by no means inevitable, and listeners borrowed from the vocabularies of other cultural structures of the period. These vocabularies may well have played a part in shaping the emergent musical experiences.

Some understood their oceanic experiences in religious terms, echoing the humanistic language of any number of utopians, from neo-Catholic, to Saint-Simonian, to socialist.[31] In its intimate associations music touched the common human essence, they said, weaving social and temperamental differences together into a harmonious fabric. One thinks of Mme Quinet needing to remind herself that the Conservatoire was not a church and its musicians not a college of priests celebrating divine service. In his book *A New Faith Sought in Art from Rembrandt to Beethoven* (1850), Alfred Dumesnil claimed that the holy experience of music made all listeners brothers, giving them "a diversity of emotions in common." [32] Another listener, writing in the *Courrier des théâtres*, likened listening to prayer since both contain "something mysterious that words cannot capture, something infinite that exceeds the bounds of thought." [33]

Here the musical experience of interior communion met the language of romantic spirituality, with each guiding and shaping the other. "The religious influence that [the Allegretto of Beethoven's Seventh Symphony] exercises over its listeners," reads a review, "gave this concert a character yet more grave and lofty than usual." A chamber concert sponsored by Zimmerman was heard "in a religious silence and welcomed with lively pleasure." The public of the Athénée Musicale "listened religiously" to works by Beethoven and Mozart and then "filed out with serenity, as though it had just attended a religious ceremony."[34]

Still, romantic universalism in musical experience contained a paradox: for how could social unity come from profound subjectivity? Subjectivity, after all, was precisely what the revolutionaries forty years earlier had tried to purge from musical experience as divisive. Now listeners called it the very keystone of cohesion. Two new realities made the turnabout possible. First, the full legitimation of musical harmony gave listeners a potent metaphor for conceptualizing a smooth merging of social differences; and, second, those who shared the July Monarchy's vision of democracy, which relied upon hierarchy and distinction to ensure social solidity, thought of social coherence as a composite of necessarily heterogeneous parts. Both variables declared cooperative individuality—not the radical egalitarianism of the Jacobins—to be the sine qua non of unity.

Heinrich Heine used the metaphor of harmony to call Meyerbeer's music the consummate expression of the July Monarchy. Rossini's Italian operas with their glorious solo passages had been perfectly suited to the Restoration, he wrote, an age characterized by self-seeking and greed. The modern period, by contrast, was the age of the masses, a time to find common political and social ground. "In Meyerbeer . . . we find the sovereign power of harmony. In the river of harmonic masses, melodies melt into one another, they flow together, just as the personal sentiments of every individual lose themselves in the general sentiment of a single people."[35] That social application would have been unthinkable to a listener convinced that musical harmony was arid or scientific.

Genuinely wanting reconciliation and mindful perhaps of the message of visionaries who promised a better state of affairs, spectators saw an ideal for society in musical experience. Music made the public one, it unified society spiritually without denying differences. As Usmar Bonnaire wrote, musical harmony was "the instrument most suited for harmony among men."[36] Music was "a respectable and indeed distinguished *juste milieu*," wrote the *Revue et gazette musicale*, "an art of reconciliation between all the classes of society."[37]

There are ideological reverberations in this language, sustained as it is by an undertone of concord. What were the preoccupations that produced such writing? Distress over social inequities? despair in the century's emptiness? defiance of the regime's smug certainties? As always the silence of the vast majority thwarts and frustrates. Still, the accounts show how aesthetic perceptions created musical experience particularly susceptible to social applications. And more: they tell how musical harmony encouraged humanitarianism among the bourgeoisie.

Well, maybe. But we shouldn't forget that the language of social harmony—and for that matter the language of the July Monarchy—is particularly elusive precisely because it does not necessarily imply equality. That the *Revue et gazette musicale* used the phrase *juste milieu* to describe social reconciliation is telling. The term was used primarily by supporters of the July Monarchy to characterize the regime's middle way between monarchical despotism and revolutionary excess.[38] *Juste milieu* conveyed all the liberal middle-class virtues of the day—freedom, popular sovereignty, the spirit of '89. Its associations cast society as a harmonious whole, a happy, inclusive, interdependent unity.[39]

The government had good reason to emphasize these principles. There were plenty who felt betrayed by the regime, and they were ready to take to the streets to show it. Mindful of the discontent, liberals moved quickly to explain—ideally, explain *away*, and in a fashion that would keep their own footing secure—the revolution that swept them to power. The July days became at once less and more revolutionary. If the violence was best papered over and forgotten, its effects were exaggerated and declared a bounty for all. It was, after all, a *bourgeois* revolution, and who wasn't bourgeois in this new age?[40] The master stroke of liberals after 1830 was to transform the ill-defined term into a watchword of social inclusiveness. Traditional privilege was abolished, they trumpeted, meritocracy replaced venality, education would be secularized and the bureaucracy opened to talent. Best of all, the king was really a populist.

But in truth the so-called bourgeois revolution was far from being as inclusive as the adjective implied. In fact French society after Louis-Philippe's changes took effect looked remarkably similar to French society of the late Restoration.[41] Despite the broadening of the electorate (suffrage was still apportioned by payment of the *cens*, a tax on property) and a lower voting age, the populace who voted and the deputies they elected after July had roughly the same political complexion as before. Landed proprietors and bureaucrats from Napoleon's administration returned to key governmental posts.[42] Even the citizen-king's ingratiating ordinariness rang slightly false. Louis-Philippe played up the superficial details of his daily life—the green umbrella, the visits to prostitutes, the casual strolls in public—while obscuring the more significant continuities with the Restoration.[43]

Like the phrase "bourgeois revolution," "harmony" cut both ways, excluding even as it included, hiding as much as it revealed. Alongside spectators in the hall who felt imminent social salvation were listeners who used the same aesthetic experience to assuage their fears and congratulate their successes. These listeners were experts in enforcing a code of etiquette that denounced all who deviated from its rules even as they rejoiced in its reputed equality; they swelled up when they thought of the social harmony music brought, even as rioters died in the streets. Of course they weren't hypocrites, far from it: to succeed nowadays demanded practicality, a level head, uprightness, and a hard line against the agitators. And anyway, that's what harmony meant—leaders and followers, melody and accompaniment, individuals perfectly free to follow their own path so long as they stayed where they belonged. Above all, order.

The acceptance of harmony, more than anything else, defined romantic musical experience. Aesthetically, it turned listeners inward to produce absorbed silence and attention. Socially, it made the hall a metaphor for the street. And its political applications spanned the ideological spectrum. Harmony momentarily suspended the mistrust. It permitted spectators to tell themselves that all men really were brothers, just as the chorus sang out in Beethoven's Ninth at the Conservatoire. It sanctified individuality without sacrificing the community.

For those most hopeful, those who shared Heine's vision of society as a single people, harmony truly fostered fellow-feeling. And for the rest it was a sop to the conscience when you had to pass the street people shivering outside the theater. The genius of the July Monarchy—though admittedly its demise, too—was in creating phrases that didn't always mean what they seemed.

Afterword

To generalize about listening is to place collective experience within two independent but related historical fields, the socially acceptable and the aesthetically accessible. These are the structures that circumscribe experience, defining the possibilities for behavior and gently pushing back the boundaries of the conceivable. The pace of change in listening is dependent upon the pace of change in political ideologies, social structures, and musical innovations. And because there are always possibilities for musical innovation and change in patterns of sociability, listening continues to evolve.

An expanding horizon of musical meaning, like expanding rings on the water's surface, still contains what earlier boundaries enclosed. Musically literate spectators, especially since the time when concerts featured the work of dead composers, have carried within them a library of symphonies, sonatas, operas, and concertos that spectators before them could not have possessed. By 1840 in France spectators were aware of the imitative devices in music, of music deliberately programmatic, and of music that defied all programs. Familiar with a range of expressive techniques, the listener could choose among (or employ simultaneously) several ways of listening that had each appeared at particular moments in the past. Hector Berlioz makes this point at the end of a long, spirited toast to music in "The Farewell Dinner." By turns damning the philistines and praising the artist who resists the lure of easy fame, Berlioz gives what amounts to a history of listening in France over the previous hundred years: music can be experienced sensuously, producing "a voluptuous feeling"; it can be associated with ideas, proving "a pleasant diversion for the mind"; and it can transcend discursive thought, launching listeners "into the infinite."[1]

Ways of listening are cumulative. Musical innovations supplement the store of aesthetic possibilities over time. A *New York Times* review makes the point eloquently in a piece on Beethoven's Sixth Symphony.

> The "Pastoral" is like an opera, in that it has a "program," a narrative line hinted at in the movement titles and in more specific indications (identifications of particular bird calls) within each movement. Beethoven's music can therefore be heard as the illustration of an actual narrative tale. . . . But the true drama of a good musical performance lies on a musical level, not a verbal or narrative one. It is the sensuous beauty of flutes counterpointed with oboes and clarinets, the gathering energy of a vigorous Allegro, the climactic power of terpsichorean repetition, that thrills the music lover, not some vision of carousing peasants.[2]

But if all approaches are possible, they are not equally appealing. From the spectators who condemned the birds in the *Pastoral* to this critic for the *Times*, listeners who have discovered the irreducible language of harmonies, rhythms, and melodies have deemed imitations and programs artistically inferior. Berlioz called the irreducible language of tones music's "proper realm," the experience of which makes us as gods.[3]

There is a related movement in descriptions of musical meaning. As long as spectators believed that meaning was limited to sounds, images, and emotions, the description of that meaning was limited only by the verbal precision of an author. Under such assumptions, the flutes in the garden scene of Lully's *Armide* were obviously birds, and the shifting prologue to *The Creation* was undeniably primordial chaos. The moment spectators acknowledged an irreducible language of musical logic, such attempts at objective description became inadequate. As with ways of listening, various possibilities from the past exist for describing musical meaning (e.g., the *Pastoral* as "carousing peasants"), but once we've acknowledged the irreducibility of musical meaning, the more precise our verbal descriptions are, the more naive they seem.

The only solution is to resort to the language of metaphor, with its inevitable approximations, to discuss musical meaning.[4] Without metaphor we are reduced either to silence or to highly technical structural analyses like those of Heinrich Schenker—analyses that tell us about as much about musical meaning as a purely grammatical analysis might reveal about the meaning of Saint John's Gospel.[5] Groping to convey our experience of the pure language of tones we feel rather like Dante in the *Paradiso*—thwarted by words, resorting more and more to analogy, frustrated that he must rely upon the intellect to relate his vision of God. "Passing beyond the human cannot be worded," he writes; "let this example serve until grace grant you the experience."[6]

Marcel Proust understood the difficulty of conveying musical meaning verbally, and he gives what is at once the most and least direct account of musical experience imaginable—most in its immediacy of feeling, least in the virtual absence of any musical reference. Here the metaphors themselves assume quasi-musical form with their variations and reiterations:

Whereas the sonata opened upon a dawn of lilied meadows, parting its slender whiteness to suspend itself over the frail and yet consistent mingling of a rustic bower of honeysuckle with white geraniums, it was upon continuous, level surfaces like those of the sea that, in the midst of a stormy morning beneath an already lurid sky, there began, in an eerie silence, in an infinite void, this new masterpiece, and it was into a roseate dawn that, in order to construct itself progressively into me, this unknown universe was drawn from silence and from night. This so novel redness, so absent from the tender, rustic, pale sonata, tinged all the sky, as dawn does, with a mysterious hope. And a song already thrilled the air, a song on seven notes, but the strangest, the most different from any that I had ever imagined, from any that I could ever have been able to imagine, at once ineffable and piercing, no longer the cooing of a dove as in the sonata, but rending the air, as vivid as the scarlet tinge in which the opening bars had been bathed, something like the mystical crow of a cock, an ineffable but over-shrill appeal of the eternal morning. The cold atmosphere, soaked in rain, electric—of a quality so different, feeling wholly other pressures, in a world so remote from that, virginal and endowed only with vegetable life, of the sonata— charged at every moment, obliterating the empurpled promise of Dawn.[7]

This necessary imprecision is more than a historical observation. It is now, for all who acknowledge it, an inalterable feature of musical experience. It may well mean that the community in musical experience dreamed of by the French revolutionaries is now impossible. Deprived of the means to describe musical meaning, spectators are left with their own incommunicable experiences.

Even harmony now seems a bit shopworn. The various polarizing ideologies that have successfully supplanted that dominant metaphor in musical experience since the 1840s—nationalism in the nineteenth century, fascism and communism in the twentieth (the Nazis' descriptions of listening to Wagner and *Pravda*'s scathing reviews of Shostakovich come to mind)—would apparently deny any necessary equation between profound musical engagement and a feeling of spiritual connection with all of humanity. In our own atomized, eclectic, post-everything society the metaphor more likely to give voice to our own ineffable impressions and bridge the inner experiences of a fragmented public is the culture of *technique*—the acoustics of the hall, fidelity in recording and reproduction, the perfect sound, all the right notes. Harmony is still within the border of experience, but it has lost the rich resonance that made it so potent in the romantic decades.

All of which makes the point that, unlike the expanding horizons of musical sense, the social aspects of experience are successive, not cumulative. What remains constant on the social side is the pressure to adhere to a particular generation's expectations. In 1758 Jacques Lacombe wrote that the arts "oblige men . . . to change their savage manners, to assume a more sociable exterior, to make themselves more affable." Few listeners more or less integrated into their society could disagree—not the eighteenth-century bachelor who spent the opera strolling up and down the parterre eyeing ladies through his lorgnette, nor revolutionary spectators who sang and danced as the soldier-singers set off cannons, nor the banker sitting perfectly still next to his wife because even whispering during Beethoven was frowned upon. It's just a matter of knowing which manners are savage and which are affable.

We are not immune to social conditioning. In 1985 I attended a performance of Gluck's *Iphigénie en Tauride* at the cavernous Palais Garnier. Having purchased one of the few remaining tickets, I climbed to the highest row of the uppermost balcony. The seats were surely the farthest from the stage in the entire house—and in that hall the distance is considerable. The lights dimmed, the curtain rose, the music began, and a spectator sitting next to me rattled a candy wrapper. Instantly a lady on the other side emitted a ferocious *shh!* and shot the poor spectator a terrible scowl. Several moments later she turned to me with a wide, triumphant smile. She had done her duty in the service of Art!

Romantic musical experience lives on in unexpected ways. Alongside genuine musical absorption is a package of reflexes set on a trip-wire to protect the aesthetic moment, nudging the dozers, discouraging applause between movements, glaring at the coughers. It almost seems that profound engagement has passed from aesthetic consequence to social imperative. Like the eighteenth-century listener observed weeping during a comic opera, we consider it our duty to be moved every time we listen. Of course the prevailing patterns of behavior are a boon to listening, and I suppose we should be grateful: the climate-

controlled, soundproofed halls with their comfortable seats and unobstructed views permit utter, undistracted communion as never before.
But ever since romanticism made a religion of art and raised worship to
a social virtue, it's not always been possible to tell true belief from mere
fascination with the sacraments.

Notes

Introduction

1. See Hans-Georg Gadamer, *Truth and Method* (New York: Crossroad Publishing Co., 1988), 238–53.

2. Carl Dahlhaus emphasizes this point in his essay "Problems in Reception History." "The forces that condition reception are the final arbiter in understanding musical meaning," he writes, "a meaning not contained within an abstract text but one which takes concrete form, and in turn 'concretises' the text, only in the course of reception" (*Foundations of Music History*, trans. J. B. Robinson [Cambridge: Cambridge University Press, 1967], 151). See also Mark Evan Bonds, *Wordless Rhetoric: Musical Form and the Metaphor of the Oration* (Cambridge: Harvard University Press, 1991), esp. 181–204.

For more general historical treatments of the social production of meaning, see Roger Chartier, "Intellectual History or Sociocultural History?: The French Trajectories," in Dominick LaCapra and Stephen L. Kaplan, eds., *Modern European Intellectual History: Reappraisals and New Perspectives* (Ithaca: Cornell University Press, 1982); idem, *Cultural History* (Ithaca: Cornell University Press, 1988); Lynn Hunt, ed., *The New Cultural History* (Berkeley: University of California Press, 1989).

3. Wolfgang Iser, *The Act of Reading: A Theory of Aesthetic Response* (Baltimore: University of Maryland Press, 1978).

4. This is in part why I must differ most strongly with the way such music historians as Lawrence Kramer and Susan McClary locate a prevailing misogyny in much of the classical tradition. I have no reason to doubt that Kramer perceives a "phallicized gaze" when listening to the Gretchen section of Liszt's *Faust* Symphony or an "objectivist-masculinist epistemology" embodied in Haydn's *The Creation*; likewise, I cannot doubt McClary when she claims to

hear a narrative of rape and murder in Beethoven's Ninth Symphony, whose final choral movement, she writes, "forces closure by bludgeoning the cadence and the piece to death."

But such a view of musical meaning, which I think neglects the actual musical features that frame our perceptions and delimit possible musical content, is arguably as one-sided as its opposite extreme, which dismisses listeners' own aesthetic and ideological expectations as irrelevant in deriving some supposedly fixed musical meaning. My larger objection to the approach of Kramer and McClary (who might respond that the meanings they perceive are indeed embedded in the musical structure) is that, lacking evidence that others in the past have also heard this meaning, its historical claims—that Haydn has reinforced a masculinist ideology, that the violence of nineteenth-century symphonists is more devastating than heavy metal—remain without foundation (see Lawrence Kramer, *Music as Cultural Practice, 1800–1900* [Berkeley: University of California Press, 1990], esp. 106–20; idem, "Haydn's Chaos, Schenker's Order; or, Hermeneutics and Musical Analysis: Can They Mix?" *19th-Century Music* 16 (1992): 3–17; Susan McClary, *Feminine Endings: Music, Gender, and Sexuality* [Minneapolis: University of Minnesota Press, 1991], esp. 127–30).

5. See Hans Robert Jauss, *Toward an Aesthetic of Reception*, trans. Timothy Bahti (Minneapolis: University of Minnesota Press, 1982); E. H. Gombrich, *Art and Illusion: A Study in the Psychology of Pictorial Representation* (Princeton: Princeton University Press, 1960); Reinhart Koselleck, "'Space of Experience' and 'Horizon of Expectation': Two Historical Categories," in *Futures Past: On the Semantics of Historical Time*, trans. Keith Tribe (Cambridge: MIT Press, 1985).

6. See Norbert Elias, *The Civilizing Process*, trans. Edmund Jephcott, 2 vols. (New York: Urizen Books, 1978; Pantheon Books, 1982), esp. vol. 2, *Power and Civility*, pt. 2, "Synopsis: Towards a Theory of Civilizing Processes."

7. Dahlhaus, *Foundations of Music History*, 154.

8. Claude Lévi-Strauss, *The Savage Mind* (Chicago: University of Chicago Press, 1966), 262.

Chapter 1. Opera as Social Duty

1. *Almanach des spectacles* (Paris: Chez Duchesne, 1759), 19. All translations are my own unless otherwise indicated.

2. Bridard de la Garde, *Lettres à Thérèse*, quoted in Elizabeth Giuliani, "Le Public de l'Opéra de Paris de 1750 à 1760," *International Review of the Aesthetics and Sociology of Music* 8 (1977): 175; see also John Lough, *Paris Theatre Audiences in the Seventeenth and Eighteenth Centuries* (London: Oxford University Press, 1957), esp. 206–71.

3. "Sentiments des parisiens sur la presence du roi et de sa famille royale à la représentation de l'Opéra de Roland, le 3 janvier 1744," *Mercure de France*, Feb. 1744, quoted in Henri Lagrave, *Le Théâtre et le public à Paris de 1715 à 1750* (Paris: Librairie C. Klincksick, 1972), 213.

4. Nicolas Bricaire de la Dixmérie, *Lettres sur l'état présent de nos spectacles, avec des vues nouvelles sur chacun d'eux; particulièrement sur la Comédie Française et l'Opéra* (Amsterdam: Chez Duchesne, 1765), 48: "The supporters of the Opéra Comique are constantly complaining about the *dignity* of our great Opéra. They compare it to Court etiquette. . . . But they should remember that the Opéra is the spectacle of magnificence."

5. Five academies were formed in a single decade: Académie Royale de Danse (1661), Académie des Inscriptions et Belles Lettres (1663), Académie des Sciences (1666), Académie Royale de Musique (1669), and Académie Royale d'Architecture (1671). The Académie Française was establised in 1635, and the Académie Royale de Peinture et de Sculpture in 1648. See Robert Isherwood, *Music in the Service of the King: France in the Seventeenth Century* (Ithaca: Cornell University Press, 1972); Philippe Beaussant, *Lully, ou le musicien du Soleil* (Paris: Éditions Gallimard, 1992).

6. Graham Sadler, "Rameau's Singers and Players at the Paris Opéra: A Little-Known Inventory of 1738," *Early Music* 11 (1983): 458.

7. Spire Pitou, *The Paris Opera: An Encyclopedia of Operas, Ballets, Composers, and Performers*, 4 vols. (Westport, Conn.: Greenwood Press, 1983), 1:12–13.

8. "Mémoire des ouvrages de peinture faits au théâtre de l'Académie Royale de Musique" (1750), Archives Nationales (hereafter A. N.), AJ[13] 6.

9. Ibid.

10. [Pierre] Patte, *Essai sur l'architecture théâtrale* (Paris: Chez Moutard, 1782), 194.

11. Letter dated 1784, A. N. O[1] 628.

12. "Mémoire des ouvrages de peinture," A. N. AJ[13] 6. See also Gösta Bergman, *Lighting in the Theatre* (Stockholm: Almqvist and Wiksell, International, l977), 125.

13. "A Monsieur le prévost des marchands" (ca. 1766), A. N. AJ[13] 6.

14. "Loges louées à l'année et des abonnements d'entrée à l'Opéra" (1750–51), A. N. AJ[13] 8.

15. A. N. AJ[13] 12.

16. A. N. O[1] 618.

17. "She also asked Mother if she could take me to the Opéra the day after tomorrow, in her box; she said that we would be alone there, and that we could talk the whole time without having to worry about anyone hearing us: I like that even more than the Opéra" (Cecile Volanges to Sophie Carnay, in Choderlos de Laclos, *Les Liaisons dangereuses* [Paris: Editions Gallimard, 1972], 93).

18. "Loges louées à l'année et des abonnements d'entrée à l'Opéra" (1750–51), A. N. AJ[13] 8.

19. *Mémoire relatif aux places du spectacle de l'Opéra et à leur prix* (1780), quoted in Elizabeth Giuliani, "Le Public et le repertoire de l'Opéra à l'époque de Jean-Jacques Rousseau, 1749–57" (Mémoire de Maîtrise, Université de Paris X, 1970–71), 57.

20. "Loges louées à l'année et des abonnements d'entrée à l'Opéra" (1750–51), A. N. AJ[13] 8.

21. Ibid.

22. Giuliani, "Le Public et le repertoire," 47–48.

23. "A Monsieur le prévost des marchands" [c. 1766], A. N. AJ[13] 6; Mme la comtesse de Genlis, *Dictionnaire critique et raisonné des étiquettes de la cour, et des usages du monde*, 2 vols. (Paris: Imprimerie de Fain, 1818), 2:311.

24. The number 1,000 is contained in "Notice de ce qui a été fait et observé à l'Opéra pour la représentation où Monseigneur le Dauphin et Madame la Dauphine sont venus le mardy 15 juin 1773," A. N. O[1] 120, quoted in *Recherches sur la musique française classique* 19 (1979): 255.

25. René Louis de Voyer de Paulmy, marquis d'Argenson, *Mémoires et journal inédit*, 5 vols. (Paris: Chez P. Jannet, 1857), 4:161 (Dec. 1753); Jean-Jacques Rousseau, "Lettre sur la musique française," in Denise Launay, ed., *La Querelle des bouffons: Texte des pamphlets avec introduction, commentaires et index*, 3 vols. (Geneva: Minkoff Reprints, 1973), 1:764.

26. Louis-Sebastien Mercier, *Du Théâtre, ou nouvel essai sur l'art dramatique* (Amsterdam: n.p., 1773), 347; *L'Esprit du "Mercure de France," depuis son origine jusqu'à 1792*, 5 vols. (Paris: Chez Barba, 1810), 3:74.

27. Jean-Marie Bernard Clément, *Anecdotes dramatiques*, 2 vols. (Paris: Chez la Veuve Duchesne, 1775), 1:4–5.

28. [Dubuisson], *Lettres du commissaire Dubuisson au marquis de Caumont, 1735–41*, ed. A. Rouxel (Paris: E. Soye et Fils, 1882), 2.

29. See for instance the haughty description of the parterre in *Réponse du coin du roi au coin de la reine* (1753), 4–5: "You might imagine yourself in a Republic; in the parterre you'll meet a lot of witty gentlemen who do nothing but say clever things; but we know that clever words aren't always a good thing" (in Launay, ed., *La Querelle des bouffons*).

30. See James H. Johnson, "The Encyclopedists and the Querelle des Bouffons: Reason and the Enlightenment of Sentiment," *Eighteenth-Century Life* 10 (1986): 12–27; Launay, ed., *La Querelle des bouffons*; Louisette Reichenburg, *Contribution à l'histoire de la querelle des bouffons* (Philadelphia: University of Pennsylvania Press, 1937).

31. "Entrées à l'Opéra" (1725), A. N. AJ[13] A3-V.

32. "Mémoire concernant l'Académie Royale de Musique, donné à M. Berger en 1744," A. N. O[1] 628.

33. For Louis XIV's edict forbidding "all persons, regardless of their qualities and conditions—including officials of his household, his guards, his gendarmes, his light troops, musketeers and others—from entering without paying," see "De par le roi, et monsieur le prévost de Paris: ou monsieur son lieutenant général de police" (1699), Bibliothèque Nationale (hereafter B. N.), Collection Delamare, Ms. 21625, fol. 241.

34. "État des entrées à l'Opéra ordonnées par le roi, 1750," A. N. AJ[13] 3.

35. "The number of these entries successively granted is considerable," the director of the Opéra Berger wrote to the comte de Maurepas in 1744, "and if the practice continues the Opéra will not be able to support itself" (A. N. AJ[13] 3); see also "État des entrées à l'Opéra ordonnées par le roi, 1750."

36. The portrait of a bustling, rambunctious, minimally attentive audience that emerges from eighteenth-century memoirs, police records, and pamphlets stands in sharp contrast to traditional scholarly depictions of the Old Regime French musical public. For altogether laudable reasons—though with very little evidence—scholars have assumed that the seriousness of the music must have

brought an appropriately respectful silence from the public. This passage from Paul-Marie Masson, the noted Rameau scholar, is typical:

> It is obvious that the Lullian overture is no mere formal lucubration designed to give the audience time to settle down at their leisure. It is an introduction of solemn brilliance, designed to capture and hold the attention of the spectator and prepare him for the magnificance of the performance that is about to take place before his eyes. It must condition the spectator to tragic emotion and in this respect has an expressive role.
> *(From Masson, "French Opera from Lully to Rameau," in Gerald Abraham et al., eds., The New Oxford History of Music, vol. 5, Opera and Church Music, 1630–1750, ed. Anthony Lewis and Nigel Fortune [London: Oxford University Press, 1975], 223.)*

37. See James R. Anthony, "The French Opera-Ballet in the Early Eighteenth Century: Problems of Definition and Classification," *Journal of the American Musicolocigal Society* 18 (1965): 197–206.

38. See ibid., 203–5.

39. For a listing of all the works performed at the Académie Royale de Musique in the period 1749–56, see Giuliani, "Le Public et le repertoire," 66–70.

40. Robert Fajon, *L'Opéra à Paris du roi soleil à Louis le bien-aimé* (Geneva: Slatkine, 1984), 141.

41. Théodore de Lajarte, *Bibliothèque musicale du théâtre de l'Opéra: Catalogue historique, chronologique, anecdotique*, 2 vols. (Paris: Librairie des Bibliophiles, 1878; reprint ed., Hildesheim: Georg Olms Verlag, 1969), 1:24–27, 46–47, 52–53.

42. See Caroline Wood, "Orchestra and Spectacle in the *Tragédie en Musique* 1643–1715: Oracle, *Sommeil* and *Tempête*," *Proceedings of the Royal Musical Association* 108 (1981–82): 26.

43. See Joyce Newman, *Jean-Baptiste de Lully and His Tragédies-Lyriques* (Ann Arbor: UMI Research Press, 1979), 26.

44. Jean-Baptiste Lully, *Alceste*, ed. Henri Prunières (Paris: Édition de la Revue Musicale, 1932), 166–67, 260–70, 286.

45. The chorus is from Lully, *Armide*, ed. Théodore de Lajarte (Paris: Editions Michaelis, n.d.; reprint ed., New York: Broude Brothers, 1971), 126.

Incongruously, the spirit of youthfulness dominates the first two-thirds of *Atys*, the darkest of Lully's works, before the mood suddenly turns somber with Atys mistakenly killing his lover and then himself in remorse. This rare, genuinely tragic ending was nevertheless followed in performance by the accustomed divertissement. The abbé de Villiers recorded the reaction of his fellow spectators to this jarring contrast:

> Mais on rit tout à coup, quand on les voit soudain
> Changer leur triste scène en spectacle badin,
> Et finir le récit de leurs peines secrètes,
> Par les gaillards refrains de fades chansonettes.
>
> But everyone laughs when they suddenly see
> The characters change from sadness to glee
> And finish the tale of their terrible pains
> With jolly tunes and insipid refrains.
> *(Quoted in Lully, Atys, ed. Lajarte [Paris: Éditions Michaelis, n.d.; reprint ed., New York: Broude Brothers, 1971], 2.)*

"Enjoy the bliss . . ." comes from Lully, *Armide*, 294. For Boileau's condemnation, see Nicolas Boileau, *Satires*, quoted in Cuthbert Girdlestone, *Jean-Philippe Rameau: His Life and Work* (New York: Dover Publications, 1969), 122.

46. See Isherwood, *Music in the Service of the King*, 220ff.

47. *Le Mercure de France*, Dec. 1733, 679–80.

48. Girdlestone, *Jean-Philippe Rameau*, 320.

49. Lajarte, *Bibliothèque musicale du théâtre de l'Opéra*, 1 : 191–92, 1 : 182–84.

50. See Girdlestone, *Jean-Philippe Rameau*, 130, 199, 277.

51. For a discussion of changing post-Regency patterns of aristocratic sociability in France, see Michel Antoine, *Louis XV* (Paris: Fayard, 1989), 262–63.

52. Jérome de La Gorce, "Décors et machines à l'Opéra de Paris au temps de Rameau: Inventaire de 1748," *Recherches sur la musique française classique* 21 (1983): 145–57.

53. Beaussant, *Lully*, 580, 717; Bergman, *Lighting in the Theatre*, 128; Charles Collé, *Journal et mémoires sur les hommes de lettres, les ouvrages dramatiques et les événements les plus mémorables du règne de Louis XV*, 3 vols. (Paris: Didot Frères, 1868), 1 : 70.

54. See Aubrey S. Garlington, Jr., "*Le Merveilleux* and Operatic Reform in Eighteenth-Century French Opera," *Musical Quarterly* 49 (1963): 484–97; see also Catherine Kintzler, *Poétique de l'Opéra français de Corneille à Rousseau* (Paris: Minerve, 1991), 259–77.

55. Toussaint Rémond de Saint-Mard, *Réflexions sur l'opéra* (The Hague: Chez Jean Neaulme, 1741), 20.

56. François Antoine de Chevrier, *Les Ridicules du siècle* (London: n.p., 1752), 60.

57. Charles Dufresny, *Les Amusements sérieux et comiques* (1731), quoted in Lagrave, *La Théâtre et le public à Paris*, 509–10.

58.   Souvent au plus beau char le contrepoids résiste
       Un dieu pend à cord et crie au machiniste;
       Un reste de forêt demeure dans la mer,
       Ou la moitié de ciel au milieu de l'enfer.
       (From Jean de La Fontaine, "Sur l'Opéra," in
       Oeuvres complètes, *ed. Pierre Clarac,*
       2 vols. [Paris: Gallimard, 1958], 2 : 617.)

59. Ivor Guest, *Le Ballet de l'Opéra de Paris* (Paris: Théâtre National de l'Opéra, 1976), 26.

60. Ibid., 38.

61. Ibid., 30.

62. Pidansat de Mairobert, *L'Espion anglais, ou correspondance secrète entre Milord All'eye et Milord All'ear*, 3 vols. (London: John Adamson, 1779), 3 : 218–19.

63. Chevrier, *Les Ridicules du siècle*, 65–66.

64. Ibid., 46.

65. Mme Lévesque, *Le Siècle, ou les Mémoires du comte de S * * * * (1736),

quoted in Lagrave, *Le Théâtre et le public à Paris*, 515; marquis de Surville, quoted in Isherwood, *Music in the Service of the King*, 317–18.

66. François Mayeur de Saint Paul, *Le Vol plus haut, ou l'espion des principaux théâtres de la capitale* . . . (Memphis: Chez Sincère, Libraire Réfugié au Puits de la Vérité, 1784), 21; J. B. Boyer, marquis d'Argens, *Lettres juives, ou correspondance philosophique, historique et critique, entre un juif voyageur en différents états de l'Europe, et ses correspondants en divers endroits* (The Hague: Chez Pierre Paupie, 1738), 184.

67. Beaussant, *Lully*, 538; Georges Snyders, *Le Goût musical en France aux XVIIᵉ et XVIIIᵉ siècles* (Paris: J. Vrin, 1968), 34.

68. See Lois Rosow, "How Eighteenth-Century Parisians Heard Lully's Operas: The Case of *Armide*'s Fourth Act," in John Hajdu Heyer, ed., *Jean-Baptiste Lully and the Music of the French Baroque: Essays in Honor of James R. Anthony* (Cambridge: Cambridge University Press, 1989), 213–37; on the general practice of adding divertissements to earlier stage works for their eighteenth-century revivals, see Rosow, "Lully's *Armide* at the Paris Opéra: A Performance History, 1686–1766" (Ph.D. diss., Brandeis University, 1981), esp. chaps. 6–7.

69. Lajarte, *Bibliothèque musicale du théâtre de l'Opéra*, 1:31, 45.

70. Rémond de Saint-Mard, *Réflexions sur l'opéra*, 96.

71. *Voltaire's Correspondence*, ed. Theodore Bestermann, 107 vols. (Geneva: Institut et Musée Voltaire, 1953), 2:387.

72. *Almanach des spectacles*, 1759, 20.

73. Ibid.

74. "Garde de l'Opéra," A. N. O¹ 620.

75. Jean-Philippe Rameau, *Observations sur notre instinct pour la musique*, quoted in Giuliani, "Le Public et le repertoire," 52; see also Girdlestone, *Jean-Philippe Rameau*, 124, 350.

76. B. N., Collection Delamare, Ms. 21625, fol. 256 (1728).

77. P. Lacome, "Les Pétits mémoires du parterre," in *Le Ménéstrel*, 6 April 1873, No. 19, 149.

78. Clément, *Anecdotes dramatiques*, 1:19.

79. Métra, Imbert, et al., *Correspondance secrète, politique et littéraire*, 18 vols. (London: Chez John Adamson, 1787), 3:283.

80. Collé, *Journal et mémoires*, 310.

81. [Chevalier de Moulay?], *Mémoires d'Anne-Marie de Moras, comtesse de Courbon*, 4 vols. (The Hague: Chez Pierre de Hondt, 1740), 3:36–37.

82. *Paris vu tel qu'il est* (Paris: n.p., 1781), 19.

83. Nicolas Edme Rétif de la Bretonne, *Tableaux de la bonne compagnie, ou traits caractéristiques, anecdotes secrètes, politiques, morales et littéraires, receuillies dans les sociétés du bon ton, pendant les années 1786 et 1787*, 2 vols. (Paris: n.p., 1787), 1:77–83.

84. *Un Provincial à Paris, pendant une partie de l'année 1789* (Strasbourg: Imprimerie de la Sociéte Typographique, n.d.), 92.

85. *Tableau du siècle par un auteur connu* (Geneva: n.p., 1759), 206.

86. Cazotte, "La Guerre de l'Opéra" (Paris: n.p., 1753), 12 (in Launay, ed., *La Querelle des bouffons*); Jacques Rochette de La Morlière, *Angola: Histoire indienne*, 2 vols. (Paris: n.p., 1746), 1:67.

87. Chevrier, *Les Ridicules du siècle*, 21.

88. Boyer, *Lettres juives*, 17.

89. [Moulay?], *Mémoires d'Anne-Marie de Moras, comtesse de Courbon*, 3:31.

90. *Almanach musical* (1775–79, 1781–83), 8 vols. (Geneva: Minkoff Reprints, 1972), 6:74–76.

91. Emmanuel duc de Croÿ, *Journal inédit*, 4 vols. (Paris: Flammarion, 1906), 1:54–55; La maréchale princesse de Beauvau and maréchal prince de Beauvau, *Souvenirs* (Paris: Léon Techener, 1872), Appendix, 22–23.

92. Croÿ, *Journal inédit*, 1:55.

93. *Almanach musical*, 6:74–76.

94. Pidansat de Mairobert, *L'Espion anglais*, 3:229.

95. François Antoine de Chevrier, *Paris: Histoire véridique, anecdotique, morale et critique, avec la clef* (The Hague: n.p., 1767), 79.

96. Albert de Lasalle, *Les Treize salles de l'Opéra* (Paris: Librairie Sartorius, 1875), 93.

97. Lagrave, *Le Théâtre et le public à Paris*, 423–24.

98. Marville to Maurepas, 17 Nov. 1745, quoted in Lagrave, ibid., 57.

99. La Morlière, *Angola*, 1:80: "They were in a most tender moment in their conversation when Almair, a scrupulous observer of *bienséance*, let them know they were in the fifth act, and as there is nothing *so indecent* as staying to the end, . . . they left."

100. Letter to *Mercure*, Nov. 1774, quoted in Nicole Wild, "La Vie musicale en France sous la régence, d'après le 'Mercure' " (Mémoire présenté pour l'obtention du diplôme de Musicologie sous la direction de Monsieur N. Dufourq, 22 juin 1961), 36–37.

101. *Un Provincial à Paris*, 95.

102. La Morlière, *Angola*, 1:69.

103. *Mercure*, Oct. 1718, quoted in Nicole Wild, "La Vie musicale en France sous la régence d'après le 'Mercure,' " 17.

104. La Morlière, *Angola*, 1:70.

105. Collé, *Journal et mémoires*, 2:116–17.

106. Voyer de Paulmy, *Mémoires*, 3:188.

107. See Orest Ranum, "Courtesy, Absolutism, and the Rise of the French State, 1630–1660," *Journal of Modern History* 52 (1980): 426–51.

108. Norbert Elias, *The Court Society* (New York: Pantheon Books, 1983), 20. See also Michael Curtin, "A Question of Manners: Status and Gender in Etiquette and Courtesy," *Journal of Modern History* 57 (1985): 395–423, for a general treatment of etiquette and books of etiquette on the Continent and in England.

109. "A man who knows the court is a master of his gestures, of his eyes, and of his face," writes La Bruyère. "He is profound, impenetrable; he dissimulates bad offices, smiles at his enemies, controls his irritation, disguises his passions, belies his heart, speaks and acts against his feelings" (*Oeuvres complètes* [Paris: Bibliothèque de la Pléiade, 1951], 235).

110. Alfred Franklin, *La Civilité, l'étiquette, la mode, le bon ton du XVIIe au XIXe siècle* (Paris: Émile-Paul, 1908), 131–32, 146.

111. Chevalier de Méré, *Oeuvres complètes du Chevalier de Méré*, ed. Charles

H. Boudhors. 3 vols. (Paris: Éditions Fernand Roches, 1930), 2 : 27–28.

112. Louis de Rouvroy, duc de Saint-Simon, *Mémoires,* quoted in Elias, *The Court Society,* 100.

113. Antoine de Courtin, *The Rules of Civility, Nouveau traité de la civilité* (London: R. Chiswell, T. Sawbridge, G. Wells, and R. Bentley, 1681), 47–48.

114. Le Cerf de la Vieville, *Comparaison de la musique italienne et de la musique française,* quoted in William Weber, "Learned and General Musical Taste in Eighteenth-Century France," *Past and Present* 39 (1980): 71; see also Girdlestone, *Jean-Philippe Rameau,* 58.

115. La Morlière, *Angola,* 1 : 70.

116. *Nouvelles de la cour et de la ville concernant le monde, les arts, les théâtres et les lettres 1734–1738, Publiées d'après une correspondance inédite conservées à la Bibliothèque Nationale* (Paris: n.p., 1879), 57.

117. "Lettre d'un philosophe moitié gai, moitié chagrin, sur quelques-uns de nos sottises, au baron de ***" (1770), 18 (in Launay, ed., *La Querelle des bouffons*).

118. François Antoine de Chevrier, *Observations sur le théâtre, dans lesquelles on examine avec impartialité l'état actuel des spectacles de Paris* (Paris: Chez Debure le Jeune, 1755), 33–34.

119. For an articulation of this notion of a public structured by representation, see Jürgen Habermas, *The Structural Transformation of the Public Sphere,* trans. Thomas Burger and Frederick Lawrence (Cambridge: MIT Press, 1989), chaps. 1 and 2; see also Ralph E. Giesey, "The King Imagined," in Keith Michael Baker et al., eds., *The French Revolution and the Creation of Modern Political Culture,* 3 vols., vol. 1, *The Political Culture of the Old Regime,* ed. Keith Michael Baker (Oxford: Pendragon Press, 1987), 41–59.

120. Letter dated 23 Dec. 1735, quoted in *Nouvelles de la cour et de la ville,* 57.

121. "It is not at all necessary to know the character of people, but only their interests, to guess more or less what they will say about everything. . . . Thus no one says what he thinks, but what suits him best to make others think; and the apparent zeal for truth is nothing other than a mark of interest. . . . Find out their societies, their coteries, their friends, the ladies they see, the authors they know; from that you can know in advance their opinion on a book about to appear which they have not read, a play about to open which they have not seen, a certain author whom they do not know, or a philosophical system about which they know nothing. . . . These people go out each night to learn in their little societies what to think the next day" (Jean-Jacques Rousseau, *Julie, ou la nouvelle Héloïse* [Paris: Édition Garnier-Flammarion, 1967], 164–65).

Chapter 2. Expression as Imitation

1. Rousseau, *Julie, ou la nouvellle Héloïse,* 85.

2. Boyé, *L'Expression musicale mise au rang des chimères* (Paris: Chez Veuve Duchesne, 1779), 23–24.

3. Pons-Augustin Alletz, *Manuel de l'homme du monde, ou connaissance générale des principaux états de la société, et de toutes les matières qui font le sujet des conversations ordinaires* (Paris: Chez Guillyn, 1761), 397.

4. "As long as composers of instrumental music do not have an action or expression to paint (one might cite, for example, the famous Tartini), they will produce hopeless noise. . . . Our operas should therefore contain expressive symphonies, that is, those whose meaning and spirit are always indicated in detail, whether by the scenery, the action, or the overall spectacle" (Jean le Rond d'Alembert, "De la liberté de la musique," in *Mélanges de littérature, d'histoire, et de philosophie* [Amsterdam: Chez Zachairie Chatelain et Fils, 1759], 455–56).

5. Jean François Marmontel, *Examen des réflexions de M. Dalembert sur la liberté de la musique*, and Charles Bâton, *Examen de la lettre de M. Rousseau*, quoted in Paul-Marie Masson, *L'Opéra de Rameau* (Paris: Henri Laurens, 1930; reprint ed., New York: Da Capo Press, 1972), 424. See also Snyders, *Le Goût musical en France*, 17–34; Maria Rika Maniates, " 'Sonate, que me veux-tu?': The Enigma of French Musical Aesthetics in the Eighteenth Century," *Current Musicology* 9 (1969): 117–40; Alfred Richard Oliver, *The Encyclopedists as Critics of Music* (New York: Columbia University Press, 1947), 16–19; John Neubauer, *The Emancipation of Music from Language: Departure from Mimesis in Eighteenth-Century Aesthetics* (New Haven: Yale University Press, 1986), 60–75.

6. André Morellet, *De l'expression en musique*, described in Snyders, *Le Goût musical en France*, 26.

7. Jean-Laurent Lecerf de la Viéville, *Comparaison de la musique italienne et de la musique francaise*, quoted in Snyders, *Le Goût musical en France*, 25, 27.

8. [Abbé d'Arnauld?], *Réflexions sur la musique en général, et sur la musique française en particulier* (n.p., 1754), 7.

9. Ibid., 13.

10. [De Rulhière], *Jugement de l'orchestre de l'Opéra* (n.p., [1753]), 5. "Although music can paint everything," he reasoned, "there are nevertheless paintings that good taste should avoid."

11. A. J. Labbet, abbé de Morambert, et A. Léris, *Sentiments d'un harmonophile, sur différents ouvrages de musique* (Amsterdam: n.p., 1756; reprint ed., Geneva: Minkoff Reprints, 1972), 65–75.

12. Cazotte, "La Guerre de l'Opéra," 13.

13. Charles Batteux, *Les Beaux-arts réduits à un même principe* (Paris: Durand, 1746), 266–67.

14. See Cazotte, "La Guerre de l'Opéra," 14–15.

15. Pierre Clément, *Les Cinq années littéraires, ou nouvelles littéraires, 1748–52*, 4 vols. (The Hague: Chez Ant. de Groot et Fils, 1754), 2:16; summary of overture quoted in Masson, "French Opera from Lully to Rameau," in Abraham et al., eds., *The New Oxford History of Music*, 257.

16. D'Aquin de Châteaulyon, *Siècle littéraire de Louis XV ou Lettres sur les hommes célèbres* (1753), Clément, *Les Cinq années littéraires*, and Michel-Paul-Guy de Chabanon, *Éloge de M. Rameau*, quoted in Girdlestone, *Jean-Philippe Rameau*, 300, 301, 307.

17. Jean-Baptiste Dubos, *Critical Reflections on Poetry, Painting and Music* (1719), trans. Thomas Nugent, 3 vols. (London: Norse, 1748; reprint ed., New York: AMS Press, 1978), 1:364.

18. [Arnauld?], *Réflexions sur la musique en général*, 25.

19. [Jacques] Lacombe, *La Spectacle des beaux arts; ou considérations touchant leur nature, leurs objets, leurs effets et leurs règles principales* (Paris: Chez Hardy Libraire, 1758), 307.

20. Gabriel Bonnot de Mably, *Lettres à Madame la Marquise de P*** sur l'Opéra* (Paris: Chez Didot, 1741), 152–53.

21. Batteux, *Les Beaux-arts réduits à un même principe*, 269.

22. *Mercure*, November 1714, quoted in Wild, "La Vie musicale en France," 36–37.

23. For two excellent discussions of the philosophes' approach in reworking the concept of imitation in musical expression, see Béatrice Didier, *La Musique des Lumières: Diderot, "L'Encyclopédie," Rousseau* (Paris: Presses Universitaires de France, 1985),19–39, and Catherine Kintzler, *Poétique de l'Opéra français de Corneille à Rousseau* (Paris: Minerve, 1991), 433–80.

24. Jean-Jacques Rousseau, "Imitation," in *Dictionnaire de musique* (Paris: Chez A. Belin, 1817), 197–98. See also Neubauer, *The Emancipation of Music from Language*, 85–102.

25. Denis Diderot, "Leçons de clavecin," in *Oeuvres complètes*, ed. Robert Lewinter, 15 vols. (Paris: Le Club Français du Livre, 1969–73), 9:506. See Neubauer, *Emancipation of Music from Language*, 109–20.

26. Rousseau develops this point in *Essai sur l'origine des langues* (Paris: Chez A. Belin, 1817).

27. Rousseau, "Mélodie" and "Harmonie," in *Dictionnaire de musique*, 216, 191.

28. Rousseau, "Imitation," in ibid., 198.

29. Kintzler, *Poétique de l'Opéra français*, 461.

30. Diderot, "Lettre sur les sourds et les muets," in *Oeuvres complètes*, 2: 562.

31. Diderot, "Lettre à Mademoiselle," in *Oeuvres complètes*, 2:581.

32. See Jean Ehrard, *L'Idée de nature en France dans la première moitié du XVIIIᵉ siècle*, 2 vols. (Paris: École Pratique des Hautes Études, 1963), 1:251–328; see also Ernst Cassirer, *The Philosophy of the Enlightenment*, trans. C. A. Koelln and James P. Pettegrove (Princeton: Princeton University Press, 1951), 275–360.

33. See Didier, *La Musique des lumières*, 22.

34. See James R. Anthony, *French Baroque Music from Beaujoyeulx to Rameau* (New York: W. W. Norton, 1974), 67–89; see also Anthony, "Jean-Baptiste Lully," *The New Grove Dictionary of Music and Musicians*, ed. Stanley Sadie, 20 vols. (London: MacMillan Publishers, Ltd., 1980), 11:323–24.

35. For a discussion of Lully's harmonic style, see Lionel de La Laurencie, *Lully* (Paris: Félix Alcan, 1919), 199ff.

36. "I waited for the aria," Goldoni writes. "The dancers appeared: I thought the act was over, not an aria. I spoke of this to my neighbour who scoffed at me and assured me that there had been six arias in the different scenes which I had just heard" (Carlo Goldoni, *Memoirs*, quoted in Anthony, *French Baroque Music*, 82).

37. André-Cardinal Destouches, *Omphale* (Paris: Éditions Michaelis, n.d.; reprint ed., New York: Broude Brothers, 1971), 111.

38. See Michel-Richard Delalande and André-Cardinal Destouches, *Les Éléments* (Paris: Éditions Michaelis, n.d.; reprint ed., New York: Broude Brothers, 1971), 268ff. Other instances appear in Campra's *Les Fêtes Vénitiennes* and Destouches's *Issé*.

39. Lully, *Alceste*, 101–4. The melismas occur in the phrase: "Et laissez régner sur les ondes les zéphirs les plus doux."

40. Rousseau, "Imitation," in *Dictionnaire de musique*, 197.

41. Lully, *Alceste*, "Les Vents," 98; *Cadmus et Hermione*, ed. Henri Prunières (Paris: Édition de la Revue Musicale, 1930), 29.

42. See Wood, "Orchestra and Spectacle in the *Tragédie en Musique* 1673–1715," 40–43.

43. Lully, *Thésée*, ed. Théodore de Lajarte (Paris: Imprimerie Lemercier, n.d.), 49–52.

44. André-Cardinal Destouches, *Issé* (Paris: Éditions Michaelis, n.d.; reprint ed., New York: Broude Brothers, 1971), 14–18.

45. Lully, *Armide*, ed. Lajarte, 117–25.

46. On this point see Masson, "French Opera from Lully to Rameau," in Abraham et al., eds., *The New Oxford History of Music*, 236.

47. Quoted in Catherine Kintzler, *Jean-Philippe Rameau: Splendeur et naufrage de l'esthétique du plaisir à l'âge classique* (Paris: Le Sycomore, 1983), 109.

48. See Masson, *L'Opéra de Rameau*, 287–312.

49. Collé, *Journal et mémoires*, 2:221.

50. Quoted in Louis Laloy, *Rameau* (Paris: Félix Alcan, 1908), 212.

51. Contre la moderne musique
Voilà ma dernière réplique:
Si la difficile est beau,
C'est un grand homme que Rameau.
Mais si le beau, par aventure,
N'était que la simple Nature,
Dont l'art doit être le tableau;
C'est un pauvre homme que Rameau.
(Quoted in Clément, Anecdotes dramatiques,
1:180.)

52. Desfontaines, *Observations sur les écrits modernes*, quoted in Girdlestone, *Jean-Philippe Rameau*, 349.

53. For a comprehensive treatment of this theme, see Masson, *L'Opéra de Rameau*, 326–44.

54. Rameau, *Hippolyte et Aricie*, ed. Vincent d'Indy (Paris: A. Durand et Fils, 1900), 395–400.

55. Rameau, *Les Indes galantes*, ed. Paul Dukas (Paris: A. Durand et Fils, 1902), 17–24.

56. Jean-Philippe Rameau to the abbé d'Arnauld, quoted in Girdlestone, *Jean-Philippe Rameau*, 138.

57. Jean-Philippe Rameau, *A Treatise on Harmony*, ed. and trans. Philip Gossett (New York: Dover Publications, 1971), 154; *Observations sur notre instinct pour la musique*, quoted in Masson, *L'Opéra de Rameau*, 466.

58. Jean-Philippe Rameau, *Dardanus*, ed. Vincent d'Indy (Paris: A. Durand et Fils, 1905), 310–19; *Castor et Pollux*, ed. Théodore de Lajarte (Paris: Éditions Michaelis, n.d.; reprint ed., New York: Broude Brothers, 1971), 181–95; *Hippolyte et Aricie*, 164–68. On this point see also Julien Tiersot, "Rameau," *Musical Quarterly* 14 (1928): 77–107.

59. Cf. this passage from the Rameau obituary that appeared in the *Mercure de France* in 1764: "This opera [*Hippolyte et Aricie*] was the time when the revolution took place in music in France and there was fresh progress. People were at first astonished by music much more laden and richer in images than they were wont to hear on the stage. But they appreciated this new kind and they ended by applauding it" (quoted in Girdlestone, *Jean-Philippe Rameau*, 191).

60. Quoted in Masson, *L'Opéra de Rameau*, 426.

61. Rémond de Saint-Mard, *Réflexions sur l'opéra*, 77.

62. Boyé, *L'Expression musicale*, 39.

Chapter 3. Tears and the New Attentiveness

1. Nicolas Karamzin, *Letters of a Russian Traveler, 1789–1790*, trans. Florence Jonas (New York: Columbia University Press, 1957), 228–31.

2. "Loges à l'année,..." 1788–89, A. N. O¹ 624; Ernest Boysse, *Les Abonnés de l'Opéra (1783–1786)* (Paris: A. Quantin, 1881), 1–5.

3. Boysse, *Les Abonnés de l'Opéra*, 26.

4. "Loges à l'année,..." 1788–89, A. N., O¹ 624.

5. Ibid.; "A Monsieur le prévost des marchands" [ca. 1766], A. N. AJ¹³ 6.

6. "Loges à l'année,..." 1788–89, A. N., O¹ 624.

7. Frédéric-Melchior, baron de Grimm, *Correspondance littéraire*, 16 vols. (Paris: Garnier Frères, 1877), 9:129; see also Métra, *Correspondance secrète*, quoted in Boysse, *Les Abonnés de l'Opéra*, 102.

8. "Loges à l'année,..." 1781–82, A. N. O¹ 624; Boysse, *Les Abonnés de l'Opéra*, 195–198.

9. "Loges à l'année,..." 1788–89, A. N. O¹ 624; document [1786?] without title, A. N. O¹ 624.

10. A. N. O¹ 618.

11. Ibid.

12. Grimm, *Correspondance littéraire*, 8:451.

13. Letter from "le Baron de Thunder," *Almanach musical*, 1789, 9:44. The correspondent went on to express wonder that anyone would choose to sit in the paradise: "I don't know what you can see from the paradise, and I won't write what one smells there."

14. *Almanach des spectacles*, 1769–70, 140.

15. It was in the Théâtre de la Porte Saint-Martin were Karamzin encountered Gluck.

16. Patte, *Essai sur l'architecture théâtrale*, 3.

17. "A Monsieur le prévost des marchands" [c. 1766], A. N. AJ¹³ 6.

18. "Mémoire," A. N. O¹ 628.

19. Charles-Nicolas Cochin, *Lettres sur l'opéra* (Paris: L. Cellot, 1781). I am grateful to Downing A. Thomas for bringing this work to my attention.

20. Bricaire de la Dixmérie, *Lettre sur l'état présent de nos spectacles* (Amsterdam: Chez Duchesne, 1765), 71–72.

21. "A Monsieur le prévost des marchands," A. N. AJ¹³ 6.

22. "Mémoire," A. N. O¹ 628.

23. Grimm, *Correspondance littéraire*, 8:450.

24. Patte, *Essai sur l'architecture théâtrale*, 166.

25. Alexis Donnet, *Architectonographie des théâtres de Paris* (Paris: Chez Orgiazzi, 1821), 113.

26. Ibid., 111–12. See also Germain Bapst, *Essai sur l'histoire du théâtre, la mise en scène, le décor, la costume, l'architecture, l'éclairage, l'hygiène* (Paris: Librairie Hachette, 1893), 451.

27. Ibid., 451; Donnet, *Architectonographie des théâtres de Paris*, 113.

28. *Almanach des spectacles*, 1771, 6; Donnet, *Architectonographie des théâtres de Paris*, 114.

29. "Notice sur la salle de l'Opéra au Palais Royal" [1771?], A. N. AJ¹³ 6; *Almanach des spectacles*, 1771, 7.

30. "L'Ombre de Poinsinet," *Journal de musique* (Feb. 1770), ed. François Lesure, 3 vols. (Geneva: Minkoff Reprints, 1972), 1:46–47.

31. Bergman, *Lighting in the Theatre*, 197–98.

32. Tawfik Mekka-Barrada, ed., *Correspondance littéraire secrète*, 2 vols. (Göteborg: Acta Universitatis Gothoburgensis, 1986), 2:42.

33. Jean-François Laharpe, ed., *Correspondance littéraire*, 6 vols. (Paris: Chez Mignaret, 1804–7), 1:225.

34. Ibid., 2:76.

35. Métra, *Correspondance secrète*, 2:112 (1775).

36. *Journal de politique et littérature*, n.d., in François Lesure, ed., *Querelle des gluckistes et des piccinnistes*, 2 vols. (Geneva: Minkoff Reprints, 1984), 1:108.

37. *Mercure*, 18 April 1779, quoted in Edouard G. J. Grégoire, ed., *Souvenirs artistiques: Documents pour servir à l'histoire de la musique*, 3 vols. (Anvers: Imprimerie L. de la Montagne, 1888), 2:102.

38. *Almanach musical*, 7:93.

39. *Calendrier musical universel, suite de l'Almanach musical*, 10 vols. (Geneva: Minkoff Reprints, 1971), 10:44.

40. J. H. Marchand, *Les Vues simples d'un bon homme* (London: n.p., 1776), 110–11.

41. Jean de La Bruyère, *Oeuvres complètes*, 101: "Why is it that one laughs so freely in the theater but is ashamed to cry? Is sympathy for the pitiable any less a part of our nature than exploding over the ridiculous? Is it the change in our expression that holds us back? But that change is greater in an immoderate laugh than in the bitterest sorrow, and in any case one averts one's face to laugh and to cry in the presence of the *grands* and all others whom one respects."

42. *Journal de politique et de littérature*, n.d. [1777?], in Lesure, ed., *Querelle des gluckistes et piccinnistes*, 1:108–9; "Vers sur l'Opéra d'*Alceste*, adressé à M. le Chevalier Gluck," in ibid., 1:93; "Vers d'un ignorant, comme des trois quarts du monde, en musique, et sans doute en poésie; mais sensible autant que personne," *Journal de Paris*, 17 Nov. 1777, from ibid., 1:378.

43. Louis-Sebastien Mercier, *Tableau de Paris*, 12 vols. (Amsterdam: n.p., 1782–88), 7:272.

44. Rousseau to Gluck, 17 April 1774, quoted in André Pirro, "Mémoires sur la musique à Paris à la fin du règne de Louis XV," *Revue musicale* 149 (1934): 167; Métra, *Correspondance secrète*, 5:405. According to Laharpe, the discovery of Gluck brought Rousseau temporarily out of the depression that marked his final years: "As long as one can enjoy such a pleasure for two hours," he was reported to have said, "I suppose that life is still worth something" (Laharpe, *Correspondance littéraire*, 1:25).

45. *Almanach musical*, 3:45; *Correspondance des amateurs musiciens rédigée par le citoyen Cocatrix . . .* (Geneva: Minkoff Reprints, 1972), 256.

46. *Correspondance des amateurs musiciens*, 256.

47. For a thorough treatment of the appeal of the new Opéra Comique and popular entertainments to elites in the 1750s and 1760s, see Robert M. Isherwood, *Farce and Fantasy: Popular Entertainment in Eighteenth-Century Paris* (New York: Oxford University Press, 1986).

48. Grimm, *Correspondance littéraire*, 5:44, 10:271.

49. Ibid., 10:416.

50. See Norman Demuth, *French Opera: Its Development to the Revolution* (Sussex: The Artemis Press, 1963), 230–36.

51. *Almanach musical*, 4:36–37.

52. Grimm, *Correspondance littéraire*, 11:460.

53. Ibid; Laharpe, *Correspondance littéraire*, 2:393:

Ce Marmontel, si lourd, si lent, si lourd,
Qui ne parle pars, mais qui beugle,
Juge les couleurs en aveugle
Et la musique comme un sourd.

54. Grimm, *Correspondance littéraire*, 1:461.

55. Métra, *Correspondance secrète*, 7:30.

56. Ibid., 2:263.

57. Ranieri Calzabigi, in Alfred Einstein, *Gluck*, trans. Eric Bloom (New York: McGraw-Hill Book Co., 1972), 66–67.

58. See Patricia Howard, *Gluck and the Birth of Modern Opera* (London: Barrie and Rockliff, 1963), 54–71; Winton Dean, "Gluck," in *New Grove Dictionary of Music and Musicians*, ed. Stanley Sadie, 20 vols. (London: MacMillan, 1980), 7:455–75; Robert M. Isherwood, "The Third War of Musical Enlightenment," *Studies in Eighteenth-Century Culture* 4 (1975): 223–45; Julien Tiersot, "Gluck and the Encyclopedists," *Musical Quarterly* 16 (1930): 336–57.

59. Laharpe, *Correspondance littéraire*, 2:371.

60. Grimm, *Correspondance littéraire*, 10:416; "Réponse de l'anonyme de Vaugirard, à M. le chevalier Gluck," *Journal de Paris*, 23 Oct. 1777, in Lesure, ed., *Querelle des gluckistes et des piccinnistes*, 1:291; "Essai sur les révolutions de la musique en France," *Journal de Paris*, 3 June 1777, in ibid., 1:184.

61. According to figures based upon a monthly accounting of revenue in tickets and subscriptions, the total in receipts of the 1750–51 season was 304,556 livres; the total in 1777–78 was 494,734 livres. (A. N. AJ[13] 8 [1750–51] and O[1] 625 [1777–78]).

62. From Claude Labrosse, *Lire au XVIIIe siècle. "La Nouvelle Héloïse" et ses lecteurs* (Lyon: Presses Universitaires de Lyon, 1985), 29; see also Robert Darnton, "Readers Respond to Rousseau," in *The Great Cat Massacre and Other Episodes in French Cultural History* (New York: Basic Books, Inc., 1984).

63. Quoted in Fernand Baldensperger, *Goethe en France*, 2 vols. (Paris: Hachette, 1904), 1:415–16. See also A. Tedeschi, *Ossian: L'Homère du Nord en France* (Milan: Tipografia Sociale, 1911), and Anita Brookner, *Greuze: The Rise and Fall of an Eighteenth-Century Phenomenon* (London: Paul Elek, Ltd., 1972).

64. Baldensperger, *Goethe en France*, 1:83. The professional gossip Métra relates that in 1779 a man was seen weeping uncontrollably during a comic opera (Métra, *Correspondance secrète*, 7:393). See also Anne Vincent-Buffault, *Histoire des larmes: XVIIIe–XIXe siècles* (Paris: Éditions Rivages, 1986).

65. See Charles Rosen, *The Classical Style: Haydn, Mozart, Beethoven* (New York: W. W. Norton, 1972), 171–72.

66. Julian Rushton discusses the debate among Gluck's contemporaries over *deus ex machina* endings, particularly concerning the Paris production of *Iphigénie en Aulide*, in "'Royal Agamemnon': The Two Versions of Gluck's *Iphigénie en Aulide*," in Malcolm Boyd, ed., *Music and the French Revolution* (Cambridge: Cambridge University Press, 1992), 15–36.

67. Christoph Willibald Gluck, *Alceste* (Leipzig: C. F. Peters, n.d.), 17, 53–56.

68. Niccolò Piccinni, *Roland* (Paris: Éditions Michaelis, n.d.; reprint ed., New York: Broude Brothers, 1971), 12–30, 144–70.

69. Grimm, *Correspondance littéraire*, 13:321; *Almanach musical*, 7:64–65.

70. A. N. O¹ 627.

71. *Calendrier musical universel*, 9:69.

72. Pierre Augustin Caron de Beaumarchais, "Aux abonnés de l'Opéra qui voudraient aimer l'Opéra," in *Théâtre: Lettres relatives à son théâtre* (Paris: Gallimard, 1956), 381.

73. *Almanach musical*, 6:116, 2:36.

74. Grimm, *Correspondance littéraire*, 11:406; *Almanach des spectacles*, 1778, 53. See also Rushton, "'Royal Agamemon,'" 31.

75. Mekki-Berrada, *Correspondance littéraire secrète*, 28:41.

76. Laharpe, *Correspondance littéraire*, 2:169; 3:150.

77. Grimm, *Correspondance littéraire*, 11:12. One spectator suggested that the hot-air balloons so popular in Paris made the flying chariots at the Opéra with their ill-covered ropes and pulleys seem all the more ridiculous (*Calendrier musical universel*, 9:43).

78. See William Weber "'La Musique ancienne' in the Waning of the Ancien Régime," *Journal of Modern History* 56 (1984): 58–88. "As Lully disappeared from the active repertoire of the Opéra in the early 1770s," Weber writes, "the state lost the ability to celebrate itself in opera; no one in the royal house nurtured new works which might bring it international glory, and Lully's operas became so dated they could no longer successfully recall the *grandeur* of Louis XIV" (82).

79. Grimm, *Correspondance littéraire*, 11:12.

80. Laharpe, *Correspondance littéraire*, 5:192, 3:194; see also *Almanach musical*, 7:154, for the earliest instance I have seen of the audience demanding the performers to repeat an aria (1781).

81. Baronne d'Oberkirch, *Mémoires*, 2 vols. (Paris: Charpentier, 1835), 2:223.

82. Ibid., 1:218.

83. "La Soirée perdue à l'Opéra," in Lesure, ed., *Querelle des gluckistes et piccinnistes*, 1:52. For an excellent discussion of the negative connotations sometimes associated with the "connoisseur"—the underlying sentiments of which the author of this pamphlet seems to share—see William Weber, "Learned and General Musical Taste in Eighteenth-Century France," *Past and Present* 89 (1980): 58–85.

84. *Almanach musical*, 7:81.

Chapter 4. Concerts in the Old Regime

1. See Michel Brenet [Marie Bobillier], *Les Concerts en France sous l'ancien régime* (Paris: Librairie Fischbacher, 1900), 115ff.

2. For descriptions of the Salle des Suisses, see Luc-Vincent Thiéry, *Guide des amateurs et des étrangers voyageurs à Paris*, 2 vols. (Paris: Chez Hardouin et Gattey, 1780), 1:383–84; *Mercure de France* (March 1725), quoted in Brenet, *Les Concerts en France*, 118.

3. See Brenet, *Les Concerts en France*, 257–59; Pierre Daval, *La Musique en France au XVIIIe siècle* (Paris: Payot, 1961), 135ff, 236; *Almanach des spectacles*, 1758, 2–3. Programs appear regularly in the *Almanach des spectacles* throughout the eighteenth century.

4. "First, one performs only music in Latin," reads a review of the *concert spirituel* from 1771; "this genre is made only for true connoisseurs, and connoisseurs in Paris are quite rare. Our women, on whose taste one must always focus if one wants to succeed, like to hear only texts that they can understand and arias they can repeat. Such are the obstacles that are by no means inconsequential; nor are they the only ones." *Journal de musique*, 2:206–7; see also *Année littéraire*, ed. Elie Fréron, 37 vols. (Geneva: Slatkine Reprints, 1966), 31:237, for descriptions of performances by a blind harpsichordist, a seventeen-year-old violinist, a clarinetist, and a cellist.

5. *Almanach musical*, 6:102. On the *symphonie concertante*, see Barry S. Brook, *La Symphonie française dans la seconde moitié du XVIIIe siècle*, 3 vols. (Paris: Institut de Musicologie de l'Université de Paris, 1962).

6. See Neal Zaslow, *Mozart's Symphonies* (Oxford: Oxford University Press, 1989), 318.

7. *Annonce, affiches et avis divers* (25 April 1764), quoted in Brenet, *Les Concerts en France*, 299.

8. Mayeur de Saint Paul, *Le Vol plus haut*, 27.

9. M. le prince de Montbarey, *Mémoires autobiographiques*, 3 vols. (Paris: A. Eymery, 1826–27), 1:110–11; d'Oberkirch, *Mémoires*, 2:221; Ancelet, *Observations sur la musique*, quoted in Brenet, *Les Concerts en France*, 230.

10. *Mémoires secrètes* (20 Feb. 1782), quoted in Brenet, *Les Concerts en France*, 353–54.

11. Grimm, *Correspondance littéraire*, 8:166; Elisabeth Vigée Le Brun, *Souvenirs*, 2 vols. (Paris: Gallimard, 1984), 1:79.

12. Brenet, *Les Concerts en France*, 351–55, 167.

13. Collé, *Journal et mémoires*, 1:26–27.

14. The duc de Richelieu describes in gloating detail this particular seduction. For 2400 livres he rented the *hôtel* adjacent La Poplinière's and paid a concierge to live there. He then engaged two carpenters, whom he blindfolded and led to the *hôtel* at night, to work as silently as possible. Richelieu claims to have made weekly visits once the door was finished, emerging from the fireplace "like a salamander." He always brought along his valet Stephano, whose job it was to win the confidence of Mme de La Popelinière's chambermaid. In a stroke worthy of Laclos, Richelieu dismissed Stephano as a dangerous risk when he realized he had grown too fond of the chambermaid and convinced Mme de La Popelinière to fire her, too (duc de Richelieu, *Mémoires* [Paris: Gustave Barba, n.d.], 211ff).

15. Ibid., 210. See also Georges Cucuel, *La Pouplinière et la musique de chambre au XVIIIᵉ siècle* (Paris: Librairie Fischbacher, 1913).

16. Stéphanie-Félicité, comtesse de Genlis, *Mémoires*, 16 vols. (Paris: Ladvocat, 1825), 1:95.

17. Collé, *Journal et mémoires*, 1:31.

18. Grimm, *Correspondance littéraire*, 9:442.

19. See Laharpe, *Correspondance littéraire*, 1:73; Brenet, *Les Concerts en France*, 355ff. There is precious little material on the Concert des Abonnés and no adequate treatment of any of these concert societies that appeared in the late eighteenth century.

20. Grimm, *Correspondance littéraire*, 9:442.

21. Laharpe, *Correspondance littéraire*, 1:73.

22. Ibid.; see also *Almanach musical*, 7:61.

23. Thiéry, *Guide des amateurs*, 1:278–79.

24. Haydn joined the Viennese lodge "Zur wahren Eintracht" on 11 February 1785, roughly the period when he was in communication with d'Ogny about the Loge Olympique; in letters just before his initiation he spoke warmly of the "humanitarian and wise principles" of freemasonry (see David P. Schroeder, *Haydn and the Enlightenment: The Late Symphonies and Their Audience* [Oxford: Oxford University Press, 1990], 35). See also H. C. Robbins-Landon, *Haydn: Chronicle and Works*, 5 vols. (Bloomington: Indiana University Press, 1978), 2:591–92; and A. Elwart, *Histoire de la Société des Concerts du Conservatoire Impérial de Musique* (Paris: S. Castel, 1860), 53ff.

25. Thiéry, *Guide des amateurs*, 1:278–79.

26. According to Daniel Roche, most provincial academies at the end of the *ancien régime* remained aristocratic in general orientation while exhibiting democratic tendencies; this split personality stemmed from their self-conception as republics of letters. Rather than organs of uniquely aristocratic culture, such academies described their goals in terms of utility and progress in science, knowl-

edge, and the arts, encouraging an overall egalitarian sociability in meetings. (See Daniel Roche, *Le Siècle des lumières en province: Académies et académiciens provinciaux, 1680–1789,* 2 vols. [Paris: École des Hautes Études en Sciences Sociales, 1978].)

Humphrey Burton describes the same general pattern in provincial "académies de musique" in the eighteenth century. In order to supplement the "pleasure of the music" with "the pleasure of a true society of honorable men," reports a member of the Académie des Lyriques de Bordeaux, "we always observed a certain equality and *politesse* among all members," so that "the humblest musician" was welcomed in the same way as "those who were distinguished by birth and rank." See Humphrey Burton, "Les Académies de musique en France au XVIII e siècle," *Revue de musicologie* 37 (1955): 122–47.

27. Membership lists of the lodge from 1788 can be found in the manuscript division of the Bibliothèque Nationale, Baylot FM² 153. See also "Loge Olympique de la Parfaite Estime—Correspondance avec le Grand Orient, 1781– 1805," B. N. ms. Baylot FM² 91, and [Pierre] Chevallier, "Nouvelles lumières sur la Société Olympique" (n.d.), B. N. FM Impr. 3204.

28. Thiéry, *Guide des amateurs,* 1:279.

29. Métra, *Correspondance secrète,* 17:286; "Tableau des membres qui composent la R. L. de la Parfaite-Estime et Société Olympique, avec leurs qualités civiles et demeures" (1788), B. N. ms. Baylot FM² 153.

30. See Robbins-Landon regarding the Österreich Freimaurerlogen (*Haydn: Chronicle and Works,* 2:593); "Tableau des membres qui composent la R. L. de la Parfaite-Estime" (1788), B. N. ms. Baylot FM² 153.

31. "Tableau des membres qui composent la R. L. de la Parfaite-Estime"; see *Almanach des spectacles,* 1789, for a listing of the Opéra orchestra's members.

32. Ancelet, *Observations sur la musique,* quoted in Burton, "Les Académies de musique en France au XVIII e siècle," 139.

33. Grimm, *Correspondance littéraire,* 5:411–12.

34. Mozart to Leopold Mozart, 1 May 1778, E. Anderson, ed., *The Letters of Mozart and His Family,* 2 vols. (London: MacMillan, 1961), 2:531.

35. Vigée Le Brun, *Souvenirs,* 1:79; Cucuel, *La Pouplinière et la musique de chambre,* 390. M. de Cheveigné writes in his *Mémoires* that "at all dinners [at the residence of La Popelinière] we had the pleasure of hearing horns that played quartets throughout the dinner until the entremets" (quoted in Cucuel, 390).

36. Even with evidence as clear as this, some scholars still find it unthinkable that spectators talked during eighteenth-century performances. Barbara R. Hanning, for instance, contends that Saint-Aubin's engraving isn't really intended to depict inattentive spectators but that Saint-Aubin, realizing he could attain greater compositional grace by having the spectators turn toward one another, has "ensemblisized" an entire afternoon of aristocratic activities into a single moment. (See Barbara R. Hanning, "Conversation and Musical Style in the Late Eighteenth-Century Parisian Salon," *Eighteenth-Century Studies* 22 [1989]: 329–50.)

37. *Année littéraire,* 31:238, 32:724.

38. *Tablettes de renommée des musiciens, auteurs, compositeurs . . . pour servir à l'Almanach Dauphin* (Paris: n.p., 1785) [no page numbers].

39. Métra, *Correspondance secrète*, 4:226.

40. Mozart to Leopold Mozart, 3 July 1778, in Anderson, ed., *Letters of Mozart and His Family*, 2:558.

41. These two phrases, played by the first violins in measures 105–16, are repeated in slightly varied form after the recapulation in measures 251–56 and 270–75. The triplets in other orchestral parts when these phrases appear—in a movement otherwise characterized by a strong duple feel—immediately draw attention to the motif and contribute to its plodding, sing-song quality. Nikolaus Harnoncourt suggests that the passage that drew applause may be measures 65–73 (recurring at 220–27), while Stanley Sadie proposes measures 84–92, recurring at 238–50 and 257–69. Both are possible, although the phrase I have identified stands out from the texture more clearly than the other two and, I think, would have been noticed more readily. (See Neal Zaslaw, *Mozart's Symphonies*, 311–14.) The last movement of the Piano Sonata in F (K. 300 k/332), which also dates from Mozart's stay in Paris, similarly trips up inattentive or distracted listeners with its unexpected turns and false finales.

Chapter 5. Harmony's Passions and the Public

1. *Correspondance des amateurs musiciens*, 27 April 1804, 256; *Almanach musical*, 7:93; Grimm, *Correspondance littéraire*, 10:417.

2. "La Soirée perdue à l'Opéra," in Lesure, ed., *Querelle des gluckistes et piccinnistes*, 1:54.

3. "Réponse d'un anonyme de Vaugirard à M. le chevalier Gluck," in ibid., 1:291.

4. For a discussion of the differences between seeking musical painting and sensing musical emotions, see Carl Dahlhaus, *Esthetics of Music*, trans. William Austen (Cambridge: Cambridge University Press, 1982), 26–28.

5. C. P. Coquéau, "Entretiens sur l'état actuel de l'Opéra de Paris," in Lesure, ed., *Querelle des gluckistes et piccinnistes*, 2:11–12.

6. "Lettre de M. L. A. au P. Martini," in ibid., 1:246.

7. "Lettre de M. L'A*** à Madame d'***," in ibid., 1:30–31.

8. Métra, *Correspondance secrète*, 7:398.

9. "Le Souper des enthousiastes," in Lesure, ed., *Querelle des gluckistes et piccinnistes*, 1:63.

10. "Here the orchestra is so filled with the spirit and fire of a burning fury that even if the words did not describe it verbally, one would immediately see how much the musical sentiment has in common with the language of the passions it imitates" (*Almanach musical*, 7:177).

11. Coquéau, "Entretiens sur l'état actuel de l'Opéra de Paris," in Lesure, ed., *Querelle des gluckistes et piccinnistes*, 2:476–77.

12. *Almanach musical*, 7:187. There also exists a cornucopia of keyboard works from the period ostensibly representational: among them, *La Séduisante*, *L'Auguste*, *Les Vergers fleuris*, *Les Moissonneurs*, *Les Petites âges*, and *Les Folies françaises* by Couperin, and *La Poule*, *Les Sauvages*, *L'Égyptienne*, *Les Soupirs*,

La Boiteuse, and *Les Cyclopes* by Rameau—so many images for listeners to visualize as they listened, even where there seemed few imitations present.

13. *Journal de Paris* (30 Nov.–27 Dec. 1783), quoted in Brenet, *Les Concerts en France*, 320.

14. *Mercure de France* (Jan. 1778), quoted in ibid., 308.

15. Ducharger's description comes in an unpublished manuscript that recounts conversations about music with one Prince Stalkoff, a visitor to France from Russia. The work also contains a somewhat parodic description of provincial concert performances and recommendations for improving them. Was Stalkoff anything other than a creation of Ducharger, who used the conceit to offer frank advice to the prince de Condé without appearing presumptuous? See Ducharger, *Stalkoff gentilhomme russe en France et amateur de musique . . .* , Bibliothèque du Château de Chantilly, n.d. I am grateful to M. Pierre for his kind assistance in making this manuscript available to me.

16. Ibid., 57, 67.

17. *Mercure* (May 1779), quoted in Brenet, *Les Concerts en France*, 335.

18. Ibid.

19. Ducharger, *Stalkoff gentilhomme russe*, 78.

20. B. -G. -D. de Lacépède, *La Poétique de la musique*, 2 vols. (Paris: L'Imprimerie de Monsieur, 1785), 1 : 8–9. "These works of harmony also form a language, for the same reason that melodies constitute one; or better, they insert new words into the language of airs and melodies; they enlarge it, . . . which permits the musician to achieve the sorts of tableaux that we have undertaken to teach him to design" (1 : 101–2).

21. *Tablettes de renommées des musiciens, auteurs, compositeurs . . . pour servir à l'Almanach Dauphin* (Paris: n.p., 1785), n.p.

22. *Almanach musical*, 7 : 93–94.

23. Lacépède, *La Poétique de la musique*, 1 : 9.

24. Lacombe, *Le Spectacle des beaux arts*, 50.

25. "Le Souper des enthousiastes," in Lesure, ed., *Querelle des gluckistes et piccinnistes*, 1 : 87.

26. The orchestral storm that opens *Iphigénie en Tauride* is one such occasion, although the text that follows ("in the depths of my heart the storm rages on") points to a psychological reading. (Gluck, *Iphigénie en Tauride* [Zurich: Ernst Eulenburg, Ltd., n.d.], 45–46.)

27. From Preface (1769) to *Alceste*, quoted in Dean, "Gluck," in *New Grove Dictionary of Music and Musicians*, 7 : 467; see also Bruce Alan Brown, *Gluck and the French Theatre in Vienna* (Oxford: Clarendon Press, 1991).

28. See Christoph Willibald Gluck, *Armide*, ed. Klaus Hortschansky (Kassel: Bärenreiter, 1987), 28–29.

29. Christoph Willibald Gluck, *Alceste*, ed. Rudolf Gerber (Kassel: Bärenreiter, 1957), 35–44.

30. Gluck, *Iphigénie en Tauride*, 62–68; *Alceste*, ed. Gerber, 280–82.

31. Gluck, *Iphigénie en Tauride*, 129–32. During rehearsals for the Paris premiere of the opera the orchestra played this section softly. "Forte! Forte!" Gluck called out from the audience. One of the musicians replied that if they played the passage any louder they would destroy the sense of the text. "He's lying!" Gluck shouted back. "He's killed his mother!" The anecdote demon-

strates how reluctant even musicians were at the time of Gluck's appearance to see the orchestral parts as equal to the text in expression. (Related in La comtesse de Genlis, *Dictionnaire critique et raisonné des étiquettes de la cour*, in a footnote to the article "Opera," 2:12–13).

32. A chorus of sailors in Piccinni's *Roland* sings that the waves and the winds look kindly upon lovers to the accompaniment of an incessant lapping motif, and a storm scene in his *Iphigénie en Tauride* unleashes not just wind and thunder but an earthquake. In Gossec's *Nativité* a shepherdess sings an aria that imitates nightingales, just as spectators reported, and one of Gossec's most popular symphonies, the Symphony in D Major, Opus 13, No. 2 (ca. 1773), was subtitled "La Chasse" for its imitations of baying dogs and galloping horses and its use of hunting-horn motifs to denote the progress of the chase. Guillaume-Antoine Calvière mimicked wind and thunder in his *Te Deum*, and in the motet *Regina coeli* François Giroust included a musical painting intended to "depict the movement of the sepulchral stone at the instant Christ leaves his tomb." (See Niccolò Piccinni, *Roland*, 209–21; idem, *Iphigénie en Tauride* [Happenheim: Gregg International Publishers, Ltd., 1972], 71–89; Robert James MacDonald, "François-Joseph Gossec and French Instrumental Music in the Second Half of the Eighteenth Century," 3 vols. [Ph.D. diss., University of Michigan, 1968], 1:331–40; Mme Giroust, *Notice historique sur Fr. Giroust*, quoted in Brenet, *Les Concerts en France*, 296–97.)

33. This episode illustrates why I believe that a history of perception cannot be deduced solely from change in artistic form or intention. The dominant perceptual categories of the particular historical moment, gleaned from accounts of the public, must also be considered. For a stimulating study of late-eighteenth-century painting and its public, an account that concentrates chiefly on the perceptual effects of changes in artistic form, see Michael Fried, *Absorption and Theatricality: Painting and Beholders in the Age of Diderot* (Berkeley: University of California Press, 1980).

34. "Observations sur la nécessité de construire une salle provisoire pour l'Académie Royale de Musique," A. N. O¹ 628.

35. See, inter alia, Keith Michael Baker, "Public Opinion as Political Invention," in *Inventing the French Revolution* (Cambridge: Cambridge University Press, 1990), 167–99; Roger Chartier, "The Public Sphere and Public Opinion," in *The Cultural Origins of the French Revolution*, trans. Lydia Cochrane (Durham: Duke University Press, 1991), 20–37; Thomas E. Crow, *Painters and Public Life in Eighteenth-Century Paris* (New Haven: Yale University Press, 1985); Daniel Gordon, "'Public Opinion' and the Civilizing Process in France: The Example of Morellet," *Eighteenth-Century Studies* 22 (1989): 302–28; Jürgen Habermas, *The Structural Transformation of the Public Sphere*; James H. Johnson, "Musical Experience and the Formation of a French Musical Public," *Journal of Modern History* 64 (1992): 191–226; Joan Landes, *Women in the Public Sphere in the Age of the French Revolution* (Ithaca: Cornell University Press, 1988); Benjamin Nathans, "Habermas's 'Public Sphere' in the Era of the French Revolution," *French Historical Studies* 16 (1990): 620–44; Mona Ozouf, "'Public Opinion' at the End of the Old Regime," *Journal of Modern History* 60 (1988): S1-S21.

36. Baker, "'Public Opinion' as Political Invention," 168.

37. See Ozouf, "'Public Opinion' at the End of the Old Regime," S3-S4.

38. Habermas, *Structural Transformation of the Public Sphere*, 31–43.

39. "The issues discussed became 'general' not merely in their significance, but also in their accessibility: everyone had to *be able* to participate" (ibid., 37). See also Nina Rattner Gelbart, *Feminine and Opposition Journalism in Old Regime France: Le Journal des Dames* (Berkeley: University of California Press, 1987), and Jack R. Censer and Jeremy D. Popkin, eds., *Press and Politics in Pre-Revolutionary France* (Berkeley: University of California Press, 1987).

40. Quoted in Landes, *Women in the Public Sphere*, 16.

41. "Lettre d'un anonyme de Vaugirard," from *Journal de Paris*, 30 Oct. 1777, in Lesure, ed., *Querelle des gluckistes et piccinnistes*, 1:315. Cf. also the evaluation of the *Courrier de l'Europe et des spectacles* of the opera *Céphale et Procris*: "The public cannot pronounce upon the merit of the work because the actors performed it so badly from start to finish" (quoted in *Almanach des spectacles*, 1778, 55).

42. "Lettres d'un amateur" (1776), quoted in Weber, "Learned and General Musical Taste in Eighteenth-Century France," 67.

43. *Almanach musical*, 7:67–68.

44. Ducharger, *Stalkoff gentilhomme russe*, 40.

45. On the role of protodemocratic sociability in academies, lodges, and salons see Auguste Cochin, *Les Sociétés de pensée et la démocratie: Études d'histoire révolutionnaire* (Paris: Plon-Nourrit, 1921), 3–23; Daniel Roche, *La Siècle des lumières en province*; Reinhart Koselleck, *Critique and Crisis: Enlightenment and the Pathogenesis of Modern Society* (Cambridge: MIT Press, 1988); Dena Goodman, "Governing the Republic of Letters: The Politics of Culture in the French Enlightenment," *History of European Ideas* 13 (1991): 183–99. See also Chartier, "A Desacralized King," in *Cultural Origins of the French Revolution*, 111–35.

46. Similarly, the putative equality in recruitment of masonic lodges near the end of the Old Regime existed within a framework of traditional corporate distinctions that the lodges deliberately maintained: "the brothers were sincerely convinced that, in order to promote the experience of equality most effectively, they had to maintain the limits fixed by the society of orders" (see Gérard Gayot, *La Franc-maçonnerie française: Textes et pratiques [XVIIIᵉ –XIXᵉ siècles]* [Paris: Gallimard, 1980], 177–78).

47. Marie-Joseph Chénier, *De la Liberté du théâtre en France* (Paris: n.p., 1789), 39–40, 35.

Chapter 6. Entertainment and the Revolution

1. Donnet, *Architectonographie des théâtres de Paris*, 209–18.

2. Ibid.; Albert de Lasalle, *Les Treize salles de l'Opéra* (Paris: Librairie Sartorius, 1875), 182.

3. *La Décade philosophique*, 30 thermidor, an II, 171.

4. *Almanach des spectacles*, 1794, 55.

5. *Le Moniteur universel*, 30 Aug. 1973, 515.

6. *Journal des spectacles*, 20 floréal, an II, 254.

7. *Almanach des spectacles*, 1794, 55.

8. *Journal de Paris*, 28 Aug. 1793, 966.

9. See *Almanach des spectacles*, 1794, 53–57; Donnet, *Architectonographie des théâtres de Paris*, 208.

10. "One might have wished that they had been painted on a much larger area . . . so they could be distinguished by spectators, who are able to see the details only with the aid of opera glasses; as for ourselves, we made them out only with the greatest trouble" (*Almanach des spectacles*, 1794, 57).

11. Marvin Carlson, *The Theater of the French Revolution* (Ithaca: Cornell University Press, 1966), 199–200.

12. *Moniteur universel*, 30 Aug. 1793, 515; *Journal des spectacles*, 28 Aug. 1793, 461.

13. *Journal des spectacles*, 28 Aug. 1793, 515.

14. Letter from Antoine Dauvergne, 12 July 1789, A. N. O¹ 619; see also Adélaïde de Place, *La Vie musicale en France au temps de la Révolution* (Paris: Fayard, 1989), 54.

15. Letter from Dauvergne, 14 July 1789, A. N. O¹ 619.

16. Letter from Dauvergne, 10 Aug. 1789, A. N. O¹ 619.

17. *Cahiers de doléance, remonstrances, et instructions: L'Assemblée de tous les ordres des Théâtres Royaux de Paris*, 10 April 1789.

18. See Nicholas Étienne Framery, *De l'Organisation des spectacles de Paris* (Paris: Buisson Librairie, 1790), 170; *Discours et motions sur les spectacles* (Paris: Chez Donné, 1789), 5–7.

19. *Discours et motions sur les spectacles*, 6.

20. Laharpe, ed., *Correspondance littéraire*, 5:349.

21. "État des loges louées à l'année 1791–92," A. N. AJ¹³ 44.

22. Ultimately this randomness would be dressed up in fraternal trappings and promoted as a revolutionary principle: since all were equal, all should be equally visible. "Why hide yourself to enjoy an innocent pleasure?" reads one such articulation in 1794. "Every citizen in the midst of his brothers ought to see them and be seen by them." In the early years of the Revolution the lack of a discernable order in seating seems to have been more from the continuing decay of Old Regime etiquette and taste (*Décade philosophique*, 30 floréal, an II, 139).

23. "État des loges louées à l'année 1791–92," A. N. AJ¹³ 44.

24. De Besseuil to M. de la Ferté, 9 April 1786, A. N. O¹ 624.

25. Letter dated 9 April 1786, A. N. O¹ 624.

26. Deurent to M. de la Ferté, 26 April 1786, A. N. O¹624.

27. "État des loges louées à l'année 1791–92," A. N. AJ¹³ 44.

28. Ibid.

29. See Robert M. Isherwood, *Farce and Fantasy*, 129–30.

30. See David Charlton, *Grétry and the Growth of Opéra-Comique* (Cambridge: Cambridge University Press, 1986), 62–67, 207-16.

31. See Clarence D. Brenner, *The Theatre Italian: Its Repertory, 1716–*

1793, University of California Publications in Modern Philology, vol. 63 (Berkeley: University of California Press, 1961); Martine de Rougemont, *La Vie théâtrale en France au XVIIIᵉ siècle* (Paris: Librairie Honoré Champion, 1988), 247–52.

32. André-Modeste Grétry, *Mémoires, ou Essais sur la musique*, 3 vols. (Paris: Imprimerie de la République, an V; reprint ed., New York: Da Capo Press, 1971), 1:360.

33. Nous sommes nés pour l'esclavage;
    Nul n'est libre dans l'universe.
    Des hommes tel est le partage,
    Les rois mêmes portent les fers.
    . . . Des maîtres que chacun se donne,
    L'Amour me semble le plus doux.
    (André-Modest Grétry, La Caravane du Caire
    [Paris: Éditions Michaelis, n.d.; reprint ed.,
    New York: Broude Brothers, 1971], 141ff.)

34. Ibid., 177–83.
35. Ibid., 235–37.
36. See Rougemont, *La Vie théâtrale en France*, 29–32.
37. Grétry, *La Caravane du Caire*, 245–47.
38. See Jean Mongrédien, *La Musique en France des lumières au romantisme, 1789–1830* (Paris: Harmoniques Flammarion, 1986), 87–105.
39. Jean-François Le Sueur, *La Caverne*, [1793?], French Opera in the Seventeenth and Eighteenth Centuries, ed. Barry S. Brook, vol. 74 (New York: Pendragon Press, 1985); Maria Luigi Cherubini, *Lodoïska* [1791?], Early Romantic Opera, ed. Philip Gossett and Charles Rosen, vol. 33 (New York: Garland Publishing, 1978); Nicolas-Étienne Méhul, *Mélidore et Phrosine*, French Opera in the Seventeenth and Eighteenth Centuries, ed. Brook, vol. 73 (New York: Pendragon Press, 1990]). See also David Charlton, "On Redefinitions of 'Rescue Opera,' " in Boyd, ed., *Music and the French Revolution*, 169–88.
40. Similar themes surfaced during the Revolution in the black novel, melodrama, and various forms of pornography. See Emmet Kennedy, *A Cultural History of the French Revolution* (New Haven: Yale University Press, 1989), 130–39; Lynn Hunt, *The Family Romance of the French Revolution* (Berkeley: University of California Press, 1992), esp. 29–36, 89–150.
41. Minutes of sansculottes *comité* meeting, March 1793, quoted in Richard C. Cobb, *The Police and the People: French Popular Protest, 1789–1820* (Oxford: Oxford University Press, 1970), 331.
42. Quoted in Mongrédien, *La Musique en France*, 98.
43. *Chronique de Paris*, 12 Dec. 1790, 1,383; for an account of the incident by the German playwright August von Kotzebue see Place, *La Vie musicale en France*, 59.
44. *Chronique de Paris*, 8 Feb. 1792, 154–55.
45. See Laura Mason, "'Ça ira' and the Birth of the Revolutionary Song," *History Workshop* 28 (1989): 22–38.
46. *Chronique de Paris*, 27 Feb. 1792, 231.

47. O Louis, O mon Roi!
Notre amour t'environne;
Pour notre coeur c'est une loi
D'être fidèle à ta personne.
(From Carlson, The Theater of
the French Revolution, *114–15.)*

48. Ibid., 115.

49. Ibid., 123.

50. Ibid., 147.

51. *Chronique de Paris,* 5 Aug., 10 Aug., 11 Aug., 16 Aug. 1790; see also Béatrice Didier, *Écrire la révolution, 1789–1799* (Paris: Presses Universitaires de France, 1989), 161–69.

52. *Chronique de Paris,* 10 Aug. 1790, 886.

53. By now the interior guard at the Opéra had grown to sixty soldiers, two sergeants, and four corporals (see *Almanach des spectacles,* 1788, 28).

54. Isaac-René-Guy Le Chapelier in speech reported in *Le Moniteur universel,* 15 Jan. 1791, quoted in M. Elisabeth C. Bartlet, "Étienne-Nicolas Méhul and Opera during the French Revolution, Consulate, and Empire: A Source, Archival, and Stylistic Study," 5 vols. (Ph.D. diss., University of Chicago, 1982), 1:275; see also Paul d'Estrée [Paul Quentin], *Le Théâtre sous la terreur (théâtre de la peur) 1793–94* (Paris: Émile-Paul Frères, 1913), 4.

55. See *Journal de Paris,* 8 March 1793, 268, for a detailed description of the pomp of *Jugement de Paris.* After the first performance of *Psyché* in 1791 Grimm wrote that it was "perhaps the most magical spectacle that has ever been performed on any stage" (Grimm, *Correspondance,* 16:135–36, quoted in Judith Chazin-Bennahum, *Dance in the Shadow of the Guillotine* [Carbondale: Southern Illinois University Press, 1988], 49).

56. *Chronique de Paris,* 15 May 1792, 542–43.

57. François-Joseph Gossec, *L'Offrande à la liberté: Composé de l'air Veillons au salut de l'empire et de la marche des Marseillois* (Paris: Chez Imbault, n.d.).

58. "Three hundred persons were on the stage when the curtain rose," the account begins. "At the stanza beginning with the verses, 'Amour sacré de la patrie,' the people and the warriors knelt, lowered their lances, and with an adagio this hymn that had been so sublimely martial assumed a religious character. Suddenly, when the choir sounded the terrible battle cry, 'Aux armes citoyens,' the 300 men, women, and children rose spontaneously to the sound of the tocsin and of the drums beating" (quoted in Mongrédien, *La Musique en France,* 43–44); see also Grimm, ed., *Correspondance littéraire,* July 1792, 6:161; Place, *La Vie musicale en France,* 101–2.

59. François-Joseph Gossec, *Le Triomphe de la République, ou le Camp de grand-pré* (Paris: Chez Mogin, n.d.).

60. *Journal de Paris,* 4 April 1793, 378.

61. "The smoke has blackened the decorations and the furniture and is clearly destroying them," the director of the Théâtre Français wrote of *La Prise de la Bastille* (*Chronique de Paris,* 7 March 1792, 266).

62. Bernardo Porta, *La Réunion du dix août, ou l'Inauguration de la République Française,* 1793, Bibliothèque de l'Opéra ms. My thanks to Mme Nicole Wild for her assistance in procuring this manuscript. See also Henri

Welschinger, *Le Théâtre de la révolution, 1789–1799, avec documents inédits* (Paris: Charavay Frères, 1880), 491-92; Chazin-Bennahum, *Dance in the Shadow of the Guillotine*, 113; Mona Ozouf, *Festivals and the French Revolution*, trans. Alan Sheridan (Cambridge: Harvard University Press, 1988), 84.

63. See Ozouf, *Festivals and the French Revolution*, 271, 306, 327–29.

64. *Chronique de Paris*, 12 July 1790, 770.

65. Ibid., 771.

66. Fiévée, *Les Rigueurs du Cloître* (Paris: Imprimerie de l'Auteur, n.d.), 37; *Almanach des spectacles*, 1791, 228–29; see also Matthias Brzoska, "De l'anti-cléricalisme révolutionnaire au cléricalisme anti-révolutionnaire chez M. Berton de 1790 à 1799," in Jean-Rémy Julien and Jean-Claude Klein, eds., *Le Tambour et la harpe: Oeuvres, pratiques et manifestations musicales sous la révolution, 1788–1800* (Paris: Éditions du May, 1991), 257–66.

67. D'Estrée, *Le Théâtre sous la terreur*, 4.

68. Ibid., 6.

69. Ibid., 8, 288.

Chapter 7. Musical Experience of the Terror

1. D'Estrée, *Le Théâtre sous la terreur*, 52–53; Aurélien Vivie, *Histoire de la terreur à Bordeaux*, 2 vols. (Bordeaux: Feret et Fils, 1877), 2:111–20; Arthur Pougin, *L'Opéra Comique pendant la Révolution* (Paris: Albert Savine, 1891), 103. The offending lines of Pedro Calderón de la Barca's *La vida es sueño* (1636), which appeared in French translation in 1733, come in the third act when supporters of the reigning King Basilio attempt to prevent his son Sigismundo from overthrowing him.

While there is no reason to doubt d'Estrée's account of Arouch and his execution, I have been unable to find additional references to the actor in the press or in secondary literature. Vivie's *Histoire de la terreur à Bordeaux* lists the name as a victim of the guillotine but gives no circumstances of arrest.

2. For descriptions of the *Pamela* incident, see Georges Duval, *Souvenirs thermidoriens*, 2 vols. (Paris: Victor Magen, 1844), 1:278–88; *Almanach des spectacles*, 1794, 1:122–25; Carlson, *The Theater of the French Revolution*, 159–61; d'Estrée, *Le Théâtre sous la terreur*, 18–20. See also François de Neuf-château, *Pamela, ou la vertu récompensée* (Paris: Chez Barba, an III).

These two incidents, along with a third of an another actor denounced from the stage for portraying a counter-revolutionary, open my essay "Revolutionary Audiences and the Impossible Imperatives of Fraternity," in Bryant T. Ragan, Jr., and Elizabeth A. Williams, eds., *Re-Creating Authority in Revolutionary France* (New Brunswick: Rutgers University Press, 1992). Since that publication I have decided that the third denunciation and arrest of the actor Dugazon did not in fact take place during a performance of *Le Modéré*, as I asserted in the piece; the newspaper account is not clear, but I now believe that Dugazon wrote and acted in the play *after* his arrest and subsequent release to demonstrate his political purity, which he did by lampooning the behavior that brought about his denunciation. I regret the error and any misunderstanding it has caused.

3. See Place, *La Vie musicale en France*, 116–18.

4. D'Estrée, *Le Théâtre sous la terreur*, 19–20.

5. *Feuille du salut public*, quoted in *Almanach des spectacles*, 1794, 1:124.

6. "Extrait d'une lettre écrite par les représentants du peuple à Bordeaux au ministre de l'intérieure," *Moniteur universel*, 13 December 1793.

7. *Journal des spectacles*, 2 Oct. 1793, 733.

8. *Almanach des spectacles*, 1794, 1:119; d'Estrée, *Le Théâtre sous la terreur*, 288.

9. *Journal de Paris*, 9 Nov. 1793, 1260; Pierre Caron, *Paris pendant la terreur: Rapports des agents secrets du ministre de l'intérieur*, 6 vols. (Paris: Librairie Alphonse Picard et Fils, 1910), 1:317.

10. Quoted in M. Elisabeth C. Bartlet, "From Académie Royale de Musique to Opéra National: The Republican 'Regeneration' of an Institution," (typescript, Dept. of Music, Duke University), 36; Jean-Baptiste Lemoyne, *Toute la Grèce, ou ce que peut la liberté* (Paris: n.p., an II); see also Albert Bier, "La Pipe de Socrate: L'Antiquité dans l'opéra de l'époque révolutionnaire," in Jean-Rémy Julien and Jean-Claude Klein, eds., *L'Orphée phrygien: Les Musiques de la révolution* (Paris: Éditions du May, 1989), 177–82.

11. Welschinger, *Le Théâtre de la révolution*, 144–46.

12. Ibid.

13. *Feuille du salut public*, 25 vendémiaire, an II, 3.

14. *Révolutions de Paris*, 5–12 Nov. 1793, regarding *Miltiade à Marathon* (Lemoyne, 1793), quoted in Beatrice F. Hyslop, "The Theater during a Crisis: The Parisian Theater during the Reign of Terror," *Journal of Modern History* 17 (1945): 343.

15. Barré, Léger, Rosières, *L'Heureuse décade* (Paris: Librairie de la Vaudeville, n.d.), 30.

16. [Jean-Baptiste] Rochefort, *Toulon soumis*. Opéra en un acte. Paroles de Favre Olivot [sic], musique de Rochefort. Représenté le 17 ventose an 2. Par ordre du Comité du salut publique au dit théâtre. Bibliothèque de l'Opéra, ms.; [Louis-Emmanuel] Jadin, *Le Siège de Thionville* (1793), Bibliothèque de l'Opéra, ms.; Gossec, *L'Offrande à la liberté*.

17. Caron, *Paris pendant la terreur*, 3:83.

18. *Affiches, annonces et avis divers*, 12 Jan. 1794, quoted in M. Elisabeth C. Bartlet, "The New Repertory at the Opéra during the Reign of Terror: Revolutionary Rhetoric and Operatic Consequences," in Boyd, ed., *Music and the French Revolution* (Cambridge: Cambridge University Press, 1992), 148.

19. See Jean-Jacques Rousseau, *Lettre à M. d'Alembert sur son article Genève*, trans. Allan Bloom as *Politics and the Arts: Letter to M. d'Alembert on the Theatre* (Glencoe, Ill,: The Free Press, 1960), 126; see also Jean Starobinski, *Jean-Jacques Rousseau: Transparency and Obstruction*, trans. Arthur Goldhammer (Chicago: University of Chicago Press, 1988), esp. 92–97; David Marshall, "Rousseau and the State of Theater," *Representations* 13 (1986): 84–114.

20. *Feuille du salut public*, 9 brumaire, an II, 4.

21. Rousseau raised a version of this complaint against the hypocrisy of actors in *Lettre à d'Alembert*: "Of what does the actor's skill consist? It is the art of counterfeit, of assuming a character other than one's own, of appearing dif-

ferent than one actually is, of speaking passionately in cold blood, of saying the things one does not believe as naturally as the things one does, and of ultimately forgetting one's own place for having taken on that of another" (163).

22. François Furet, *Interpreting the French Revolution*, trans. Elborg Forster (Cambridge: Cambridge University Press, 1978), 53–57.

23. Letter from Aristide Valcour to *Journal de la Montagne*, reprinted in *Journal des spectacles*, 9 Sept. 1793, 558.

24. *Feuille du salut public*, 4 Sept. 1793, quoted in Arthur Pougin, *La Comédie-Française et la Révolution* (Paris: Gaultier, Magnier, 1902), 116.

25. *Journal des spectacles*, 9 Sept. 1793, 559.

26. *Feuille du Salut Public*, 20 Sept. 1793, 647.

27. D'Estrée, *Le Théâtre sous la terreur*, 90–91.

28. Caron, *Paris pendant la terreur*, 2:321.

29. Bibliothèque de l'Arsenal, Fonds Rondel, Rt. 720, "Extrait des registres des arrêtés du Comité de Salut Public de la Convention nationale," 5 messidor an II.

30. *Moniteur universel*, 15 July 1794, 211.

31. Report by Joseph Payan to Committee of Public Instruction, quoted in d'Estrée, *Le Théâtre sous la terreur*, 43–44; see also Michèle Root-Bernstein, *Boulevard Theater and Revolution in Eighteenth-Century Paris* (Ann Arbor: UMI Research Press, 1984), 229–33. Mona Ozouf describes the same dissatisfaction with inauthenticity among festival audiences: some found the mountains and altars inappropritely artificial, others claimed that the actresses were prostitutes made up to look virtuous, and others found the ritual oaths and declarations hollow (*Festivals and the French Revolution*, 27–32).

32. Antoine Christophe Merlin, *Opinion de Merlin (de Thionville) sur les fêtes publiques* (Paris: Imprimerie Nationale, an III), 2.

33. Charles-Alexandre de Moy, *Des Fêtes, ou quelques idées d'un citoyen français relatives aux fêtes publiques et à un culte national* (Paris: Chez Garnery, an VII), 2; see Ozouf, *Festivals and the French Revolution*, 280.

34. De Moy, *Des Fêtes*, 43.

35. See Ozouf, *Festivals and the French Revolution*.

36. *Journal de Paris*, Nov. 1793, quoted in James Leith, "Music as an Ideological Weapon in the French Revolution," *Canadian Historical Association Annual Report* (1966), 129.

37. Merlin, *Opinion de Merlin*, 5

38. See Michel Lassabathie, *Histoire du Conservatoire Impériale de Musique et de Déclamation, suivie de documents inédits, receuillies et mis en ordre* (Paris: Chez Lévi Frères, 1860), 20.

39. L. M. La Revellière-Lépeaux, *Essai sur les moyens de faire participer l'universalité des spectateurs à tout ce qui se pratique dans les fêtes nationales* (Paris: Chez H. J. Jansen, an VI), 15; see also Mongrédien, *La Musique en France*, 45–47.

40. François Antoine Boissy d'Anglas, *Essai sur les fêtes nationales* (Paris: Imprimerie Polyglotte, an II), 13.

41. Edouard Lefebvre, *Considérations politiques et morales, sur la France constituée en république* (Paris: Chez Bertrand, 1798), 102; La Revellière-Lépeaux, *Essai sur les moyens de faire participer l'universalité des spectateurs*, 14.

42. P. C. F. Daunou, *Rapport sur l'organisation des écoles spéciales* (Paris: n.p., an V), 28–29.

43. Jean Louis Thomas Heurtault, comte de Lamerville, *Sur l'organisation nouvelle du conservatoire de musique, au nom des commissions d'instruction publique et des institutions républicaines* (Paris: n.p., an VIII), 6.

44. Boissy d'Anglas, *Essai sur les fêtes*, 18, 14.

45. Jean-Baptiste Leclerc, *Essai sur la propagation de la musique en France, sa conservation, et ses rapports avec le gouvernement* (Paris: Imprimerie Nationale, an VI), 24; *Décade philosophique*, 20 floréal, an II, 71.

46. Nicolas Étienne Framery, *Avis aux poètes lyriques*, quoted in Ora Frishberg Saloman, "French Revolutionary Perspectives on Chabanon's *De la musique* of 1785," in Malcolm Boyd, ed., *Music and the French Revolution* (Cambridge: Cambridge University Press, 1992), 218.

47. For a discussion of these and other miraculous effects attributed to music, see Nicolas Étienne Framery and Pierre-Louis Ginguené, eds., *Encyclopédie méthodique: Musique*, 2 vols. (Paris: Chez Panckoucke, 1791–1818), "Effets de la musique chez les anciens," 1:491–95.

48. "Lycurgus," in Plutarch, *The Lives of the Noble Grecians and Romans*, trans. Dryden (Chicago: University of Chicago Press, 1952), 44.

49. Chevalier de Méré, *Conversations*, "Seconde Conversation" (1668–69), in *Oeuvres complètes du chevalier de Méré*, ed. Charles H. Boudhors, 3 vols. (Paris: Éditions Fernand Roches, 1930), 1:27.

50. Framery and Ginguéné, "Effets de la musique," 1:492.

51. *Décade philosophique*, 20 thermidor, an VI, 257–62.

52. Ibid., 258–59.

53. Ibid., 259.

54. Ibid., 262.

55. Ibid.

56. Ibid.

57. Ibid., 30 thermidor, an IV, 328–29. What Thompson recounts having seen that night is visible in the background of Houël's engraving, with the elephants in the positions Thompson describes. Subsequent research has revised this somewhat anthropocentric understanding. See J. F. Eisenberg, G. M. McKay, and M. R. Jainudeen, "Reproductive Behaviour of the Asiatic Elephant (*Elephas maximus* L.)," *Behaviour* 38 (1971): 193–225.

58. François de Neufchâteau in speech to Conservatory students and faculty, quoted in Pierre, *Le Conservatoire National de Musique et de déclamation: Documents historiques et administratifs recueillis ou reconstitués* (Paris: Imprimerie Nationale, 1900), 900.

59. On the ways republican virtue reshaped the language, calendar, dress, and behavior of citizens, see Lynn Hunt, *Politics, Culture, and Class in the French Revolution* (Berkeley: University of California Press, 1984), 56–57, 72; Hunt, "The Unstable Boundaries of the French Revolution," in Philippe Arès and Georges Duby, eds., *A History of Private Life*, trans. Arthur Goldhammer, vol. 4, *From the Fires of the French Revolution to the Great War*, ed. Michelle Perrot (Cambridge: Harvard University Press, 1990), 13–45.

60. See Cynthia M. Gessele, "The Conservatoire de Musique and National Music Education in France, 1795–1801," in Boyd, ed., *Music and the French*

Revolution, 191–210; Lassabathie, *Histoire du Conservatoire Impériale de Musique,* 19.

61. See Constant Pierre, *Musique des fêtes et cérémonies de la révolution française* (Paris: Imprimerie Nationale, 1899).

62. Quoted in Lassabathie, *Histoire du Conservatoire Impériale de Musique,* 21.

63. Quoted in Constant Pierre, *Le Magasin de Musique à l'usage des fêtes nationales et du conservatoire* (Paris: Librairie Fischbacher, 1895), 15–16.

64. Quoted ibid., 23.

65. "These clauses [of the social contract], properly understood, may be reduced to one—the total alienation of each associate, together with all his rights, to the whole community; for, in the first place, as each gives himself absolutely, the conditions are the same for all; and, this being so, no one has any interest in making them burdensome to others. . . .

"In order then that the social compact may not be an empty formula, it tacitly includes the undertaking, which alone can give force to the rest, that whoever refuses to obey the general will shall be compelled to do so by the whole body. This means nothing less than that he will be forced to be free; for this is the condition which, by giving each citizen to his country, secures him against all personal dependence. In this lies the key to the working of the political machine; this alone legitimizes civil undertakings, which, without it, would be absurd, tyrannical and liable to the most frightful abuses" (Jean-Jacques Rousseau, *The Social Contract,* trans. G. D. H. Cole [London: J. M. Dent and Sons, 1973], 174–77).

66. I am employing the distinction from the essay "Two Concepts of Liberty" in Isaiah Berlin, *Four Essays on Liberty* (Oxford: Oxford University Press, 1969).

67. Saint-Just, quoted in Mona Ozouf, "Liberté," in François Furet and Mona Ozouf, eds., *Dictionnaire critique de la Révolution française* (Paris: Flammarion, 1988), 772.

68. Marat, in *Le Publiciste de la révolution française,* 15 June 1793, quoted in Michel Vovelle, *La Mentalité révolutionnaire: Société et mentalités sous la révolution française* (Paris: Éditions Sociales, 1985), 25.

69. Robespierre, in a speech given 21 Nov. 1793, quoted in Carol Blum, *Rousseau and the Republic of Virtue: The Language of Politics in the French Revolution* (Ithaca: Cornell University Press, 1986), 223.

70. Jean-Baptiste Leclerc, *Sur l'établissement d'écoles spéciales de musique* (Paris: n.p., an VII), 3.

71. Leclerc, *Essai sur la propagation de la musique en France,* 22.

72. Ibid.

Chapter 8. Musical Expression and Jacobin Ideology

1. *Moniteur universel,* 11 March 1790, 4:333.

2. *Feuille du salut public,* 5 ventose, an II, 11.

3. Ibid., 4 pluviose, an II.

4. *Journal des théâtres et des fêtes nationales*, 2 Nov. 1794, as quoted in Place, *La Vie musicale en France*, 131.

5. Mme Jullien de La Drome, *Journal d'une bourgeoise pendant la Révolutioin*, quoted in André Monglond, *Le Préromantisme français*, 2 vols. (Grenoble: Editions B. Arthaud, 1930), 2:409-10.

6. *Feuille du salut public*, 20 floréal, an II, 4.

7. J. N. Bouilly, *Mes récapitulations*, 2 vols. (Paris: Louis Janet, 1836-37), 2:5, 7-8.

8. *Feuille du salut public*, 4 pluviose, an II, 4.

9. Winton Dean, "French Opera," in Gerald Abraham et al., eds., *The New Oxford History of Music*, vol. 8, *The Age of Beethoven, 1790-1830*, ed. Gerald Abraham (New York: Oxford University Press, 1982), 51; see also Ora Frishberg Saloman, "The Orchestra in Le Sueur's Musical Aesthetics," *Musical Quarterly* 40 (1974): 616-625.

10. *Affiches, annonces et avis divers*, 17 Feb. 1791, 3 Aug. 1791, quoted in Place, *La Vie musicale en France*, 82, 84.

11. *Journal de Paris*, 17 July 1794, 2274.

12. *Journal de la municipalité*, 17 July 1790, quoted by Bruno Brévan, "La Révolution et ses publics," in Julien and Klein, eds., *L'Orphée phrygien: Les Musiques de la révolution*, 32.

13. *Journal des théâtres et des fêtes nationales*, 19 Sept. 1794, quoted in Place, *La Vie musicale en France*, 212.

14. Mme de Genlis, *Nouvelle méthode pour apprendre à jouer de la harpe*, quoted in Brévan, "La Révolution et ses publics," in Julien and Klein, eds., *L'Orphée phrygien*, 32-33; Nicolas Ruault, *Gazette d'un Parisien sous la Révolution*, quoted by Place, *La Vie musicale en France*, 166.

15. *Chronique de Paris*, 5 June 1792, quoted by Place, *La Vie musicale en France*, 175.

16. Report of the Commission Temporaire des Arts, Dec. 1793, quoted in François Sabatier, "Musique et vandalisme: Le Destin de l'orgue en France entre 1788 et 1795," in Julien and Klein, eds., *Le Tambour et la harpe*, 52.

17. *Décade philosophique*, 30 frimaire, an III, 530. Was the work Haydn's Symphony No. 103, the "Drum Roll?"

18. Ibid.

19. *Moniteur universel*, 24 Jan. 1795, quoted in Jean-Louis Jam, "Le Clairon de l'avenir," in Julien and Klein, eds., *L'Orphée phrygien*, 23-24.

20. Grétry, *Mémoires*, 1:35.

21. Ibid., 2:280.

22. Ibid., 1:342-43.

23. Ibid., 2:284, 248.

24. Ibid., 2:14, 191, 367, 373.

25. Ibid., 3:264. Grétry's contemporary Jean-François Le Sueur expresses his views on musical expression of the passions in virtually identical terms: the function of imitation is not to give a literal copy of the human passions but to evoke in the hearer "the sensations which one experiences in looking at an ob-

ject" (Jean Mongrédien, "Jean-François Le Sueur," in *The New Grove Dictionary of Music and Musicians*, 10:695).

26. Grétry, *Mémoires*, 3:268.

27. Ibid., 3:270.

28. See for instance the overtures to Cherubini's *Démophon* and *Lodoïska*.

29. Johann Friedrich Reichardt, *Vertraute Briefe aus Paris*, quoted in Margery Juliet Stomne Selden, "The French Operas of Luigi Cherubini," 2 vols. (Ph.D. diss., Yale University, 1951), 1:98.

30. Méhul, *Euphrosine, ou le tyran corrigé*, in Early Romantic Opera, ed. Philip Gossett and Charles Rosen, vol. 38 (New York: Garland Publishing, 1980), 111–32.

31. Méhul, *Mélidore et Phrosine*, 233–37.

32. Méhul, *Euphrosine, ou le tyran corrigé*, 60–96.

33. Méhul, *Mélidore et Phrosine*, 179–94.

34. Cherubini, *Lodoïska*, 361–81.

35. There is one two-page section of two-part singing with different words and rhythms in the work (Lemoyne, *Toute la Grèce*, 337–38); otherwise the words of all ensemble parts are sung at the same time.

36. Ibid., 51–70, 151–63, 236–59.

37. Porta, *La Réunion du dix août*, 177–233.

38. Méhul, *Horatius Coclès*, ed. Louis Saguer (Paris: Éditions Française de Musique, 1974).

39. [Louis-Emmanuel] Jadin, *Le Siège de Thionville*, Bibliothèque de l'Opéra ms. (1793), 454–76.

40. The manifest simplicity of the hymns performed at festivals and published in the *Ouvrage périodique* stems from similar factors, both practical and ideological. Writing for citizen-choruses and the need to project across large distances simplified them still more.

41. See Jam, "Le Clairon de l'avenir," in Julien and Klein, eds., *L'Orphée phrygien*, 25–26.

Epilogue to Part 3.   Thermidor and the Return of Entertainment

1. Louis-Sebastien Mercier, *Le Nouveau Paris* (Paris: A. Gènes, an III), xxxxiv.

2. See François Furet and Denis Richet, *La Révolution française* (Paris: Librairie Arthème Fayard, 1973), 445–77; Henrion, *Les Incroyables et les merveilleuses, ouvrage impayable* (Paris: Chez Graffe, an V); Martyn Lyons, *France under the Directory* (Cambridge: Cambridge University Press, 1975), 143–44.

3. *Journal des spectacles*, 1797.

4. "Lettre sur un fameux concert," signed Polyscope, in *La Décade philosophique*, 30 frimaire, an III, 527.

5. *La Sentinelle*, 17 April 1797, in Alphonse Aulard, ed., *Paris pendant la réaction thermidorienne et sous le directoire*, 5 vols. (Paris: Léopold Cerf, 1898), 1:492; *La Vedette*, 1 ventose, an III, quoted in ibid., 4:63.

6. Police report 17 frimaire, an IV, quoted in Welschinger, *Le Théâtre de la révolution*, 164.

7. Duval, *Souvenirs thermidoriens*, 1:355–56; Aulard, ed., *Paris pendant la réaction thermidorienne*, 1:438.

8. Mercier, *Le Nouveau Paris*, 127; Aulard, ed., *Paris pendant la réaction thermidorienne*, 1:296–97.

9. Aulard, ed., *Paris pendant la réaction thermidorienne*, 2:82–83.

10. Ibid., 2:317.

11. Ibid., 3:7, 21–23, 44–45, 251.

12. Frederic Jean Laurent Meyer, *Fragments sur Paris*, trans. Le Général Dumouriez (Hamburg: n.p., 1798), 137, 139.

13. *La Décade philosophique*, 30 prairial, an IV, 535.

14. Meyer, *Fragments sur Paris*, 81.

15. *La Décade philosophique*, 10 vendémiaire, an IX.

16. See Place, *La Vie musicale en France*, 131–35.

17. *Le Moniteur universel*, 26 Feb. 1795, 637.

18. *Le Moniteur universel*, 11 July 1795, 179; *Journal des théâtres et des fêtes nationales*, 10 vendémiaire, an III, 358.

19. *Le Moniteur universel*, 21 Dec. 1794, 8.

20. Letter of André-Modest Grétry dated 14 Feb. 1796, quoted in Michel Noiray, "L'Opéra de la Révolution (1790–1794): Un tapage de chien?" in J. C. Bonnet, ed., *La Carmagnole des muses: L'Homme de lettres et l'artiste dans la révolution* (Paris: Armand Colin, 1988), 359.

21. *Feuille de la république* (formerly *Feuille du salut public*), 5 sansculottide, an II, 4.

22. The correspondent clinched his point with an elaborate analogy appropriate to the ostentation that followed Thermidor: "Doesn't anyone have the good sense to realize and the good faith to show us that the abuse of the poetic arts is much like the abuse of the art of cooking, and that theatrical relevance and a fancy stew are often an artificial and ruinous resource for apathetic souls and exhausted palates?" (Letter from "Votre concitoyen, Alceste" to *L'Abréviateur universel*, 4 Sept. 1794, quoted in Aulard, ed., *Paris pendant la réaction thermidorienne*, 1:82.)

23. *Le Moniteur universel*, 26 Dec. 1795, 35. Crying, so widespread among musical audiences in the 1770s and 1780s, had been criticized during the Revolution as contrary to "strong republican morals" (*Journal des spectacles*, 15 July 1793, 120).

24. *Journal de Paris*, 30 July 1796, 1,250.

25. *Journal des théâtres et des fêtes nationales*, 13 brumaire, an III, 626.

26. *Vedette*, 1 ventose, an III, quoted in Aulard, ed., *Paris pendant la réaction thermidorienne*, 1:492.

27. Ibid., 4:418.

28. J. B. Poncet, who was present at the performance, relates that after the announcement the choir sang the chorus "Poursuivons jusqu'au trépas l'ennemi

qui nous outrage" "with transport" and the audience "felt and applauded" their enthusiasm. (Edouard Forestié, ed., "Notes sur les spectacles et les musées de Paris en l'an VII et en l'an VIII" [Extraits du journal de J.-B. Poncet], in *Bulletin de la société de l'histoire de Paris et de l'Ile-de-France, 1891* (Paris: Chez H. Champion, 1891), 60.

Chapter 9. Napoleon's Show

1. *La Décade philosophique*, 10 nivôse, an IX, 45.
2. *Le Rédacteur*, 1 nivôse, an IV, as quoted in Aulard, ed., *Paris pendant la réaction thermidorienne*, 4:516.
3. Stendhal, *Journal*, 14 July 1804, in *Oeuvres intimes* (Paris: Bibliothèque de la Pléiade, 1981), 97–98; Alphonse Aulard, ed., *Paris pendant le consulat*, 4 vols. (Paris: Léopold Cerf, 1903), 2:324.
4. Letters from government officials to Opéra administrators concerning press notices of Napoleon's planned visits to the theater can be found in the carton A. N. AJ[13] 76.
5. *Le Journal de l'empire*, 5 March 1812, 2–4; *Gazette de France*, 20 July 1805, quoted in Alphonse Aulard, ed., *Paris sous le premier empire*, 3 vols. (Paris: Léopold Cerf, 1912), 2:64.
6. *Gazette de France*, 25 Sept. 1802, quoted in Alphonse Aulard, ed., *Paris pendant le consulat*, 4 vols. (Paris: Léopold Cerf, 1903), 3:270–71; *Gazette de France*, 9 April 1813, 420.
7. Patrick Barbier, *La Vie quotidienne à l'Opéra au temps de Rossini et de Balzac* (Paris: Hachette, 1987), 154, 22; Maurice Guerrini, *Napoleon and Paris: Thirty Years of History*, trans. Margery Weiner (New York: Walker and Company, 1970), 88, 105.
8. *La Décade philosophique*, 10 nivôse, an IX, 44–46; *Journal des débats*, 23 Dec. 1800, quoted in Aulard, ed., *Paris sous le consulat*, 2:84; report from the Ministère de la Police, 25 Dec. 1800, quoted in Aulard, ed., *Paris sous le consulat*, 2:85.
9. See J. G. Prod'homme, "Napoleon, Music, and Musicians," *Musical Quarterly* 7 (1921): 579–605.
10. Auguste Kotzebue, *Souvenirs de Paris en 1804*, 2 vols. (Paris: Chez Barba, 1805), 2:239; "Manière d'éclairer la partie de la salle sans beaucoup nuire à l'effect du théâtre" (an XI), A. N. AJ[13] 95.
11. "État des loges louées à l'année au Théâtre de l'Opéra," A. N. AJ[13] 44.
12. "État nominatif des personnes occupantes des loges à l'année au premier janvier, 1812," A. N. AJ[13] 44.
13. This shift from social rank to state office is reflected in the Opéra's 1812 subscription rolls, which list the titles of government officials but not their names.
14. See for example "Registres d'abonnement, 1809–1814," which lists

the names of subscribers in the order of their requests (Bibliothèque de l'Opéra, CO 239).

15. "Tableau des loges et des places de l'Académie Impériale de Musique, 1810," A. N. AJ¹³ 76.

16. Pierre Jouhaud, *Paris dans le dix-neuvième siècle, ou réflexions d'un observateur sur les nouvelles institutions* . . . (Paris: J. G. Dentu, Imprimeur, 1809), 304; *Courrier de l'Europe et des spectacles*, 11 Oct. 1807, 2.

17. "Loges louées à l'année à l'Opéra, 1788–89," A. N. O¹624; "État nominatif des personnes occupantes des loges à l'année au premier janvier 1812," A. N. AJ¹³ 76.

18. See comparisons of receipts by year, A. N. AJ¹³ 76.

19. Among them were Jean-Antoine-Claude-Adrien de Mun, comte de l'empire, 1809; Jean-Andoche Junot, duc d'Abrantes, 1809; Anne-Gilbert de Laval, baron de l'empire, 1810; François-Jérome-Léonard de Mortmart de Boisse, chevalier de l'empire, 1811; Louis Friant, comte de l'empire, 1808; Jacques-François Gay, baron de l'empire, 1808; Hubert-Joseph-Vincent Perrin, chevalier de l'empire, 1810; Antoine-François-Adolphe Renaud, baron de l'empire, 1810; Jean-Pierre-Chrysostome Colin, chevalier de l'empire, 1808; Anne-Jean-Marie-René Savary, duc de Rovigo, 1808; Benjamin Gault, baron de l'empire, 1808. "Registres d'abonnement, 1809–1814," Bibliothèque de l'Opéra, CO 239; A. Révérand, *Armorial du premier empire*, 4 vols. (Paris: Honoré Champion, 1894–97).

20. See Barbier, *La Vie quotidienne à l'Opéra*, 46.

21. Boullet, "Restauration à faire au Théâtre des Arts," 15 prairial, an XI, A. N. AJ¹³ 95.

22. Aulard, ed., *Paris sous le premier empire*, 2:65; Aulard, ed., *Paris pendant le consulat*, 4:16

23. *Correspondance des professeurs et amateurs de musique*, 7 April 1804, 229.

24. *Les Tablettes de Polymnie: Journal consacré à tout ce qui interésse l'art musical*, June 1810, 7–11. *Les Bayadères* seems to have been calculated to draw just such a response ("Remember that an entire lifetime can occur in but a few days," the Bayadères croon). The plot concerns the sacred wedding choice the raja of Benares, a man named Démaly, must make. Tradition would have him choose from the harem (and the three leading candidates amply display their virtues), but, unhappily, Démaly is in love with the Bayadère Laméa, one of the sacred Hindu dancing girls who must remain chaste. A foreign army overruns the city, but its soldiers are slaughtered when the Bayadères' sweet songs cause them to unbuckle their swords in anticipation, leaving them vulnerable to the loyalists' counterattack. Démaly's confidant announces that the raja has been injured in battle and will probably die, but he must still make the sacred wedding selection. Of course the wife will be obliged to burn herself on his funeral pyre. The three leading candidates respectfully withdraw, Laméa comes forward to pledge her love, and the marriage is approved. After much mourning and as Laméa is preparing herself for death, Démaly arrives in perfect health: it was all a hoax to avoid marrying from the harem! Happiness abounds! (Charles-Simon

Catel, *Les Bayadères* [Paris: Éditions Michaelis, n.d. (reprint ed., New York: Broude Brothers, 1971)]).

25. *Memorandums of a Residence in France, in the Winter of 1815–16* (London: Longman, Hurst, Rees, Orme, and Brown, 1816), 289.

26. Ms. signed Boullet, "Restauration à faire au Théâtre des Arts," A. N. AJ[13] 95.

27. In a letter from Lecerf, "Au Préfet du Palais chargé de la surveillance et direction générale du Théâtre des Arts," 23 nivôse, an XI, A. N. AJ[13] 95.

28. Aulard, ed., *Paris pendant le consulat*, 1:127.

29. Ibid., 4:658.

30. Ibid., 4:680. Defly probably should have considered himself lucky: four years later there would be a formalized procedure to place political opponents under administrative arrest whereby detainees could be held indefinitely without trial (D. M. G. Sutherland, *France 1789–1815: Revolution and Counterrevolution* [Oxford: Oxford University Press, 1986], 391).

31. See Lasalle, *Les Treize salles de l'Opéra*, 191; Sutherland, *France 1789–1815*, 351.

32. Aulard, ed., *Paris pendant le consulat*, 3:48.

33. *La Décade philosophique*, 10 prairial, an X, 419–22.

34. Louis-Damien Emeric, *De la Politesse, ouvrage critique, moral et philosophique, avec des notes suivis d'un petit aperçu littéraire* (Paris: Imprimerie de Renaudière, 1819), 148.

35. Ibid., 148–49.

36. *Tablettes de Polymnie*, June 1810, 7–11.

37. *Memorandums of a Residence in France*, 289.

38. Aulard, ed., *Paris pendant le consulat*, 3:790.

39. Jouhaud, *Paris dans le dix-neuvième siècle*, 304.

40. J. T. Merle, *De l'Opéra* (Paris: Baudouin Frères, 1827), 31, 37, 35; for additional complaints about the brightness of the hall, see "Manière d'éclairer la partie de la salle sans beaucoup nuire à l'effet du théâtre," A. N. AJ[13] 95; Kotzebue, *Souvenirs de Paris*, 2:238.

41. Barbier, *La Vie quotidienne à l'Opéra*, 20.

42. M. Vivien and Edmond Blanc, eds., *Traité de la législation des théâtres . . .* (Paris: Brissot-Thivars, 1830), 402.

43. Ibid., 360.

44. Ibid., 363.

45. A decree of 8 June 1806, covering all Paris theaters, reads: "no new piece can be performed without the authorization of the Minister of Police" (ibid., 360).

46. Napoleon in letter dated 13 Feb. 1810, quoted in Barbier, *La Vie quotidienne à l'Opéra*, 26; see also Guerrini, *Napoleon and Paris*, 162.

47. Napoleon in 1806 letter to Champagny, quoted in Guerrini, *Napoleon and Paris*, 162.

48. *Journal de l'empire*, 21 Feb. 1811, 2.

49. Jouhard, *Paris dans le dix-neuvième siècle*, 331.

50. See Lajarte, *Bibliothèque musicale du théâtre de l'Opéra*, 369.

51. M. le comte Fortia de Piles, *Quelques refléxions d'un homme du monde, sur les spectacles, la musique, le jeu et le duel* (Paris: Porthmann, 1812), 31.

52. "*Iphigénie en Aulide* needs a ballet," urged the *Journal de l'empire* in 1811. "Gardel is protecting Gluck," *Journal de l'empire*, 21 Feb. 1811, 2. See also *Gazette de France*, 25 May 1813, 589.

53. *Journal de l'empire*, 26 March 1812, 1.

54. G. A. Villoteau, *Recherches sur l'analogie de la musique avec les arts qui ont pour objet l'imitation du langage*, 2 vols. (Paris: L'Imprimerie Impériale, 1807), 1:85.

55. For details on the plot of *Les Mystères d'Isis*, see Adolphe Jullien, *Paris dilettante au commencement du siècle* (Paris: Didot, 1889), 115–16; see also Mongrédien, *La Musique en France*, 72; Barbier, *La Vie quotidienne à l'Opéra*, 87–88; Lasalle, *Les Treize salles de l'Opéra*, 195; Louis Spohr, *Louis Sphor's Autobiography* (London: Longman, Green, Longman, Roberts, and Green, 1865; reprint ed., New York: Da Capo Press, 1969), 110.

56. *Journal des débats*, 19–20 Oct. 1805, quoted in Mongrédien, *La Musique en France*, 326; Aulard, ed., *Paris sous le premier empire*, 2:188.

57. *Revue musical*, 2:538. François Henri Joseph Blaze, music critic of the *Journal des débats* from 1822 to 1832, wrote under the name Castil-Blaze.

58. Catherine Join-Diéterle, *Les Décors de scène de l'Opéra de Paris à l'époque romantique* (Paris: Picard, 1988), 284.

59. See Jean-François Le Sueur, *Ossian, ou les bardes*, in Early Romantic Opera, ed. Philip Gossett and Charles Rosen, vol. 37 (New York: Garland Publishing, 1979), 384–433; David Charlton, "Ossian, Le Sueur, and Opera," *Studies in Music* 11 (1977): 37–48.

60. *Courrier de l'Europe et des spectacles*, 5 July 1807, 2.

61. "Comte général de la situation morale et politique du Département de la Seine, pendant le mois de pluviose, an VII," quoted in Aulard, ed., *Paris sous le consulat*, 1:164.

62. See Gaspare Spontini and Étienne de Jouy, *La Vestale*, Early Romantic Opera, ed. Philip Gossett and Charles Rosen, vol. 42 (New York: Garland Publishing, 1979).

63. *Courrier de l'Europe et des spectacles*, 8 Nov. 1807, 2.

64. See Aulard, ed., *Paris sous le premier empire*, 3:382–83.

65. *Courrier de l'Europe et des spectacles*, 8 Nov. 1804, 2.

66. Ibid., 2–3.

67. The recognition comes when Trajan burns a letter containing a plot on his life, apparently a reference to Napoleon's decision to commute a death sentence for treason given to Prince Hatzfeldt, a Prussian nobleman who had condemned the French entry into Berlin in a letter to Frederick William III. Napoleon burned the letter in a dramatic gesture of clemency when the Princess Hatzfeldt came to his quarters to beg for her husband's life. (See Baron Claude-François de Méneval, *Memoirs Illustrating the History of Napoleon I*, 3 vols. [New York: D. Appleton and Co., 1894], 2:63–64; William Milligan Sloane, *Life of Napoleon Bonaparte*, 4 vols. [New York: The Century Co., 1909], 3:3.)

68. *Courrier de l'Europe et des spectacles*, 29 Oct. 1807, 3–4.

69. See A. N. AJ[13] 76.

70. Emmanuel Dupaty and [Rodolphe] Kreutzer, *Le Triomphe du mois de mars, ou le berceau d'Achille* (Paris: Masson, 1811), 30.

71. See Mongrédien, *La Musique en France*, 56.

72. Gaspare Spontini, *Fernand Cortez, ou la conquête du Mexique*, Early Romantic Opera, ed. Philip Gossett and Charles Rosen, vol. 43 (New York: Garland Publishing, 1980), 484–90.

73. Prefatory dedication in Le Sueur, *Ossian*, 496–519.

74. Spontini, *Fernand Cortez*, 2:490–503.

75. See Gerald Abraham, "The Best of Spontini," *Music and Letters* 23 (1942): 168.

76. "Historic truth demanded that the guilty Vestale should suffer the death to which her sin had exposed her; but was this fearful catastrophe—which might have been introduced by means of a narrative in regular tragedy—of such a nature that it could be consummated before the eyes of the specatator? I do not think so." (V. J. Étienne de Jouy, quoted in Karin Pendle, *Eugène Scribe and French Opera of the Nineteenth Century* [Ann Arbor: UMI Research Press, 1979], 369.)

77. Spontini and de Jouy, *La Vestale*, 453–56; Mongrédien, *La Musique en France*, 57.

78. "Bonaparte's Speech to the Council of Elders, 19 Brumaire, Year VIII (10 Nov. 1799)," in Keith Michael Baker, ed., *The Old Regime and the French Revolution* (Chicago: University of Chicago Press, 1987), 406.

79. Joseph-Alphonse Esménard, *Le Triomphe de Trajan*, in Lepeintre, ed., *Suite du répertoire du théâtre français avec un choix des pièces de plusieurs autres théâtres*, 80 vols. (Paris: Mme Veuve Dabo, 1822), 15:286.

80. It "raised French souls to the heights of admiration while at the same time enchanting their eyes and ears with its magnificent spectacle and beautiful verse" (*Gazette de France*, 7 March 1811, 261).

81. See Mme de Chastenay, *Mémoires* (Paris: Librairie Académique Perrin, 1987), 508.

Chapter 10. The Théâtre Italien and Its Elites

1. See René Rémond, *The Right Wing in France from 1815 to De Gaulle*, trans. James M. Laux (Philadelphia: University of Pennsylvania Press, 1966), esp. 55–80.

2. Castil-Blaze, *L'Opéra Italien de 1548 à 1856* (Paris: Castil-Blaze, 1856), 423.

3. Honoré de Balzac, "De l'Eau-de-Vie," from *Traité des excitants modernes*, in *La Comédie humaine*, 12 vols. (Paris: Bibliothèque de la Pléiade, 1976–81), 12:311–15.

4. *Courrier de l'Europe et des spectacles*, 25 Dec. 1807, 2.

5. Castil-Blaze, *L'Opéra Italien*, 293–94.

6. *Gazette de France*, 25 May 1813, 590; Barbier, *La Vie quotidienne à l'Opéra*, 229.

7. On the reception of Mozart at the Théâtre Italien, see Mongrédien, *La Musique en France*, 117–18; Castil-Blaze, *L'Opéra Italien*, 352–60.

8. See Castil-Blaze, *L'Opéra Italien*, 391–424.

9. Barbier, *La Vie quotidienne à l'Opéra*, 231; J. G. Prod'homme, "Rossini and His Works in France," *Musical Quarterly* 17 (1931): 110–37.

10. See Jullien, *Paris dilettante*, 71–84; letter quoted in Florence Fabricant, "Celebrating Rossini's Birthday and His Truly Operatic Tastes," *New York Times*, 26 Feb. 1992, C3.

11. Nicholas Till, *Rossini: His Life and Times* (New York: Hippocrene Books, 1983), 11.

12. Stendhal, *Vie de Rossini*, 2 vols. (Paris: Librairie Ancienne Honoré Champion, 1922), 1:3.

13. See Jullien, *Paris dilettante*, 83–84; *Guerre aux rossinistes! par un amateur de Morvan* (1821), quoted in Philip Gossett, "Music at the Théâtre Italien," in Peter Bloom, ed., *Music in Paris in the Eighteen-Thirties*, vol. 4, Musical Life in Nineteenth-Century France (Stuyvesant, N.Y.: Pendragon Press, 1987), 330.

14. *Il n'y a qu'un Paris dans le monde . . .* (Paris: Imprimerie Laurens, 1815), 58.

15. For an excellent discussion of the Opéra's repertoire under the Restoration, see Catherine Join-Diéterle, "La Monarchie, source d'inspiration de l'Opéra à l'époque romantique," *Revue d'histoire du théâtre* 35 (1983–84): 430–41.

16. On the formation of a canon, understood as such, in the nineteenth century, see William Weber, "The Rise of the Classical Repertoire in Nineteenth-Century Orchestral Concerts," in Joan Peyser, ed., *The Orchestra: Origins and Transformations* (New York: Charles Scribner's Sons, 1986), 361–86. See also idem, *The Rise of Musical Classics in Eighteenth-Century England: A Study in Canon, Ritual, and Ideology* (Oxford: Clarendon Press, 1992).

17. See Sophie Augustine Leo, "Musical Life in Paris (1817–1848): A Chapter from the Memoirs of Sophie Augustine Leo," trans. W. Oliver Strunk, *Musical Quarterly* 17 (1931): 261. The one active genre was ballet, where tried and true formulas from the Old Regime still succeeded. Among the most popular titles were *Nina, ou la folle pour amour* (1813), *Flore et Zéphire* (1815), *La Carnaval de Venise* (1816), and *La Rossignol* (1816).

18. *Nouveau tableau de Paris, ou observations sur les moeurs et usages des parisiens au commencement du XIXe siècle*, 2 vols. (Paris: Chez Pillet Ainé, 1828), 2:132; *Le Mercure du XIXe siècle*, 1829, quoted in Join-Diéterle, *Les Décors de scène de l'Opéra*, 105.

19. *Le Pandore*, quoted in Join-Diéterle, *Les Décors de scène de l'Opéra*, 105.

20. Stendhal, *Vie de Rossini*, 1:270.

21. "Loges louées à l'année à l'Opéra, 1788–89," A. N. O^1 624; "Loges louées à l'année, 1819;" "Loges louées à l'Opéra, 1820," A. N. AJ^13 144.

22. "I remember that at these performances [of the operas of Gluck in the

late 1810s] the audience might easily have been counted," writes Sophie Leo. "It consisted almost entirely of those to whom these works brought pleasant memories of departed youth. The aged Gossec, taking his place in the first row of the balcony, was to be seen regularly at the Gluck operas" (Leo, "Musical Life in Paris," 261–62).

23. L. Montigny, *Le Provincial à Paris: Esquisse des moeurs Parisiennes*, 2 vols. (Paris: Chez Ladvocat, 1825), 2:46.

24. Stendhal, *Vie de Rossini*, 2:50, n. 1.

25. The 1820 budget for the Opéra is contained in A. N. AJ[13] 144; "Recette générale, Recettes à la Porte, 1823," Théâtre Italien, A. N. AJ[13] 147.

26. See Mongrédien, *La Musique en France*, 129.

27. Heinrich Heine, *Lutezia*, quoted in Francis Claudon, "L'Idée et l'influence de la musique, chez quelques romantiques français et notamment Stendhal" (Thèse, Université de Paris IV, 1979), 35.

28. Join-Diéterle, *Les Décors de scènes de l'Opéra*, 118; Stendhal, *Vie de Rossini*, 1:17; 1835 letter from Balzac cited in Claudon, "L'Idée et l'influence de la musique," 34.

29. *Courrier des théâtres*, 1 Jan. 1826, 3.

30. Castil-Blaze, *L'Opéra-Italien*, 292; Jal [Gabriel Fictor], *Manuscrit de 1905* (1827), quoted in Prod'homme, "Rossini and His Works in France," 128.

31. "Théâtre Royal Italien, Instruction sur la service de la salle," n.d., A. N. AJ[13] 144.

32. Lubbert to La Rouchefoucault, 24 March 1827, quoted in Janet Lynn Johnson, "The Théâtre-Italien and Opera and Theatrical Life in Restoration Paris, 1818–27," 3 vols. (Ph.D. diss., University of Chicago, 1988), 3:442.

33. "Théâtre Royal Italien, location des loges, 1821," A. N. AJ[13] 147.

34. "Décompte du prix des locations de loges à l'année, restante à servir à l'époque du 1er octobre 1827," "Théâtre Royal Italien, location des loges, 1821," A. N. AJ[13] 147.

35. "Entrées de droit" gave recipients the privilege to sit in any of the theater's open seating but its first balcony. "Entrées de service" and "entrées de faveur" restricted their recipients to the floor seats or the galleries; the latter could not be used for the first two performances or the first reengagement of a work that had already appeared ("Théâtre Royal Italien, Instruction sur la service de la salle," n.d., A. N. AJ[13] 144).

36. Marie d'Agoult, *Mémoires*, quoted in Join-Diéterle, *Les Décors de scène de l'Opéra*, 195.

37. Business directories such as Bottin's give liberal professions that correspond to many of the untitled names on the rolls of the Théâtre Italien. Anne Martin-Fugier identifies several of the subscribers in *La Vie élégante, ou la formation du Tout-Paris, 1815–1848* (Paris: Librairie Arthème Fayard, 1990): a Davilliers was a "grand industriel" living on the boulevard Poissonnière, for example, and Charles Bocher made a fortune in banking (104–5). Most positive identifications of subscribers to the Théâtre Italien are impossible, however, as the subscription lists lack both first names and addresses. See Joseph François Michaud, *Biographie universelle* (Paris: C. Desplaces, 1854–65), and Sébastien Bottin, *Annuaire du commerce de Paris* (Paris: Didot) for individual years.

38. Honoré de Balzac, *Père Goriot*, trans. E. K. Brown (New York: Modern Library, 1950), 138.

39. Lagrave, *Le Théâtre et le public à Paris*, 83; Lasalle, *Les Treize salles de l'Opéra*, 182; Johnson, "The Théâtre-Italien and Opera and Theatrical Life," 2: 289.

40. Bergman, *Lighting in the Theatre*, 252; see also various documents regarding the hall of the Théâtre Italien, dated 1824, in A. N. AJ[13], 147, and letter to *Miroir des spectacles*, 17 Dec. 1827, 3. Compare also A. J.-J. Deshayes, *Idées générales sur l'Académie Royal de Musique* (1822): "This light is perfect for the stage. By means of the gas one can obtain a gradation of the brightness that is really magical, and one does not have to make something offendingly improbable when action passes from day to night; one can also advantageously present illuminations and transparencies, etc." (quoted in Bergman, *Lighting in the Theatre*, 252).

41. Stendhal, *Le Rouge et le noir*, in *Romans*, 2 vols. (Paris: Bibliothèque de la Pléiade, 1952), 1:618–19.

42. Montigny, *Le Provincial à Paris*, 2:46.

43. *Nouveaux tableaux de Paris, ou observations sur les moeurs*, 2:136.

44. *Journal des débats*, 19 March 1831, quoted in Joseph-Marc Bailbé, *Le Roman et la musique en France sous la monarchie de juillet* (Paris: Minard, 1969), 24.

45. Stendhal, *Notes d'un dilettante*, in *Oeuvres intimes*, 2:374. Mainvielle-Fodor was of Hungarian descent, though born in Paris.

46. *Le Globe*, 25 Feb. 1825, quoted in Johnson, "The Théâtre-Italien and Opera and Theatrical Life," 3:383.

47. Stendhal, *Notes d'un dilettante*, 2:287–88.

48. The psychiatric hospital.

49. *Tablettes de Polymnie*, 5 Nov. 1810, 168–69.

50. Joseph d'Ortigue, *De la Guerre des dilettanti, ou de la révolution opérée par M. Rossini dans l'opéra français; et des rapports qui existent entre la musique, la littérature et les arts* (Paris: Imprimerie de Béthune, 1829), 23.

51. *Pandore*, 7 June 1824, quoted in Johnson, "The Théâtre-Italien and Opera and Theatrical Life," 3:443.

52. H. N. Raisson and A. Romieu, *Code civil: Manuel complet de la politesse, du ton, des manières de la bonne compagnie . . .* (Paris: G. Doyen, 1828), 92.

53. Ibid.

54. Stendhal, *Life of Rossini*, trans. Richard N. Coe (Seattle: University of Washington Press, 1970), 315–16.

55. Stendhal to Adolphe de Mareste, 15 April 1819, Stendhal, *Correspondance*, 3 vols. (Paris: Bibliothèque de la Pléiade, 1962), 1:963.

56.   Harmonie, ange d'or! comme toujours tes nimbes
          Savent mon cerveau rasséréner, les limbes!
          Harmonie, harmonie, oh! quel amour puissant
          Pour tes miracles saints fermente dans mon sang!
          Si jamais la rigueur de mon sort me décide
          A chercher un refuge aux bras du suicide,
          Mon exaltation d'artiste choisira

Pour le lieu de ma mort l'Italique Opéra.
Je m'enfermerai seul dans une loge à grilles;
Et quand les violons, les hautbois et les strilles [sic],
Au grand contentement de maint dilettante,
Accompagneront l'air du basso-cantante,
L'oeil levé hardiment vers les sonores voûtes,
D'un sublime opium j'avalerai cent gouttes;
Puis je m'endormirai sous les enivrements
Dont la Musique, almé voluptueuse et chaste,
Sur ma belle agonie épanchera le faste.
(Philothée O'Neddy [Théophile Dondey],
"Nuit septième—Dandyisme," from Feu et flamme
[Paris: Éditions Presses Françaises, 1926], 34-37.)

57. *La Revue musicale* 5 (Feb.-July 1829): 520-21.
58. Ibid., 3 (Feb.-July 1828): 538.
59. Ibid., 421.
60. Stendhal, *Notes d'un dilettante*, 2:333-34.
61. Stendhal, *Vie de Rossini*, 1:107.

Chapter 11. The Birth of Public Concerts

1. *Allgemeine musikalische Zeitung*, May 1800, quoted in Boris Schwarz, *French Instrumental Music between the Revolutions (1789-1830)* (New York: Da Capo Press, 1987), 16.

2. *Journal de l'empire*, 20 March 1810, quoted in Mongrédien, *La Musique en France*, 227-28.

3. See ibid., 212-18; Schwarz, *French Instrumental Music*, 21-22.

4. *Allgemeine musikalische Zeitung*, Feb. 1805, quoted in Schwarz, *French Instrumental Music*, 21-22; *Allgemeine musikalische Zeitung*, 10 Feb. 1802, quoted in Mongrédien, *La Musique en France*, 213.

5. *Correspondance des amateurs musiciens*, 7 Jan. 1803, 2.

6. *Paris et ses modes, ou les soirées parisiennes* (Paris: Chez Michelet, 1803), 13.

7. "No other musician who did not live in this country," writes the French musicologist François Lesure, "and who had no apparent affinity with its language or culture, received as sudden, official, spontaneous, and enthusiastic a public reception as Haydn" (*Haydn en France* [Budapest: Akadémiai Kiado, 1961], 79). Jean Mongrédien writes, "With the possible exception of Haydn's symphonies, instrumental music—*pure music*—was not truly appreciated by the public of the large concerts, which preferred vocal music" (*La Musique en France*, 201).

8. *Journal des débats*, 3 April 1808, quoted in Grégoire, ed., *Souvenirs artistiques*, 3:15; *Tablettes de Polymnie*, 5 April 1811, 329; *Correspondance des amateurs musiciens*, 13 March 1803, 3.

9. Lesure, *Haydn en France*, 83.

10. Ibid., 79.

11. See Mongrédien, *La Musique en France*, 214.

12. *Correspondance des amateurs musiciens*, 29 Jan. 1803, n.p.; Mongrédien, *La Musique en France*, 216.

13. *Correspondance des professeurs et amateurs de musique*, 18 Feb. 1804, 115.

14. Fortia de Piles, *Quelques refléxions d'un homme du monde*, 60.

15. *Correspondance des professeurs et amateurs de musique*, 1803, quoted in Mongrédien, *La Musique en France*, 200.

16. *Journal de l'empire*, 16 May 1812, 4.

17. See Mongrédien, *La Musique en France*, 212–13.

18. See *Correspondance des professseurs et amateurs de musique*, 26 Jan. 1805, 29.

19. Ibid.

20. Ibid., 8 Feb. 1805, 45; 23 Feb. 1805, 60.

21. See Schwarz, *French Instrumental Music*, 23.

22. Ibid.

23. See Mongrédien, *La Musique en France*, 219.

24. *Courrier des spectacles*, no. 2536, quoted in Pierre, *Le Conservatoire National de Musique*, 462.

25. *Journal de Paris*, 12 April 1814, quoted in Schwarz, *French Instrumental Music*, 27.

26. Pierre, *Le Conservatoire National de Musique*, 465.

27. Schwarz, *French Instrumental Music*, 29.

28. *Journal de l'empire*, 21 March 1811, 1.

29. *Tablettes de Polymnie*, 5 Sept. 1811, 481.

30. *Gazette de France*, 26 June 1818, 693.

31. *Allgemeine musikalische Zeitung*, Feb. 1804, quoted in Schwarz, *French Instrumental Music*, 29.

32. Geoffroy in *Journal de l'empire*, quoted in Grégoire, *Souvenirs artistiques*, 3:172.

33. See for example programs for the Exercices listed in the pages of *Gazette de France*, 1813–15; see also Schwarz, *French Instrumental Music*, 29.

34. *Journal de l'empire*, 20 Oct. 1905, quoted in Mongrédien, *La Musique en France*, 315.

35. See Schwarz, *French Instrumental Music*, 78–79; see also Pierre, *La Conservatoire National de Musique*, 466.

36. Schwarz, *French Instrumental Music*, 79.

37. *Allgemeine musikalische Zeitung*, Feb. 1805, quoted in Schwarz, *French Instrumental Music*, 23–24.

38. Fortia de Piles, *Quelques refléxions d'un homme du monde*, 58.

39. From François Perne, *Exposé des moyens que l'ou peut prendre pour mettre en évidence des travaux de l'école royale* (1816), reprinted in Pierre, *La Conservatoire National de Musique*, 471.

40. Schwarz, *French Instrumental Music*, 54.

41. For details on the programs of Baillot's series, see Joël-Marie Faguet,

Les Sociétés de musique de chambre à Paris de la restauration à 1870 (Paris: Aux Amateurs de Livres, 1986), 51; see also idem, "La Musique de chambre à Paris dans les années 1830," in Bloom, ed., *Music in Paris in the Eighteen-Thirties,* 299–326.

42. *Le Miroir des spectacles,* 28 Jan. 1822, 3.

43. *Revue musicale,* 7 March 1827, 191.

44. *Revue musicale* 2 (Aug. 1827–Jan. 1828):607.

45. Ibid., 523–24.

Chapter 12. In Search of
Harmony's Sentiments

1. *Tablettes de Polymnie,* 1810, 3; *Correspondance des amateurs musiciens,* 12 Feb. 1803, 3.

2. In his typically intemperate manner, the critic Geoffroy declared that "our orchestras are killing our operas" with harmony. In 1804 the high-minded *Correspondance des professeurs et amateurs de musique* published an article that concluded with essentially the same point: the recent "profusion of instruments," it claimed, has damaged the capacity of music to paint its objects of expression (*Journal de l'empire,* 1805, 2:157; *Correspondance des professeurs et amateurs de musique,* 27 Oct. 1984, 693). David Charlton has compiled statistics concerning the instrumentation of operas of the period, and they confirm these listeners' perceptions. Surveying some 4,000 numbers from works at the Académie Royale de Musique staged during the years 1780–1810, Charlton concludes that operatic scores employed on average 33 percent of available instruments in any given number before 1789 and 54 percent of available instruments in 1810 (Charlton, "Les Instruments à vent: Les sons et les gestes," in Julien and Klein, eds., *Le Tambour et la harpe,* 213. See also David Charlton, "Orchestration and Orchestral Practice in Paris, 1789–1810" (Ph.D. diss., Cambridge University, 1973).

3. Villoteau, *Recherches sur l'analogie de la musique avec les arts,* 1:xviii.

4. Quatremère de Quincy, *Essai sur la nature, le but et les moyens de l'imitation dans les beaux-arts* (1823), quoted in Fernand Baldensperger, *Sensibilité musicale et romantisme* (Paris: Les Presses Françaises, 1925), 112.

5. François Henri Joseph Blaze [Castil-Blaze], *De l'Opéra en France,* 2 vols. (Paris: A. Egron, 1820), 1:124.

6. Letter signed R—h, in *Journal de l'empire,* 3 July 1812, 2.

7. It seems unlikely that the explanation lies in "nationalist pressure" that opposed Mozart because of his Austrian origins, as Jean Mongrédien has suggested, for such a solution would make the case of Haydn still more inexplicable (see Mongrédien, *La Musique en France,* 317).

8. *Journal des débats* 4 April 1808, quoted in Grégoire, ed., *Souvenirs artistiques,* 3:15.

9. *Tablettes de Polymnie,* 5 April 1811, 329, 321–22.

10. Quoted in Mongrédien, *La Musique en France,* 257.

11. Quoted in James Webster, *Haydn's "Farewell" Symphony and the Idea of Classical Style: Through-Composition and Cyclic Integration in His Instrumental Music* (Cambridge: Cambridge University Press, 1991), 230.

12. *Décade philosophique,* 10 nivôse, an IX, 45.

13. Ibid.

14. *Journal de l'empire,* 19 April 1811, 4.

15. Ibid.

16. Georg Griesinger, *Biographische Notizen über Joseph Haydn,* quoted in Webster, *Haydn's "Farewell" Symphony,* 234.

17. See ibid., 236–37.

18. See Mongrédien, *La Musique en France,* 215–16.

19. "De l'expression musicale," *Revue musicale* 1 (Feb.–July 1827): 372.

20. *Tablettes de Polymnie,* May 1810, 13.

21. *Journal de l'empire,* 5 March 1812, 2.

22. *Journal de l'empire,* March 1811, quoted in Grégoire, *Souvenirs artistiques,* 3:172.

23. *Mercure de France,* quoted in Robbins-Landon, *Haydn: Chronicle and Works,* 2:593.

24. "Spontini was the last link in a chain of composers whose first link was Gluck; what Gluck aimed at, and first seriously attempted, the most complete possible dramatization of the opera-cantata, was achieved by Spontini—in so far as it is possible to achieve it in the form of opera. . . . Spontini is dead and with him a great, noble and much to be respected artistic period has manifestly gone to its grave: it and he no longer belong to life, but solely to the history of art. Let us bow low and reverently before the tomb of the creator of the 'Vestale,' of 'Cortez' and of 'Olympie' " (Wagner quoted in Abraham, "The Best of Spontini," 163).

25. Spontini, *Fernand Cortez,* 1:50, 91, 99, 147.

26. Amazily first relates the news that the life of Cortez's brother has been spared through Montezuma's intervention (half note = 80); she then voices her fear of the sinister priests who still hold him (quarter note = 84); finally, she recounts the glory of Cortez (quarter note = 80) (ibid., 186–90).

27. Spontini, *Fernand Cortez,* 1:108–26.

28. Edward J. Dent, *The Rise of Romantic Opera* (Cambridge: Cambridge University Press, 1976), 105–6.

29. Le Sueur, *Ossian,* 76–85, 261–73. See also Charlton, "Ossian, Le Sueur, and Opera," 42–43; Winton Dean, "French Opera," in Abraham et al., eds., *The New Oxford History of Music,* 88–89.

30. Dean, "French Opera," in Abraham et al., eds., *The New Oxford History of Music,* 89–90.

31. *Revue musicale* 3 (Feb.–July 1828): 413–14.

32. *Tablettes de Polymnie,* 5 April 1811, 329.

33. See Martin H. Tartak, "The Italian Comic Operas of Rossini" (Ph.D. diss., University of California, Berkeley, 1968).

34. For a discussion of the structure of Rossini's finales, see Philip Gossett, "The Candeur Virginale of *Tancredi*," *Musical Times* 112 (1971): 326–29.

35. See Tartak, "Italian Comic Operas of Rossini," 83–86.

36. See Gioacchino Rossini, *L'italiana in Algeri*, ed. Arzo Corghi (Milan: G. Ricordi, 1982), 152–236. A similar sort of controlled pandemonium reigns in the Finale to *Il barbiere di Siviglia*.

37. Rossini, *Il barbiere di Siviglia* (New York: G. Schirmer, 1951), 31–41; idem, *Semiramide*, 2 vols., in Early Romantic Opera, ed. Philip Gossett and Charles Rosen, vol. 13 (New York: Garland Publishing Co., 1978), 1:152–65; idem, *L'italiana in Algeri*, 379–94; idem, *Tancredi*, ed. Philip Gossett (Milan: G. Ricordi, 1991), 288–309; idem, *Otello* (New York: Edwin F. Kalmus, n.d.), 112–16.

38. Gluck in Preface to *Alceste*, quoted in Dean, "Gluck," *New Grove Dictionary of Music and Musicians*, 7:467.

39. Augustin Thierry quoted in Jean-Louis Causson, *Gioacchino Rossini: L'Homme et son oeuvre* (Paris: Slatkine, 1982), 176.

40. Philip Gossett, "Gioacchino Rossini and the Conventions of Composition," *Acta Musicologica* 42 (1970): 57; Tartak, "Italian Comic Operas of Rossini," 81–83.

41. See Dean, "Italian Opera," in Abraham et al., eds., *The New Oxford History of Music*, esp. 413–26.

42. Dean, "French Opera," in Abraham et al., eds., *The New Oxford History of Music*, 103; Stendhal quoted in Causson, *Gioacchino Rossini*, 172; Dent, *Rise of Romantic Opera*, 118.

43. Dean, "Italian Opera," in Abraham et al., eds., *The New Oxford History of Music*, 422.

44. *Journal des débats*, 15 Feb. 1829, quoted in Francis Claudon, "L'Idée et l'influence de la musique," 397–98.

45. La comtesse Merlin, *Madame Malibran* (Brussels: Société Typographique Belge, 1838), 62–64.

46. Quoted in Claudon, "L'Idée et l'influence de la musique," 369.

47. *Observations désintéressées sur l'administration du Théâtre Italien, adressées à M. Viotti, directeur de ce théâtre par un dilettante* (Paris: Chez Anth^e. Boucher, 1821), 14.

Chapter 13. The Social Roots of Silence

1. Richard Sennett, *The Fall of Public Man: On the Social Psychology of Capitalism* (New York: Random House, 1974), 209. See esp. part 3, "The Turmoil of Public Life in the Nineteenth Century," 123–255.

2. Ibid., 210.

3. David Higgs, *Nobles in Nineteenth-Century France: The Practice of Inegalitarianism* (Baltimore: Johns Hopkins University Press, 1987), 16.

4. François August Mignet, "Notice historique sur la vie et les travaux de M. comte Merlin," *Mémoires de l'Académie des Sciences Morales* (1844), quoted in Adeline Daumard, *Les Bourgeois et la bourgeoisie en France depuis 1815* (Saint-Amand: Aubier-Montagne, 1987), 242.

5. Louis Bergeron, *France under Napoleon*, trans. R. R. Palmer (Princeton: Princeton University Press, 1981), 69, 70.

6. Higgs, *Nobles in Nineteenth-Century France*, 8.

7. Adeline Daumard, *La Bourgeoisie parisienne de 1815 à 1848* (Paris: École Pratique des Hautes Études, 1963), 244.

8. Bergeron, *France under Napoleon*, 70.

9. Letter written by Paty, maître des requêtes, 2 June 1821, quoted in Daumard, *La Bourgeoisie parisienne*, 147.

10. Ibid., 149.

11. Daumard, *Les Bourgeois et la bourgeoisie*, 134.

12. Ibid., 117; see also Higgs, *Nobles in Nineteenth-Century France*, 217.

13. *Le Constitutionnel*, 27 Dec. 1823, quoted in Daumard, *La Bourgeoisie parisienne*, 29; *Journal des débats*, 13 Sept. 1830, quoted in Daumard, *Les Bourgeois et la bourgeoisie*, 129. In the discussion that follows I have relied heavily on Daumard's discussion of the bourgeoisie's collective psychology.

14. *Revue française*, June 1838, quoted in Daumard, *Les Bourgeois et la bourgeoisie*, 45.

15. See Pierre Rosanvallon, *Le Moment Guizot* (Paris: Gallimard, 1985), 114

16. Duc de Broglie, speech on the proposed electoral law of 1820, quoted in ibid., 121.

17. General de Pelleport, quoted in Daumard, *Les Bourgeois et la bourgeoisie*, 177.

18. Alexis de Tocqueville, *The Old Regime and the French Revolution*, trans. Stuart Gilbert (Garden City: Anchor Books, 1955), 118. Rémusat reports that Roger [sic] Collard, trying for several days to find the right compliment for a friend who had been made a duke, finally replied, "You are too considerable a man for this to diminish you" (quoted in Daumard, *Les Bourgeois et la bourgeoisie*, 177).

19. See Jesse R. Pitts, "Continuity and Change in Bourgeois France," in Stanley Hoffmann et al., eds., *In Search of France* (Cambridge: Harvard University Press, 1963), 252.

20. *Journal des débats*, 17 Dec. 1847, quoted in Daumard, *La Bourgeoisie parisienne*, 246.

21. [Abel Goujon], *Manuel de l'homme de bon ton, ou cérémonial de la bonne société* (Paris: Chez Andin, [1822]), 8–9.

22. Ibid., 110. Goujon begins his book with a description of "good society," consistent with contemporary views of an open elite accessible to those with the proper qualities: "Good education and personal merit, together with good manners and probity, distinguish men from one another and form a particular class called good society" (5).

23. Emeric, *De la Politesse*, 148.

24. And it's no longer just applause. I attended a Paris recital by Alfred Brendel in 1985 that included Schubert's B-flat Opus posthumous Sonata. Between

the first two movements—both of them introspective and hushed—spectators began coughing and clearing their throats. Brendel hesitated, then turned to the hall with his hands drawn up as if to plead for silence. Instantly the spectators who hadn't coughed *shh*-ed those who had ("We know better than to do *that!*"), destroying any magic not already wrecked by the coughing. This enraged Brendel, who rose slightly from the piano bench and coldly snapped back his tuxedo tails before starting the second movement.

25. *Le Miroir des spectacles*, 31 Jan. 1823, 3.

26. Edmond Goblot, *La Barrière et le niveau: Étude sociologique sur la bourgeoisie française moderne* (Paris: Presses Universitaires de France, 1967).

27. Balzac, "Traité de la vie élégante," published in *La Mode*, 1830, quoted in Martin-Fugier, *La Vie élégante*, 23.

28. Raisson and Romieu, *Code civil*, 52.

29. *Correspondance des professeurs et amateurs de la musique*, 18 Feb. 1804, 115.

30. Goblot, *La Barrière et le niveau*, 57.

31. For further development of these themes along similar lines, see Robert A. Nye, *Masculinity and Male Codes of Honor in Modern France* (Oxford: Oxford University Press, 1993), esp. 31–46.

32. Alexis de Tocqueville, *Democracy in America*, trans. Henry Reeve, rev. Brown and Bradley, 2 vols. (New York: Random House, 1945), 2:11.

Chapter 14. Operatic Rebirth and the Return of Grandeur

1. Albéric Second, *Les Petits mystères de l'Opéra* (Paris: Kugelmann, 1844), 25; Duverger, "Quelques indications sur la mise en scène de Guillaume Tell," in H. Robert Cohen, ed., *The Original Staging Manuals for Twelve Parisian Operatic Premières* (Stuyvesant, N.Y.: Pendragon Press, 1991), 211–13.

2. Charles de Forster, *Quinze ans à Paris (1832–1848): Paris et les parisiens*, 2 vols. (Paris: Imprimeur de l'Institut, 1849), 2:212.

3. See *Revue musicale* 4 (Aug. 1828–Jan. 1829): 91; D. Kern Holoman, "The Emergence of the Orchestral Conductor in Paris in the 1820s," in Bloom, ed., *Music in Paris in the Eighteen-Thirties*, 394.

4. M. Locatelli was responsible for dimming the light in the hall beginning in the 1829–30 operatic season, introducing a chandelier that gave no more light, in his words, than "a night-light [*veilleuse*] in a tomb" (see Bergman, *Lighting in the Theatre*, 298). See also *Revue musicale* 11 (Feb. 1831–Jan. 1832): 142; Allan Keiler, "Liszt and Beethoven: The Creation of a Personal Myth," *19th-Century Music* 12 (1988), 8; report from Commission de Sureté Publique, July 1844, A. N. AJ[13] 222.

5. *L'Artiste: Journal de la littérature et des beaux-arts*, (1ère série, t. 2, 1832): 1:184.

6. The government of Louis-Philippe made provision for a "director-entre-preneur" to manage the Opéra "at his own risk and fortune." The plan was an attempt to stanch the flow of governmental funds to an institution that was per-petually on the brink of bankruptcy during the Restoration. While the director was free in assembling a staff, he would nevertheless be considered an agent of the state (see William L. Crosten, *French Grand Opera: An Art and a Business* [New York: King's Crown Press, 1948], 17).

7. *La Mode: Revue des modes, galerie de moeurs, album des sâlons*, April–June 1831, 7:239–41.

8. Philarète Chasles, quoted in G. I. C. de Courcy, *Paganini the Genoese*, 2 vols. (Norman: University of Oklahoma Press, 1957; reprint ed., New York: Da Capo Press, 1977), 2:11.

9. *Courrier des théâtres*, 1 Jan. 1826, 3; untitled ms. A. N. AJ [13] 222. See also Steven Huebner, "Opera Audiences in Paris, 1830–1870," *Music and Letters* 70 (1989): 206–25.

10. Véron, *Mémoires d'un bourgeois de Paris*, quoted in Crosten, *French Grand Opera*, 28.

11. André Lejeune and Stéphane Wolff, *Les Quinze salles de l'Opéra de Paris, 1669–1955* (Paris: E. Ploix, 1955), 28.

12. "Chauffage par la vapeur," A. N. AJ [13], 222.

13. "Appendice à l'état du mobilier par suite d'un récolement fait en juin 1844," in A. N. AJ [13], 222.

14. *Revue musicale* 11 (Feb. 1831–Jan. 1832): 142. See also Bapst, *Essai sur l'histoire du théâtre*, 535.

15. *Revue musicale* 11 (Feb. 1831–Jan. 1832): 135.

16. Ibid.

17. Victor de Balabine, *Journal* (Paris: Émile Paul Frères, 1914), 6–7.

18. *Revue musicale* 11 (Feb. 1831–Jan. 1832): 142.

19. de Forster, *Quinze ans à Paris*, 2:212.

20. *Courrier des théâtres*, 4 July 1831, 3; Frédéric Soulié, *Deux séjours: Prov-ince et Paris*, 2 vols. (Paris: Hippolyte Souverain, 1836), 2:251.

21. Charles de Boigne, *Petits mémoires de l'Opéra* (Paris: Librairie Nouvelle, 1857), 103.

22. *Courrier des théâtres*, 4 July 1831, 3.

23. Soulié, *Deux séjours*, 2:250.

24. Véron, *Mémoires d'un bourgeois de Paris*, quoted in Crosten, *French Grand Opera*, 20.

25. See Huebner, "Opera Audiences in Paris, 1830–1870," 208. Huebner rightly observes that these percentages form a microcosm of "the aristocracies of birth, fortune, and education" that according to René Rémond constituted a socially and politically powerful elite after 1830 (ibid., 218; see also Rémond, *The Right Wing in France*, 79–125).

26. "Location pour la saison d'hiver, 1833–1834," A. N. AJ [13] 228.

27. The lion, according to George Matoré, replaced the dandy in the 1830s as the elegant man of the world, with the one difference that the former did not push his originality to the point of eccentricity. "The dandy wants to make him-

self seen, the lion is someone people want to see" (George Matoré, *Le Vocabulaire et la société sous Louis-Philippe*, [Geneva: Slatkine, 1967], 46); Second, *Les Petits mystères de l'Opéra*, 82.

28. Crosten, *French Grand Opera*, 42.

29. Letter from Auguste Levasseur to Le Duc, reproduced in Boigne, *Petits mémoires de l'Opéra*, 90.

30. Second, *Les Petits mystères de l'Opéra*, 111–12.

31. See Hector Berlioz, *Evenings with the Orchestra*, trans. Jacques Barzun (Chicago: University of Chicago Press, 1956), 77–78.

32. See Jules Lau, *Mémoires d'un chef de claque: Souvenirs des théâtres* (Paris: Librairie Nouvelle, 1883), 17–23.

33. Ibid., 5.

34. Théophile Gautier, *Histoire de l'art dramatique en France*, quoted in Crosten, *French Grand Opera*, 45.

35. *La France musicale*, 23 Oct. 1838, n.p.

36. Edouard Fétis, "Le Romantisme en musique," *Revue musicale* 7 (Feb.–March 1830): 236.

37. *La France musicale*, 7 Aug. 1842, 278.

38. Soulié, *Deux séjours*, 2:251.

39. *Revue musicale* 2 (Aug. 1827–Jan. 1828): 543.

40. Police report dated 7 Feb. 1843, A. N. AJ¹³ 180.

41. M. A. Bazin, *L'Epoque sans nom: Esquisses de Paris, 1830–1833*, 2 vols. (Paris: Alexandre Mesnier, 1833), 2:110.

42. *Revue musicale* 11 (Feb. 1831–Jan. 1832): 336–37.

43. *Revue des deux mondes*, quoted in Catherine Join-Diéterle, "*Robert le diable*: Le premier opéra romantique," *Romantisme* 28–29 (1980), 150.

44. Scenes, respectively, from *La Muette de Portici* (Auber), *Les Huguenots* (Meyerbeer), and *La Juive* (Halévy).

45. *Revue des deux mondes*, 29 Nov. 1831, quoted in Join-Diéterle, "*Robert le diable*," 152.

46. Giacomo Meyerbeer, *Robert le diable*, 2 vols., in Early Romantic Opera, ed. Philip Gossett and Charles Rosen, vol. 19 (New York: Garland Publishing, 1980), 2:604.

47. Letter from Mendelssohn dated 19 Nov. 1831, quoted in Joseph-Marc Bailbé, "Mendelssohn à Paris," in Bloom, ed., *Music in Paris in the Eighteen-Thirties*, 30.

48. "Quel plaisir de voir ces femmes légères qui s'agitent au milieu de cette douteuse lumière!" (*Revue des deux mondes*, 29 Nov. 1831, quoted in Join-Diéterle, "*Robert le diable*," 152).

49. Berlioz, *Evenings with the Orchestra*, 108–9.

50. See Crosten, *French Grand Opera*, 64–65.

51. M. L. Palianti, "La Juive," in Cohen, ed., *The Original Staging Manuals for Twelve Parisian Operatic Premières*, 141.

52. Véron, *Mémoires d'un bourgeois de Paris*, quoted in Crosten, *French Grand Opera*, 129–30.

53. Winton Dean observes, for example, that the "jauntiness" of Sultan Ma-

ometo is smoothed out considerably for *Le Siège* (Dean, "French Opera," in Abraham et al., eds., *The New Oxford History of Music*, 106).

54. Alfred de Vigny, "Réflexions sur la vérité dans l'art," quoted in Donald Geoffrey Charlton, "Prose Fiction," in Donald Geoffrey Charlton, ed., *The French Romantics*, 2 vols. (Cambridge: Cambridge University Press, 1984), 1:189.

55. Sosthène de la Rochefoucauld to Charles X, 20 Oct. 1826, quoted in Anselm Gerhard, "Une véritable révolution opérée à l'Opéra français," *L'Avant scène opéra* 81 (1985): 19; Adolphe Adam, "Académie Royale de Musique: *Le Siège de Corinthe* de Rossini," in *Revue et gazette musicale de Paris*, 22 Nov. 1835, quoted in Karen Pendle, *Eugène Scribe and French Opera of the Nineteenth Century* (Ann Arbor: UMI Research Press, 1979), 424.

56. Louis Rainier Lanfranchi, *Voyage à Paris, ou esquisses des hommes et des choses* (Paris: Lepetit, 1830), 345; *Revue musicale* 13 (Feb. 1833–Jan. 1834): 85.

57. See Jane F. Fulcher, *The Nation's Image: French Grand Opera as Politics and Politicized Art* (Cambridge: Cambridge University Press, 1987), 33–36; M. Solomé, "Indications générales et observations pour la mise en scène de *La Muette de Portici*," in Cohen, ed., *The Original Staging Manuals for Twelve Parisian Operatic Premières*, 13–72.

58. *Revue musicale* 3 (Feb.–July 1828): 155.

59. "One could, I see, call you Mr. Microcosm" (Blaze de Bury, in *Revue des deux mondes*, 1859). "[His] coat of arms belongs to all races. He . . . forgot only one thing, to give himself any ancestors" (Victor Planche, in *Chronique de Paris*, 1836). Both quoted in Kerry Murphy, *Hector Berlioz and the Development of French Music Criticism* (Ann Arbor: UMI Research Press, 1988), 123, 124.

60. Giacomo Meyerbeer, *Les Huguenots*, 2 vols., Early Romantic Opera, ed. Philip Gossett and Charles Rosen, vol. 20 (New York: Garland Publishing Co., 1990), 1:242–47.

61. Robert Schumann, "Un huguenot contre *Les Huguenots*," reprinted in *L'Avant scène opéra* 134 (Sept.–Oct. 1990): 98.

62. See Meyerbeer, *Robert le diable*, 2:529–40. For a brief commentary on Meyerbeer's innovations in orchestral timbre, see David Charlton, "Romantic Opera: 1830–1850," in Gerald Abraham et al., eds., *The New Oxford History of Music*, vol. 9, *Romanticism*, ed. Gerald Abraham (Oxford: Oxford University Press, 1990), 94–96.

63. Meyerbeer, *Les Huguenots*, 2:525–85.

64. See Rey Morgan Longyear, "La Muette de Portici," *Music Review* 19 (1958): 37–46. In her book *The Nation's Image* Jane F. Fulcher similarly calls *La Muette* destabilizing for the royalist regime, although for different reasons. In this sophisticated and rich study Fulcher looks for political meaning in Grand Opera. Her method is to read politics into virtually every aesthetic detail—from the greater historical accuracy of plots (the monarchical regime's attempt "to co-opt the revolutionary spirit" [25]) to the eruption of Vesuvius at the end of *La Muette* (a political semiotic of "eruption after compression" [36]). The view that emerges in *The Nation's Image* is an audience on the verge of revolution ready to seize the slightest subversive nuance (often declared to be sub-rosa in

the text or music) and a reactionary administration unable to control the political passions it has unwittingly unleashed. But in the absence of clear and convincing evidence that the Opéra's administration undertook to make *La Muette* into "subtle propaganda" (43), that it came to fear "thinly veiled political demonstrations" at its performance (80), or that the opera produced "tumultuous" (66) responses and stirred up "revolutionary sentiments" (79), *The Nation's Image* overstates the extent and nature of Grand Opera's politicization.

65. Daniel François Auber, *La Muette de Portici*, 2 vols., in Early Romantic Opera, ed. Philip Gossett and Charles Rosen, vol. 30 (New York: Garland Publishing, 1980), 2:486–87.

66. For an excellent intellectual biography of Scribe in political context, see Pendle, *Eugène Scribe and French Opera of the Nineteenth Century*.

67. Meyerbeer, *Les Huguenots*, 2:681–718.

68. Schumann's vitriolic attack on the entire opera first appeared in the *Neue Zeitschrift für Musik*. See Schumann, "Un Huguenot contre *Les Huguenots*."

69. See Crosten, *French Grand Opera*, 67.

70. *Revue musicale* 13 (Feb. 1833–Jan. 1834): 85.

71. *Courrier des théâtres*, 24 Nov. 1831, 4.

72. *Le Temps*, 26 Feb. 1835, quoted in Crosten, *French Grand Opera*, 66.

Chapter 15. Beethoven Triumphant

1. A. Elwart to François-Antoine Habeneck, 10 Aug. 1845, in A. Elwart, *Histoire de la Société des Concerts du Conservatoire Impérial de Musique* (Paris: S. Castel, 1860), 346.

2. Eugène Delacroix, *Journal* (7 March 1847), trans. Walter Pach (New York: Crown Publishers, 1948), 156.

3. Maîson du Roi to Luigi Cherubini, Director of the Conservatoire, 22 Feb. 1828, Archives of the Société des Concerts, B. N. D 17337.

4. *Revue musicale* 3 (Feb.–July 1828): 145–48; *Journal des débats*, quoted in J. G. Prod'homme, *Les Symphonies de Beethoven* (Paris: Delagrave, 1906; reprint ed., New York: Da Capo Press, 1977), 124–25.

5. *Revue musicale* 3 (Feb.–July 1828): 206, 274.

6. Ibid., 274–76, 344.

7. Ibid., 277, 12:69. Cf. also the account Berlioz filed for *La Revue et gazette musicale* of an 1838 concert featuring the Ninth: "During the performance of the Scherzo and the Adagio . . . the assembly seemed to be strongly moved; at every instant exclamations of admiration rose up from various parts of the hall, and at the end of the long Adagio . . . the enthusiasm burst out in an explosion" (*La Revue et gazette musicale* 5:161).

8. *Gazette musicale de Paris* 1:72.

9. *Revue musicale* 3 (Feb.–July 1828): 315.

10. See Schwarz, *French Instrumental Music*, 30, which lists the following performances of Beethoven at Conservatoire Exercises: Symphony No. 1, 22

Feb. 1807; No. 1 (probably), 10 May 1807; No. 1 (probably), 10 April 1808; No. 2 (probably), 25 March 1810; No. 2 (probably), 10 March 1811; No. 3, 5 May 1811; No. 1 or No. 2 (unknown), 2 May 1813; No. 1 or No. 2 (unknown), 21 July 1814; Overture to *The Creatures of Prometheus*, 28 July 1814; Symphony No. 1, 21 March 1819; No. 1, 2 December 1819; Overture to *Fidelio*, 25 April 1824.

11. See Mongrédien, *La Musique en France*, 313; reviews quoted in Leo Schrade, *Beethoven in France* (New Haven: Yale University Press, 1942), 3, 25.

12. Prod'homme, *Les Symphonies de Beethoven*, 21; Robin Wallace, *Beethoven's Critics: Aesthetic Dilemmas and Resolutions During The Composer's Lifetime* (Cambridge: Cambridge University Press, 1986), 108.

13. See Prod'homme, *Les Symphonies de Beethoven*, 125; *Revue musicale 7* (Feb.–May 1830): 234.

14. [Hermione] Quinet, *Ce que dit la musique* (Paris: Imprimerie Paul Brodard, 1893), 5. Quinet specifies that her reminiscences of the Société des Concerts date from before 1848. Description of the hall taken from A. Bellaigue, *Impressions musicales et littéraires*, as quoted in *Auber et l'opéra romantique*, compiled by Délégation à l'Action Artistique de la Ville de Paris (Aleçon: Imprimerie Alençonnaise, 1982), 49.

15. François-Joseph Fétis, quoted in Peter Anthony Bloom, "Critical Reaction to Beethoven in France: François-Joseph Fétis," *Revue belge de musicologie* 26–27 (1972–73): 74.

16. Jean-Michel Nectoux, "Trois Orchestres Parisiens en 1830: L'Académie Royal de Musique, le Théâtre Italien et la Société des Concerts du Conservatoire," in Bloom, ed., *Music in Paris in the Eighteen-Thirties*, 483.

17. Prod'homme, *Les Symphonies de Beethoven*, 124–25.

18. Heinrich Heine, "Lettres confidentielles" (reprint of letter from Heine to Auguste Lewald), *Revue et gazette musicale*, 4 Feb. 1838, 41. The concert, given 9 Dec. 1832, marked the beginning of public acclaim for Berlioz. Its audience included Alexandre Dumas, Eugène Sue, Paganini, Liszt, and Hugo, reviews were carried in two dozen newspapers, and Berlioz was thereafter recognized and saluted by strangers in the street (see D. Kern Holoman, *Berlioz* [Cambridge: Harvard University Press, 1989], 135).

19. See Holoman, *Berlioz*, 135–36.

20. General outlines of the social profile of Société audiences, however imprecise, emerge from matching names and addresses found on subscription rolls (e.g., "Adresses des abonnées aux concerts, 1837," B. N. D 17257) with listings in Bottin, *Annuaire de Commerce* and Michaud, *Biographie universelle*.

21. "Adresses des abonnées aux concerts, 1837," B. N. D 17257. See also Elisabeth Bernard, "Les Abonnées à la Société des Concerts du Conservatoire en 1837," in Bloom, ed., *Music in Paris in the Eighteen-Thirties*, 41–54.

22. Original prices for tickets can be found in the document dated 15 Jan. 1828, Statutes of the Société des Concerts, B. N. D 17338. For discussion of the domination of concert life by the upper middle class in the 1830s, see William Weber, *Music and the Middle Classes* (New York: Holmes and Meier Publishers, 1975); see also Elwart, *Histoire de la Société des Concerts du Conservatoire*, 116.

23. See David Owen Evans, *Social Romanticism in France, 1830–1848* (New York: Octagon Books, 1969), 5.

24. *L'Artiste* (1ère série, t. 3, 1832), 1:152.

25. "Décision du Comité," 22 Nov. 1837, in Statutes of the Société des Concerts, B. N. D 17337; see also Elwart, *Histoire de la Société des Concerts*, 64.

26. *La France musicale*, 18 Feb. 1838, n.p.

27. Joseph Louis d'Ortigue, *Le Balcon de l'Opéra* (Paris: Librairie d'Eugène Renduel, 1833), 343–44.

28. *La France musicale*, 21 Jan. 1844, 18.

29. For her help in securing a reproduction of the watercolor *La Première audition de la Septième Symphonie de Beethoven* (Figure 21), by Eugène Lami, I am especially grateful to Mme Florence Gétreau of the Musée de la Musique.

30. *Revue et gazette musicale*, 19 Feb. 1837, 63.

31. Ibid., 5 March 1837, 81.

32. *La France musicale*, 17 Jan. 1838, n.p.

33. See A. Dandelot, *La Société des Concerts du Conservatoire de 1828 à 1897* (Paris: G. Havard, 1898), 160.

34. See Joël-Marie Fauguet, "La Musique de chambre à Paris dans les années 1830," in Bloom, ed., *Music in Paris in the Eighteen-Thirties*, 299–326. Faguet estimates that aristocrats living in the Marais or the faubourg Saint Germain constituted one-third of the audience; the rest were persons employed in finance, commerce, or the legal professions.

35. *Revue musicale* 5 (Feb.–July 1829): 18.

36. See ibid., 3 (Feb.–July 1828): 232.

37. *La France musicale*, 17 June 1838, n.p.; *Revue musicale* 2 (Aug. 1827–Jan. 1828): 607.

38. *L'Artiste* (1ère série, t. 3, 1832), 1:109.

39. Jules Janin in *Revue et gazette musicale*, 26 Feb. 1837, quoted in Bailbé, *Le Roman et la musique en France*, 5.

40. "It was here that princes, despite the pride they took in their rank, *grandes dames*, despite the vanity of their titles, and pretty women and dainty gentlemen, despite their delicacy, all climbed to the fifth floor for the first time in their lives, to hear the celestial music of Boccherini performed by M. Viotti. And that nothing might take away from the triumph of the Artist, they descended the stairs regretfully after the concert to return to their sumptuous dwellings, where talent, however refined at times, was often stifled or unrecognized by cold dignity and sad ceremony, and where constraint and boredom reigned amidst magnificence and etiquette" (*La Décade philosophique*, 16 Sept. 1797, 523–24).

41. See Jerrold Seigel, *Bohemian Paris: Culture, Politics, and the Boundaries of Bourgeois Life, 1830–1930* (New York: Viking Press, 1986), 14–15.

42. Franz Liszt, "De la Situation des artistes et de leur condition dans la société," quoted in Ralph P. Locke, "Liszt's Saint-Simonian Adventure," *19th-Century Music* 4 (1981): 220.

43. See *L'Artiste* (1ère série, t. 3, 1832), 1:309, 163–64.

44. According to Paganini's biographer G. I. C. de Courcy, the rumors, apparently false, of Paganini's imprisonment started as early as 1814. De Courcy quotes a passage written that year from Colonel Maxwell Montgomery's mem-

oirs, *My Adventures*. "I have become acquainted with the most outré, most extravagant, and strangest character I ever beheld, or heard, in the musical line. He has just been emancipated from durance vile where he has been incarcerated on suspicion of murder. His long figure, long neck, long face, and long forehead, his hollow and deadly pale cheek, large black eyes, hooked nose, and jet black hair, which is long and more than half hides his expressive Jewish face—all these rendered him the most extraordinary person I ever beheld" (de Courcy, *Paganini the Genoese*, 1:131).

45. Quoted in ibid., 2:13.

46. *Revue musicale* 11 (Feb. 1831–Jan. 1832): 94–96.

47. Letter from Paganini to *L'Annoteur de Boulogne*, reprinted in *Revue musicale* 13 (Feb. 1834–Jan. 1835): 220.

48. *Gazette musicale de Paris*, 6 July 1834, 214; see also de Courcy, *Paganini the Genoese*, 2:160–69.

49. Gustave Flaubert to Jules Duplan, 3 or 4 Oct. 1857, quoted in Charles Rosen and Henri Zerner, *Romanticism and Realism: The Mythology of Nineteenth-Century Art* (New York: W. W. Norton & Co., 1984), 15.

50. De Courcy, *Paganini the Genoese*, 2:14.

51. See, inter alia, F.-J. Fétis, *Biographical Notice of Nicolo Paganini* (London: Schott & Co., 1876; reprint ed., New York: AMS Press, 1976), 73; de Courcy, *Paganini the Genoese*, 2:15.

52. *Revue musicale* 11 (Feb. 1831–Jan. 1832): 41–42; d'Ortigue, *Le Balcon de l'Opéra*, 247.

53. *Revue musicale* 11 (Feb. 1831–Jan. 1832): 43.

54. Ibid.; d'Ortigue, *Le Balcon de l'Opéra*, 250.

55. *L'Entracte*, 28 March 1831, quoted in Danièle Pistone, "Paganini et Paris: Quelques témoignages," in "Dossier: Paganini et Paris," *Revue internationale de musique française* 9 (1982): 8.

56. *La France musicale*, 21 April 1844, 125; Heinrich Heine, *Letters on the French Stage*, quoted in Arnold Benedict Perris, "Music in France during the Reign of Louis-Philippe: Art as 'A Substitute for the Heroic Experience,'" (Ph.D. diss., Northwestern University, 1967), 224. Having finished a concert at the Hôtel de Ville, a twenty-four-year-old Franz Liszt collapsed, "exhausted by the emotions and the demands of the evening," and had to be carried from the stage (*Gazette musicale de Paris*, 12 April 1835, 131). "Nothing stops him, nothing bars his way," wrote Joseph d'Ortigue about Liszt. "These aren't his hands playing the piano, but his mind, his soul, his heart. He pounces upon this wondrous instrument, he cries, weeps, succumbs, and emerges proudly; he dreams and sighs, excites himself to the point of frenzy, coils like a young tiger; he dazzles you, entrances you, crushes you, and then tosses you aside with a concluding bolt of lightning to produce stupefaction with his genius" (d'Ortigue, *Le Balcon de l'Opéra*, 293). See also Robert Wangermée, "Conscience et inconscience du virtuose romantique: A propos des années parisiennes de Franz Liszt," in Bloom, ed., *Music in Paris in the Eighteen-Thirties*, 553–73.

57. Castil-Blaze, quoted in de Courcy, *Paganini the Genoese*, 2:15.

58. *Revue musicale* 10 (Nov. 1830–Jan. 1831): 151.

59. Holoman, *Berlioz*, 36.

60. See ibid., 50–51, 612; see also Jacques Barzun, *Berlioz and the Romantic Century*, 2 vols. (New York: Columbia University Press, 1969), 1:88.

61. Ibid., 1:237, 241, 258.

62. See Holoman, *Berlioz*, 57.

63. *Charivari* 1 (Nov. 1840), quoted in ibid., 271–72.

64. See *Revue musicale* 13 (Feb. 1833–Jan. 1834): 349.

65. Père Enfantin, *Oeuvres*, quoted in Locke, "Liszt's Saint-Simonian Adventure," 221. See also Ralph P. Locke, *Music, Musicians, and the Saint-Simonians* (Chicago: University of Chicago Press, 1986), esp. 15–67.

66. Jules Michelet, *Le Peuple*, quoted in Donald Geoffrey Charlton, *Secular Religions in France, 1815–1870* (London: Oxford University Press, 1963), 36.

67. Ibid., 25, 26.

68. See Maxime Leroy, *Histoire des idées sociales en France*, 3 vols. (Paris: Gallimard, 1946–54), 2:382.

69. *Le Globe*, 26 Sept. 1831, quoted in Murphy, *Hector Berlioz and the Development of French Music Criticism*, 31.

70. *L'Artiste* (1ᵉʳᵉ série, t. 3, 1832), 164. Elsewhere the newspaper wrote that only music could heal the malaise of "'minds that know everything except how to love, that understand all but are plunged in doubt, and have an excess of faith without an ounce of conviction" (ibid., [1ᵉʳᵉ série, t. 5, 1833], 199). Franz Liszt describes the religious role of art in "Religious Music of the Future" (see Franz Liszt, *An Artist's Journey: Lettres d'un bachelier ès musique 1835–1841*, trans. and annotated by Charles Suttoni [Chicago: University of Chicago Press, 1989], 236–37).

Chapter 16. The Musical Experience of Romanticism

1. François-Joseph Fétis, "De l'influence de la musique instrumentale sur les révolutions de la musique dramatique," in *Revue musicale* 10 (Nov. 1830–Jan. 1831): 131.

2. M. P. Lahalle, *Essai sur la musique, ses fonctions dans les moeurs, et sa véritable expression; suivi d'une bibliographie musicale* (Paris: Imprimerie de Casimir, 1825), 48.

3. *La Revue indépendante*, 25 Nov. 1844, 277, 276.

4. *La France musicale*, 10 Nov. 1844, 321.

5. Ibid., 322.

6. A program dated 15 March 1829 survives in the archives of the Société des Concerts at the Bibliothèque Nationale. It contains the following message to audiences: "Notice on the Pastoral Symphony of Wan Beethoven: In composing this symphony Beethoven wished to represent a wholly dramatic action. His imagination occupied itself depicting the pleasure found in a bustling countryside; it has attempted to imitate the songs of birds, a murmuring brook, a crashing storm that interrupts village dances, and finally the calm that follows the

impact of these forces. In order to appreciate this rather original composition, it is necessary for the public to absorb this brief analysis that faithfully reproduces Beethoven's ideas." The text of Beethoven's notes then follows in the program. A quotation from Rousseau's *Dictionnaire de musique* is cited in a footnote: "Music paints all things, even those objects that are merely visible." (B. N. D 17337.)

7. "De la musique pittoresque et des symphonies de Beethoven," *La France musicale*, 7 Jan. 1838, n.p.; *Journal des débats*, 24 March 1829, quoted in Prod'homme, *Les Symphonies de Beethoven*, 270; *Revue musicale* 5 (Feb.–July 1829): 173.

8. *Revue et gazette musicale de Paris*, 4 Feb. 1838, 49.

9. Paul Scudo, *De l'Influence du mouvement romantique sur l'art musical et du role qu'a voulu jouer M. H. Berlioz* (Paris: La Revue indépendente, 1846), 17.

10. Berlioz's program appears in the printed score (Hector Berlioz, *Fantastic Symphony*, ed. Edward T. Cone [New York: W. W. Norton & Co., 1971], 23–35).

11. "What a good thing it isn't music," Rossini said of the *Symphonie fantastique* (quoted in Holoman, *Berlioz*, 109).

12. *L'Artiste* (1ère serie., t. 13, 1837), 294–95; *Revue musicale* 12 (Feb. 1832–Jan. 1833): 367. Berlioz defended his *Symphonie fantastique* by claiming he had done nothing more than approximate poetically the vague moods the work conveyed. "The purpose of the program is not, as some have affected to believe, to give a detailed account of what the composer has tried to do by means of the orchestra," Berlioz wrote in letter distributed to spectators at the work's second performance on 5 Dec. 1830. "The composer knows quite well that music is a substitute neither for speech nor for the art of drawing. He has never had the absurd pretension of reproducing abstract ideas or moral qualities, but only passions and impressions" (quoted in Barzun, *Berlioz and the Romantic Century*, 2:197–98).

13. *L'Artiste* (1ère série, t. 14, 1838), 161.

14. Katherine Kolb Reeve discusses the emergence of metaphor in musical descriptions after 1830 in "Rhetoric and Reason in French Music Criticism of the 1830s," in Bloom, ed., *Music in Paris in the Eighteen-Thirties*, 537–51.

15. Quoted in Katherine Kolb Reeve, "The Poetics of the Orchestra in the Writings of Hector Berlioz" (Ph.D. diss., Yale University, 1978), 165.

16. Quinet, *Ce qu dit la musique*, 29–30. Had she recently seen *Robert le diable* when she wrote this?

17. François Stoepel, "Beethoven et sa musique," in *Gazette musicale de Paris*, 9 Feb. 1834, quoted in Katherine Kolb Reeve, "Rhetoric and Reason in French Music Criticism of the 1830s," in Bloom, ed., *Music in Paris in the Eighteen-Thirties*, 539–40.

18. Crétien Urhan, writing in *Le Temps*, quoted in Prod'homme, *Les Symphonies de Beethoven*, 459; *L'Artiste* (1ère série, t. 7, 1834), 26; letter from Baillot to Galitzine, quoted in Fouquet, *Les Sociétés de musique de chambre à Paris*, 98.

19. *L'Artiste* (1ère série, t. 7, 1834) 2:5; Quinet, *Ce que dit la musique*, 7.

20. Quatremère de Quincy, *Essai sur la nature, le but et les moyens de l'imi-

tation dans les beaux-arts, quoted in Baldensperger, *Sensibilité musicale et romantisme*, 112.

21. Adophe Guéroult, "L'Eglise et l'Opéra," *L'Artiste* (1ère série, t. 4, 1832), 78; d'Ortigue, *De la guerre des dilettanti*, 17.

22. *L'Artiste*, (1ère série, t. 9, 1835), 1:160; Fétis, "Des Sensations musicales," *Revue musicale* 12 (Feb. 1832–Jan. 1833): 26.

23. Honoré de Balzac, *Massimilla Doni*, trans. G. Burnham Ives (Philadelphia: George Barrie and Son, 1899), 175.

24. Fétis, "Des Sensations musicales," 26.

25. Charles Baudelaire, "Qu'est-ce que le romantisme?" from *Salons de 1846*, in *Oeuvres complètes*, ed. Y.-G. Le Dautec (Paris: Bibliothèque de la Pléiade, 1954), 610.

26. E. T. A. Hoffmann, "Beethoven's Instrumental Music" (1810), trans. Martyn Clarke, in *E. T. A. Hoffmann's Musical Writings: Kreisleriana, The Poet and the Composer, Musical Criticism*, ed. David Charlton (Cambridge: Cambridge University Press, 1989), 96, 98.

27. Balzac, *Seraphita* and 1837 letter, quoted in Jean-Pierre Barricelli, "Balzac and Beethoven: The Growth of a Concept," *Modern Language Quarterly* 25 (1964): 415–18; see also Pierre Citron, "'Gambara,' Strunz and Beethoven," in *L'Année balzacienne* (1967): 165–70.

28. Leo Schrade's 1942 *Beethoven in France* set out the terms of this explanation. Romanticism first struck the literary world of Émile Deschamps, Hugo, Balzac, and Sand, and from there its ideas spread to critics and journalists, who passed the themes and attitudes on to the public: "How did it happen that in 1811 the *Eroica* was performed without leaving any trace of an impression, except for opposition, while in 1828 the same work suddenly aroused enthusiasm and literary inspiration? Romanticism loomed behind the latter production. In 1811, on the other hand, there was no idea that could play escort to Beethoven; there were only traditional ideas of classicism ready to repulse him" (Leo Schrade, *Beethoven in France*, 28). More recently William S. Newman has offered a substantially similar argument for Beethoven's acceptance in France after twenty years of neglect. Like E. T. A. Hoffmann and Bettina von Arnim in Germany, Newman writes, the French romantics convinced audiences to accept Beethoven through their writings; the dreamy musical accounts left by spectators are thus understood as imitations, conscious or not, of the romantics' descriptions of music. (See William S. Newman, "The Beethoven Mystique in Romantic Art, Literature, and Music" *Musical Quarterly* 69 [1983]: 354–87.) I discuss the reasons I find these explanations inadequate to explain Beethoven's rehabilitation in France in "Beethoven and the Birth of Romantic Musical Experience in France," *19th-Century Music* 15 (1991): 23–55.

29. See Émile Deschamps, *La Préface des études françaises et étrangères*, ed. Henri Girard (Paris: Les Presses Françaises, 1923); Marcel Breuillac, "Hoffmann en France," *Revue d'histoire littéraire de la France* 13 (1906): 427–57; James Smith Allen, *Popular French Romanticism* (Syracuse, N.Y.: Syracuse University Press, 1981), 45–73; see also José-Luis Diaz, "L'Artiste romantique en perspective," *Romantisme* 54 (1986): 5–23, for a discussion of the appearance and evolution of the concept of the romantic artist in France.

30. Carl Dahlhaus, *The Idea of Absolute Music*, trans. Roger Lustig (Chicago: University of Chicago Press, 1989), 146.

31. See Paul Bénichou, *Le Temps des prophètes: Doctrines de l'âge romantique* (Paris: Gallimard, 1977).

32. Quinet, *Ce que dit la musique*, 6; Alfred Dumesnil, *La Foi nouvelle cherchée dans l'art de Rembrandt à Beethoven* (Paris: E. Thunot et Cie., 1850), 407, 45.

33. *Courrier des théâtres*, 5 May 1827, 3.

34. *L'Artiste* (1ère série, t. 15, 1839), 34; *La France musicale*, 7 Jan. 1838, n.p.; ibid., 28 Jan. 1838.

35. Heinrich Heine, in *Revue et gazette musicale de Paris*, 21 Jan. 1838, 18. For Heine's associations with Saint-Simonianism, see Lloyd S. Kramer, *Threshold of a New World: Intellectuals and the Exile Experience in Paris, 1830–1848* (Ithaca: Cornell University Press, 1988), esp. 87–102.

36. Usmar Bonnaire, *De l'influence de la musique sur les moeurs* (Vienna: n.p., 1856), 13–14

37. *Revue et gazette musicale*, 27 March 1842.

38. Charles Rosen and Henri Zerner trace the first use of the phrase *juste milieu* in an artistic context to a critic in 1831 who urged painters to steer a path between the "moribund Classicism of the school of David and the wild-eyed Romanticism of the more audacious younger artists" (Rosen and Zerner, *Romanticism and Realism*, 116).

39. See Linda Orr, *Headless History: Nineteenth-Century French Historiography of the Revolution* (Ithaca: Cornell University Press, 1990), esp. 18ff.

40. Ultra royalists of the late Restoration had nourished this class-based reading of society by casting the industrial and commercial middle classes (the "bourgeoisie") as inimical to traditional society and the monarchy. Intellectuals such as Guizot, Tocqueville, and Rémusat contributed to the myth by describing the 1789 Revolution and imperial years as the true period of growth for the "bourgeoisie." Socialists and republicans, meantime, used the term pejoratively to denounce liberals—the "bourgeoisie"—for stealing 1830 from its rightful possessors, the workers. (See Pamela Pilbeam, *The 1830 Revolution in France* [New York: St. Martin's Press, 1991], 124, 131–32; Louis Blanc, *The History of Ten Years*, 2 vols. [London: Chapman & Hall, 1845; reprint ed., New York: Augustus M. Kelley, 1969], 1:266.)

41. André Tudesq's analysis of the elites of the July Monarchy emphasizes the continued predominance of large landowners, whose power and political presence easily outstripped that of middle-class professionals and businessmen. (See André-Jean Tudesq, *Les Grands notables en France, 1840–1849*, 2 vols. [Paris: Presses Universitaires de France, 1964]; see also Alfred Cobban, "The 'Middle Class' in France, 1815–1848," *French Historical Studies* 5 [1967]: 41–56; William Weber, "The Muddle of the Middle Classes," *19th-Century Music* 3 [1979]: 175–85.)

42. See Pilbeam, *The 1830 Revolution in France*, 134–35; David H. Pinkney, *The French Revolution of 1830* (Princeton: Princeton University Press, 1972), esp. 290–93.

43. Pilbeam, *The 1830 Revolution in France*, 147.

Afterword

1. Hector Berlioz, "The Farewell Dinner," from *Evenings with the Orchestra*, 308–9.

2. John Rockwell, "The Roles of Artist and Listener," *New York Times*, 9 Aug. 1987, section 2, 21.

3. Berlioz, "The Farewell Dinner," 309.

4. "Just as we transfer an experience of movement to music (which does not move)," writes Roger Scruton, "so do we transfer an experience of passion to music (which has no passions). We project into the music the inner life that is ours, and that is *how* we hear it there" (Roger Scruton, *The Aesthetic Understanding: Essays in the Philosophy of Art and Culture* [Manchester: Carcanet Press, 1983], 95).

5. I have adapted this point from Leo Treitler, *Music and the Historical Imagination* (Cambridge: Harvard University Press, 1989), 32ff; see also Nicolas Cook, *Music, Imagination, and Culture* (Oxford: Clarendon Press, 1990).

6. Dante Alighieri, *Paradiso*, trans. Allen Mandelbaum (New York: Bantam Books, 1984), 6–7. I have slightly altered Mandelbaum's translation.

7. Marcel Proust, *Remembrance of Things Past*, trans. C. K. Scott Moncrieff, 2 vols., *The Captive* (*Albertine disparue*) (New York: Random House, 1932), 2:554.

Bibliography

Unpublished Manuscripts

Archives Nationales
 Series AD VIII
 Series AJ¹³
 Series AJ³⁷
 Series O¹ 618
 Series O¹ 619
 Series O¹ 624
 Series O¹ 628
Bibliothèque de l'Arsenal
 Fonds Rondel
Bibliothèque du Château de Chantilly
 Ducharger. *Stalkoff gentilhomme russe en France et amateur de musique.*
  Ou, idée des concerts de province. Ouvrage dévisé en trois parties dédiés à
  S. A. S. Monseigneur le Prince de Condé, Prince de Sang & Gouverneur
  de la Province de Bourgogne. Par M. Ducharger Pensionnaire de la ville
  de Dijon. n.d.
Bibliothèque Nationale
 Baylot Series FM²
 Collection Delamare
 Cahiers de doléance, remonstrances, et instructions; L'Assemblée de tous les
  ordres des Théâtres Royaux de Paris
 Statutes of the Société des Concerts
Bibliothèque de l'Opéra
 Jadin, [Louis-Emmanuel]. *Le Siège de Thionville.* 1793.
 Porta, Bernardo. *La Réunion du dix août, ou l'inauguration de la répu-*
  blique française. 1793.

Registres, CO 239

Rochefort, [Jean-Baptiste]. *Toulon soumis.* Opéra en un acte. Paroles de Favre Olivot [sic], musique de Rochefort. Représenté le 17 ventose an 2. Par ordre du Comité du salut publique au dit théâtre."

Periodicals and Newspapers

Almanach des spectacles
L'Artiste: Journal de la littérature et des beaux-arts
Chronique de Paris
Courrier de l'Europe et des spectacles
Courrier des théâtres: Littérature, beaux-arts, sciences, moeurs, variétés, nouvelles et modes
La Décade philosophique, littéraire et politique; par une société de républicains
Le Dilettante: Journal de musique, de littérature, de théâtres et de beaux-arts
Le Drapeau blanc
Feuille du salut public
Feuille de la république
La France musicale
Gazette de France
Gazette nationale
Le Globe
Journal de l'empire
Journal de musique
Journal des dames et des modes
Journal des débats
Journal des spectacles
Le Ménestrel
Le Mercure de France
Miroir des spectacles
La Mode: Revue des modes, galerie de moeurs, album des salons
Le Moniteur universel
La Musique: Gazette universelle des artistes et amateurs
La Revue et gazette musicale
La Revue indépendante
La Revue musicale
Les Tablettes de Polymnie: Journal consacré à tout ce qui intéresse l'art musical

Published Sources

Abraham, Gerald. "The Best of Spontini." *Music and Letters* 23 (1942): 163–71.

Abraham, Gerald, et al., eds. *The New Oxford History of Music*. 11 vols. London: Oxford University Press, 1957–75.

Alembert, Jean le Rond d'. "De la liberté de la musique." In *Mélanges de littérature, d'histoire, et de philosophie*. Amsterdam: Chez Zachairie Chatelain et Fils, 1759.

———. *Oeuvres philosophiques, historiques et littéraires de d'Alembert*. 17 vols. Paris: Jean-François Bastien, 1805.

Allen, James Smith. *In the Public Eye: A History of Reading in Modern France, 1800–1940*. Princeton: Princeton University Press, 1991.

———. *Popular French Romanticism*. Syracuse: Syracuse University Press, 1981.

Alletz, Pons-Augustin. *Manuel de l'homme du monde, ou connoissance générale des principaux états de la société, et de toutes les matières qui font le sujet des conversations ordinaires*. Paris: Chez Guillyn, 1761.

Almanach musical. 8 vols. Geneva: Minkoff Reprints, 1972.

Anderson, E., ed. *The Letters of Mozart and His Family*. London: MacMillan, 1961.

André, Yves-Marie. *Essai sur le beau*. Amsterdam: J. H. Schneider, 1759.

Année littéraire. Ed. Elie Fréron. 37 vols. Geneva: Slatkine Reprints, 1966.

Anthony, James R. *French Baroque Music from Beaujoyeulx to Rameau*. New York: W. W. Norton & Co., 1974.

———. "The French Opera-Ballet in the Early Eighteenth Century: Problems of Definition and Classification." *Journal of the American Musicological Society* 18 (1965): 197–206.

Antoine, Michel. *Louis XV*. Paris: Fayard, 1989.

———. *Le Gouvernement et l'administration sous Louis XV*. Paris: Éditions du Centre National de la Recherche Scientifique, 1978.

Aquin de Châteaulyon, Pierre Louis d'. *Siècle littéraire de Louis XV, ou lettres sur les hommes célèbres*. Amsterdam: Duchesne, 1754.

Arago, Jacques. *Mémoires d'un petit banc de l'Opéra*. Paris: D. Ebrard, 1844.

[d'Arnauld, abbé?]. *Réflexions sur la musique en général, et sur la musique française en particulier*. N.p., 1754.

Auber, Daniel François. *La Muette de Portici*. 2 vols. Early Romantic Opera, ed. Philip Gossett and Charles Rosen, vol 30. New York: Garland Publishing, 1980.

Aulard, Alphonse, ed. *Paris pendant la réaction thermidorienne et sous le directoire*. 5 vols. Paris: Léopold Cerf, 1898.

———. *Paris pendant le consulat*. Paris: Léopold Cerf, 1903.

———. *Paris sous le premier empire*. 3 vols. Paris: Léopold Cerf, 1912.

Bailbé, Joseph-Marc. "Mendelssohn à Paris." In *Music in Paris in the Eighteen-Thirties*, ed. Peter Bloom. Musical Life in Nineteenth-Century France, vol. 4. Stuyvesant, N.Y.: Pendragon Press, 1987.

———. *Le Roman et la musique en France sous la monarchie de juillet*. Paris: Minard, 1969.

Baker, Keith Michael. *Inventing the French Revolution*. Cambridge: Cambridge University Press, 1990.

———, ed. *The Old Regime and the French Revolution*. Chicago: University of Chicago Press, 1987.

Baker, Keith Michael, et al., eds. *The French Revolution and the Creation of Modern Political Culture*. 3 vols. Oxford: Pendragon Press, 1987.

Balabine, Victor de. *Journal*. Paris: Émile-Paul Frères, 1914.

Baldensperger, Fernand. *Goethe en France*. 2 vols. Paris: Librairie Hachette, 1904.

———. *Sensibilité musicale et romantisme*. Paris: Les Presses Françaises, 1925.

Balzac, Honoré de. *La Comédie humaine*. 12 vols. Paris: Bibliothèque de la Pléiade, 1976–1981.

———. *Massimilla Doni*. Trans. G. Burnham Ives. Philadelphia: George Barrie and Son, 1899.

———. *Père Goriot*. Trans. E. K. Brown. New York: Modern Library, 1950.

Bapst, Germain. *Essai sur l'histoire du théâtre, la mise en scène, le décor, la costume, l'architecture, l'éclairage, l'hygiène*. Paris: Librairie Hachette, 1893.

Barbier, Patrick. *La Vie quotidienne à l'Opéra au temps de Rossini et de Balzac*. Paris: Hachette, 1987.

Barré, et al. *L'Heureuse décade*. Paris: Librairie de la Vaudeville, n.d.

Barricelli, Jean-Pierre. "Balzac and Beethoven: The Growth of a Concept." *Modern Language Quarterly* 25 (1964): 415–18.

Bartlet, M. Elisabeth C. "Étienne-Nicolas Méhul and Opera during the French Revolution, Consulate, and Empire: A Source, Archival, and Stylistic Study." 5 vols. Ph.D. diss., University of Chicago, 1982.

———. "The New Repertory at the Opéra during the Reign of Terror: Revolutionary Rhetoric and Operatic Consequences." In *Music and the French Revolution*, ed. Malcolm Boyd. Cambridge: Cambridge University Press, 1992.

Barzun, Jacques. *Berlioz and the Romantic Century*. 2 vols. New York: Columbia University Press, 1969.

Batteux, Charles. *Les Beaux-arts réduits à un même principe*. Paris: Durand, 1746.

Baudelaire, Charles. *Oeuvres complètes*. Ed. Y.-G. Le Dautec. Paris: Bibliothèque de la Pléiade, 1954.

Bazin, M. A. *L'Époque sans nom: Esquisses de Paris 1830–1833*. 2 vols. Paris: Alexandre Mesnier, 1833.

Beaumarchais, Pierre Augustin Caron de. *Théâtre: Lettres relatives à son théâtre*. Paris: Gallimard, 1956.

Beaussant, Philippe. *Lully, ou le musicien du soleil*. Paris: Éditions Gallimard, 1992.

Beauvau, La Maréchale Princesse de, and Le Maréchal Prince de Beauvau. *Souvenirs*. Paris: Léon Techener, 1872.

Bellaigue, Camille. *Impressions musicales et littéraires*. Paris: Librairie Ch. Delagrave, [1900].

Bénichou, Paul. *Les Mages romantiques*. Paris: Gallimard, 1988.

———. *Le Temps des prophètes: Doctrines de l'âge romantique*. Paris: Gallimard, 1977.

Bergeron, Louis. *France under Napoleon*. Trans. R. R. Palmer. Princeton: Princeton University Press, 1981.

Bergman, Gösta. *Lighting in the Theatre*. Stockholm: Almqvist and Wiksell, International, 1977.

Berkheim, K. G. de. *Lettres sur Paris.* Heidelberg: n.p., 1809.

Berlin, Isaiah. "Two Concepts of Liberty." In *Four Essays on Liberty.* Oxford: Oxford University Press, 1969.

Berlioz, Hector. *Evenings with the Orchestra.* Trans. Jacques Barzun. New York: Knopf, 1956.

———. *Fantastic Symphony.* Ed. Edward T. Cone. New York: W. W. Norton & Co., 1971.

———. *The Memoires of Hector Berlioz, Member of the French Institute, Including His Travels in Italy, Germany, Russia and England, 1803–1865.* Trans. David Cairnes. New York: W. W. Norton & Co., 1969.

Bernard, Elisabeth. "Les Abonnées à la Société des Concerts du Conservatoire en 1837." In *Music in Paris in the Eighteen-Thirties,* ed. Peter Bloom. Musical Life in Nineteenth-Century France, vol. 4. Stuyvesant, N.Y.: Pendragon Press, 1987.

Berret, Paul. "Comment la scène du théâtre du XVIII siècle a été débarassée de la présence des Gentilshommes." *Revue d'histoire littéraire de la France* 18 (1908): 456–60.

Bier, Albert. "La Pipe de Socrate: L'Antiquité dans l'opéra de l'époque révolutionnaire." In *L'Orphée phrygien: Les Musiques de la Révolution,* ed. Jean-Rémy Julien and Jean-Claude Klein. Paris: Éditions du May, 1989.

Blainville, C. H. *L'Esprit de l'art musical, ou réflexions sur la musique, et ses différentes parties.* Geneva: n.p., 1754.

Blanc, Louis. *The History of Ten Years.* 2 vols. London: Chapman & Hall, 1845. Reprint ed., New York: Augustus N. Kelley, 1969.

Blaze, François Henri Joseph [Castil-Blaze]. *De l'Opéra en France.* 2 vols. Paris: A. Egron, 1820.

———. *L'Opéra Italien de 1548 à 1856.* Paris: Castil-Blaze, 1856.

Blessington, Marguerite (Power) Farmer Gardiner, countess of. *The Idler in France.* Paris: A. and W. Galignani and Co., 1841.

Bloom, Peter Anthony. "Critical Reaction to Beethoven in France: François-Joseph Fétis." *Revue belge de musicologie* 26–27 (1972–73): 67–83.

———, ed. *Music in Paris in the Eighteen-Thirties.* Musical Life in Nineteenth-Century France, vol 4. Stuyvesant, N.Y.: Pendragon Press, 1987.

Blum, Carol. *Rousseau and the Republic of Virtue: The Language of Politics in the French Revolution.* Ithaca: Cornell University Press, 1986.

Boigne, Charles de. *Petits mémoires de l'Opéra.* Paris: Librairie Nouvelle, 1857.

Boissy d'Anglas, François Antoine. *Essai sur les fêtes nationales.* Paris: Imprimerie Polyglotte, an II.

Bollioud-Mermet, Louis. *De la corruption du goust dans la musique françoise.* Lyon: n.p., 1746.

Bonds, Mark Evan. *Wordless Rhetoric: Musical Form and the Metaphor of the Oration.* Cambridge: Harvard University Press, 1991.

Bonnaire, Usmar. *De l'influence de la musique sur les moeurs.* Vienna: n.p., 1856.

Bonnet, J. F., ed. *La Carmagnole des Muses: L'homme de lettres et l'artiste dans la révolution.* Paris: Armand Colin, 1988.

Bonnet, Jacques. *Histoire de la musique, et de ses effets, depuis son origine jusqu'à présent.* Paris: Chez Jean Cochart, 1715.

Bottin, Sébastien. *Annuaire du commerce de Paris.* Paris: Didot,

Bouilly, J. N. *Mes récapitulations.* 2 vols. Paris: Louis Janet, 1836–37.

Bouloiseau, Marc. *The Jacobin Republic, 1792–1794.* Trans. Jonathan Mandelbaum. Cambridge: Cambridge University Press, 1983.

Boyd, Malcolm, ed. *Music and the French Revolution.* Cambridge: Cambridge University Press, 1992.

Boyé. *L'Expression musicale, mise au rang des chimères.* Paris: Chez La Veuve Duchesne, 1779.

Boyer, J. B., Marquis d'Argens. *Lettres juives, ou correspondance philosophique, historique et critique, entre un juif voyageur en différents états de l'Europe, et ses correspondants en divers endroits.* The Hague: Chez Pierre Paupie, 1738.

Boysse, Ernest. *Les Abonnés de l'Opéra (1783–1786).* Paris: A. Quantin, 1881.

Bredvald, Louis. *The Natural History of Sensibility.* Detroit: Wayne State University Press, 1962.

Brenet, Michel [Bobillier, Marie]. *Les Concerts en France sous l'ancien régime.* Paris: Librairie Fischbacher, 1900.

Brenner, Clarence D. *The Theatre Italien: Its Repertory, 1716–1793.* University of California Publications in Modern Philology, vol. 63. Berkeley: University of California Press, 1963.

Breuillac, Marcel. "Hoffmann en France." *Revue d'histoire littéraire de la France* 13 (1906): 427–57.

Brévan, Bruno. *Les Changements de la vie musicale parisienne de 1774 à 1779.* Paris: Presses Universitaires de France, 1980.

———. "La Révolution et ses publics." In *L'Orphée phrygien: Les Musiques de la révolution,* ed. Jean-Rémy Julien and Jean-Claude Klein. Paris: Éditions du May, 1989.

Bricaire de la Dixmérie, Nicolas. *Lettres sur l'état présent de nos spectacles, avec des vues nouvelles sur chacun d'eux; particulièrement sur la Comédie Françoise et l'Opéra.* Amsterdam: Chez Duchesne, 1765.

Brook, Barry S. *La Symphonie française dans la seconde moitié du XVIIIe siècle.* 3 vols. Paris: Institut de Musicologie de l'Université de Paris, 1962.

Brookner, Anita. *Greuze: The Rise and Fall of an Eighteenth-Century Phenomenon.* London: Paul Elek, Ltd., 1972.

Brown, Bruce Alan. *Gluck and the French Theatre in Vienna.* Oxford: Clarendon Press, 1991.

Brzoska, Matthias. "De l'anticléricalisme révolutionnaire au cléricalisme anti-révolutionnaire chez M. Berton de 1790 à 1799." In *Le Tambour et la harpe: Oeuvres, pratiques et manifestations musicales sous la révolution, 1788–1800,* ed. Jean-Rémy Julien and Jean-Claude Klein. Paris: Éditions du May, 1991.

Budd, Malcolm. *Music and the Emotions: The Philosophical Theories.* London: Routledge & Kegan Paul, 1985.

Buisson, F. *Le Spectateur français avant la révolution.* Paris: Imprimerie de la Croix, an IV.

Burney, Charles. *The Present State of Music in France and Italy.* London: T. Becket and Co., 1773.

Burton, Humphrey. "Les Académies de musique en France au XVIIIe siècle." *Revue de musicologie* 37 (1955): 122–47.

Calendrier musical universel, suite de l'Almanach musical. 10 vols. Geneva: Minkoff Reprints, 1971.

Caraccioli, Louis A. de. *Paris, le modèle des nations étrangères, ou l'Europe française.* Paris: Chez Duchesne, 1777.

Carlson, Marvin. *The Theater of the French Revolution.* Ithaca: Cornell University Press, 1966.

Caron, Pierre. *Paris pendant la terreur: Rapports des agents secrets du ministre de l'intérieur.* 6 vols. Paris: Librairie Alphonse Picard et Fils, 1910.

Cartaud de La Vilate, François. *Essais historiques et philosophiques sur le goût.* The Hague: Chez Pierre de Hondt, 1737.

Cassirer, Ernst. *The Philosophy of the Enlightenment.* Trans. C. A. Koelln and James P. Pettegrove. Princeton: Princeton University Press, 1951.

Catel, Charles-Simon. *Les Bayadères.* Paris: Éditions Michaelis, n.d. Reprint ed., New York: Broude Brothers, 1971.

Causson, Jean-Louis. *Gioacchino Rossini: L'Homme et son oeuvre.* Paris: Slatkine, 1982.

Censer, Jack, and Jeremy Popkin, eds. *Press and Politics in Pre-Revolutionary France.* Berkeley: University of California Press, 1987.

Chabanon, Michel-Paul-Guy de. *De la Musique considérée en elle-même et dans ses rapports avec la parole, les langues, la poésie et le théâtre.* Paris: Chez Pissot, 1785.

———. *Éloge de M. Rameau.* Paris: Imprimerie de M. Lambert, 1764.

———. *Observations sur la musique, et principalement sur la metaphysique de l'art.* Paris: Chez Pissot, 1779.

Charlton, David. *Grétry and the Growth of Opéra-Comique.* Cambridge: Cambridge University Press, 1986.

———. "Les Instruments à vent: Les sons et les gestes." In *Le Tambour et la harpe: Oeuvres, pratiques et manifestations musicales sous la révolution, 1788–1800,* ed. Jean-Rémy Julien and Jean-Claude Klein. Paris: Éditions du May, 1991.

———. "On Redefinitions of 'Rescue Opera.'" In *Music and the French Revolution,* ed. Malcolm Boyd. Cambridge: Cambridge University Press, 1992.

———. "Orchestration and Orchestral Practice in Paris, 1789–1810." Ph.D. diss., Cambridge University, 1973.

———. "Ossian, Le Sueur, and Opera." *Studies in Music* 11 (1977): 37–48.

———. "Romantic Opera: 1830–1850." In *The New Oxford History of Music,* ed. Gerald Abraham et al. Vol. 9. *Romanticism,* ed. Gerald Abraham. Oxford: Oxford University Press, 1990.

Charlton, Donald Geoffrey. *Secular Religions in France, 1815–1870.* London: Oxford University Press, 1963.

———, ed. *The French Romantics.* 2 vols. Cambridge: Cambridge University Press, 1984.

Chartier, Roger. *Cultural History.* Trans. Lydia G. Cochrane. Ithaca: Cornell University Press, 1988.

———. *The Cultural Origins of the French Revolution.* Trans. Lydia G. Cochrane. Durham: Duke University Press, 1991.

———. "Intellectual History or Sociocultural History?: The French Trajectories." In *Modern European Intellectual History: Reappraisals and New Perspectives*, ed. Dominick LaCapra and Steven L. Kaplan. Ithaca: Cornell University Press, 1982.

Chastellux, J. Fr. *Essai sur l'union de la poésie et de la musique*. The Hague: n.p., 1765.

Chastenay, Mme de. *Mémoires*. Paris: Librairie Académique Perrin, 1987.

Chaussard, P. *Essai philosophique sur la dignité des arts*. Paris: Imprimerie des Sciences et Arts, an VI.

Chaussard, P. J. B. Publicola. *Le Nouveau diable boiteux, tableau philosophique et moral de Paris*. 2 vols. Chez Buisson, 1799.

Chaussinard-Nougaret, Guy. *The French Nobility in the Eighteenth Century*. Trans. William Doyle. Cambridge: Cambridge University Press, 1985.

Chazin-Bennahum, Judith. *Dance in the Shadow of the Guillotine*. Carbondale: Southern Illinois University Press, 1988.

Chénier, M[arie]-J[oseph]. *De la liberté du théâtre en France*. Paris: n.p., 1789.

Cherubini, Maria Luigi. *Lodoïska*. [1791?]. Early Romantic Opera, ed. Philip Gossett and Charles Rosen, vol. 33. New York: Garland Publishing, 1978.

Chevrier, François Antoine de. *Paris: Histoire véridique, anecdotique, morale et critique, avec le clef*. The Hague: n.p., 1767.

———. *Observations sur le théâtre, dans lesquelles on examine avec impartialité l'état actuel des spectacles de Paris*. Paris: Chez Debure le Jeune, 1755.

———. *Les Ridicules du siècle*. London: n.p., 1752.

Choron, A. E., and Lafage, J. Adrien. *Manuel complet de musique vocale et instrumentale, ou encyclopédie musicale*. 3 vols. Paris: Imprimerie et Fonderie de Fain, 1836.

Chouillet, Jacques. *L'Esthétique des lumières*. Paris: Presses Universitaires de France, 1974.

Citron, Pierre. "'Gambara,' Strunz and Beethoven." *L'Année balzacienne* (1967): 165–70.

Claudon, Francis. "L'Idée et l'influence de la musique, chez quelques romantiques français et notamment Stendhal." Thèse devant l'Université de Paris IV. Lille: Atelier reproduction des thèses, 1979.

Clément, Jean-Marie Bernard. *Anecdotes dramatiques*. 2 vols. Paris: Chez la Veuve Duchesne, 1775.

Clément, Pierre. *Les Cinq années littéraires, ou nouvelles littéraires, 1748–52*. 4 vols. The Hague: Chez Ant. de Groot et Fils, 1754.

Cobb, Richard. *The Police and the People: French Popular Protest, 1789–1820*. Oxford: Oxford University Press, 1970.

Cobban, Alfred. "The 'Middle Class' in France, 1815–1848." *French Historical Studies* 5 (1967): 41–56.

Cochin, Auguste. *Les Sociétés de pensée et la démocratie: Études d'histoire révolutionnaire*. Paris: Plon-Nourrit, 1921.

Cochin, Charles-Nicolas. *Lettres sur l'opéra*. Paris: L. Cellot, 1781.

Cohen, H. Robert, ed. *The Original Staging Manuals for Twelve Parisian Operatic Premières*. Stuyvesant: Pendragon Press, 1991.

Collé, Charles. *Journal et mémoires sur les hommes de lettres, les ouvrages drama-*

tiques et les événements les plus mémorables du règne de Louis XV. 3 vols. Paris: Didot Frères, 1868.

Condillac, Étienne Bonnard de. *Treatise on the Sensations.* Trans. Geraldine Carr. Los Angeles: University of Southern California Press, 1930.

Cook, Nicolas. *Music, Imagination, and Culture.* Oxford: Clarendon Press, 1990.

Cooper, Martin. *Gluck.* New York: Oxford University Press, 1935.

Correspondance des amateurs musiciens rédigée par le citoyen Cocatrix, suivie de la Correspondance des professeurs et amateurs de musique. Geneva: Minkoff Reprints, 1972.

Coupé, J. M. *Des Fêtes en politique et en morale.* Paris: Imprimerie de Baudouin, 1796.

Courcy, G. I. C. de. *Paganini the Genoese.* 2 vols. Norman: University of Oklahoma Press, 1957. Reprint ed., New York: Da Capo Press, 1977.

Courtin, Antoine de. *The Rules of Civility, Nouveau traité de la civilité.* London: R. Chiswell, T. Sawbridge, G. Wells, and R. Bentley, 1681.

Coyez, abbé. *Nouvelles observations sur l'Angleterre, par un voyageur.* Paris: Chez Duchesne, 1779.

Crosten, William L. *French Grand Opera: An Art and a Business.* New York: King's Crown Press, 1948.

Crousaz, J. P. *Traité du beau.* Amsterdam: Chez François l'Honoré, 1715.

Crow, Thomas E. *Painters and Public Life in Eighteenth-Century Paris.* New Haven: Yale University Press, 1985.

Croÿ, Emmanuel, duc de. *Journal inédit.* 4 vols. Paris: Flammarion, 1906.

Cucuel, Georges. *La Pouplinière et la musique de chambre au XVIIIᵉ siècle.* Paris: Librairie Fischbacher, 1913.

Cuisin, P. *Le Peintre des coulisses, salons, mansardes, boudoirs, moeurs, et mystères nocturnes de la capitale, ou Paris en miniature.* Paris: Chez François, 1822.

Curtin, Michael. "A Question of Manners: Status and Gender in Etiquette and Courtesy." *Journal of Modern History* 57 (1985): 395–423.

Dahlhaus, Carl. *Esthetics of Music.* Trans. William Austen. Cambridge: Cambridge University Press, 1982.

———. *Foundations of Music History.* Trans. J. B. Robinson. Cambridge: Cambridge University Press, 1967.

———. *The Idea of Absolute Music.* Trans. Roger Lustig. Chicago: University of Chicago Press, 1989.

Dandelot, A. *La Société des Concerts du Conservatoire de 1828 à 1897.* Paris: G. Havard, 1898.

Darnton, Robert. *The Great Cat Massacre and Other Episodes in French Cultural History.* New York: Basic Books, Inc., 1984.

———. *Mesmerism and the End of the Enlightenment in France.* Cambridge: Harvard University Press, 1968.

Daumard, Adeline. *La Bourgeoisie parisienne du 1815 à 1848.* Paris: École Pratique des Hautes Études, 1963.

———. *Les Bourgeois et la bourgeoisie en France depuis 1815.* Saint-Amand: Aubier-Montagne, 1987.

Daunou, P. C. F. *Rapport sur l'organisation des écoles spéciales.* Paris: n.p., an V.

Daval, Pierre. *La Musique en France au XVIIIe siècle*. Paris: Payot, 1961.

Dean, Winton. "French Opera." In *The New Oxford History of Music*, ed. Gerald Abraham et al. Vol. 8, *The Age of Beethoven, 1790–1830*, ed. Gerald Abraham. New York: Oxford University Press, 1982.

———. "Gluck." In *New Grove Dictionary of Music and Musicians*, ed. Stanley Sadie. 20 vols. London: MacMillan, 1980.

———. "Italian Opera." In *The New Oxford History of Music*, ed. Gerald Abraham et al. Vol. 8, *The Age of Beethoven, 1790–1830*, ed. Gerald Abraham. New York: Oxford University Press, 1982.

Delacroix, Eugène. *Journal*. Trans. Walter Pach. New York: Crown Publishers, 1948.

Délégation à l'Action Artistique de la Ville de Paris. *Auber et l'opéra romantique*. Aleçon: Imprimerie Alençonnaise, 1982.

Delalande, Michel-Richard, and André-Cardinal Destouches. *Les Éléments*. Paris: Éditions Michaelis, n.d. Reprint ed., New York: Broude Brothers, 1971.

Demuth, Norman. *French Opera: Its Development to the Revolution*. Sussex: The Artemis Press, 1963.

Dent, Edward J. *The Rise of Romantic Opera*. Cambridge: Cambridge University Press, 1976.

[De Rulhière]. *Jugement de l'orchestre de l'Opéra*. N.p., [1753].

Deschamps, Émile. *La Préface des études françaises et étrangères*. Ed. Henri Girard. Paris: Les Presses Françaises, 1923.

Desessarts. *Réflexions sur la musique, considerée comme moyen curatif*. Paris: n.p., an XI.

Destouches, André-Cardinal. *Issé*. Paris: Éditions Michaelis, n.d. Reprint ed., New York: Broude Brothers, 1971.

———. *Omphale*. Paris: Éditions Michaelis, n.d. Reprint ed., New York: Broude Brothers, 1971.

Diaz, José-Luis. "L'Artiste romantique en perspective." *Romantisme* 54 (1986): 5–23.

Diderot, Denis. *Oeuvres complètes*. Ed. Roger Lewinter. 15 vols. Paris: Le Club Français du Livre, 1969–73.

Didier, Béatrice. *Écrire la révolution, 1789–1799*. Paris: Presses Universitaires de France, 1989.

———. *La Musique des Lumières: Diderot, "L'Encyclopédie," Rousseau*. Paris: Presses Universitaires de France, 1985.

Discours et motions sur les spectacles. Paris: Chez Donnet, 1789.

Dixmérie, Nicolas Bricaire de la. *Lettre sur l'état présent de nos spectacles . . . particulièrement sur la Comédie-Française et l'Opéra*. Amsterdam: Chez Duchesne, 1765.

Donakowski, Conrad. *A Muse for the Masses: Ritual and Music in an Age of Democratic Revolution, 1770–1870*. Chicago: University of Chicago Press, 1977.

Donnet, Alexis. *Architectonographie des théâtres de Paris*. Paris: Chez Orgiazzi, 1821.

Dormeuil. *Réflexions sur la liberté des théâtres, soumises à MM. les membres de la commission dramatique*. Paris: R. Riga, 1830.

Doyle, William. *Origins of the French Revolution.* Cambridge: Cambridge University Press, 1980.

Dubos, Jean-Baptiste. *Critical Reflections on Poetry, Painting and Music.* Trans. Thomas Nugent. 3 vols. London: Norse, 1748. Reprint ed., New York: AMS Press, Inc., 1978.

[Dubuisson]. *Lettres du Commissaire Dubuisson au marquis de Caumont, 1735–1741.* Ed. A. Rouxel. Paris: E. de Soye et Fils, 1822.

Dumesnil, Alfred. *La Foi nouvelle cherchée dans l'art de Rembrandt à Beethoven.* Paris: E. Thunot et Cie., 1850.

Dupaty, Emmanuel, and [Rodolphe] Kreutzer. *Le Triomphe du mois de mars, ou le berceau d'Achille.* Paris: Masson, 1811.

Durey de Noinville, Jacques Bernard. *Histoire du Théâtre de l'Académie Royale de Musique en France, depuis son établissement jusqu'à présent.* Paris: Chez Duchesne, 1757.

Duval, Georges. *Souvenirs thermidoriens.* 2 vols. Paris: Victor Magen, 1844.

Duverger. "Quelques indications sur la mise en scène de Guillaume Tell." In *The Original Staging Manuals for Twelve Parisian Operatic Premières,* ed. H. Robert Cohen. Stuyvesant, N.Y.: Pendragon Press, 1991.

Ehrard, Jean. *L'Idée de nature en France dans la première moitié du XVIIIe siècle.* 2 vols. Paris: École Pratique des Hautes Études, 1963.

Ehrard, Jean, and Paul Viallaneix, eds. *Les Fêtes de la révolution.* Paris: Société des Études Robespierristes, 1977.

Einstein, Alfred. *Gluck.* Trans. Eric Bloom. New York: McGraw-Hill Book Co., 1972.

Elias, Norbert. *The Civilizing Process.* 2 vols. Trans. Edmund Jephcott. New York: Urizen Books, 1978; Pantheon Books, 1982.

———. *The Court Society.* New York: Pantheon Books, 1983.

Elwart, A. *Histoire de la Société des Concerts du Conservatoire Impérial de Musique.* Paris: S. Castel, 1860.

Emeric, Louis-Damien. *De la Politesse, ouvrage critique, moral et philosophique, avec des notes suivis d'un petit aperçu littéraire.* Paris: Imprimerie de Renaudière, 1819.

Encylopédie, ou dictionnaire raisonné des sciences, des arts et des métiers. Stuttgart-Bad Cannstatt: Freidrich Frommann Verlag, 1966.

Entretiens galans, ou conversations sur la solitude, la teste à teste, le bon-goust, la coqueterie. Paris: n.p., 1681.

Esménard, Joseph-Alphonse. *Le Triomphe de Trajan.* Vol 15 of *Suite du répertoire du théâtre français avec un choix des pièces de plusieurs autres théâtres,* ed. Lepeintre. 80 vols. Paris: Mme Veuve Dabo, 1822.

Essais sur la necessité et sur les moyens de plaire. Paris: Chez Prault, 1738.

Estrée, Paul [Paul Quentin] d'. *Le Théâtre sous la terreur (théâtre de la peur) 1793–1794.* Paris: Émile-Paul Frères, 1913.

Evans, David Owen. *Social Romanticism in France, 1830–1848.* New York: Octagon Books, 1969.

Fabricant, Florence. "Celebrating Rossini's Birthday and His Truly Operatic Tastes." *New York Times,* 26 Feb. 1992, C3.

Faguet, Joël-Marie. "La Musique de chambre à Paris dans les années 1830."

In *Music in Paris in the Eighteen-Thirties*, ed. Peter Bloom. Musical Life in Nineteenth-Century France, vol. 4. Stuyvesant, N.Y.: Pendragon Press, 1987.

———. *Les Sociétés de musique de chambre à Paris de la restauration à 1870.* Paris: Aux Amateurs de Livres, 1986.

Fajon, Robert. *L'Opéra à Paris du roi soleil à Louis le bien-aimé.* Geneva: Slatkine, 1984.

Falco, Robert. *Le Spectateur au théâtre.* Paris: Laval, 1907.

Fétis, Edouard. "Le Romantisme en musique." *Revue musicale* 7 (Feb.–March 1830): 235.

Fétis, F. J. *Biographical Notice of Nicolo Paganini.* London: Schott & Co., 1876. Reprint ed., New York: AMS Press, 1976.

———. "De l'influence de la musique instrumentale sur les révolutions de la musique dramatique." *Revue musicale* 10 (Nov. 1830–Jan. 1831): 131–32.

———. "Des Sensations musicales." *Revue musicale,* 25 Feb. 1832, 26.

Fiévée. *Les Rigueurs du cloître.* Paris: Imprimerie de l'Auteur, n.d.

Fleischmann, Théo. *Napoléon et la musique.* Brussels: Éditions Brepols, 1965.

Forster, Charles de. *Quinze ans à Paris (1832–1848): Paris et les parisiens.* 2 vols. Paris: Imprimeur de l'Institut, 1849.

Fortia de Piles, Alphonse Toussaint Joseph André Marie Marseille, comte de. *Quelques réflexions d'un homme du monde, sur les spectacles, la musique, le jeu et le duel.* Paris: Porthmann, 1812.

Framery, Nicholas Étienne. *De l'Organisation des spectacles de Paris.* Paris: Buisson Libraire, 1790.

Framery, Nicholas Étienne, and Pierre-Louis Ginguené, eds. *Encyclopédie méthodique: Musique.* 2 vols. Paris: Chez Panckoucke, 1791–1818.

Franklin, Alfred. *La Civilité, l'étiquette, la mode, le bon ton du XVIIe au XIXe siècles.* Paris: Émile-Paul Frères, 1908.

Fried, Michael. *Absorption and Theatricality: Painting and Beholders in the Age of Diderot.* Berkeley: University of California Press, 1980.

Fulcher, Jane F. *The Nation's Image: French Grand Opera as Politics and Politicized Art.* Cambridge: Cambridge University Press, 1987.

Funt, David. "Diderot and the Esthetics of the Enlightenment." *Diderot Studies 11.* Geneva: Librairie Droz, 1968.

Furet, François. *Interpreting the French Revolution.* Trans. Elborg Forster. Cambridge: Cambridge University Press, 1981.

Furet, François, and Mona Ozouf, eds. *Dictionnaire critique de la révolution française.* Paris: Flammarion, 1988.

Furet, François, and Denis Richet. *La Révolution française.* Paris: Librairie Arthème Fayard, 1973.

Gadamer, Hans-Georg. *Truth and Method.* New York: Crossroad Publishing Co., 1988.

Garcins, Laurens. *Traité du melodrame, ou réflexions sur la musique dramatique.* Paris: Chez Vallat-La-Chapelle, 1772.

Garlington, Aubrey S., Jr. "*Le Merveilleux* and Operatic Reform in Eighteenth-Century French Opera." *Musical Quarterly* 49 (1963): 484–97.

Gaudet, Fr. *Bibliothèque des petits-maîtres, ou mémoires pour servir à l'histoire du bon ton et de l'extrêmement bonne compagnie.* Paris: Chez la Petite Lalo, 1762.

Gayot, Gérard. *La Franc-maçonnerie française: Textes et pratiques (XVIIIe – XIXe siècles).* Paris: Gallimard, 1980.

Gelbart, Nina Rattner. *Feminine and Opposition Journalism in Old Regime France: Le Journal des Dames.* Berkeley: University of California Press, 1987.

Genlis, Stéphanie-Félicité, Mme la comtesse de. *Dictionnaire critique et raisonné des étiquettes de la cour, et des usages du monde.* Paris: Imprimerie de Fain, 1818.

———. *De l'Esprit des étiquettes de l'ancienne cour et des usages du monde de ce temps.* Rennes: Caillière Libraire-Editeur, 1885.

———. *Mémoires.* 16 vols. Paris: Ladvocat, 1825.

Gerhard, Anselm. "Une véritable révolution opérée à l'Opéra français." *L'Avant scène opéra* 81 (1985): 19–23.

Geringer, Karl. *Haydn: A Creative Life in Music.* Los Angeles: University of California Press, 1968.

Gessele, Cynthia M. "The Conservatoire de Musique and National Music Education in France, 1795–1801." In *Music and the French Revolution,* ed. Malcolm Boyd. Cambridge: Cambridge University Press, 1992.

Giesey, Ralph E. "The King Imagined." In *The French Revolution and the Creation of Modern Political Culture,* ed. Keith Michael Baker et al. 3 vols. Vol. 1, *The Political Culture of the Old Regime,* ed. Keith Michael Baker. Oxford: Pendragon Press, 1987.

Girdlestone, Cuthbert. *Jean-Philippe Rameau: His Life and Work.* New York: Dover Publications, 1969.

Giuliani, Elizabeth. "Le Public de l'Opéra de Paris de 1750 à 1760." *International Review of the Aesthetics and Sociology of Music* 8 (1977): 159–81.

———. "Le Public et le répertoire de l'Opéra à l'époque de Jean-Jacques Rousseau, 1749–57." Mémoire de Maîtrise, Université de Paris X, 1970–71.

Gjertz, Marie. *La Musique au point de vue moral et religieux.* Paris: Jacques Lecoffre et Cie., 1859.

Gluck, Christoph Willibald. *Alceste.* Leipzig: C. F. Peters, n.d.

———. *Alceste.* Ed. Rudolf Gerber. Kassel: Bärenreiter, 1957.

———. *Armide.* Ed. Klaus Hortschansky. Kassel: Bärenreiter, 1987.

———. *The Collected Correspondence and Papers of Christoph Willibald Gluck.* Ed. Hedwig and E. H. Mueller van Asow. Trans. Stewart Thomson. London: Barrie and Rockliff, 1962.

———. *Iphigénie en Tauride.* Zurich: Ernst Eulenburg, Ltd., n.d.

Goblot, Edmond. *La Barrière et le niveau: Étude sociologique sur la bourgeoisie française moderne.* Paris: Presses Universitaires de France, 1967.

Gombrich, E. H. *Art and Illusion: A Study in the Psychology of Pictorial Representation.* Princeton: Princeton University Press, 1960.

Goodman, Dena. "Governing the Republic of Letters: The Politics of Culture in the French Enlightenment." *History of European Ideas* 13 (1991): 183–99.

Gordon, Daniel. "'Public Opinion' and the Civilizing Process in France: The Example of Morellet." *Eighteenth-Century Studies* 22 (1989): 302–28.

Gossec, François-Joseph. *L'Offrande à la liberté: Composé de l'air Veillons au salut de l'empire et de la marche des Marseillois.* Paris: Chez Imbault, n.d.

——. *Le Triomphe de la République, ou le Camp de Grand-Pré.* Paris: Chez Mogin, n.d.

Gossett, Philip. "The Candeur Virginale of *Tancredi.*" *Musical Times* 112 (1971): 326–29.

——. "Gioacchino Rossini and the Conventions of Composition." *Acta Musicologica* 42 (1970): 48–58.

——. "Music at the Théâtre Italien." In *Music in Paris in the Eighteen-Thirties,* ed. Peter Bloom. Musical Life in Nineteenth-Century France, vol. 4. Stuyvesant, N.Y.: Pendragon Press, 1987."

[Goujon, Abel]. *Manuel de l'homme de bon ton, ou cérémonial de la bonne société.* Paris: Chez Andin, [1822].

Grégoire, Edouard G. J., ed. *Souvenirs artistiques: Documents pour servir à l'histoire de la musique.* 3 vols. Anvers: Imprimerie L. de la Montagne, 1888.

Grétry, André-Modest. *La Caravane du Caire.* Paris: Éditions Michaelis, n.d. Reprint ed., New York: Broude Brothers, 1971.

——. *Mémoires, ou Essais sur la musique.* 3 vols. Paris: Imprimerie de la République, an V. Reprint ed., New York: Da Capo Press, 1971.

Grimm, Frédéric-Melchior, baron de. *Correspondance littéraire.* 16 vols. Paris: Garnier Frères, 1877.

Guerrini, Maurice. *Napoleon and Paris: Thirty Years of History.* Trans. Margery Weiner. New York: Walker and Company, 1970.

Guest, Ivor. *Le Ballet de l'Opéra de Paris.* Paris: Théâtre National de l'Opéra, 1976.

Habermas, Jürgen. *The Structural Transformation of the Public Sphere.* Trans. Thomas Burger and Frederick Lawrence. Cambridge: MIT Press, 1989.

Hamiche, Daniel. *Le Théâtre de la révolution, la lutte de classes au théâtre en 1789 et en 1793.* Paris: Union Général d'Éditions, 1973.

Hanning, Barbara. "Conversation and Musical Style in the Late Eighteenth-Century Parisian Salon." *Eighteenth-Century Studies* 22 (1989): 329–50.

[Hartig, François de.] *Lettres sur la France, l'Angleterre et l'Italie.* Geneva: n.p., 1785.

Henrion. *Encore un tableau de Paris.* Paris: Chez Favre, an VIII.

——. *Les Incroyables et les merveilleuses, ouvrage impayable.* Paris: Chez Graffe, an V.

L'Hermite de la chaussée d'Antin. 3 vols. Paris: Imprimerie de Pillet, 1813.

Heyer, John Hajdu, ed. *Jean-Baptise Lully and the Music of the French Baroque: Essays in Honor of James R. Anthony.* Cambridge: Cambridge University Press, 1989.

Higgs, David. *Nobles in Nineteenth-Century France: The Practice of Inegalitarianism.* Baltimore: Johns Hopkins University Press, 1987.

Hippeau, Edmond. *Berlioz et son temps.* Paris: Paul Ollendorf, 1890.

Hoffmann, E. T. A. *E. T. A. Hoffmann's Musical Writings: Kreisleriana, The Poet and the Composer, Musical Criticism.* Ed. David Charlton. Cambridge: Cambridge University Press, 1989.

Hoffmann, Stanley, et al., eds. *In Search of France.* Cambridge: Harvard University Press, 1963.

Holoman, D. Kern. *Berlioz.* Cambridge: Harvard University Press, 1989.

———. "The Emergence of the Orchestral Conductor in Paris in the 1820s." In *Music in Paris in the Eighteen-Thirties,* ed. Peter Bloom. Musical Life in Nineteenth-Century France, vol. 4. Stuyvesant, N.Y.: Pendragon Press, 1987.

Howard, Patricia. *Gluck and the Birth of Modern Opera.* London: Barrie and Rockliff, 1963.

Huebner, Steven. "Opera Audiences in Paris, 1830–1870." *Music and Letters* 70 (1989): 206–25.

Hunt, Lynn. *The Family Romance of the French Revolution.* Berkeley: University of California Press, 1992.

———. *Politics, Culture, and Class in the French Revolution.* Berkeley: University of California Press, 1984.

———. "The Unstable Boundaries of the French Revolution." In *A History of Private Life,* ed. Philippe Arès and Georges Duby, Vol. 4, *From the Fires of the French Revolution to the Great War,* ed. Michelle Perrot, trans. Arthur Goldhammer. Cambridge: Harvard University Press, 1990.

Hunt, Lynn, ed. *The New Cultural History.* Berkeley: University of California Press, 1989.

Huray, Peter le, and James Day, eds. *Music and Aesthetics in the Eighteenth and Early Nineteenth Centuries.* Bath: Cambridge University Press, 1981.

Hyslop, Beatrice F. "The Theater during a Crisis: The Parisian Theater during the Reign of Terror," *Journal of Modern History* 17 (1945): 332–55.

Il n'y a qu'un Paris dans le monde, croquis, ou littéraire, ou politique, ou moral, ou plaisant, comme on voudra, propre à figurer dans les opuscules du jour. Paris: Imprimerie Laurens, 1815.

Ingarden, Roman. *The Work of Music and the Problem of Its Identity.* Trans. Adam Czerniawski. Berkeley: University of California Press, 1986.

Iser, Wolfgang. *The Act of Reading: A Theory of Aesthetic Response.* Baltimore: University of Maryland Press, 1978.

Isherwood, Robert. *Farce and Fantasy: Popular Entertainment in Eighteenth-Century Paris.* New York: Oxford University Press, 1986.

———. *Music in the Service of the King: France in the Seventeenth Century.* Ithaca: Cornell University Press, 1972.

———. "The Third War of Musical Enlightenment." *Studies in Eighteenth-Century Culture* 4 (1975): 223–45.

Jam, Jean-Louis. "Le Clairon de l'avenir." In *L'Orphée phrygien: Les Musiques de la révolution,* ed. Jean-Rémy Julien and Jean-Claude Klein. Paris: Éditions du May, 1989.

Jauss, Hans Robert. *Toward an Aesthetic of Reception.* Trans. Timothy Bahti. Minneapolis: University of Minnesota Press, 1982.

Johnson, James H. "Beethoven and the Birth of Romantic Musical Experience in France." *19th-Century Music* 15 (1991): 23–35.

———. "The Encyclopedists and the Querelle des Bouffons: Reason and the Enlightenment of Sentiment." *Eighteenth-Century Life* 10 (1986): 12–27.

———. "Musical Experience and the Formation of a French Musical Public." *Journal of Modern History* 64 (1992): 191–226.

———. "Revolutionary Audiences and the Impossible Imperatives of Fraternity." In *Re-Creating Authority in Revolutionary France*, ed. Bryant T. Ragan, Jr., and Elizabeth A. Williams. New Brunswick: Rutgers University Press, 1992.

Johnson, Janet Lynn. "The Théâtre-Italien and Opera and Theatrical Life in Restoration Paris, 1818–27." 3 vols. Ph.D. diss., University of Chicago, 1988.

Join-Diéterle, Catherine. *Les Décors de scène de l'Opéra de Paris à l'époque romantique*. Paris: Picard, 1988.

———. "La Monarchie, source d'inspiration de l'Opéra à l'époque romantique." *Revue d'histoire du théâtre* 35 (1983–84): 430–41.

———. "*Robert le diable*: Le premier opéra romantique." *Romantisme* 28–29 (1980): 147–66.

Jouhaud, Pierre. *Paris dans le dix-neuvième siècle, ou réflexions d'un observateur sur les nouvelles institutions, les embellissements, l'esprit public, la société, les ridicules, les femmes, les journaux, le théâtre, la littérature, etc.*. Paris: J. G. Dentu, Imprimeur, 1809.

Jouy, Étienne de. *L'Hermite de la Guiane, ou observations sur les moeurs et les usages français au commencement du XIXe siècle*. Paris: Chez Pillet, 1816.

Julien, Jean-Rémy, and Jean-Claude Klein, eds. *L'Orphée phrygien: Les Musiques de la révolution*. Paris: Éditions du May, 1989.

———, eds. *Le Tambour et la harpe: Oeuvres, pratiques et manifestations musicales sous la révolution, 1788–1800*. Paris: Éditions du May, 1991.

Jullien, Adolphe. *Paris dilettante au commencement du siècle*. Paris: Didot, 1889.

———. *Les Spectateurs sur le théâtre: Établissement et suppression des bancs sur les scènes de la Comédie-Française et de l'Opéra*. Paris: A. Detaille, 1875.

Karamzin, Nicolas. *Letters of a Russian Traveler, 1789–1790*. Trans. Florence Jonas. New York: Columbia University Press, 1957.

Keane, Michaela Maria. *The Theoretical Writings of Jean-Philippe Rameau*. Washington, D.C.: Catholic University of America Press, 1961.

Keiler, Allan. "Liszt and Beethoven: The Creation of a Personal Myth." *19th-Century Music* 12 (1988): 116–31.

Kennedy, Emmet. *A Cultural History of the French Revolution*. New Haven: Yale University Press, 1989.

Kintzler, Catherine. *Jean-Philippe Rameau: Splendeur et naufrage de l'esthétique du plaisir à l'âge classique*. Paris: Le Sycomore, 1983.

———. *Poétique de l'Opéra français de Corneille à Rousseau*. Paris: Minerve, 1991.

Kisch, Eve. "Rameau and Rousseau." *Music and Letters* 22 (1941): 97–114.

Kivy, Peter. *The Corded Shell: Reflections on Musical Expression*. Princeton: Princeton University Press, 1980.

———. *Music Alone: Philosophical Reflections on the Purely Musical Experience*. Ithaca: Cornell University Press, 1990.

———. *Osmin's Rage: Philosophical Reflections on Opera, Drama, and Text*. Princeton: Princeton University Press, 1988.

———. *Sound and Semblance: Reflections on Musical Representation*. Princeton: Princeton University Press, 1984.

Koselleck, Reinhart. *Critique and Crisis: Enlightenment and the Pathogenesis of Modern Society*. Cambridge: MIT Press, 1988.

———. *Futures Past: On the Semantics of Historical Time*. Trans. Keith Tribe. Cambridge: MIT Press, 1985.

Kotzebue, Auguste. *Souvenirs de Paris en 1804*. 2 vols. Paris: Chez Barba, 1805.

Kramer, Lawrence. "Haydn's Chaos, Schenker's Order; or, Hermeneutics and Musical Analysis: Can They Mix?" *19th-Century Music* 16 (1992): 3–17;

———. *Music as Cultural Practice, 1800–1900*. Berkeley: University of California Press, 1990.

Kramer, Lloyd S. *Threshold of a New World: Intellectuals and the Exile Experience in Paris, 1830–1848*. Ithaca: Cornell University Press, 1988.

Labbet, A. J., abbé de Morambert, and A. Léris. *Sentiments d'un harmonophile, sur différents ouvrages de musique*. Amsterdam: n.p., 1756. Reprint ed., Geneva: Minkoff Reprints, 1972.

Labrosse, Claude. *Lire au XVIIIᵉ siècle: "La Nouvelle Héloïse" et ses lecteurs*. Lyon: Presses Universitaires de Lyon, 1985.

La Bruyère, Jean de. *Les Caractères*. Paris: Librairie Hachette, 1904.

———. *Oeuvres complètes*. Paris: Bibliothèque de la Pléiade, 1951.

LaCapra, Dominick, and Steven L. Kaplan, eds. *Modern European Intellectual History: Reappraisals and New Perspectives*. Ithaca: Cornell University Press, 1982.

Lacépède, B.-G.-D. *La Poétique de la musique*. 2 vols. Paris: L'Imprimerie de Monsieur, 1785.

Laclos, Choderlos de. *Les Liaisons dangereuses*. Paris: Gallimard, 1972.

Lacombe, [Jacques]. *Le Spectacle des beaux arts; ou considérations touchant leur nature, leurs objets, leurs effets et leurs règles principales*. Paris: Chez Hardy Libraire, 1758.

La Fontaine, Jean de. *Oeuvres complètes*. Ed. Pierre Clarac. 2 vols. Paris: Gallimard, 1958.

La Gorce, Jérome de. "Décors et machines à l'Opéra de Paris au temps de Rameau: Inventaire de 1748." *Recherches sur la musique française classique* 21 (1983): 145–57.

Lagrave, Henri. *Le Théâtre et le public à Paris de 1715 à 1750*. Paris: Librairie C. Klincksick, 1972.

Lahalle, M. P. *Essai sur la musique, ses fonctions dans les moeurs, et sa véritable expression; suivi d'une bibliographie musicale*. Paris: Imprimerie de Casimir, 1825.

Laharpe, Jean-François, ed. *Correspondance littéraire*. 6 vols. Paris: Chez Mignaret, 1804–7.

Lajarte, Théodore de. *Bibliothèque musicale du théâtre de l'Opéra: Catalogue historique, chronologique, anecdotique*. 2 vols. Paris: Librairie des Bibliophiles, 1878. Reprint ed., Hildesheim: Georg Olms Verlag, 1969.

La Laurencie, Lionel de. *Le Goût musical en France au XVIIIᵉ siècle*. Paris: A. Joanin et Cie., 1905.

———. *Lully*. Paris: Félix Alcan, 1919.

Laloy, Louis. *Rameau*. Paris: Félix Alcan, 1908.

Lamerville, Jean Louis Thomas Heurtault, comte de. *Sur l'organisation nouvelle du conservatoire de musique, au nom des commissions d'instruction publique et des institutions républicaines.* Paris: n.p., an VIII.

La Morlière, Jacques Rochette de. *Angola: Histoire indienne.* 2 vols. Paris: n.p., 1746.

Landes, Joan. *Women in the Public Sphere in the Age of the French Revolution.* Ithaca: Cornell University Press, 1988.

Lanfranchi, Louis Rainier. *Voyage à Paris, ou esquisses des hommes et des choses.* Paris: Lepetit, 1830.

Langer, Susanne Katherina Knauth. *Philosophy in a New Key: A Study in the Symbolism of Reason, Rite, and Art.* Cambridge: Harvard University Press, 1951.

La Revellière-Lépeaux, L. M. *Essai sur les moyens de faire participer l'universalité des spectateurs à tout ce qui se pratique dans les fêtes nationales.* Paris: Chez H. J. Jansen, an VI.

Lasalle, Albert de. *Les Treize salles de l'Opéra.* Paris: Librairie Sartorius, 1875.

Lassabathie, Michel. *Histoire du Conservatoire Impérial de Musique et de Déclamation, suivie de documents inédits recueillis et mis en ordre.* Paris: Chez Lévy Frères, 1860.

Lau, Jules. *Mémoires d'un chef de claque: Souvenirs des théâtres.* Paris: Librairie Nouvelle, 1883.

Launay, Denise, ed. *La Querelle des bouffons: Texte des pamphlets avec introduction, commentaires et index.* Geneva: Minkoff Reprints, 1973.

Leclerc, J. B. *Essai sur la propagation de la musique en France, sa conservation, et ses rapports avec le gouvernement.* Paris: Imprimerie Nationale, an VI.

———. *Sur l'établissement d'écoles spéciales de musique.* Paris: n.p., an VII.

Lefebvre, Edouard. *Considérations politiques et morales, sur la France constituée en république.* Paris: Chez Bertrand, 1798.

Legreville Saint-Alme, Auguste de. *Des journaux et des théâtres.* Paris: n.p., 1828.

Leith, James. "Music as an Ideological Weapon in the French Revolution." *Canadian Historical Association Annual Report* (1966): 126–40.

Lejeune, André, and Stéphane Wolff. *Les Quinze Salles de l'Opéra de Paris, 1669–1955.* Paris: E. Ploix, 1955.

Lemoyne, Jean-Baptiste. *Toute la Grèce, ou ce que peut la liberté.* Paris: n.p., an II.

Leo, Sophie Augustine. "Musical Life in Paris (1817–1848): A Chapter from the Memoirs of Sophie Augustine Leo." Trans. W. Oliver Strunk. *Musical Quarterly* 17 (1931): 259–71.

Léon, Guillemin. *Physiologie du Parterre: Types du spectateur.* Paris: Imprimerie de Guiraudet, 1841.

Leroy, Maxime. *Histoire des idées sociales en France.* 3 vols. Paris: Gallimard, 1946–1954.

Le Sueur, Jean-François. *La Caverne.* [1793?] French Opera in the Seventeenth and Eighteenth Centuries, ed. Barry S. Brook, vol. 74. New York: Pendragon Press, 1985.

———. *Ossian, ou les bardes.* Early Romantic Opera, ed. Philip Gossett and Charles Rosen, vol. 37. New York: Garland Publishing, 1979.

Lesure, François. *Haydn en France.* Budapest: Akadémiai Kiado, 1961.

———, ed. *Querelle des gluckistes et des piccinnistes.* 2 vols. Geneva: Minkoff Reprints, 1984.

Létissier, Mme [Marie Benigne Esther ?]. *La Société parisienne: Esquisse de moeurs.* Paris: Imprimerie de H. Fournier, 1842.

*Lettre d'un amateur de l'Opéra à M. de ***, dont la tranquille habitude est d'attendre les événements pour juger du mérite des projets.* Amsterdam: n.p., 1776.

*Lettre d'un philosophe moitié gai, moitié chagrin, sur quelques-unes de nos sottises, au Baron de ***.* Paris: Chez Sébastien Jorry, 1770.

Levinson, Jerrold. *Music, Art, and Metaphysics: Essays in Philosophical Aesthetics.* Ithaca: Cornell University Press, 1990.

Lévi-Strauss, Claude. *The Savage Mind.* Chicago: University of Chicago Press, 1966.

Liszt, Franz. *An Artist's Journey: Lettres d'un bachelier ès musique 1835–1841.* Trans. and annot. Charles Suttoni. Chicago: University of Chicago Press, 1989.

Locke, Ralph P. "Liszt's Saint-Simonian Adventure." *19th-Century Music* 4 (1981): 209–26.

———. *Music, Musicians, and the Saint-Simonians.* Chicago: University of Chicago Press, 1986.

Longyear, Rey Morgan. "*La Muette de Portici.*" *Music Review* 19 (1958): 37–46.

Lough, John. *Paris Theatre Audiences in the Seventeenth and Eighteenth Centuries.* London: Oxford University Press, 1957.

Lovejoy, A. O. "Nature as Aesthetic Norm." *Modern Language Notes* 42 (1927): 444–50.

Lucas, Colin. "Noble, Bourgeois and the Origins of the French Revolution." *Past and Present* 60 (1973): 84–126.

Luchet, [Jean Pierre Louis de la Roche du Maine, marquis de]. *Paris en miniature, d'après les dessins d'un nouvel argus.* Paris: Chez Pichard, 1784.

Lully, Jean-Baptiste. *Alceste.* Ed. Henri Prunières. Paris: Édition de la Revue Musicale, 1932.

———. *Armide.* Ed. Théodore de Lajarte. Paris: Éditions Michaelis, n.d. Reprint ed., New York: Broude Brothers, 1971.

———. *Atys.* Ed. Théodore de Lajarte. Paris: Éditions Michaelis, n.d. Reprint ed., New York: Broude Brothers, 1971.

———. *Cadmus et Hermione.* Ed. Henri Prunières. Paris: Éditions de la Revue Musicale, 1930.

———. *Thésée.* Ed. Théodore de Lajarte. Paris: Imprimerie Lemercier, n.d.

Lyons, Martyn. *France under the Directory.* Cambridge: Cambridge University Press, 1975.

McClary, Susan. *Feminine Endings: Music, Gender, and Sexuality.* Minneapolis: University of Minnesota Press, 1991.

Mably, Gabriel Bonnot de. *Lettres à Madame la Marquise de P*** sur l'Opéra.* Paris: Chez Didot, 1741.

MacDonald, Robert James. "François-Joseph Gossec and French Instrumental Music in the Second Half of the Eighteenth Century." 3 vols. Ph.D. diss., University of Michigan, 1968.

Mairobert, Mathieu François Pidansat de. *L'Espion anglais, ou correspondance secrète entre Milord All'eye et Milord All'ear.* 3 vols. London: Chez John Adamson, 1779.

Maniates, Maria Rika. " 'Sonate, que me veux-tu?': The Enigma of French Musical Aesthetics in the Eighteenth Century." *Current Musicology* 9 (1969): 117–40.

Marchand, J. H. *Les Vues simples d'un bon homme.* London: n.p., 1776.

Marshall, David. "Rousseau and the State of Theater." *Representations* 13 (1986): 84–114.

Martin-Fugier, Anne. *La Vie élégante, ou la formation du Tout-Paris, 1815–1848.* Paris: Librairie Arthème Fayard, 1990.

Mason, Laura. " 'Ça ira' and the Birth of the Revolutionary Song," *History Workshop* 28 (1989): 22–38.

Masson, Paul-Marie. "French Opera from Lully to Rameau." In *The New Oxford History of Music*, ed. Gerald Abraham et al. Vol. 5, *Opera and Church Music, 1630–1750*, ed. Anthony Lewis and Nigel Fortune. London: Oxford University Press, 1975.

———. *L'Opéra de Rameau.* Paris: Henri Laurens, 1930. Reprint ed., New York: Da Capo Press, 1972.

Matoré, George. *Le Vocabulaire et la société sous Louis-Philippe.* Geneva: Slatkine, 1967.

Maugain, Gabriel. "Le Silence au théâtre en France et en Italie, au XVIII siècle." *Ausonia, cahiers franco-italiens* 3 (1936): 125–32.

Mayeur de Saint Paul, François Marie. *Le Vol plus haut, ou l'espion des principaux théâtres de la capitale; Contenant une histoire abrégée des acteurs et actrices de ces mêmes théâtres, enrichis d'observations philosophiques et d'anecdotes récréatives.* Memphis: Chez Sincère, Libraire Réfugié du Puits de la Verité, 1784.

Mekka-Barrada, Tawfik, ed. *Correspondance littéraire secrète.* 2 vols. Göteborg: Acta Universitatis Gothoburgensis, 1986.

Méhul, Nicolas-Étienne. *Euphrosine, ou le tyran corrigé.* Early Romantic Opera, ed. Philip Gossett and Charles Rosen, vol. 38. New York: Garland Publishing, 1980.

———. *Horatius Coclès.* Ed. Louis Saguer. Paris: Éditions Française de Musique, 1974.

———. *Mélidore et Phrosine.* French Opera in the Seventeenth and Eighteenth Centuries, ed. Barry S. Brook, vol. 73. New York: Pendragon Press, 1990.

Mélèse, Pierre. *Le Théâtre et le public à Paris sous Louis XIV, 1659–1715.* Paris: Librairie E. Droz, 1934.

Memorandums of a Residence in France, in the Winter of 1815–16. London: Longman, Hurst, Rees, Orme, and Brown, 1816.

Méneval, Baron Claude-François de. *Memoirs Illustrating the History of Napoleon I.* 3 vols. New York: D. Appleton and Co., 1894.

Mercier, Louis-Sebastien. *Du Théâtre, ou nouvel essai sur l'art dramatique.* Amsterdam: n.p., 1773.

———. *Tableau de Paris.* 12 vols. Amsterdam: n.p., 1782–88.

Méré, Antoine Gombaud, Chevalier de. *Oeuvres complètes du chevalier de Méré.* Ed. Charles H. Boudhors. 3 vols. Paris: Éditions Fernand Roches, 1930.

Merle, J. T. *De l'Opéra.* Paris: Baudouin Frères, 1827.

Merlin, Antoine Christophe. *Opinion de Merlin (de Thionville) sur les fêtes nationales.* Paris: Imprimerie Nationale, an III.

Merlin, la comtesse. *Madame Malibran.* Brussels: Société Typographique Belge, 1838.

Mésangère. *Le Voyageur à Paris: Tableau pittoresque et moral de cette capitale.* 3 vols. Paris: Chez Chaignieau, 1797.

Métra, Imbert, et al. *Correspondance secrète, politique et littéraire.* 18 vols. London: Chez John Adamson, 1787.

Meyer, Frederic Jean Laurent. *Fragments sur Paris.* Trans. Le Général Dumouriez. Hamburg: n.p., 1798.

Meyer, Leonard B. *Emotion and Meaning in Music.* Chicago: University of Chicago Press, 1956.

———. *Music, the Arts, and Ideas.* Chicago: University of Chicago Press, 1967.

Meyerbeer, Giacomo. *Les Huguenots.* 2 vols. Early Romantic Opera, ed. Philip Gossett and Charles Rosen, vol. 20. New York: Garland Publishing, 1980.

———. *Robert le diable.* 2 vols. Early Romantic Opera, ed. Philip Gossett and Charles Rosen, vol. 19. New York: Garland Publishing, 1980.

Michaud, Joseph François. *Biographie universelle.* Paris: C. Desplaces, 1854–65.

Momigny, Jérôme-Joseph de. *Cours complet d'harmonie et de composition.* Paris: Bailleul, 1803.

Montbarey, M. le prince de. *Mémoires autobiographiques.* 3 vols. Paris: A. Eymery, 1826–1827.

Monglond, André. *Le Préromantisme français.* 2 vols. Grenoble: Éditions B. Arthaud, 1930.

Mongrédien, Jean. *La Musique en France des lumières au romantisme, 1789–1830.* Paris: Harmoniques Flammarion, 1986.

Montigny, L. *Le Provincial à Paris: Esquisse des moeurs parisiennes.* 2 vols. Paris: Chez Ladvocat, 1825.

Morgan, Sydney Owenson, Lady. *La France.* 2 vols. Paris: Chez Treuttel, 1817.

———. *La France en 1829 et 1830.* 2 vols. Paris: H. Fournier, 1830.

Morellet, André. *Observations sur un ouvrage nouveau, intitulé: "Traité du Melo-Drame," ou réflexions sur la musique dramatique.* Paris: Chez Vallat-La-Chapelle, 1771.

Un mot sur tout le monde, ou La Revue de Paris, pour l'an dix, almanach chantant; par les auteurs des Diners du Vaudeville. Paris: n.p., n.d.

[Moulay, chevalier de?]. *Mémoires d'Anne-Marie de Moras, comtesse de Courbon.* 4 vols. The Hague: Chez Pierre de Hondt, 1740.

Mousnier, Roland. *The Institutions of France*. Trans. Brian Pearce. 2 vols. Chicago: University of Chicago Press, 1979.

Moy, Charles-Alexandre de. *Des fêtes, ou quelques idées d'un citoyen français relatives aux fêtes publiques et à un culte national*. Paris: Chez Garnery, an VII.

Murphy, Kerry. *Hector Berlioz and the Development of French Music Criticism*. Ann Arbor: UMI Research Press, 1988.

Nathans, Benjamin. "Habermas's 'Public Sphere' in the Era of the French Revolution." *French Historical Studies* 16 (1990): 620–44.

Nectoux, Jean-Michel. "Trois orchestres parisiens en 1830: L'Académie Royale de Musique, le Théâtre Italien et la Société des Concerts du Conservatoire." In *Music in Paris in the Eighteen-Thirties*, ed. Peter Bloom. Musical Life in Nineteenth-Century France, vol. 4. Stuyvesant, N.Y.: Pendragon Press, 1987.

Neubauer, John. *The Emancipation of Music from Language: Departure from Mimesis in Eighteenth-Century Aesthetics*. New Haven: Yale University Press, 1986.

Neufchâteau, François de. *Pamela, ou la vertu récompensée*. Paris: Chez Barba, an III.

———, ed. *Recueil des lettres circulaires, instructions, programmes, discours, et autres actes publics*. 2 vols. Paris: Imprimerie de la République, an VII.

Newman, Ernest. *Gluck and the Opera*. London: Victor Gallancy Ltd., 1964.

Newman, Joyce. *Jean-Baptiste de Lully and His Tragédies Lyriques*. Ann Arbor: UMI Research Press, 1979.

Newman, William S. "The Beethoven Mystique in Romantic Art, Literature, and Music." *Musical Quarterly* 69 (1983): 354–87.

Noiray, Michel. "L'Opéra de la révolution (1790–1794): Un tapage de chien?" In J. C. Bonnet, ed., *La Carmagnole des muses: L'Homme de lettres et l'artiste dans la révolution*. Paris: Armand Colin, 1988.

Nougaret, P. J. B. *Aventures parisiennes, avant et depuis la révolution*. 3 vols. Paris: Imprimerie de Maugeret Fils, 1808.

———. *Paris, ou le rideau levé: Anecdotes singulières, bizarres et sentimentales; pour servir à l'histoire de nos moeurs anciennes et nouvelles; avec des faits, qui n'avaient point encore été publiés*. 3 vols. Paris: n.p., an VIII.

Nouveau tableau de Paris au XIX siècle. Paris: Imprimerie de Bourgogne et Martinet, 1835.

Nouveau tableau de Paris, ou observations sur les moeurs et usages des parisiens au commencement du XIXe siècle. 2 vols. Paris: Chez Pillet Aîné, 1828.

Nouvelles de la cour et de la ville concernant le monde, les arts, les théâtres et les lettres, 1734–1738 . . . Paris: n.p., 1879.

Nye, Robert A. *Masculinity and Male Codes of Honor in Modern France*. Oxford: Oxford University Press, 1993.

Oberkirch, baronne d'. *Mémoires*. 2 vols. Paris: Charpentier, 1835.

Observations désintéressées sur l'administration du Théâtre Italien, adressées à M. Viotti, directeur de ce théâtre par un dilettante. Paris: Chez Anth^e. Boucher, 1821.

Oliver, Alfred Richard. *The Encyclopedists as Critics of Music*. New York: Columbia University Press, 1947.

O'Neddy, Philothée [Théophile Dondey]. *Feu et flamme*. Paris: Éditions Presses Françaises, 1926.

Orr, Linda. *Headless History: Nineteenth-Century French Historiography of the Revolution*. Ithaca: Cornell University Press, 1990.

Ortigue, Joseph Louis d'. *Le Balcon de l'Opéra*. Paris: Librairie d'Eugène Renduel, 1833.

———. *De la guerre des dilettanti, ou de la révolution opérée par M. Rossini dans l'opéra français; et des rapports qui existent entre la musique, la littérature et les arts*. Paris: Imprimerie de Béthune, 1829.

Ozouf, Mona. *Festivals and the French Revolution*. Trans. Alan Sheridan. Cambridge: Harvard University Press, 1988.

———. "'Public Opinion' at the End of the Old Regime." *Journal of Modern History* 60 (1988): S1–S21.

Palianti, M. L. "La Juive." In *The Original Staging Manuals for Twelve Parisian Operatic Premières*, ed. H. Robert Cohen. Stuyvesant, N.Y.: Pendragon Press, 1991.

Paris et ses modes, ou les soirées parisiennes. Paris: Chez Michelet, 1803.

Paris vu tel qu'il est. Paris: Chez les Libraires qui vendent les Nouveautés, 1781.

Patte, [Pierre]. *Essai sur l'architecture théâtrale*. Paris: Chez Moutard, 1782.

Paul, Charles G. "Music and Ideology: Rameau, Rousseau and 1789." *Journal of the History of Ideas* 32 (1971): 395–410.

Pendle, Karin. *Eugène Scribe and French Opera of the Nineteenth Century*. Ann Arbor: UMI Research Press, 1979.

Perris, Arnold Benedict. "Music in France during the Reign of Louis-Philippe: Art as 'A Substitute for the Heroic Experience.'" Ph.D. diss., Northwestern University, 1967.

Pestelli, Giorgio. *The Age of Mozart and Beethoven*. Trans. Eric Cross. Cambridge: Cambridge University Press, 1984.

Pétition d'un membre de la Bazoche aux très honorables membres des assemblées du Palais-Royal. Paris: n.p., 1789.

Peyser, Joan, ed. *The Orchestra: Origins and Transformations*. New York: Charles Scribner's Sons, 1986.

Piccinni, Niccolò. *Iphigénie en Tauride*. Happenheim: Gregg International Publishers, Ltd., 1972.

———. *Roland*. Ed. Gustave Lefevre. Paris: Éditions Michaelis, n.d. Reprint ed., New York: Broude Brothers, 1971.

Pierre, Constant. *Le Conservatoire National de Musique et de déclamation: Documents historiques et administratifs recueillis ou reconstitués*. Paris: Imprimerie Nationale, 1900.

———. *Le Magasin de Musique à l'usage des fêtes nationales et du conservatoire*. Paris: Librairie Fischbacher, 1895.

———. *Musique des fêtes et cérémonies de la révolution française*. Paris: Imprimerie Nationale, 1899.

Pilbeam, Pamela. *The 1830 Revolution in France*. New York: St. Martin's Press, 1991.

Pinkney, David H. *The French Revolution of 1830*. Princeton: Princeton University Press, 1972.

Pirro, André. "Mémoires sur la musique à Paris à la fin du règne de Louis XV." *Revue musical* 149 (1934): 111–19.

Pistone, Danièle. "Paganini et Paris: Quelques témoignages." In "Dossier: Paganini et Paris." *Revue internationale de musique française* 9 (1982): 7–16.

———. "Réflexions sur l'évolution du public musical parisien." *Romantisme* 38 (1982): 19–23.

Pitou, Spire. *The Paris Opera: An Encyclopedia of Operas, Ballets, Composers, and Performers.* 4 vols. Westport, Conn.: Greenwood Press, 1983.

Pitts, Jesse R. "Continuity and Change in Bourgeois France." In *In Search of France*, ed. Stanley Hoffmann et al. Cambridge: Harvard University Press, 1963.

Place, Adélaïde de. *La Vie musicale en France au temps de la Révolution.* Paris: Fayard, 1989.

Pompey, Edouard de. *Beethoven: Sa vie, son caractère, sa musique.* Paris: n. p., 1865.

Pougin, Arthur. *La Comédie-Française et la Révolution.* Paris: Gaultier, Magnier, 1902.

———. *L'Opéra-Comique pendant la Révolution.* Paris: Albert Savine, 1891.

Prod'homme, J. G. "Napoleon, Music, and Musicians." *Musical Quarterly* 7 (1921): 579–605.

———. "Rossini and His Works in France." *Musical Quarterly* 17 (1931): 110–37.

———. *Les Symphonies de Beethoven.* Paris: Delagrave, 1906. Reprint ed., New York: Da Capo Press, 1977.

Un Provincial à Paris, pendant une partie de l'année 1789. Strasbourg: Imprimerie de la Société Typographique, n.d.

Pujoulx, J. B. *Paris à la fin du XVIIIᵉ siècle, ou esquisse historique et morale des monuments et des ruines de cette capitale; de l'État des sciences, des arts de l'industrie à cette époque, ainsi que des moeurs et des ridicules de ces habitants.* Paris: Chez Mathé, an IX.

Querelle des gluckists et des piccinnistes. Ed. François Lesure. 2 vols. Geneva: Minkoff Reprints, 1984.

Quinet, [Hermione]. *Ce que dit la musique.* Paris: Imprimerie Paul Brodard, 1893.

Ragan, Jr., Bryant T., and Elizabeth A. Williams, eds. *Re-Creating Authority in Revolutionary France.* New Brunswick: Rutgers University Press, 1992.

Raisson, H. N., and A. Romieu. *Code civil: Manuel complet de la politesse, du ton, des manières de la bonne compagnie, contenant les lois, règles, applications, et exemples de l'art de se présenter et de se conduire dans le monde.* Paris: Imprimerie G. Doyen, 1828.

Rameau, Jean-Philippe. *Castor et Pollux.* Ed. Théodore de Lajarte. Paris: Éditions Michaelis, n.d. Reprint ed., New York: Broude Brothers, 1971.

———. *Complete Theoretical Writings.* Ed. Erwin R. Jacobi. 6 vols. New York: American Institute of Musicology, 1967.

———. *Dardanus.* Ed. Vincent d'Indy. Paris: A. Durand et Fils, 1905.

———. *Hippolyte et Aricie.* Ed. Vincent d'Indy. Paris: A. Durand et Fils, 1900.

————. *Les Indes galantes.* Ed. Paul Dukas. Paris: A. Durand et Fils, 1902.

————. *A Treatise on Harmony.* Ed. and trans. Philip Gossett. New York: Dover Publications, 1971.

Ranum, Orest. "Courtesy, Absolutism, and the Rise of the French State, 1630–1660." *Journal of Modern History* 52 (1980): 426–51.

Reeve, Katherine Kolb. "The Poetics of the Orchestra in the Writings of Hector Berlioz." Ph.D. diss., Yale University, 1978.

————. "Rhetoric and Reason in French Music Criticism of the 1830s." In *Music in Paris in the Eighteen-Thirties,* ed. Peter Bloom. Musical Life in Nineteenth-Century France, vol. 4. Stuyvesant, N.Y.: Pendragon Press, 1987.

Reichenburg, Louisette. *Contribution à l'histoire de la querelle des bouffons.* Philadelphia: University of Pennsylvania Press, 1937.

Rémond, René. *The Right Wing in France from 1815 to De Gaulle.* Trans. James M. Laux. Philadelphia: University of Pennsylvania Press, 1966.

Rémond de Saint-Mard, Toussaint. *Réflexions sur l'opéra.* The Hague: Chez Jean Neaulme, 1741.

Rétif de la Bretonne, Nicolas Edme. *Tableaux de la bonne compagnie, ou traits caractéristiques, anecdotes secrètes, politiques, morales et littéraires, recueillies dans les sociétés du bon ton, pendant les années 1786 et 1787.* 2 vols. Paris: n.p., 1787.

Révérand, A. *Armorial du premier empire.* 4 vols. Paris: Honoré Champion, 1894–97.

Richelieu, duc de. *Mémoires.* Paris: Gustave Barba, n.d.

Ringer, Alexander L. "A French Symphonist at the Time of Beethoven: Étienne-Nicholas Méhul." *Musical Quarterly* 37 (1951): 543–65.

————. "J. J. Barthélemy and Musical Utopia in Revolutionary France." *Journal of the History of Ideas* 22 (1961): 355–68.

Robbins-Landon, H. C. *Haydn: Chronicle and Works.* 5 vols. Bloomington: Indiana University Press, 1978.

Robespierre, Maximilien. *Sur les rapports des idées religieuses et morales avec les principes républicaines, et sur les fêtes nationales.* Paris: Imprimerie Nationale, an II.

Roche, Daniel. *Le Siècle des lumières en province: Académies et académiciens provinciaux, 1680–1789.* 2 vols. Paris: École des Hautes Études en Sciences Sociales, 1978.

Root-Bernstein, Michèle. *Boulevard Theater and Revolution in Eighteenth-Century Paris.* Ann Arbor: UMI Research Press, 1984.

Rosanvallon, Pierre. *Le Moment Guizot.* Paris: Gallimard, 1985.

Rosen, Charles. *The Classical Style: Haydn, Mozart, Beethoven.* New York: W. W. Norton, 1972.

Rosen, Charles, and Henri Zerner. *Romanticism and Realism: The Mythology of Nineteenth-Century Art.* New York: W. W. Norton & Co., 1984.

Rosow, Lois. "How Eighteenth-Century Parisians Heard Lully's Operas: The Case of *Armide*'s Fourth Act." In *Jean-Baptiste Lully and the Music of the French Baroque: Essays in Honor of James R. Anthony,* ed. John Hajdu Heyer. Cambridge: Cambridge University Press, 1989.

———. "Lully's *Armide* at the Paris Opéra: A Performance History, 1686–1766." Ph.D. diss., Brandeis University, 1981.

Rossini, Gioacchino. *Il barbiere di Siviglia.* New York: G. Schirmer, 1951.

———. *L'italiana in Algeri.* Ed. Arzo Corghi. Milan: G. Ricordi, 1982.

———. *Otello.* New York: Edwin F. Kalmus, n.d.

———. *Semiramide.* 2 vols. Early Romantic Opera, ed. Philip Gossett and Charles Rosen, vol. 13. New York: Garland Publishing, 1978.

———. *Tancredi.* Ed. Philip Gossett. Milan: G. Ricordi, 1991.

———. *William Tell.* New York: Edwin F. Kalmus, n.d.

Rougemont, Martine de. *La Vie théâtrale en France au XVIIIe siècle.* Paris: Librairie Honoré Champion, 1988.

Rousseau, Jean-Jacques. *Dictionnaire de musique.* Paris: Chez A. Belin, 1817.

———. *Essai sur l'origine des langues.* Paris: Chez A. Belin, 1817.

———. *Julie, ou la nouvelle Héloïse.* Paris: Édition Garnier-Flammarion, 1967.

———. *Politics and the Arts: Letter to M. d'Alembert on the Theatre.* Trans. Allan Bloom. Glencoe, Ill.: The Free Press, 1960.

———. *The Social Contract.* Trans. G. D. H. Cole. London: J. M. Dent and Sons, 1973.

Rushton, Julian. "'Royal Agamemnon': The Two Versions of Gluck's *Iphigénie en Aulide.*" In *Music and the French Revolution.* Ed. Malcolm Boyd. Cambridge: Cambridge University Press, 1992.

Sadie, Stanley, ed. *The New Grove Dictionary of Music and Musicians.* 20 vols. London: Macmillan, 1980.

Sadler, Graham. "Rameau's Singers and Players at the Paris Opéra: A Little-Known Inventory of 1738." *Early Music* 11 (1983): 453–67.

Saloman, Ora Frishberg. "French Revolutionary Perspectives on Chabanon's *De la Musique* of 1785." In *Music and the French Revolution,* ed. Malcolm Boyd. Cambridge: Cambridge University Press, 1992.

———. "The Orchestra in Le Sueur's Musical Aesthetics." *Musical Quarterly* 40 (1974): 616–25.

Schrade, Leo. *Beethoven in France.* New Haven: Yale University Press, 1942.

Schroeder, David P. *Haydn and the Enlightenment: The Late Symphonies and Their Audience.* Oxford: Oxford University Press, 1990.

Schueller, Herbert M. "'Imitation' and 'Expression' in British Music Criticism in the Eighteenth Century." *Musical Quarterly* 34 (1948): 544–66.

Schumann, Robert. "Un Huguenot contre *Les Huguenots.*" Reprinted in *L'Avant scène opéra* 134 (Sept.–Oct. 1990): 98–99.

Schwarz, Boris. *French Instrumental Music between the Revolutions (1789–1830).* New York: Da Capo Press, 1987.

Scott, John. *A Visit to Paris in 1814; Being a Review of the Moral, Political, Intellectual, and Social Condition of the French Capital.* London: Longman, Hurst, Rees, Orme, and Brown, n.d.

Scruton, Roger. *The Aesthetic Understanding: Essays in the Philosophy of Art and Culture.* Manchester: Carcanet Press, 1983.

Scudo, Paul. *De l'Influence du mouvement romantique sur l'art musical et du rôle qu'a voulu jouer M. H. Berlioz.* Paris: La Revue Indépendante, 1846.

Second, Albéric. *Les Petits mystères de l'Opéra.* Paris: Kugelmann, 1844.

Seigel, Jerrold. *Bohemian Paris: Culture, Politics, and the Boundaries of Bourgeois Life, 1830–1930*. New York: Viking Press, 1986.

Selden, Margery Juliet Stomne. "The French Operas of Luigi Cherubini." Ph.D. diss., 2 vols, Yale University, 1951.

Sennett, Richard. *The Fall of Public Man: On the Social Psychology of Capitalism*. New York: Random House, 1974.

Sloane, William Milligan. *Life of Napoleon Bonaparte*. 4 vols. New York: The Century Co., 1909

Snyders, Georges. *Le Goût musical en France aux XVIIᵉ et XVIIIᵉ siècles*. Paris: J. Vrin, 1968.

Solomé, M. "Indications générales et observations pour la mise en scène de *La Muette de Portici*." In *The Original Staging Manuals for Twelve Parisian Operatic Premières*, ed. H. Robert Cohen. Stuyvesant, N.Y.: Pendragon Press, 1991.

Soubies, Albert. *Le Théâtre-Italien de 1801 à 1913*. Paris: Fischbacher, 1913.

Soulié, Frédéric. *Deux séjours: Province et Paris*. 2 vols. Paris: Hippolyte Souverain, 1836.

Spitzer, Alan B. *The French Generation of 1820*. Princeton: Princeton University Press, 1987.

Spohr, Louis. *Louis Spohr's Autobiography*. London: Longman, Green, Longman, Roberts, and Green, 1865. Reprint ed., New York: Da Capo Press, 1969.

Spontini, Gaspare. *Fernand Cortez, ou la conquête du Mexique*. Early Romantic Opera, ed. Philip Gossett and Charles Rosen, vol. 43. New York: Garland Publishing, 1980.

———. *La Vestale*. Early Romantic Opera, ed. Philip Gossett and Charles Rosen, vol. 42. New York: Garland Publishing, 1979.

Starobinski, Jean. *The Invention of Liberty, 1700–1789*. Geneva: Éditions d'Art Albert Skira, 1964.

———. *Jean-Jacques Rousseau: Transparency and Obstruction*. Trans. Arthur Goldhammer. Chicago: University of Chicago Press, 1988.

Starr, Anthony. *Music and the Mind*. New York: The Free Press, 1992.

Stendhal [Henri Beyle]. *Correspondance*. 3 vols. Paris: Bibliothèque de la Pléiade, 1962.

———. *Oeuvres intimes*. Paris: Bibliothèque de la Pléiade, 1981.

———. *Romans*. Paris: Bibliothèque de la Pléiade, 1952.

———. *Vie de Rossini*. 2 vols. Paris: Librairie Ancienne Honoré Champion.

Sutherland, D. M. G. *France 1789–1815: Revolution and Counterrevolution*. Oxford: Oxford University Press, 1986.

Tableau de Paris en l'an VIII. Paris: Chez Laran, n.d.

Tableau du siècle, par un auteur connu. Geneva: n.p., 1759.

Tablettes de renommée des musiciens, auteurs, compositeurs . . . pour servir à l'Almanach Dauphin. Paris: n.p., 1785.

Tartak, Martin H. "The Italian Comic Operas of Rossini." Ph.D. diss., University of California, Berkeley, 1968.

Tedeschi, A. *Ossian: L'Homère du Nord en France*. Milan: Tipografia Sociale, 1911.

Thiéry, Luc-Vincent. *Guide des amateurs et des étrangers voyageurs à Paris.* 2 vols. Paris: Chez Hardouin et Gattey, 1780.

Tiersot, Julien. "Gluck and the Encyclopedists." *Musical Quarterly* 16 (1930): 336–57.

———. *Jean-Jacques Rousseau, un maître de musique.* Paris: Alcan, 1920.

———. "Méhul, musicien des fêtes nationales et civiles." *La Révolution française: Revue d'histoire moderne et contemporaine* 72 (1919): 417–45.

———. "Rameau." *Musical Quarterly* 14 (1928): 77–107.

Till, Nicholas. *Rossini: His Life and Times.* New York: Hippocrene Books, 1983.

Tocqueville, Alexis de. *Democracy in America.* Trans. Henry Reeve, rev. Brown and Bradley. 2 vols. New York: Random House, 1945.

———. *The Old Regime and the French Revolution.* Trans. Stuart Gilbert. Garden City: Anchor Books, 1955.

Trahard, Pierre. *Les Maîtres de la sensibilité française au XVIIIᵉ siècle.* 4 vols. Paris: Boivin et Cie., 1931.

———. *La Sensibilité révolutionnaire (1978–1794).* Paris: Boivin et Cie., 1936.

Travenol, Louis. *La Galerie de l'académie royale de musique, contenant les portraits, en vers, des principaux sujets, qui la composent en la présente année, 1754.* Paris: n.p., n.d.

Treitler, Leo. *Music and the Historical Imagination.* Cambridge: Harvard University Press, 1989.

Trollope, Frances. *Paris and the Parisians.* 2 vols. Paris: Bourgogne et Martinet, 1836.

Tudesq, André-Jean. *Les Grands notables en France, 1840–1849.* 2 vols. Paris: Presses Universitaires de France, 1964.

Vigée Le Brun, Elisabeth. *Souvenirs.* 2 vols. Paris: Gallimard, 1984.

Villoteau, G. A. *Recherches sur l'analogie de la musique avec les arts qui ont pour objet l'imitation du langage.* 2 vols. Paris: L'Imprimerie Impériale, 1807.

Vincent-Buffault, Anne. *Histoire des larmes: XVIIIᵉ–XIXᵉ siècles.* Paris: Éditions Rivages, 1986.

Vivie, Aurélien. *Histoire de la terreur à Bordeaux.* 2 vols. Bordeaux: Feret et Fils, 1877.

Vivien, M., and Edmond Blanc, eds. *Traité de la législation des théâtres, ou exposé complet et méthodique des lois et de la jurisprudence relativement aux théâtres et spectacles publics.* Paris: Brissot-Thivars, 1830.

Voltaire, François Maris Arouet de. *Voltaire's Correspondence.* Ed. Theodore Besterman. 107 vols. Geneva: Institut et Musée Voltaire, 1953.

Vovelle, Michel. *The Fall of the French Monarchy, 1787–1792.* Trans. Susan Burke. Cambridge: Cambridge University Press, 1984.

———. *La Mentalité révolutionnaire: Société et mentalités sous la révolution française.* Paris: Éditions Sociales, 1985.

Voyage à Paris en 1776—Souvenir. Paris: Plon Frères, 1854.

Voyer de Paulmy, René Louis de, Marquis d'Argenson. *Mémoires et journal inédit.* 5 vols. Paris: Chez P. Jannet, 1857.

Wallace, Robin. *Beethoven's Critics: Aesthetic Dilemmas and Resolutions during the Composer's Lifetime.* Cambridge: Cambridge University Press, 1986.

Wangermée, Robert. "Conscience et inconscience du virtuose romantique: A propos des années parisiennes de Franz Liszt." In *Music in Paris in the Eighteen-Thirties,* ed. Peter Bloom. Musical Life in Nineteenth-Century France, vol. 4. Stuyvesant, N.Y.: Pendragon Press, 1987.

Weber, William. "The Contemporaneity of Eighteenth-Century Musical Taste." *Musical Quarterly* 70 (1984): 175–94.

———. "Learned and General Musical Taste in Eighteenth-Century France." *Past and Present* 89 (1980): 58–85.

———. "The Muddle of the Middle Classes." *19th-Century Music* 3 (1979): 175–85.

———. *Music and the Middle Classes.* New York: Holmes and Meier Publishers, 1975.

———. "'La Musique ancienne' in the Waning of the Ancien Régime." *Journal of Modern History* 56 (1984): 58–88.

———. "The Rise of the Classical Repertoire in Nineteenth-Century Orchestral Concerts." In *The Orchestra: Origins and Transformations,* ed. Joan Peyser. New York: Charles Scribner's Sons, 1986.

———. *The Rise of Musical Classics in Eighteenth-Century England: A Study in Canon, Ritual, and Ideology.* Oxford: Clarendon Press, 1992.

Webster, James. *Haydn's "Farewell" Symphony and the Idea of Classical Style: Through-Composition and Cyclic Integration in His Instrumental Music.* Cambridge: Cambridge University Press, 1991.

Welschinger, Henri. *Le Théâtre de la révolution, 1789–1799, avec documents inédits.* Paris: Charavay Frères, 1880.

Wild, Nicole. "La Vie musicale en France sous la régence, d'après le 'Mercure.'" Mémoire présenté pour l'obtention du diplôme de Musicologie sous la direction de Monsieur N. Dufourq, 22 juin 1961. Paris: n.p., 1961.

Wood, Caroline. "Orchestra and Spectacle in the *Tragédie en Musique* 1643–1715: Oracle, *Sommeil,* and *Tempête.*" *Proceedings of the Royal Musical Association* 108 (1981–82): 25–46.

Zaslaw, Neal. *Mozart's Symphonies.* Oxford: Oxford University Press, 1989.

Index

Compositor:	G & S Typesetters, Inc.
Text:	10/13 Galliard
Display:	Galliard
Printer:	Maple-Vail Book Mfg. Group
Binder:	Maple-Vail Book Mfg. Group